SANTIAGO DE GUATEMALA, 1541–1773

SANTIAGO DE GUATEMALA, 1541–1773

CITY, CASTE,
AND THE COLONIAL EXPERIENCE

BY CHRISTOPHER H. LUTZ

UNIVERSITY OF OKLAHOMA PRESS : NORMAN

This book is published with the generous assistance of
Edith Gaylord Harper.

Library of Congress Cataloging-in-Publication Data

Lutz, Christopher.
  Santiago de Guatemala, 1541–1773 : city, caste, and the colonial experience / by Christopher H. Lutz.
    p. cm.
  Revision of the author's thesis (doctoral—University of Wisconsin, 1976) originally published under the title: Historia sociodemográfica de Santiago de Guatemala, 1541–1773. La Antigua Guatemala : Centro de Investigaciones Regionales de Mesoamérica, 1982.
  Includes bibliographical references and index.
  ISBN: 978-0-8061-2911-2 (paper)

  1. Antigua (Guatemala)—Population—History. 2. Antigua (Guatemala)—History. I. Lutz, Christopher, 1541–1773. 1982. II. Title.
HB3539.A83L87 1994   93–46131
304.6'097281'62—dc20   CIP

The paper in this book meets the guidelines for permanence and durability of the Committee on Production Guidelines for Book Longevity of the Council on Library Resources, Inc. ∞

Copyright © 1994 by the University of Oklahoma Press, Norman, Publishing Division of the University. All rights reserved. Manufactured in the U.S.A. First paperback printing, 1997.

*For all Guatemalans
past and present
and for a future
of justice and peace*

CONTENTS

List of Illustrations	viii
List of Maps	ix
List of Tables	x
Preface	xv
1. From Conquest to Emancipation	3
2. Spanish Settlement of the Indian	19
3. The Fall of the Two Republics	45
4. Casta Origins and Growth	79
5. Marriage	113
6. Supplying the City: The Casta Economic Revolution	141
7. Conclusion	155
Appendixes	
Introduction	171
1. Marriage Tables: Santiago de Guatemala, 1577–1769	175
2. Marriage Indices	207
3. Gente Ordinaria and Spanish Baptisms: Santiago de Guatemala, 1640–1769	233
4. Population	239
5. Epidemic Disease in Santiago and Environs, 1519–1769	243
6. Case Study: The Loss of a Tributary Due to Residential Mobility	251
7. Naboría and Laborío Tribute Collection	253
Abbreviations	255
Notes	257
Glossary	311
Bibliography	319
Index	335

ILLUSTRATIONS

PLATES

Following Page 140

1. *Conquest and Reduction of Guatemala*
2. *War of Guatemala and Its Provinces*
3. Portrait of Bishop Francisco Marroquín
4. Antigua, photographed by Eadweard Muybridge in 1876
5. Map of Santiago de Guatemala and Environs dating from early eighteenth century
6. Map of "City of Guatemala," ca. 1690
7. Cabildo Building in Antigua, photographed by Eadweard Muybridge in 1876
8. Market in Central Plaza, Santiago de Guatemala, ca. 1678
9. Antigua Market, photographed by Eadweard Muybridge in 1876
10. Indian Cabildo Members of Santa María de Jesús, photographed by Eadweard Muybridge in 1876
11. Church of Santa María de Jesús, photographed by Eadweard Muybridge in 1876
12. Churches of Los Remedios Parish, 1782
13. Parish Church of Los Remedios, 1782
14. Church of San Cristóbal el Bajo, 1782

ILLUSTRATIONS

FIGURE

Page

1. Comparison of Age Pyramids: San Francisco, 1716 and 1735; San Juan del Obispo, 1755 — 77

MAPS

Audiencia of Guatemala and Southern New Spain	xii–xiii
1. Guatemalan Central Highlands	10
2. Urban Growth of Santiago de Guatemala, 1541–1773	12
3. The Valley of the City (Panchoy), ca. 1530	33
4. Santiago de Guatemala, ca. 1550	34
5. Parish Boundaries in Santiago, ca. 1770	81

TABLES

	Page
1. Indian Population of the Valley of the City, 1548–1581	65
2. Indian Population Change in Nineteen Urban Barrios and Rural Milpas, 1581–1754	67
3. Indian Barrio Tributary Population: 1638, 1670–1684, 1754	70
4. Tributario Entero Population of the Barrio of San Francisco, 1575–1754	72
5. Estimates of "Piezas de Indias" Imported into Central America, 1613–1628, Based on Payment of Royal Rights	85
6. Corrected Total Marriages by Socioracial Groups, 1570s–1760s	87
7. Population of Santiago de Guatemala ("the city and its barrios"), ca. 1740	92
8. The Spanish Population of Santiago de Guatemala, 1529–1770	104
9. Estimated Population of Santiago de Guatemala: 1590s, 1650s, 1680s, and 1750s	110
10. Santiago de Guatemala: Total Population, ca. 1770, Estimated by Cortés y Larraz	111
11. Black Slave Marriage Indices: Santiago de Guatemala, 1593–1769	116

12. Mulatto Slave Marriage Indices: Santiago de Guatemala, 1593–1769 — 118
13. Free Black Marriage Indices: Santiago de Guatemala, 1593–1769 — 121
14. Free Mulatto Marriage Indices: Santiago de Guatemala, 1593–1769 — 123
15. Indian Naboría Marriage Indices: Santiago de Guatemala, 1593–1769 — 130
16. Mestizo Marriage Indices: Santiago de Guatemala, 1593–1769 — 134
17. Spanish Marriage Indices: Santiago de Guatemala, 1590–1769 — 139
18. Marriages of Others and Unidentified: Santiago de Guatemala, 1650–1769 — 164
19. Urban Population by Ethnic Group for New Spain and Spanish Central America, 1750–ca. 1800 — 167

GULF OF
MEXICO
Mexico City
(Tenochtitlán)
Jalapa
Toluca
Puebla
Veracruz
Laguna
de
Términos
MEXICO
Isthmus
of
Tehuantepec
Oaxaca
(Antequera)
Ciudad Real
Chiapa de
los Indios
CHIAPAS
SOCONUSCO
Huehuetenango
Quezaltenango
Lake
Atitlán

HIGHLAND
GUATEMALA
Momostenango
Santa Cruz del Quiché
Utatlán
Chichicastenango
Totonicapán
Quezaltenango
Tecpán
Guatemala
Iximché
San Martín Jilotepeque
Sololá
Comalapa
San Juan Sacatepéquez
Lake
Atitlán
Patzún
Chimaltenango
Chinautla
Mixco
Guatemala City
San Lucas Sacatepéquez
Retalhuleu
Antigua Guatemala
(Santiago de
Guatemala)
San José
Pinula
Amatitlán
Petapa
Lake
Amatitlán
Palín
Escuintla
0 10 20 30 MILES
0 10 20 30 40 KILOMETERS

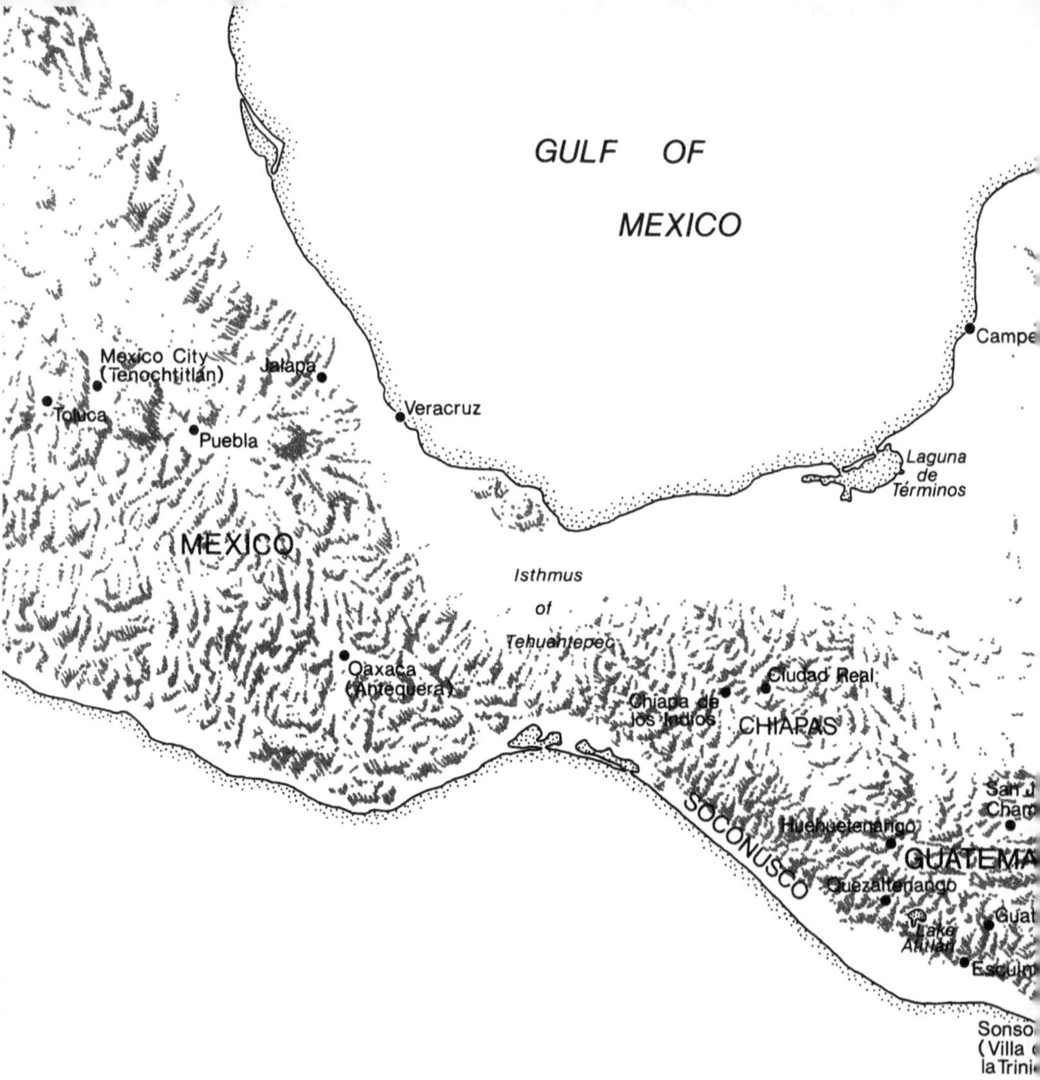

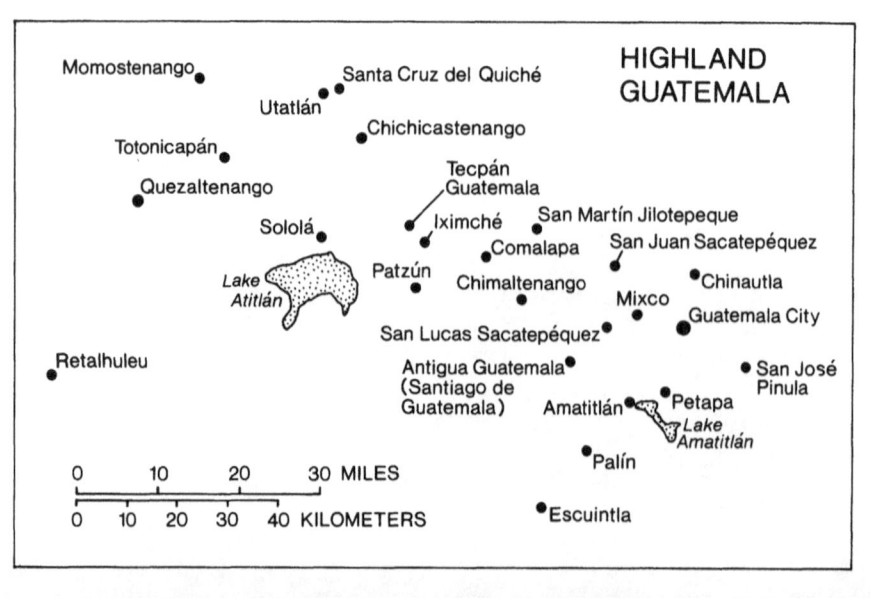

PREFACE

THE idea for this study came in 1969 from the late John L. Phelan, my mentor at the University of Wisconsin. Phelan told me that if I wanted to study colonial Latin American urban history in an area of dense Indian population, I had better go to Guatemala.

Guatemala, he said, had two notable advantages. First, compared with the major New World areas of Indian population, Mexico and the Andes, it had received little attention from colonial historians. Second, Don Joaquín Pardo—"father" of the modern national archive, the Archivo General de Centroamérica (AGCA), in Guatemala City—had almost single-handedly created a cross-indexed card catalog to the colonial documentation for Central America, most of which ended up in Guatemala because the capital of a region stretching from Chiapas to Costa Rica had been located there for most of the three centuries of colonial rule. On a visit to Latin America not long before, Phelan had passed through Guatemala, met Pardo at the AGCA, and reviewed the archivist's life work. So impressed was he that this invaluable research tool came quickly to mind when he suggested that I tackle writing about the old colonial capital of Santiago de Guatemala, the present-day city of Antigua.

As I learned upon my arrival in Guatemala, John Phelan

was right on both counts. Colonial Guatemala was indeed understudied, so much so that the beginning historian had only a few basic published chronologies and well-documented monographs on which to rely. And the AGCA card catalog, known to everybody as the *"fichero* of Don Joaquín Pardo," immediately proved indispensable, for both its scope and its organization.

Although I began my research some six years after Don Joaquín's death, I appreciated his efforts every day of the eighteen months I worked in the AGCA from July 1970 to December 1971. I also came to appreciate the kindness and assistance of the AGCA staff, especially the late Leonel Zarazúa Ramírez, who became my able research assistant, the paleographer Clodoveo Torres Moss, and Gregorio "Goyo" Concohá C'het, who became a close friend.

No less helpful were a number of Guatemalan historians I met at the archive, among them Manuel Rubio Sánchez and the brothers Luis and Jorge Luján Muñoz. John Henry Ibargüen, an American graduate student already established in the AGCA, kindly introduced me to Agustín Estrada Monroy, who was then archivist of the church archives, known today as the Archivo Histórico Arquidiocesano "Francisco Paula García Peláez" (AHA). Estrada in turn introduced me to the Mercedarian Father Ignacio Zúñiga Córres, who allowed us to use the order's newly organized archive and study key land records.

I had the good fortune as well to work at the four parish churches in Guatemala City to which parish records from the old city had been transferred soon after the earthquakes of 1773, which led to the moving of the capital. In the parish offices of the Sagrario (attached to the cathedral), San Sebastián, the Candelaria, and El Calvario (which houses the records of Los Remedios Parish), the priests and their lay secretaries generously gave us access to all of the known extant parish registers and parish censuses from the old city, allowing us to record data into notebooks and stay as late as office schedules permitted, often six days a week.

A curious and providential aspect of this research endeavor was that while virtually all of the civil and ecclesiastical archival materials pertaining to the history of the past inhabitants of Santiago de Guatemala were housed in Guatemala City, Antigua itself, the principal subject of this study, lay some thirty miles to the west. I thus took every opportunity to go to Antigua with my family, to walk its cobblestone streets, to peer into the doorways of old houses, to visit both the elegant and the impoverished *barrios* (residential districts), and, especially, to walk through the ruins of the old city's churches, convents, colonial university, Palace of the Captains General, and *cabildo* (city council) building. For me, experiencing the physical remains of the city and meeting Antigua's modern-day *vecinos* (citizens) brought to life the documents in which I was so absorbed.

Unlike most doctoral dissertations on Latin American history presented at North American universities, this work was translated and published in Spanish before an English-language version was ever contemplated. The Guatemalan edition came to fruition thanks to the early encouragement of Luis Luján Muñoz and Julio Castellanos Cambranes. Jeannie Colburn's original translation was revised by Jorge Luis Arriola and Inés Maldonado de van Oss and later subjected to the editorial skills of the late Adriaan van Oss, Cristina Zilbermann de Luján, and Jorge Luján Muñoz. The Spanish-language edition is the doctoral dissertation with only minor changes, corrections, and some inadvertent omissions. The current work is briefer, tighter, richer, and hence (I hope) more readable than its predecessors.

In general, quotations have been translated into English only if they are relatively accessible in the original Spanish. Quotations that are particularly colorful or suggest various translations are given in the original Spanish.

Chapter 1, "From Conquest to Emancipation," outlines the conquest of Guatemala, the founding and destruction of the first permanent capital, Santiago in Almolonga, and the establishment of the new city in 1541 in the Valley of Panchoy. It goes on to detail the arrival of the *audiencia* (royal court) headed by Alonso López de Cerrato and the liberation from slavery of the Indian residents of the lands immediately surrounding the two Spanish centers.

Chapter 2, "Spanish Settlement of the Indian," discusses the numerous rural and urban Indian settlements founded between ca. 1527 and 1550, both during and after slavery, as well as the labor, tribute, and land-tax obligations of these communities after emancipation. It describes "self-rule" in the Indian barrios, with a closer look at the Barrio of Santo Domingo during one short period of crisis, and the problems associated with the maintenance of law and order.

Chapter 3, "The Fall of the Two Republics," briefly examines the impact of epidemic disease on the city's outlying barrios before focusing on the impact of biological and cultural *mestizaje* (race mixture). It concludes by tracing the drastic decline of the Indian tributary population in the Barrio of San Francisco.

Chapter 4, "Casta Origins and Growth," describes the evolution of Santiago de Guatemala's diverse population, including black slaves, Indian servants, and members of the Spanish elite. The discussion ends with estimates of the size of the city's population at different periods in its history.

Chapter 5, "Marriage," follows up on the ethnic group descriptions in the previous chapter. It presents a detailed analysis of group endogamy and exogamy and the consequences of these patterns for the demographic transformation of Santiago de Guatemala from the mid-sixteenth century to the third quarter of the eighteenth century. Where necessary, the discussion moves from the city as a whole to the city's four parishes.

Chapter 6, "Supplying the City: The Casta Economic Revolution," describes the changing roles of members of different ethnic groups in providing Santiago de Guatemala with grain, meat, and drink both legally and illegally. It offers a socioeconomic perspective on the demographic transformations described in chapters 3, 4, and 5.

Chapter 7, "Conclusion," puts Santiago in the context of historian Harry Hoetink's description of the transition from a segmented to a homogeneous society. Santiago's sociodemographic patterns are compared to those of Spanish Central America and cities elsewhere in Mesoamerica. Finally, colonial socioracial relations are brought up to date.

In addition to those who assisted and befriended me in Guatemala from the early 1970s on, I wish to express my appreciation to the staff of the Archivo General de Indias (AGI) for their help during my visits to that wonderful Seville institution. Thanks, too, to Alfredo Jiménez Núñez, Salvador Rodríguez Becerra, Beatriz Suñe Blanco, Pilar Sanchiz Ochoa, and Elías Zamora Acosta of the Seminario de Antropología Americana of the Universidad de Sevilla, all of whom came to my aid in 1972 with suggestions and leads for locating valuable documentation in the Guatemalan *legajos* (files) of the AGI. I also want to thank Manuel Fuentes Mairena and Francisco Sánchez Rico, AGI *copistas* (paleographic copiers), for carefully reproducing documents my colleagues and I have used so extensively.

For more purely intellectual debts and personal encouragement I cannot forget John Smail, Peter Smith, Thomas Skidmore, and Maris Vinovskis, all still or once in Madison, William L. Sherman, and Murdo J. MacLeod. Nor can I forget Robert Carmack's kind support, first to a green researcher in the AGCA, then to a historian slow to revise his manuscript. I must also acknowledge the friendly nagging of other Guatemalanists, Sheldon Annis, Piero Gleijeses, George Lovell, and Wendy Kramer, to have this work published in English. Sheldon introduced me to David Kolkebeck, who has been invaluable in helping me tighten, reorganize, and make this work more readable; I owe a lot to David. Working over the last years on joint projects with George, Wendy, and our dear and departed colleague at CIRMA in Antigua, William Swezey, best known to his friends as "Swezey," has directly and indirectly enriched this new study.

I also want to thank Lucy Robelo, Heidi Fielder, Judy Walker, Elisabeth Siruček, and, especially, Armando Alfonzo for their never-ending support and technical assistance in preparing this manuscript for publication. Over the years their patience has been infinite. I am also grateful to Martha Davidson, Margarita Asensio de Méndez, David Jickling, and Stephen R. Elliott for advice and for helping me to obtain illustrations, and to John Cotter for the careful elaboration of the maps used in this work. Thanks go to John Drayton, Barbara Siegemund-Broka, and Mildred Logan of the University of Oklahoma Press and to Kathleen Lewis and Peter Price for all their help in seeing this manuscript through to publication.

I owe most of all to my wife, Sally, for her patience when I was "mired in the sixteenth century" and her unstinting encouragement when the task at hand seemed insurmountable. I owe as much to our children, now grown up, Sarah and Ian, who have lived through all the stages of this work from Guatemala, Seville, Madison, South Woodstock, Antigua, and beyond.

CHRISTOPHER H. LUTZ

South Woodstock, Vermont

SANTIAGO DE GUATEMALA, 1541–1773

CHAPTER ONE

FROM CONQUEST TO EMANCIPATION

PEDRO de Alvarado set out from Mexico for Guatemala on 6 December 1523. Leading an army of 120 cavalry, 300 infantry, and several hundred Mexican conscripts down the Pacific coast, he turned north below the Indian town of Retalhuleu, moved up into the piedmont through the cacao plantations and dense forests of the coastal plain, and then quickly left the piedmont behind as he scaled southern Guatemala's volcanic ridge and entered the central highlands.

In the first major battle of the Guatemalan campaign, waged in February 1524 on the broad highland plain where the city of Quezaltenango now sits, the Spanish proved themselves far superior to the K'iche', the most powerful of the highland Mayan peoples. That the K'iche' far outnumbered Alvarado and his men seems to have mattered little to their cause. Nor is it likely that they were beaten because the leaders of other highland Indian groups, including the neighboring Kaqchikel and Tz'utujil, refused their calls for a united front against the invaders.[1] Rather, as George Lovell explains, "the physical and psychological impact of cavalry on a people who had never before seen a horse and its rider in action was as devastating as the material superiority of steel and firearms over the bow and arrow."[2]

In a last-ditch attempt to stave off defeat, the K'iche' invited Alvarado northeast to Utatlán, their capital, near the present-day city of Santa Cruz del Quiché. There, under the guise of arranging the terms of their surrender, the K'iche' hoped to trap the conquistadores and then set fire to the city. But Alvarado was not fooled. Sensing the conspiracy as he entered the deserted capital, he hastily gathered his forces and managed to flee to safety; time had run out before the K'iche' could destroy the bridge that was Alvarado's only means of escape.[3] Joined by 2,000 Kaqchikel soldiers sent to bolster Spanish forces against the K'iche' at Alvarado's request, the conquistadores now showed no mercy. The conspirators were identified and burned to death, their city demolished. With K'iche' submission assured, Alvarado proceeded south to Iximché, the Kaqchikel capital, in mid-April 1524.[4] It had taken him two short months to complete the crucial first phase of the conquest of Guatemala.

But Guatemala, Alvarado must have soon discovered, would not fall as quickly as the vast Aztec tribute empire before it. Each of over a dozen highland peoples had to be conquered separately because no single individual among them enjoyed the absolute authority of Moctezuma, the Aztec ruler whose death in 1521, just two years after the arrival of the conquistadores in Mexico, marked the beginning of Aztec submission to Spanish rule. This degree of highland political fragmentation was clearly not a reflection of basic cultural or religious differences among the region's twenty-odd linguistic groups.[5] All were Mayan-speaking agrarian societies in which every aspect of daily life revolved around a similar system of beliefs and the worship of a pantheon of gods.[6] None appears to have separated secular and sacred in matters of administration: governors were priests and priests were governors. Beneath these hereditary elites was a tier of trade and craft specialists; beneath them lay a vast class of *macehuales* (peasants) who grew maize and other staples; at the bottom were the slaves of the elite.[7]

What most likely brought these highland peoples to blows, then, was a near-continuous struggle for territory, particularly lowland territory that sustained cacao and maize production almost year-round and contained such valuable resources as salt. The struggle was so fierce that the Kaqchikel, who split with the K'iche' around 1470 and vied with them for domination of the highlands until the Spaniards arrived on the scene, saw Alvarado as less of a threat to their territorial aspirations and sense of security than their highland rivals.[8] Consequently, the Kaqchikel provided warriors and supplies when Alvarado moved against the Tz'utujil, who controlled the narrow band of territory south of Lake Atitlán. Again with their assistance he next conquered the Pipil, in Cuzcatlán (in present-day El Salvador) and Escuintla (southwest of Lake Amatitlán).[9] By mid-July Alvarado had returned to Iximché, where on the twenty-fifth of the month he founded the first Spanish capital of Guatemala, which he named Santiago.

Established around 1475, Iximché was typical of late postclassic Mayan capitals throughout the central and western highlands.[10] It was built for defensive purposes on the point of a promontory lined by deep ravines and functioned as the economic, political, and religious hub of a city-state, much like the fortress towns of medieval Europe. While it normally housed members of the ruling elite and their artisans and slaves, it also could hold the large numbers of macehuales who flocked there from the surrounding villages and hamlets on market days, during religious festivals, and when under attack.[11] Thus it only appeared to Spanish chroniclers of the conquest that the Guatemalan highlands were dotted with densely populated cities; in truth, the Spanish presence itself forced the macehuales to flee their fields and hamlets for the relative safety of the fortress towns.

While Alvarado's return to Iximché seems to have provoked no such response among the Kaqchikel, it might well have, for the Spanish commander wasted little time in distributing the population of Iximché's forty or so surrounding towns in *encomiendas* (grants) to his principal soldiers.[12] Each *encomendero* (grantee) was thereby given the right to receive tribute and labor from the Indians of a specific town (or towns, if fortunate). Alvarado in addition demanded 1,200 pesos in gold of the Kaqchikel lords; if they failed to comply, he warned, they would be burned alive or hanged.[13]

To escape such treatment, the Kaqchikel secretly evacuated Iximché in August 1524, acting on the advice of what their chroniclers described (after being Christianized) as "an agent of the devil" who promised to destroy the Spanish invaders as the Kaqchikel quit the city.[14] Unimpaired by the demon, Alvarado opened hostilities against his former allies, reversing Indian roles by using Tz'utujil and K'iche' warriors to help crush the Kaqchikel revolt. The Kaqchikel were perhaps the most tenacious of the highlanders in their resistance to the conquistadores.[15] Hiding in the hills, eking out a bare subsistence, they managed to remain independent until 1530. Enslavement and resettlement awaited their surrender.

Santiago in Iximché continued for a time to serve as a center of Spanish civil and ecclesiastical administration, though it lost much of its allure after the Kaqchikel evacuation. It also continued to serve as headquarters for subsequent highland campaigns, much as Tenochtitlán (Mexico City) had during the conquest of central and southern Mexico. While the Mexican capital remained fixed, however, the Guatemalan capital did not. Resembling more a military encampment than a town,[16] it moved with Alvarado and his companions in arms until 22 November 1527, when the members of Santiago's cabildo selected a permanent site nearly a mile east of Almolonga, a pre-Hispanic Kaqchikel outpost on the lower slopes of Agua volcano.[17]

Chosen for its climate and water supply, its proximity to building materials, and its defensibility (of particular importance as the Kaqchikel rebellion wore on), Santiago in Almolonga was carefully laid out according to the accepted rules for Spanish towns in the New World. The streets were placed in a north-south and east-west grid with a *plaza mayor* (public square) at the center: two *solares* (building lots) on one side of the square were set aside for a church dedicated to Santiago (Saint James), the patron saint of the city; on the other three sides, solares were reserved for a town hall, chapel, fort, public jail, and hospital for the "lodging and curing" of pilgrims and the poor.[18]

What little we know of the capital's *traza* (urban plan)

suggests that Spanish houses were constructed in the blocks around the central plaza, with the choicest solares, those closest to the town center, going to high-ranking Spanish vecinos, as was the custom throughout the Hispanic world.[19] Most of the 100 to 150 Spanish households contained two classes of Indians—slaves, perhaps the largest group in the capital, and *naborías* (hereditary servants), wage earners who were tied to individual vecinos and enjoyed a distinct and superior status relative to the slaves.[20] To the west of the Spanish residential district, on the valley floor, lay the Indian barrio of Almolonga, home to Alvarado's Mexican auxiliaries and their families.[21] The capital's remaining few inhabitants were African slaves, held by prominent Spanish vecinos, and naborías who lived on the fringes of the Spanish settlement, raising livestock for their masters or growing vegetables on small plots.

Santiago in Almolonga grew little in its first decade. The Spaniards, at least in Guatemala, seemed to give no more than passing thought to settlement as they pressed their search for gold and extended their dominion southward, beginning the conquest of Peru by the early 1530s.[22] "This [capital] has always been inn and hospital for everyone," complained its first bishop, Francisco Marroquín, in a letter to the Spanish monarch Charles V: "It is now and it will [always] be, since it is on the way to everywhere. Everyone profits by its existence but the city receives no benefit at all."[23]

The city's second decade was its last. In the predawn hours of 11 September 1541, three days into a torrential downpour, the rain-soaked slopes of Agua volcano unleashed a tree- and boulder-laden wall of mud on the fourteen-year-old capital.[24] Channeled by Agua's natural topography, the mudslide swept away whole sections of the capital while leaving others intact. Over 600 Indian slaves, close to 100 Spaniards, and a smaller number of African slaves died in the catastrophe; only the Mexican auxiliaries on the valley floor were spared. Santiago in Almolonga was "left so damaged by the storm," Bishop Marroquín concluded, "that by necessity we moved it, since [the tragedy] was caused by water and it well could be that [other such floods] will come."[25]

PANCHOY

On 2 October 1541 a majority of Santiago's vecinos endorsed a plan to move the capital to the Valley of the Tianguesillo (market) of Chimaltenango, some nine miles north of Santiago in Almolonga.[26] Respecting the group's wishes, the new co-governors of the province—Alvarado's ally Bishop Marroquín and brother-in-law Francisco de la Cueva, who had taken power weeks before when Alvarado was killed in Jalisco (Mexico) while helping to suppress the Mixtón Indian uprising—ordered that solares be distributed there nine days hence.[27] By 22 October, however, the two had changed their minds: the new Santiago de Guatemala would be constructed instead on the level floor of the Valley of Panchoy, just a half league north of the demolished capital, on lands that had been parceled out to a number of vecinos soon after the establishment of a permanent capital in 1527.[28]

Students of colonial Guatemala have long believed that the Spanish royal engineer Don Juan Bautista Antonelli is responsible for the governors' surprising about-face.[29] It is more likely, however, that an influential group of vecinos, probably cabildo members who owned *labores* (wheat farms) and *estancias* (small cattle ranches) in Panchoy and stood to benefit from a new or continued proximity to the capital, persuaded Marroquín and de la Cueva to go against the will of the majority.

Compared with the Tianguesillo of Chimaltenango, they must have reasoned, Panchoy enjoyed a superior water supply and more abundant sources of timber and stone for construction.[30] Large numbers of Indian slaves had already been resettled on the Spanish-owned *milpas* (rural agricultural settlements) of the valley and surrounding sierra; to resettle them once again would be difficult and counterproductive.[31] One chronicler argued in addition that the Indians of the broader region would have great difficulty in changing prevailing patterns of labor and trade.[32] Finally, for a community that had yet to experience stability after seventeen years of conquest, Panchoy afforded the welcome chance to move without starting over.

Situated at 1,524 meters above sea level, the Valley of

Panchoy is surrounded by steep terrain.[33] Across its northern horizon, and to the east and west, the hills reach elevations of 2,743 meters. To the south and southwest, the land rises even more dramatically: Agua volcano, at over 3,658 meters, dominates the southern view; the twin peaks of Fuego and Acatenango, higher still though farther from the valley, rise impressively in the southwest.[34]

Panchoy's climate is temperate the year round, its average monthly temperatures ranging from 18 to 24 degrees Celsius. Rainfall is concentrated in the *invierno* (rainy season) between May and November; September, the wettest month, can account for the better part of the valley's 990-millimeter average annual rainfall. The *verano* (dry season) runs from November until May. The coldest part of the year falls between November and February, when the temperature can dip within several degrees of freezing; the hottest months are March and April, when the temperature can climb to 28 degrees Celsius.

Panchoy, which translates from the Kaqchikel as "large lake," suggesting the entire valley was once under water, is traversed by two rivers, the Guacalate (known in Spanish Guatemala as the Magdalena) and the smaller Pensativo.[35] Rising in what is today the Department of Chimaltenango, the Guacalate flows southeast into Panchoy through a corridor of land often referred to as the Valley of Jocotenango.[36] The Pensativo, which enters the Valley of Panchoy from the northeast, dropping rapidly through rugged terrain to the valley floor, joins the Guacalate at the lower end of the valley. From there, the broad stream cuts between Agua and the twin peaks of Fuego and Acatenango before descending to the Pacific coastal plain.

Most colonial visitors from Mexico City and other parts of New Spain, as well as those from such western regions of Guatemala as "los Altos" and Chiapas, entered Panchoy from the northwest, through the Valley of Jocotenango. The northeast corridor, known as the *camino de Petapa* (Petapa road), brought travelers and goods from Verapaz, the Atlantic ports (which tied the province to Spain), and the provinces of Honduras, San Salvador, and Nicaragua. The southern route, via Almolonga, opened Panchoy to the commerce of the Pacific coastal plain.[37]

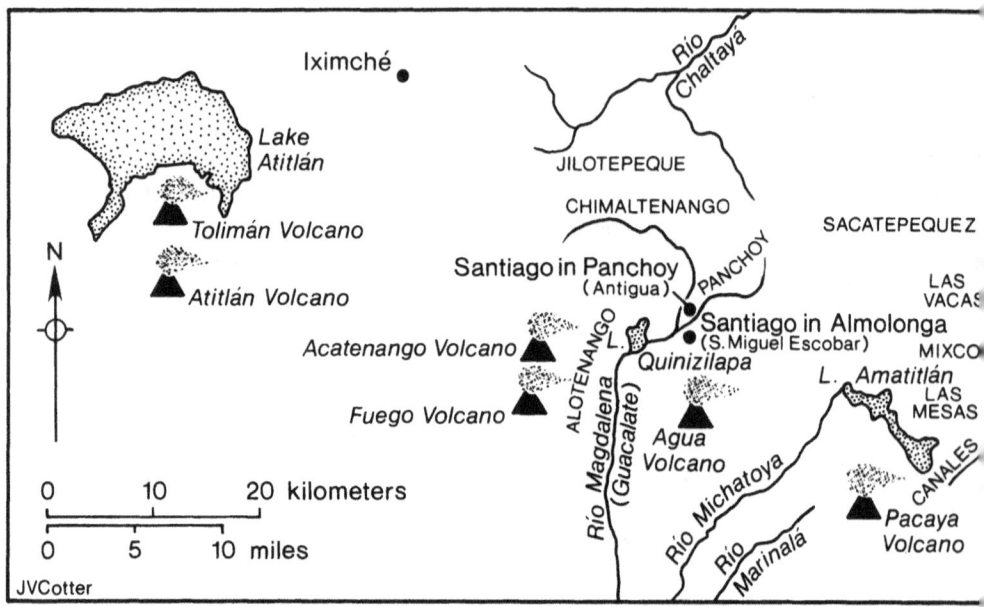

MAP 1. Guatemalan central highlands: The valleys that constituted the Corregimiento of Guatemala or the Valley of Guatemala (sites of early Spanish settlements/capitals identified).

These three corridors led also to the eight valleys that combined with Panchoy to form the *corregimiento* (jurisdiction) of the Valley of Guatemala. To the southwest, following the course of the Guacalate River, lay the Valley of Alotenango. To the north, toward the river's source, lay the large fertile valleys of Chimaltenango and Jilotepeque. To the east (from south to north) lay the valleys of Canales, Las Mesas, Mixco, Las Vacas, and Sacatepéquez (see map 1). Each would come to play a vital role in the feeding of Santiago in Panchoy.

Marking off a site just above the point at which the Pensativo joins the Guacalate, the architect (or architects) of the new capital completed work on Santiago's traza by 18 November 1541.[38] First to be laid out were the plaza mayor and blocks sufficient both to erect civil and ecclesiastical buildings and to lodge the city's vecinos. As in Santiago in Almolonga, the streets were drawn in a north-south and east-west pattern, following the cardinal points of the compass. Also as before, conquistadores, their sons, and others of wealth and distinction were ceded the most desirable solares, those nearest the town center.[39]

The early seventeenth-century Dominican Fray Antonio de Remesal—a valuable chronicler of Santiago's early years for having seen the sixteenth-century *libros de cabildo* (cabildo books), two critical volumes of which are now missing[40]—suggests that the town fathers at first followed a rudimentary traza but quickly allowed new demand for solares to dictate the pace and direction of urban expansion. Art historian Verle L. Annis, however, who assigns Antonelli a key planning role, contends that the Spanish royal engineer designed a traza "possibly intended for about five thousand inhabitants" and meant from the beginning to accommodate growth "for the foreseeable future."[41]

Antonelli, according to Annis, enclosed a central plaza 100 meters square with two tiers of blocks of equal size, eight in the first tier, sixteen in the second. To each of the north, east, and west sides of this twenty-five-block core (including the plaza) he added five rectangular blocks, followed by two large square blocks on the traza's northwest and northeast corners. In addition, Annis claims, Antonelli extended streets south of the traza to the banks of the Pensativo.[42]

Such assertions seem to be borne out by the respective placement of the Franciscan and Dominican monasteries opposite the traza's southeast and northeast corners. That the Mercedarian order did not receive a solar facing the traza's northwest corner, however, suggests that Antonelli showed less foresight than Annis gives him credit for.[43] But it is no less plausible that the Mercedarians could have taken their logical place at the corner had they not at first refused to abandon their monastery in Almolonga.[44]

Archival evidence of the city's initial growth, a body of documents Annis left untouched, is far less ambiguous. To the east of the plaza mayor, nine of thirteen solares recorded between 1558 and 1566 surely lay outside the traza defined by Annis, and three of the remaining four building lots appear to

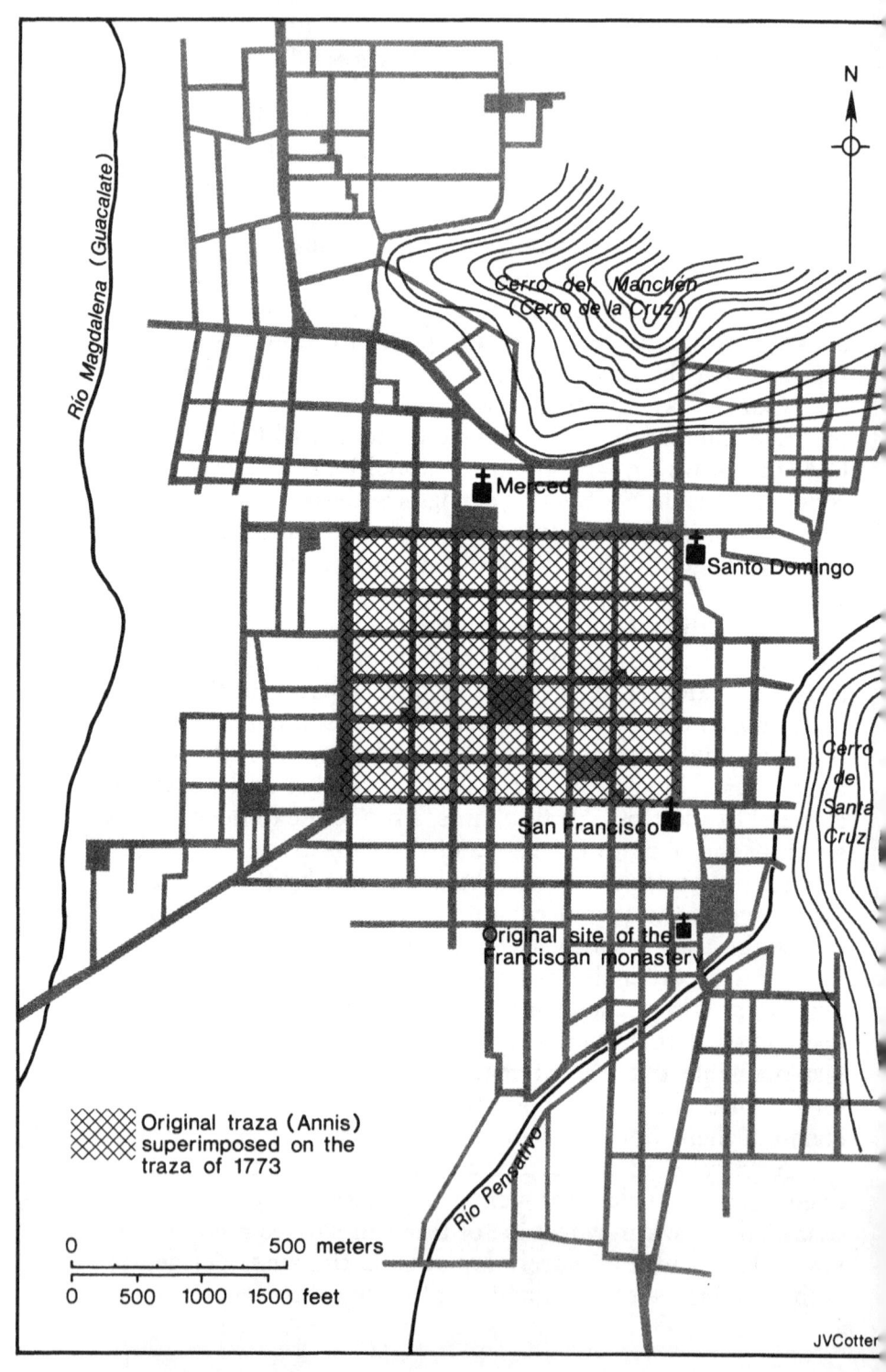

MAP 2. Urban growth of Santiago de Guatemala, 1541–1773. Original traza (Annis) superimposed on traza of 1773. Urban grid based on a map by V. L. Annis.

have been situated there as well.⁴⁵ The thirteen solares were part of a *traza nueva* (new traza) of five to ten blocks created some time between mid-1557 and 14 July 1558 in the vacant land between the monasteries of San Francisco and Santo Domingo by order of the *oidor* (judge) Antonio Mexía.⁴⁶

Expansion north of the traza defined by Annis also got under way in the late 1550s. While the extent of growth here is difficult to assess, one extant title reveals that on 11 August 1559 the widow of the vecino Juan Alvarez took possession of two solares next to the Mercedarian establishment. Coming at roughly the same time as the eastward expansion into the open lands between the Franciscan and Dominican monasteries, this Mexía grant seems to have been part of a broader plan of growth unanticipated in 1541.⁴⁷

Little more than a decade later, on 23 January 1571, Santiago's cabildo authorized the sale of solares southwest of the plaza mayor, effectively opening up to residential development two of the three tiers of blocks marked off in Annis's original traza, and then some.⁴⁸ Beyond and slightly south of the broad avenue that fixed the traza's western border, solares here in the savannah of Santa Lucía were set aside for vecinos in *censo enfiteusis* (a standard contract under which the owner, in this case the city itself, annually received 5 percent of a property's assessed value as payment for its use).⁴⁹

Claims by Annis notwithstanding, such evidence suggests that Santiago's leaders had no other choice but to extend the city limits. Residential demand by vecinos in the three decades following the founding of the city, a period well within Annis's "foreseeable future," had simply outstripped the supply of solares thought ample in 1541.

POLITICS AND SLAVERY

As construction began on the new capital in late 1541, so, too, did the business of filling the political void created by the death of Alvarado. The task would prove to be a difficult one for the Crown. "Only rarely," as William L. Sherman points out, "has one individual dominated the society of his time and place in the way that Alvarado did in Guatemala for eighteen years. Perhaps no other Spanish conqueror left his personal imprint so clearly on a colony as the conqueror of Guatemala."[50]

Surprisingly, Alvarado was able to make his mark without ever having to come to grips with his proper role as provincial governor. He devoted considerable time and effort to amassing a personal fortune in Guatemala, but none to fostering the institutions required by a new society. His keenness for all manner of military adventure (he died days before setting sail on a trans-Pacific expedition to the Spice Islands) kept him away from Santiago for long periods, making it impossible for him even to try to bring order to the chaos inevitable in any new colonial venture. Upon his return, he would disrupt what little there was in the way of administration, frequently reversing decisions made in his absence so as better to man and finance still another of his foreign campaigns. Consequently, "the average Spanish settler could not be sure of his tenure of encomienda, house plot (solar), land allotment near the city, or much else," writes Murdo J. MacLeod. "Little wonder that so many settlers left in disgust or were so ready to follow the next leader to raise a new enterprise of exploration or conquest."[51]

The Indians of Guatemala's central highlands and Pacific coastal plain, of course, had no such choice. The circumstances surrounding their enslavement produced as severe a demographic shock as the Old World diseases that would halve their numbers by mid-century. Used primarily to extract Peru's rich deposits of gold and silver, they and especially their Nicaraguan and Honduran peers represented Central America's biggest export beginning around 1530, in part because mining operations were so labor intensive, in part because so many died in transit or were worked to death when they reached their destination. Such human profligacy continued unchecked until the mid-1540s, when the Spanish slave traders and mine owners were forced to change their way of doing business, not so much because the immorality of slavery was beginning seriously to be questioned, but because there were simply no longer sufficient numbers of Indians to export.

Santiago's Spanish vecinos hastened the day when Indian labor would become a precious commodity. Acutely aware that the scarcity of gold and silver in Guatemala could be compensated for only in agricultural production, recognizing in turn that their lands were worthless without the slaves to till them, they, too, captured and purchased Indians in huge numbers, putting most to work on their milpas as field hands and *tamemes* (porters), training a select group of Indian artisans as masons, carpenters, sawyers, cartwrights, and blacksmiths. Large numbers of others were employed as miners, forced to divide their time between the milpas and small-scale mining enterprises elsewhere in Guatemala, as well as in Honduras. Although most of these milpas evolved into permanent Indian communities, some did not.[52] In certain cases, the soil proved to be infertile, the water supply inadequate. In others, the holdings fell into disuse when their owners failed to populate them with Indian slaves. In still others, entire Indian communities succumbed to disease.

The acquisition of slaves by Santiago's vecinos meant that a distinctly heterogenous Indian population came to be settled outside the capital. On the Milpa de Juan de León (later known as San Miguel Milpas Altas), for example, the Indian leaders included Juan, Pedro, and Cristóbal, all *naturales* (natives) of Momostenango; Francisco, from Oaxaca; another Francisco, from Chiquimula; and Juan, a native of Sacatepéquez (this was probably Santiago Sacatepéquez, a town north of the Valley of Panchoy). The three Momostecos (former inhabitants of Guatemala's western highlands) spoke the K'iche' tongue; Francisco from Oaxaca (New Spain) was most likely a Mixtec or Zapotec speaker; Francisco from Chiquimula (eastern lowland Guatemala) undoubtedly spoke Chorti'; and Juan from Sacatepéquez spoke Kaqchikel.[53] The vast majority of the valley's milpas appear to have exhibited a similar degree of linguistic and regional diversity as a result of Spanish resettlement practices.[54]

Alvarado's death gave the Crown its first real opportunity to end so harsh and arbitrary a system and to bring, through better government, a measure of order to labor relations in Guatemala. The time was ripe for reform because the region's militant encomenderos, those who felt they stood to lose the most if limits were put on the amount of Indian labor and tribute they could exact, now lacked effective leadership. As the Crown issued the New Laws in 1542, taking power from the governors (Marroquín and de la Cueva) and placing it in the hands of a president and his audiencia of oidores, "the time of the conquerors was about to give way to the time of the lawyers," Sherman notes, "but not before the encomenderos made their last stand."[55]

Issuing the New Laws for more humanitarian treatment of the Indian was one thing, enforcing them quite another. After a two-year delay that, according to Sherman, "afforded the encomenderos sufficient lead-time to gird for battle,"[56] the audiencia finally established itself in the town of Gracias a Dios, too far removed from Santiago to restrict the encomienda or reduce tribute payments, let alone abolish Indian slavery in the valley. Although the audiencia seat was moved to Santiago in 1548, the shift failed to give the Crown the desired upper hand in the region because the *corregidores* (magistrates) of the Valley of Guatemala served also as the *alcaldes ordinarios* of first and second vote (mayor and vice mayor, the two highest elected officials) in Santiago's cabildo.[57] As a result, control over the city and its surrounding lands and Indian towns remained in the hands of the local elite, as it had since the cabildo's inception in 1524.[58]

While the Crown was something less than a champion of the Indians in that it sought to loosen, not relinquish, the Spanish vecinos' hold on them, to ameliorate yet share in their exploitation, its earliest officials (and many later ones as well) were virtually indistinguishable from those it was supposed to control. "How can Indian slaves be liberated when the oidor himself has two or three hundred slaves?" asked Judge Alonso López de Cerrato in a letter to the king on 28 September 1548, four months after becoming president of the audiencia. "And how," Cerrato continued, "can personal service be taken away when the oidor has fifty Indians in his house, carrying water and food and fodder and other things? And how can tamemes be taken away by an oidor who has eight hundred tamemes in the mines, and when even his dogs are carried by tamemes?"[59]

In Cerrato the Crown had finally found an advocate of a

strong royal bureaucratic system, an antidote to both independent-minded governors like Alvarado and the autonomous encomendero aristocracy that would dominate much of sixteenth-century Guatemalan life. Determined to abolish native slavery in Guatemala after doing just that in Santo Domingo, Spain's first beachhead in the New World, Cerrato established in early 1549 what Sherman has called "a landmark in the history of Indian labor in the New World," cutting tribute payments by as much as 50 percent, taking Indians from particularly abusive encomenderos, curtailing tamemes' labor obligations, and ultimately winning freedom for the slaves in Santiago and its environs—all despite overwhelming opposition from both creoles (American-born Spaniards) and Spaniards. "By 1550," Sherman concludes, "the situation of the Indians was significantly altered because of Cerrato's actions, and their condition was never quite so deplorable as in the past."[60]

Cerrato, however, is not without his detractors among students of colonial Guatemala. MacLeod, for one, believes he lost much of his reformist zeal during the latter half of his seven-year presidency, raising nepotism to a fine art, applying the New Laws "only to those who lacked power in the community," and failing to execute "his other charge, that of breaking up the large encomiendas and distributing them among the poorer Spaniards."[61]

But MacLeod saves his greatest objection for the idea that Cerrato deserves most of the credit for ending the slave trade and guiding the transition to the "ordered, regulated, and careful society which emerged after 1550."[62] Indian slavery, he argues, was by then no longer a viable labor system because profit margins had narrowed and able-bodied natives were in such short supply; indeed, the severity of a new epidemic in 1545–48 "made it plain to all but the most obtuse of [Spaniards] that even in areas where Indians had been numerous their services and numbers would have to be more carefully managed." Most of the conquistadores were now dead; taking their places, increasingly, were practical leaders with business acumen and operational skills, reform-minded oidores, and a new kind of cleric who sought to defend the Indian as well as wrest "some or all of [his] diminishing services from the encomenderos and other Spaniards."[63] Cerrato, in short, was the beneficiary of broad economic, demographic, and moral forces that together marked a major watershed in the life of Guatemala and its new, nearly ten-year-old capital. Without such forces, MacLeod concludes, Indian emancipation would surely have remained beyond Cerrato's reach.[64]

CHAPTER TWO

SPANISH SETTLEMENT OF THE INDIAN

IT seems both fitting and ironic that Alvarado, not Cerrato, emancipated the first slaves. Filled with remorse for the ruthlessness with which he had acquired his native labor, Alvarado ordered Bishop Marroquín, executor of his estate, to see to it that the Indian inhabitants of all four of his milpas in the Valley of Jocotenango—the Parcialidad (community) de los Utatlecas (known as Santiago Utatleca for much of the 1540s), San Dionisio de los Pastores, San Luis de los Carreteros, and the Parcialidad de los Sacatecas—be freed upon his death.[1] In the following year, 1542, a fifth group— Guatimaltecas, mostly Kaqchikel speakers from Santa María Concepción Almolonga who claimed to be slaves of Alvarado —petitioned governors Marroquín and de la Cueva for their freedom and asked that they be granted lands nearer to their Spanish masters in Santiago in Panchoy (see the following list, "Indian Settlements in Valley of Jocotenango, 1528–42"). The governors approved the request and Santiago's cabildo ceded them lands in Jocotenango formerly occupied by Alvarado's silver mine, where they came to be called the Parcialidad de los Guatimaltecas de Jocotenango.[2]

INDIAN SETTLEMENTS IN THE VALLEY OF JOCOTENANGO, 1528-42[3]

Parcialidad de los Utatlecas de Jocotenango. *Founder:* Alvarado, ca. 1528. *Nomenclature:* After ethnolinguistic region; the Utatlecas were probably mostly K'iche', from the area around Utatlán. Alvarado populated this parcialidad not by capturing unsubjugated Indians but by taking a group of tributaries from each of the towns he held in encomienda, branding and enslaving them, and then settling them on his lands.[4] Its population was augmented, probably soon after 1 June 1543, when Marroquín emancipated Alvarado's miners after forcing them to labor one more *demora* (miners' work period during dry season) to provide an inheritance of gold for Alvarado's illegitimate heirs.[5]

San Dionisio de los Pastores. *Founder:* Alvarado, ca. 1528. *Nomenclature:* Saint's name followed by description of milpa's function. The inhabitants of this milpa were *pastores* (shepherds).[6] *Other name:* San Dionisio Pastores.

San Luis de los Carreteros. *Founder:* Alvarado, ca. 1528. *Nomenclature:* Saint's name followed by description of milpa's function. The Indians of San Luis were trained as *carreteros* (cartwrights) soon after the Spanish arrival in Guatemala and continued in that trade for generations. *Other name:* San Luis las Carretas (seventeenth century).[7]

Parcialidad de los Sacatecas de Jocotenango. *Founder:* Unknown, possibly Alvarado, ca. 1528. *Nomenclature:* After ethnolinguistic region; little is known about who the Sacatecas were or where they came from, but they probably originally lived in the central highlands' Sacatepéquez area. Whether the parcialidad dates from the period prior to Alvarado's death or soon after remains unclear.[8]

Parcialidad de los Guatimaltecas de Jocotenango. *Founder:* Marroquín, as executor of Alvarado's estate and co-governor of Guatemala, ca. 1542. *Nomenclature:* After ethnolinguistic region; "Guatimalteca" refers to a variety of subjugated ethnolinguistic groups, especially the Kaqchikel.[9] These Guatimaltecas based their petition for freedom on their status as soldiers of Alvarado. Their parcialidad, together with that of the Utatlecas, formed the *pueblo* (town) of Jocotenango. The Guatimaltecas in the pueblo were dominant both demographically and politically. While each parcialidad had its own cabildo, the Indian governor of Jocotenango appears always to have been drawn from the parcialidad of Guatimaltecas.[10]

The Indians settled in Jocotenango by Bishop Marroquín between late 1541 and the summer of 1543 were harbingers of a new urban morphology that emerged as Cerrato liberated some 3,000 to 5,000 slaves in and around Santiago in 1549.[11] In the open lands that ringed all but the south side of the city's traza, previously used by the Spanish to raise cattle and grow wheat, each of Santiago's three regular religious orders (Dominicans, Franciscans, and Mercedarians) was instrumental in founding barrios in close proximity to its monastery, peopling them with naborías and former Indian slaves, and ensuring that all of its new charges were converted to Christianity.[12]

Having spent years of captivity inside Spanish houses and workshops as servants and artisans, most of the former slaves (and all of the naborías) in this new "Republic of Indians" were more completely Hispanicized than their counterparts on the milpas and thus less likely at emancipation to have returned to the places of their birth.[13] That the diaspora was not more widespread among rural dwellers, however, serves as testimony to the agility with which vecinos and clerics alike were able to devise new methods of tying their former slaves to the land. Fearful that any new decline in the labor force would make their holdings as worthless as they had been before first settling Indians there, most moved at emancipation, and even sooner in some cases, to impose *terrazgos* (land rents) on the Indians, obligating the milpa or barrio as a whole to provide them with specified amounts of money, payable in *reales* (one real = one-eighth peso) or *tostones* (one tostón = four reales); firewood, figured by the *carga* (load, roughly 230 pounds); maize, assessed by the *fanega* (1.6 bushels or 116 pounds); and/or *gallinas de castilla* (Castilian or European chickens, valued at two reales, ca. 1580). In other cases, each family head, rather than the milpa or barrio in which the family lived, was charged with providing money or goods at a prearranged annual or weekly rate. Although the earliest known terrazgo records date from 1582, by which time a number of the valley's landholdings had passed from the estates of devout vecinos to convents, hospitals, and religious institutions like the Dominicans' College of Santo Tomás, these levies were first put in force around 1550.[14]

No less upset by real and imagined dislocations in labor and supply brought on by emancipation, including rising prices, food shortages, Indian emigration, and a new exodus of vecinos from the city, cabildo and church officials alike were further able to offset Cerrato's reforms by subjecting their former slaves to obligations of *servicio ordinario* (ordinary service) and either *mandamientos* or *repartimientos de indios* (a distribution of Indians for rural and urban labor). Designed to supply the Spanish more adequately with foodstuffs, building supplies, *sacate* (fodder), and manpower, these new institutions were in many cases as onerous as slavery itself.

The communities around Lake Quinizilapa, for example, roughly eight kilometers southwest of the capital, were designated to provide, for a pittance, sacate for the Spaniards' livestock; the attendant cutting, bundling, and then hauling (on their backs, with the aid of a tumpline) to an assigned location in the city must have occupied the better part of a day's labor. Other settlements were forced to supply fixed amounts of lumber, pork and lard, cloth, and vegetables at below-market prices. In addition, all Indian communities were required, with little or no remuneration, to supply work details (their size in proportion to total population) to perform such duties as planting, weeding, and harvesting Spanish wheat, sweeping the city's streets and government buildings, cleaning latrines, and dredging the Pensativo.

Records for the 1570s, for instance, show that the combined parcialidades of Jocotenango were ordered to supply, three times a week, thirty Indian men to clean the palace of the audiencia; forty-six *yerbateros* (grass cutters) weekly, each of whom received between two or three reales a week for his labor; three Indian wet nurses weekly; and six Indian men to clean the latrines of the city jail, without pay. This partial list says nothing of the huge construction projects that demanded hundreds of laborers (aqueducts, roads, public buildings), nor of the more routine servicio ordinario obligations (supplying water, firewood, and manual labor to Spanish households).

To lighten servicio ordinario burdens, Spanish authorities attempted to limit travel and work frequency. As audiencia President Juan Núñez de Landecho informed Philip II in 1563, no Indian was required to walk more than a half-day from his or her home to his or her assigned work detail, and no Indian was forced to take a work turn more than once every six months.[15] But such provisions were rarely observed: Spanish vecinos abused Indians with impunity in the face of a declining labor force and general economic woes. Noting more than symbolically that "all the [Spaniards] are our masters," the Indians of Jocotenango and a score of other settlements felt compelled to petition the Crown in 1572 to ease servicio ordinario requirements that had become "onerous and even unbearable."[16]

The Crown took the valley's former slaves the final step toward full subordination to Spanish rule in 1563, making each family head a tributary subject to a per capita tax both in specie and in foodstuffs, levied in such a way that milpas and barrios burdened by terrazgos paid less tribute than those burdened by none.[17] The action brought the inhabitants of the valley's Indian communities in line with the rest of Spanish Guatemala's Indian population, most of whom had first experienced the burdens of tribute payment and the introduction of Spanish forms of local rule nearly two generations before. It also meant that few of the valley's former slaves became the tributaries of individual Spaniards; the Crown, in fact, was so in need of revenue that it opposed virtually all new individual encomiendas from emancipation forward.[18]

The following two lists present the earliest existing terrazgo data (1563–96) for each of the valley's Indian communities, as well as pertinent details of their nomenclature, establishment, and varying character. Available tributary data for each are also presented; counts are of *tributarios enteros* (full tributaries or family heads), not total tributary population, and they reflect the fact that by 1590 one tributario entero was deemed equivalent to two Indian widowers, two unmarried Indian males, two Indian males married to Indian women reserved from tribute, three Indian widows, three unmarried Indian women, *or* three Indian women married to Indian men reserved from tribute.[19] Maps 3 and 4 locate each settlement.

THE REPUBLIC OF INDIANS: BARRIOS FOUNDED CA. 1550[20]

Barrio de Santo Domingo. *Founder:* Dominicans. *Nomenclature:* After Saint Dominic and the Dominican order. Santo Domingo included a parcialidad of Guatimaltecas (mostly artisans) and a parcialidad of Mexicanos (Mexicans who had accompanied Alvarado in the conquest of Guatemala and their descendants).[21] The settlement of the Guatimaltecas raised the ire of most Spanish vecinos, who believed the Dominicans took charge of these artisans to monopolize their specialized skills. *Other names:* Málaga (sixteenth century), Barrio de la Candelaria (late seventeenth century).[22] *Terrazgos:* Exempt. The Indians of the barrio purchased their lands from the Spaniard García de Salinas and were granted additional property by the Crown. *Tributary count:* 196, ca. 1595.

Barrio de San Francisco. *Founder:* Franciscans. *Nomenclature:* After Saint Francis and the Franciscan order. The Franciscans, like the Dominicans, settled a parcialidad of Guatimaltecas near their monastery.[23] These Indians were joined around 1551 by a parcialidad of Mexicanos, actually Tlaxcaltecas who had residido until then in Almolonga (Ciudad Vieja). Like the Mexicanos of Santo Domingo, they spoke Nahuatl, known popularly in Spanish Guatemala as "mexicano," hence the misidentification. Large numbers of Indians in the barrio seem to have been artisans.[24] *Terrazgos:* Exempt. The inhabitants of San Francisco were given their land outright by the Franciscans. *Tributary count:* About 90, ca. 1582.

Barrio de la Merced. *Founder:* Mercedarians. *Nomenclature:* After the Mercedarian order. Residents of La Merced and the four barrios listed immediately below, all of whom appear to have been Guatimaltecas, came under the supervision of the Mercedarians. Of the five, this community alone bears the order's name. *Terrazgos:* 1 tostón per tributary, to be paid to the Convent of La Merced. *Tributary count:* 45, ca. 1582.

Barrio de San Gerónimo. *Founder:* Mercedarians. *Nomenclature:* After Saint Jerome. *Terrazgos:* Unknown, to be paid to the Convent of La Merced. *Tributary count:* Unknown.[25]

Barrio de San Antonio. *Founder:* Unknown, probably the Mercedarians. *Nomenclature:* After Saint Anthony. *Other name*: San Antonio Jocotenango (1630s). *Terrazgos:* Unknown, with the Convent of La Merced the likely recipient. *Tributary count:* Unknown.[26]

Barrio de Santiago. *Founder:* Unknown, probably the Mercedarians. *Nomenclature:* After Saint James. *Terrazgos:* Unknown, with the Convent of La Merced the likely recipient. *Tributary count:* Unknown.

Barrio de Santa Lucía del Espíritu Santo. *Founder:* Juan Recinos, ca. 1530. *Nomenclature:* After Saint Lucía and the Holy Ghost.[27] Santiago's earliest Indian settlement, Santa Lucía came under the administration of the Mercedarians during the 1540s. Evidently, the Mercedarians gave the barrio its full name. *Other names:* Santa Lucía, Espíritu Santo. *Terrazgos:* 6 reales per tributary, with the Convent of La Merced the likely recipient. *Tributary count:* 33, ca. 1580.

Barrio de Santa Cruz. *Founders:* K'iche' *mercaderes* (merchants), ca. 1550. *Nomenclature:* Probably after the founders' native town, Santa Cruz del Quiché (also known as Santa

Cruz Utatlán in Spanish Guatemala). None of the mercaderes who settled here was a former slave, nor was one of the religious orders instrumental in founding the barrio, though, due to its geographic location, it soon came under the ecclesiastical control of the Dominicans. The Indians of Santa Cruz were unlike most of the many immigrants to Santiago after emancipation in that they came as a group and became Crown tributaries, while most arrived separately and often managed to escape tributary status. *Terrazgos:* Exempt. The mercaderes bought their land from the Spaniard Alfonso Larios, though the transaction was executed for them by their hereditary ruler, Don Juan Rojas of Santa Cruz Utatlán.[28] *Tributary count:* 29, ca. 1596.

SANTIAGO'S OTHER SETTLEMENTS[29]

Santa Ana. *Founder:* Probably Padre Juan Godínez, ca. 1530. *Nomenclature:* After Saint Ann. *Terrazgos:* Unknown; the Chapel of Nuestra Señora de la Piedad, located within the capital's cathedral, was the likely recipient. *Tributary count:* About 50, ca. 1580.

San Andrés Ceballos. *Founder:* Pedro de Ceballos, ca. 1530. *Nomenclature:* Saint's name (Andrew) followed by that of its Spanish founder. *Terrazgos:* 20 fanegas of maize, 20 chickens, and 20 tostones, to be paid annually to the heirs of Ceballos. *Tributary count:* 20, ca. 1580.

San Andrés Deán. *Founder:* Probably Padre Juan Godínez, ca. 1530. *Nomenclature:* Saint's name (Andrew) followed by title (*deán*, ecclesiastical dean) of its Spanish founder. Fuentes y Guzmán to the contrary, "deán" seems to refer not to Joan Alonso, who was never a deán of Santiago's cathedral, but to Padre Juan Godínez, the cathedral's first deán and founder of several milpas in the valley.[30] *Terrazgos:* ½ fanega of maize, 1 chicken, and 9 reales per tributary annually; recipient unknown. *Tributary count:* 23, ca. 1576.

San Antonio Aguas Calientes. *Founder:* Juan de Cháves, ca. 1530. *Nomenclature:* Saint's name (Anthony) followed by topographical description (*aguas calientes*, hot springs), an appellation that has obscured the role of its founder.[31] *Other name:* Juan de Cháves, llamada [called] San Antonio de Padua. *Terrazgos:* Exempt. In 1550 Cháves ceded the lands of the milpa to his former slaves, who had previously paid a terrazgo.[32] *Tributary count:* About 102, ca. 1580.

San Bartolomé Becerra. *Founder:* Bartolomé de Becerra, ca. 1530. *Nomenclature:* Saint's name (Bartholomew) followed by that of its Spanish founder. *Terrazgos:* Unknown. *Tributary count:* 16, ca. 1582.

San Bartolomé Carmona. *Founder:* Juan de Carmona, ca. 1530. *Nomenclature:* Saint's name (Bartholomew) followed by that of its Spanish founder. *Terrazgos:* Unknown. *Tributary count:* Figured until the seventeenth century in the total for San Juan del Obispo, below.

Santa Catalina Bobadilla. *Founder:* Ignacio de Bobadilla, ca. 1530. *Nomenclature:* Saint's name (the "fortunate" Catherine, "La Bienaventurada") followed by that of its Spanish founder. The seventeenth-century history of this milpa has been obscured as a result of its being moved in 1609, under the direction of the Dominicans, from an inaccessible site halfway between San Juan del Obispo and Santa María de Jesús Aserradero to a site just south of San Gaspar Vivar.[33] *Terrazgos:* 10 fanegas of maize annually; recipient unknown. *Tributary count:* 13, ca. 1580.

Santa Catarina Barahona. *Founder:* Sancho de Barahona, ca. 1530. *Nomenclature:* Saint's name (Catherine) followed by that of its Spanish founder. *Terrazgos:* 60 fanegas of maize and 40 chickens, to be paid annually to Barahona's son (as of 1557–59). *Tributary count:* 35–40, ca. 1580.

San Cristóbal. *Founder:* Juan Pérez Dardón, ca. 1530. *Nomenclature:* After Saint Christopher. This milpa included two communities, one in the valley (el bajo), south of Santa Isabel Godínez, the other in the eastern sierra (el alto). *Terrazgos:* 20

fanegas of maize and 35 chickens, to be paid annually to Pérez Dardón's heirs. *Tributary count:* 74, ca. 1580. The tributary payment for the milpa of San Cristóbal el Bajo went not to the Crown but to the encomenderos Cristóbal de Celada and Mateo de Zúñiga (as of 1607).[34]

Santo Domingo de los Hortelanos. *Founder:* Dominicans, probably ca. 1549. *Nomenclature:* Saint's name (Dominic) followed by description of the milpa's function. The inhabitants of this community, established on the monastic lands east of the Dominicans' monastery in Santiago in Panchoy, served the friars as *hortelanos* (gardeners) and were known more generally as *teupantecas* (Nahuatl for servants of the house of God). *Other names:* Santa Inés, Santa Inés de Monte Policiano.[35] *Terrazgos:* 120 cargas of firewood, to be paid annually to the Hospital of San Alejo (as of 1574). *Tributary count:* 38, ca. 1580.

San Felipe. *Founder:* Gaspar Arias Dávila, ca. 1528. *Nomenclature:* After Saint Philip. This milpa was located north of the future site of Santiago in Panchoy and separated from the city by Manchén Hill.[36] *Other name:* San Felipe de Jesús. *Terrazgos:* 10 reales per tributary, to be paid annually to the College of Santo Tomás. *Tributary count:* 54, ca. 1580.

San Gaspar Vivar/Barrio de los Mixtecas. *Founder:* Probably Diego de Vivar, ca. 1530. *Nomenclature:* Saint's name followed by that of its Spanish founder. The milpa of San Gaspar Vivar was populated by Vivar's former slaves and their descendants; adjoining it was a small community of Mixtec Indians (from Oaxaca) who had accompanied Alvarado to Guatemala. The only group of Mexican auxiliaries not to live in Almolonga, the Mixtecas had either disappeared or lost their separate identity by the end of the sixteenth century.[37] *Terrazgos:* 6 reales per tributary for the Mixtecas, to be paid annually to the Convent of the Concepción; unknown for San Gaspar Vivar.[38] *Tributary count:* 61, ca. 1576.

Santa Isabel Godínez. *Founder:* Padre Juan Godínez, ca. 1530. *Nomenclature:* Saint's name (Isabel) followed by that of its Spanish founder. *Terrazgos:* Unknown; payable to the Chapel of Nuestra Señora de la Piedad, located within the capital's cathedral. *Tributary count:* 18, ca. 1580.

San Juan del Obispo. *Founder:* Bishop Marroquín, ca. 1530. *Nomenclature:* Saint's name (John) followed by title (*obispo*, bishop) of its Spanish founder. *Terrazgos:* 80 tostones, to be paid annually to the Convent of the Concepción. *Tributary count:* 140 (including residents of San Bartolomé Carmona), ca. 1580.

San Juan Gascón. *Founder:* Padre Juan Gascón, ca. 1530. *Nomenclature:* Saint's name (John) followed by that of its Spanish founder; chroniclers and historians have incorrectly attributed the founding of this milpa to one Don Gascón (or Gastón) de Guzmán.[39] *Terrazgos:* Unknown, but may have been included in the neighboring San Miguel Milpas Altas total (below). The former slaves of Padre Gascón (deceased by 1550) signed a terrazgo contract with Juan de León, perhaps because the lands of San Miguel Milpas Altas were more arable than those of San Juan Gascón. *Tributary count:* 10, ca. 1580.

San Lorenzo Monroy. *Founder:* Diego de Monroy, ca. 1530. *Nomenclature:* Saint's name (Lawrence) followed by that of its Spanish founder. *Terrazgos:* 80 fanegas of maize, to be paid annually to María de Monroy (Monroy's heir as of 1576). *Tributary count:* 64, ca. 1575; 49, ca. 1582.[40]

San Lucas Cabrera. *Founder:* Gabriel de Cabrera, ca. 1530. *Nomenclature:* Saint's name (Luke) followed by that of its Spanish founder. *Terrazgos:* Unknown. *Tributary count:* 13, ca. 1580.

Santa Lucía Monterroso. *Founder:* Francisco de Monterroso, ca. 1530. *Nomenclature:* Saint's name (Lucía) followed by that of its Spanish founder. *Terrazgos:* Unknown. *Tributary count:* 49, ca. 1563.[41] As late as 1603 tribute payments were made not to the Crown but to the encomendero Luis de Monterroso.[42]

Santa María Concepción Almolonga. *Founder:* Alvarado, ca. 1527. *Nomenclature:* Saint's name (Virgin Mary) followed by Nahuatl name derived from the Kaqchikel. This milpa, the only known preconquest Kaqchikel site in the valley, was the only major settlement with an Indian name. It was divided into three parcialidades: Mexicanos, Tlaxcaltecas, and Guatimaltecas (a group reduced in population when most of its members moved to Jocotenango). Remaining Guatimaltecas (Kaqchikels) may well have been resettled in San Miguel Escobar after ca. 1542 (see entry for San Miguel Escobar in this list). *Terrazgos:* Unknown. *Tributary count:* About 168, ca. 1575: 21 Tlaxcaltecas, 23 Mexicanos, 124 Guatimaltecas.

Santa María de Jesús Aserradero. *Founder:* Possibly Dominicans and Franciscans, pre-1541. *Nomenclature:* Saint's name (Virgin Mary) followed by a description of the milpa's function (*aserradero,* saw pit). Located on the then thickly timbered northeastern slopes of Agua and overlooking Santiago in Panchoy, this milpa was known simply as "the aserradero" in the second half of the sixteenth century because its population was charged with providing lumber to the city. From its founding, the settlement was divided into two parcialidades: San Francisco, administered by the Franciscans, and Santo Domingo, under the care of the Dominicans (not to be confused with barrios of the same name).[43] *Terrazgos:* Unknown. *Tributary count:* 273, ca. 1575: 158 in San Francisco, 115 in Santo Domingo.

Santa María Magdalena. *Founder:* Unknown, pre-1541. *Nomenclature:* After Mary Magdalene. *Other name:* Santa María Magdalena Milpas Altas. *Terrazgos:* 120 fanegas of maize and 120 chickens, to be paid annually to the Royal Hospital. *Tributary count:* 52½, ca. 1590.

San Mateo Cabrera. *Founder:* Probably Gabriel de Cabrera, ca. 1530. *Nomenclature:* Saint's name (Matthew) followed by that of its Spanish founder. *Other name:* San Mateo Milpas Altas. *Terrazgos:* 20 fanegas of maize annually, plus 15 eggs and 4 cargas of firewood weekly; recipient unknown. *Tributary count:* 45, ca. 1580.

San Miguel Dueñas. *Founder:* Miguel de Dueñas, ca. 1530. *Nomenclature:* Saint's name (Michael) followed by that of its Spanish founder. Contrary to Fuentes y Guzmán's account, this Lake Quinizilapa milpa was *not* founded by Alvarado for the benefit of the conquistadores' widows and named for them as *dueñas* (owners) of the land and slaves who tilled it.[44] *Terrazgos:* 40 fanegas of maize and 20 chickens, to be paid annually to Dueñas's heirs. *Tributary count:* 63, ca. 1580.

San Miguel Escobar. *Founder:* Juan de Escobar, probably early 1540s. *Nomenclature:* Saint's name (Archangel Michael) followed by that of its Spanish founder. This milpa could only have been founded after September 1541 because the site on which it was located was occupied until then by Santiago in Almolonga. The Franciscan chronicler Francisco Vázquez states that in the late seventeenth century San Miguel was a barrio of Almolonga (Ciudad Vieja) and that its Kaqchikel population was called "los reservados," or those reserved from paying full tribute. This suggests that the original inhabitants of San Miguel and their ancestors had fought alongside the Mexicans and Pedro de Alvarado in the conquest of Guatemala.[45] *Terrazgos:* Unknown. *Tributary count:* Unknown.[46]

San Miguel Milpas Altas. *Founder:* Juan de León, 1549. *Nomenclature:* Saint's name (Michael) followed by geographical location (*milpas altas*, high milpas). *Other name:* Milpa de Juan de León. *Terrazgos:* 15 fanegas of maize and 20 chickens, to be paid annually to the Hospital of San Alejo (as of 1562). *Tributary count:* 31, ca. 1575; 20, ca. 1580.[47]

San Pedro del Tesorero. *Founder:* Francisco de Castellanos, pre-1541. *Nomenclature:* Saint's name (Peter) followed by title (*tesorero*, treasurer) of its Spanish founder. Royal treasurer Pedro de Becerra is said to have established this milpa, but it appears Castellanos was the actual founder.[48] *Other name:* San Pedro de las Huertas. *Terrazgos:* 180 tostones, to be paid annually to Alonso Hidalgo (as of 1573). *Tributary count:* Unknown.[49]

Santiago Zamora. *Founder:* Alonso de Zamora, ca. 1530. *Nomenclature:* Saint's name (James) followed by that of its

Spanish founder. *Terrazgos:* 20 fanegas of maize and 15 tostones, to be paid annually to Juan de León, "señor de las tierras" (lord or owner of the lands as of 1575). *Tributary count:* 44, ca. 1580.

BARRIO "SELF-RULE"

The separation of Indians from Spaniards was the cornerstone of early Spanish social politics in America.[50] Indeed, the Crown, as evidenced by a series of royal *cédulas* (directives) first promulgated on Spanish arrival in the New World, created the "two republics" to protect the Indians from the so-called bad example and evil ways of the Spaniards.[51] While these cédulas made explicit the Crown's desire to isolate the Indians in native towns, they were quickly incorporated into the "Laws of the Indies" and made applicable to urban Indian communities as well.

So it was that a republic of Indians ringed Santiago de Guatemala's Spanish core as the city entered the second half of the sixteenth century. Although no wall separated the two, Santiago's peripheral barrios were deemed *extramuros* (outside the walls), their Indian inhabitants barred from independent residence (but not domestic service) in the central city by Spanish wealth and distrust. Each of the two republics possessed its own language and cultural complex, its own religious institutions and racial identity, even its own governing bodies, though the Indians had long since learned whose hands held the political reins.

Acting in part on the premise that the heathen Indians needed such civilizing influences as Spanish political institutions during "the period of [their] infidelity," the Crown introduced cabildo government to Santiago's barrios and the surrounding milpas shortly after emancipation, thereby bringing to the valley a level of political Hispanicization already achieved elsewhere in Guatemala, where *principales* (members of the Indian hereditary nobility) began filling Indian cabildo offices soon after the conquest.[52] While it appears that in Santiago, too, Indian cabildo members were most often chosen from this tiny pool of principales, how they were identified remains a mystery. Would those of high birth have been able to preserve

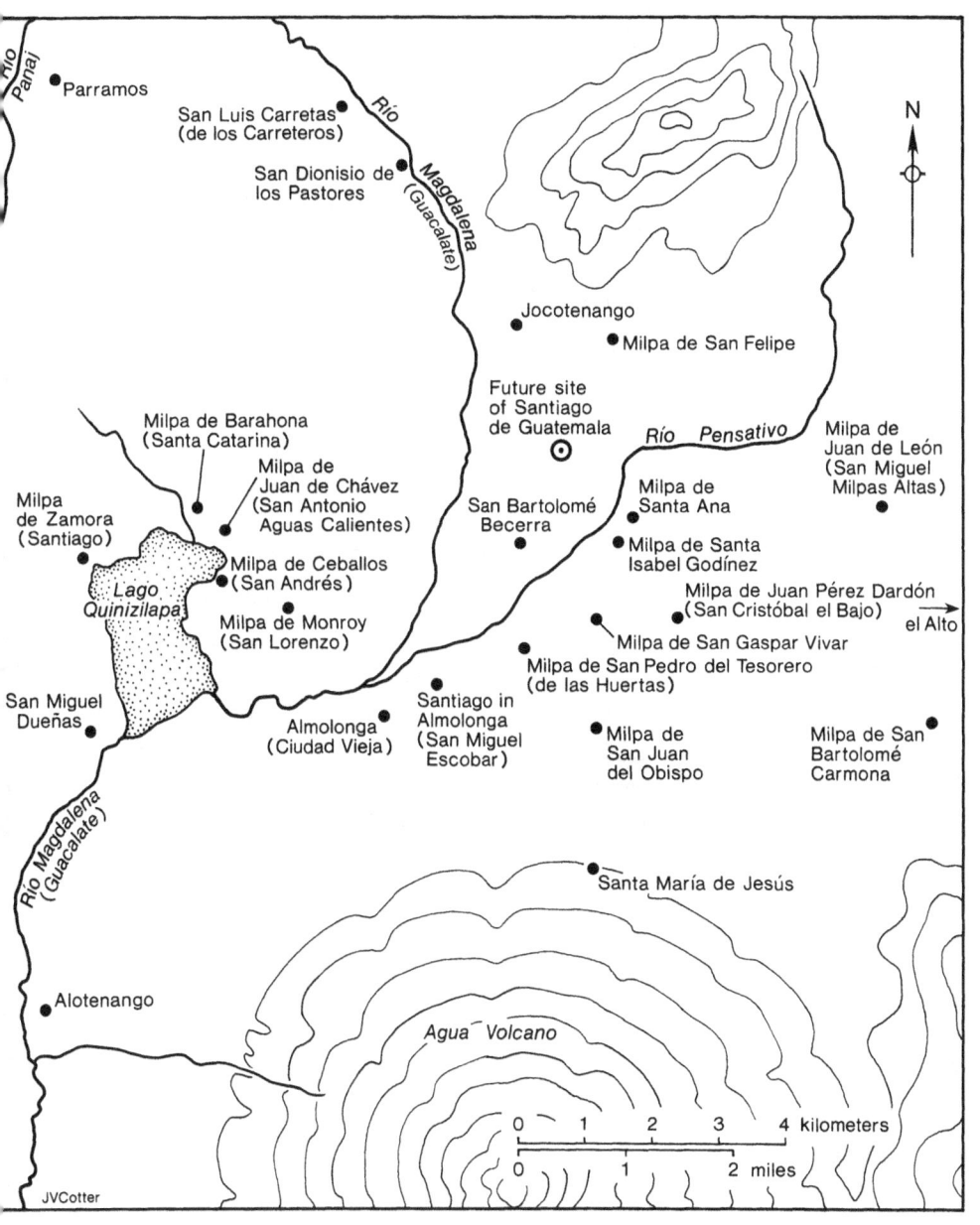

MAP 3. The Valley of the City (Panchoy), ca. 1530 (milpas founded by Spanish vecinos).

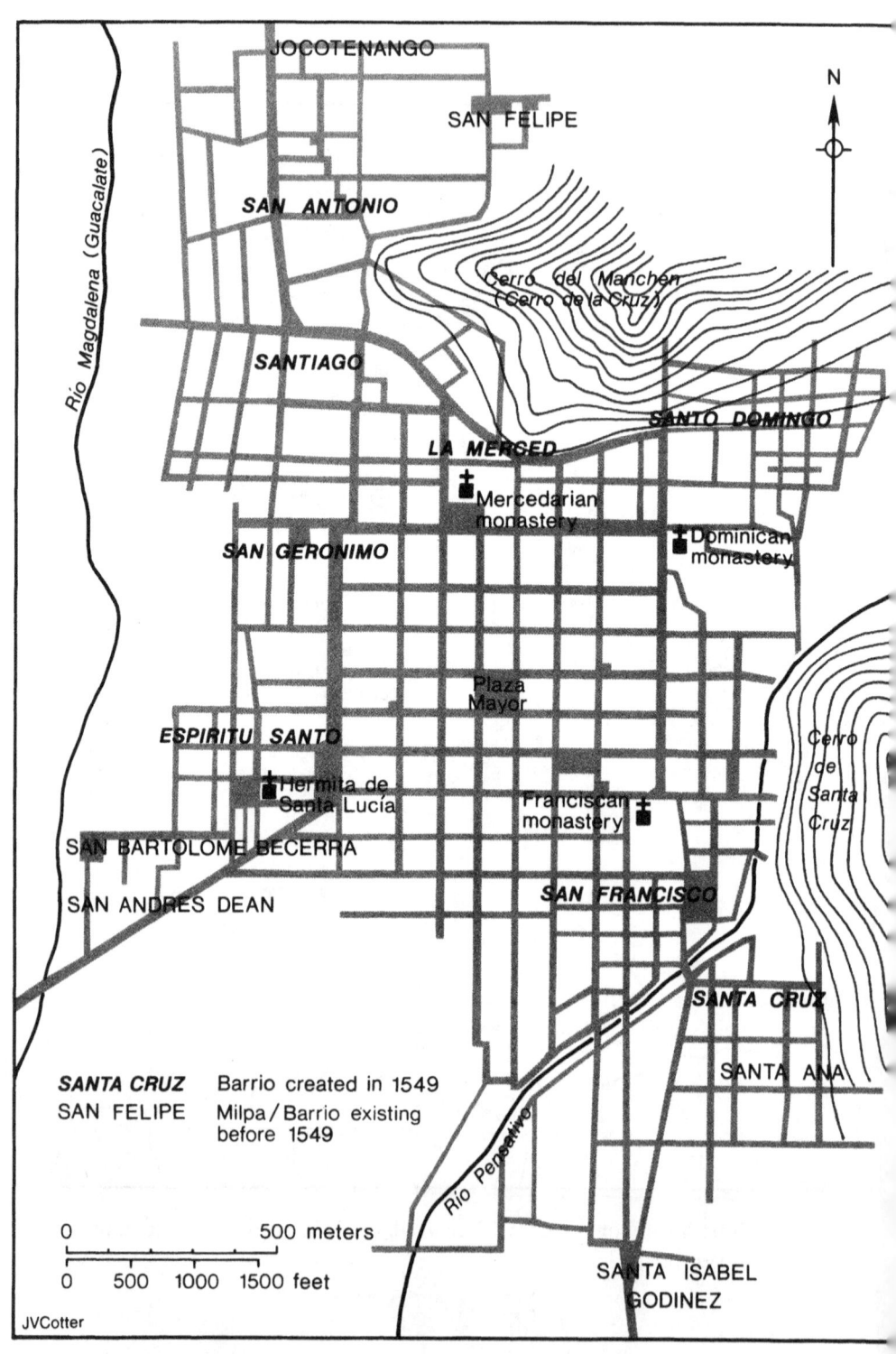

MAP 4. Santiago de Guatemala, ca. 1550, superimposed on grid of 1773 (barrios created with liberation of Indian slaves in 1549). Urban grid based on a map by V. L. Annis.

their superior social standing after two or three decades of enslavement? Could they, under such adverse conditions, have conferred noble status on their offspring, in keeping with the preconquest custom?[53] Whatever the answer, a simple comparison of surnames within particular barrios and parcialidades reveals that Indian cabildo offices in Santiago were held for generations by a small group of families.[54]

The imposition of cabildo government, of course, had less to do with saving the Indians from their presumed natural inferiority than it did with the Spaniards' desire to save themselves from the onerous (and by their estimation, risky) tasks of governing and policing the barrios and ensuring that Indian tribute obligations to the Crown were paid promptly and in full. By appointing Indian *alcaldes* (mayors, chief barrio officials), *regidores* (aldermen), and *alguaciles* (constables) and holding *them* responsible for many (though not all) of these duties, the Crown was able to control the barrios while at the same time insulating itself from the wrath of the Indian underclasses who dwelt there.

Few of Santiago's Indian barrios lacked a cabildo. Santo Domingo had one, as did San Francisco, La Merced, Espíritu Santo, Santa Cruz, Santiago, San Antonio, and San Gerónimo. So did the contiguous settlements of San Felipe, Santo Domingo de los Hortelanos, Santa Isabel Godínez, San Lucas Cabrera, the Parcialidad de los Utatlecas de Jocotenango, and the Parcialidad de los Guatimaltecas de Jocotenango (in which the Parcialidad de los Sacatecas was also representado). Each had its own cabildo building. Each had its own chapel or hermitage, except for Jocotenango, where the Utatlecas and Guatimaltecas shared a single church. The most populous barrios, the Parcialidad de los Guatimaltecas de Jocotenango, Santo Domingo, and San Francisco, even had jails under their control.[55]

Population dictated the number of cabildo offices.[56] Thus the smaller Indian jurisdictions were represented by one alcalde and one regidor, the biggest by as many as two alcaldes, four regidores, and an *alguacil mayor* (chief constable), a limit set in the early seventeenth century by Philip III. Because its residents outnumbered those of any other Indian community in Santiago, the Parcialidad de los Guatimaltecas de Jocotenango was ruled in addition by an Indian *gobernador* (governor) who presided over the pueblo's cabildo.[57] Santo Domingo and San Francisco contained two distinct ethnolinguistic groups within their jurisdictions, Guatimaltecas and Mexicanos, so each barrio was represented by two alcaldes, one from each group.[58]

ADMINISTRATION

At times such bipartite administration broke down into intra-barrio conflict. The Guatimaltecas of Santo Domingo were permanently relegated to the position of alcalde of second vote —the source of one dispute that tells us much about office-holding in the Indian communities of Santiago de Guatemala.[59] True, Santo Domingo was not wholly representative of the city's Indian barrios, being more populous and, like San Francisco alone, composed of two parcialidades.[60] But Santo Domingo functioned like the others in its dealings with church and Crown. It endured the same administrative restraints and the same lack of control over cabildo appointments. It encountered the same kinds of pressures to adopt the Spanish system as its own, to use the suit and countersuit as the sole instruments of political redress.

Claiming to represent the entire barrio, the leaders of the parcialidad of Guatimaltecas in Santo Domingo petitioned the audiencia in early September 1703 to accept a slate of officials for 1704 that would, for the first time in a century and a half, give the alcalde of first vote to the Guatimaltecas and name the alcalde of second vote from the parcialidad of Mexicanos. In the interest of barrio peace and unity, they argued, the Crown should in addition reestablish the *alternativa* (an ancient custom by which two competing groups annually rotated leadership posts), then widely used in colonial Spanish religious orders to lessen the antagonism between *peninsulares* (Spanish-born) and creoles over election to top religious offices.[61]

Unwilling to accept the Guatimalteca slate outright, the audiencia sent the petition to Fray Domingo de los Reyes, the *cura doctrinero* (priest) of Santo Domingo, who found fault not with the Guatimaltecas' attempts to institute the alternativa (his support for that was so unequivocal as to suggest he had conspired with the Guatimaltecas to wrest control of the barrio from the Mexicanos) but with their choice for alcalde of second vote. The Mexicano Matheo Ramírez, de los Reyes insisted, was too old and too undependable to take office in Santo Domingo;[62] Pascual Silvestre, a Mexicano of "good age and customs," should therefore take his place. After naming two replacements for the lesser posts of *regidor mayor* (first regidor) and alguacil mayor, neither of whom offended leaders of either parcialidad,[63] Fray de los Reyes gave the Guatimalteca slate his blessing and sent it on to the audiencia for approval.

The audiencia's decision on 19 September 1703 to endorse de los Reyes's recommendations sparked an immediate and angry protest from Santo Domingo's Mexicanos. The original petition for reinstitution of the alternativa, they argued in a petition of their own, failed to represent the views of the entire barrio, as the Guatimaltecas had reported. It violated a time-honored custom and deprived them of their birthright as descendants of those who had assisted Alvarado in the conquest of Guatemala and founded Santo Domingo. By inference, moreover, the Guatimalteca petition made the spurious claim that peace and unity were somehow lacking in the barrio, when in fact both, according to the Mexicanos, had been carefully maintained as long as they had filled the office of alcalde of first vote, an arrangement with which Guatimalteca officials had largely been content.

In response to a 15 October 1703 order from the audiencia that they justify these claims, the Mexicanos of Santo Domingo presented as witnesses two longtime Spanish residents of the barrio, one seventy-seven years of age, the other eighty, both of whom confirmed the facts set forth in the Mexicano counterpetition. But their next witness was far more damaging to the Guatimalteca cause. According to Lorenzo Pérez, a Spanish-speaking Guatimalteca born in Santo Domingo, the very same case had been decided in 1672, when the acting president of the audiencia, Bishop Juan de Santo Mathías Sáenz de Mañozca y Murillo, refused to grant the post of alcalde of first vote to the barrio's top Guatimalteca on the grounds that the move was without precedent.[64]

With the appointment of the Guatimalteca slate on hold until the interparcialidad dispute could be resolved, the audiencia agreed on 24 October to give the Guatimaltecas five days to rebut the Mexicano allegations. At the hearing, the Guatimaltecas' lawyer disputed even the most basic Mexicano claims. The Mexicanos, he argued, had neither founded Santo Domingo nor descended from the conquistadores. Rather, they were fellow slaves who had usurped Guatimalteca lands and the office of alcalde of first vote, only to claim later that the lands were originally theirs and that they held a monopoly on the chief alcalde post. The Guatimaltecas, he concluded, were now seeking merely to share that to which they held clear title; since they had been loyal vassals and tributaries of the king of Spain, performing services for Crown and church in equal measure to the Mexicanos, they therefore deserved equal alcalde status.

The evidence for the Guatimalteca rebuttal—a document from an unbound sixteenth-century volume that allegedly belonged to the Cofradía (brotherhood) del Nombre de Jesús, a Mexicano religious group—was presented to Mexicano leaders and their attorney on 7 November 1703. Under oath, all denied having seen the document, though most had served the cofradía as part of their civil and religious obligations in the barrio and thus were likely to have known its holdings intimately. Noting on closer inspection that the document was written not in Nahuatl, the language of their forebears, but in Mexicana Pipil, which they called "an adulterated and illegitimate version of Nahuatl," the Mexicano leaders claimed it was a fake.[65]

The Mexicanos were probably on the mark. The unbound volume had most recently been in the possession of Tomás de Salas, *fiscal* (local Indian official charged with enforcing Indian religious obligations) of the barrio's church and *escribano* (notary) of the opposing parcialidad of Guatimaltecas. This raised the suspicion that the document had been forged and then inserted in the unbound volume in an attempt to bolster the Guatimalteca case. In any event, the document was inconclusive. Relating the story, first, of Bishop Bartolomé de Las Casas, the Dominican reformer whose efforts in the 1540s to free the enslaved of Guatemala earned him the appellation "apostle of the Indians," it went on to describe President Cerrato's success in emancipating the slaves. Although it made no reference to the Mexicanos and thus shed no light on how and when the Mexicanos came to settle in Santo Domingo, the Guatimaltecas apparently used the document to prove that the Mexicanos' ancestors, like their own, had been slaves, not conquistadores, and that their Guatimalteca ancestors had won the right to the office of alcalde of first vote simply by being the first to settle in the barrio.[66]

The conflicting claims of the two groups are not easily resolved. It appears that both parcialidades moved to Málaga (the name of Santo Domingo ca. 1550) in 1551 and that their cabildo was started in June 1552.[67] No differentiation between the two parcialidades, or the alcaldes that served them, was made in repeated sixteenth-century petitions to the Crown complaining of abuses by local Spanish officials and vecinos.[68] Santo Domingo's tributaries were always counted as constituents of one jurisdiction, not two parcialidades.[69] Though some of the barrio's earliest inhabitants said they spoke Mexicano, a reasonably good indicator of their status as conquistadores, they claimed at the same time to be former slaves and naborías, not unlike their Guatimalteca neighbors. The barrio, in short, had once spoken in a single voice.

Why was all this forgotten in disputes over officeholding after 1672? Perhaps the answer lies in the Mexicanos' special status as both conquistadores and slaves. The record shows that the Tlaxcaltecan conquistadores, despite Spanish promises to the contrary, were distributed like so many chattels (ten or twenty to an individual) among Spanish captains and soldiers of the conquest after their military services were no longer needed in the late 1520s.[70] The Mexicanos probably suffered a similar fate, and their late seventeenth- and early eighteenth-century descendants either forgot the indignity or chose to hide it, knowing it would only tarnish their claim to preeminent alcalde status. But the Spanish had even more to hide. To admit the Mexicanos had been enslaved would be to reveal the Spaniards' treachery and shatter the belief that Alvarado's Mexican auxiliaries had been accorded special status for making the conquest of Guatemala a joint crusade.[71]

A last bit of legal wrangling preceded the audiencia's final ruling in the case, by now all but a foregone conclusion. Responding to a petition from the Mexicanos' attorney, the audiencia on 23 November 1703 ordered the Indian gobernador and alcaldes of Santa María Concepción Almolonga (Ciudad Vieja) to produce "the executories and papers that speak in favor of the Mexicans." The Mexicanos of Santo Domingo hoped to prove that, because the Mexicanos of Ciudad Vieja had aided the Spanish in conquering Guatemala, their ancestors must have done the same. Among the documents they produced was a royal provision of Philip II, signed in Madrid on 18 May 1562, which exempted from tribute Mexicanos, Tlaxcaltecas, and Zapotecas (from Oaxaca) who lived in Ciudad Vieja and had served the king in the conquest, as well as their descendants.[72] In rebuttal, the Guatimaltecas' attorney noted persuasively that the Mexicanos of Santo Domingo had paid tribute for over a century and thus must be descended from slaves.[73] The cofradía document, he reminded the audiencia, had proved his case.

The audiencia's decision, in favor of the Mexicanos, was handed down on 13 December 1703. It supported their exclusive right to the office of alcalde of first vote and voided the 19 September 1703 decree assigning that office to the Guatimaltecas and establishing the alternativa. About a week later the Mexicanos claimed that the Guatimalteca Bernardino de Cháves, the alcalde of second vote who had started the whole affair in an attempt to win the top alcalde post for himself and his fellow Guatimaltecas, was slandering the Mexicanos in the wake of the audiencia's decision. The Mexicanos, fearing Cháves would stir up more trouble, asked the audiencia to void his election and give them permission to replace him with another Guatimalteca from the barrio. The fiscal of the audiencia agreed with the Mexicanos, but the audiencia did not. Instead, it ordered Cháves to serve in peace as alcalde of second vote and warned him that any further trouble would prompt his dismissal.[74] No trouble was reported thereafter. The status quo had been preserved.

Electoral procedures in Santo Domingo, while they favored the Mexicanos by giving them exclusive claim to the office of alcalde of first vote, at least permitted both Guatimaltecas and Mexicanos to select officials from each other's parcialidades.[75] Thus Guatimalteca leaders nominated the alcalde of first vote, Mexicano leaders the alcalde of second vote, and so on down the line. Here, as in all of Santiago's Indian cabildos, nominees were designated in September and installed the following January. The intervening three months gave the barrio's cura doctrinero ample time to study the proposed slates and select appropriate replacements.[76] What seems unusual about the 1703 dispute in Santo Domingo is that the Mexicanos were able to challenge the cura's choices at all, let alone win a reversal.

On second look, however, the case was not atypical. Legal procedures were carefully observed and much was made of proper protocols in the presentation of documentary evidence, yet the evidence itself was flimsy, even irrelevant, the outcome more in line with Spanish interests than with the facts. In name only were the Indians of Santiago's barrios given justice, autonomy, or legal privilege, yet Spanish administrative procedures and legal forms remained a powerful influence upon them—so powerful, in fact, that although Indians sued Spaniards in the sixteenth and seventeenth centuries to protect their limited rights, by the eighteenth century they had come to contest each other's rights.

LAW AND ORDER

Santiago's Indian cabildos were given the same kind of nominal authority to enforce the law as they were to select officials. Within the borders of their respective barrios and nowhere else, Indian alcaldes and alguaciles were directed to intervene in minor crimes and disturbances among Indians, as well as in those involving Indians and either blacks or castas, but were not empowered to do so when such infractions as drunkenness, petty thievery, or disturbing the peace were committed by or against Spaniards. Assaults and murders, whatever the ethnic identity of the victim or assailant, were similarly exempt from Indian justice. Indian officials enjoyed perhaps their greatest autonomy during emergencies, when police powers would be thrust upon them until their Spanish counterparts arrived on the scene. At all other times Indian autonomy was limited by the prerogative of Spanish city officials to exert their own higher authority.

A preliminary survey of thousands of criminal cases in the city of Santiago from roughly 1580 to 1770 reveals few instances of Spaniards' being charged with crimes against either Indians or castas and even fewer instances of their being prosecuted for such crimes.[77] Of those cases that went to trial, Spaniards were more often prosecuted for abusing Indians than for abusing castas—proof, perhaps, that the Crown paid something more than lip service to the notion that its wards the Indians merited special protection.[78] But the fact remains that only a few Spaniards were ever convicted of crimes against Indians. As members of the dominant group within Santiago and the surrounding valley, Spaniards clearly had little difficulty in manipulating a legal system that treated Indians (not to mention blacks and castas) as second-class citizens.

Yet Spanish supremacy cannot fully explain why the vast majority of criminal cases in this preliminary survey involved non-Spanish defendants. Nor can the fact that non-Spaniards constituted an overwhelming percentage of the city's total population by as early as 1580.[79] Here, it seems, recent explanations for crime and social violence are also appropriate. Casta and Indian alike were crammed into the barrios. Such factors as abject poverty, ethnic rivalry, and alcoholism must have combined to create a fertile environment for crime.

It should logically follow, then, that most crimes committed by non-Spaniards occurred in the slums that ringed the city's Spanish core and that the overwhelming majority of the victims were non-Spaniards.[80] But this was only partly the case.

While most victims of non-Spanish assailants were indeed non-Spanish, Spaniards appear to have been the most common victims of non-Spanish larcenists. Virtually every Spanish household was staffed by Indian and casta servants and, in many cases, by black and mulatto slaves. It was probably from among these domestic workers that the great majority of larcenists came. Certainly servants and slaves had more intimate knowledge of Spanish material possessions and greater access to them than did the independent Indians and castas of the barrios.[81]

Although blacks, mulattoes, and mestizos in the capital were without their own systems of law enforcement—none of the three administered a jail or was supervised by its own alcaldes and alguaciles—each was assigned a key peacekeeping role. As early as the 1640s Santiago's militia included whole companies of *gente parda* (mulattoes) and blacks;[82] established in most of the city's principal barrios, all were commanded by mulatto officers by the eighteenth century. Mestizos and other nonmulatto castas also filled the ranks of the capital's Spanish infantry companies, founded in the sixteenth century; previously, some degree of military preparedness and contribution to the region's defense had been expected of every Spanish vecino.[83] Only the Spanish cavalry seems to have remained truly Spanish in character.

While the capital's Indian justices and Spanish magistrates performed a dual police-judicial function, the urban militia companies (especially those of gente parda) acted strictly as policemen, regularly patrolling the city at night beginning around the turn of the eighteenth century. Their orders, it seems, were to apprehend lawbreakers and to leave to Spanish officials the further task of bringing the accused to justice.[84]

To Indian barrio and pueblo officials during this period fell the new burden of manning *rondas* (patrols) *outside* their jurisdictions, under the authority of one of the city's two Spanish alcaldes.[85] On their way to report for one such ronda on a December night in 1761, the *alcalde mayor* (mayor of first vote), regidor, and alguacil of San Cristóbal el Bajo arrested a man fleeing with a *mantilla* (shawl) he had stolen from a woman on the street. The trio delivered the suspect to the Spanish alcalde on the victim's *mandato verbal* (spoken order).[86]

The decision by Santiago's town fathers to intensify rondas in the city was prompted by a growing fear that the Spanish would easily be surrounded and annihilated in any uprising by castas and Indians. They knew, after all, that the ratio of Spaniards to non-Spaniards in and around the capital had never before been so disadvantageous. Like ruling European minorities elsewhere, they sensed the critical importance of any measure to disunite their subjects. Establishing mulatto militias in the Indian barrios, recruiting nonmulattoes for other nominally Spanish infantry companies, using Indian justices to patrol predominantly casta neighborhoods—all, they believed, would work to channel the hostility of the nonelites not against the Spanish who had devised these measures but against a diversity of fellow subjects who were obligated to implement and enforce them.

By most accounts, the Spanish tactics of divide and rule worked well. Subject groups remained largely in competition. The Indian justices and pardo militiamen who served as Spanish proxies not only toed the Spanish line but showed no overt favoritism toward members of their own groups. Direct force, though often threatened, was rarely used against Santiago's multiracial majority population. Yet the Spanish strategy was as much a product of necessity as it was a product of fear.[87] Unwilling to assume the task of policing the barrios alone when faced with a rapidly declining pool of Indian officials— itself the result of a fast-decaying urban Indian population— the Spanish left themselves no other choice but to burden still further the few remaining Indian justices and to enlist the aid of the castas who had come to desegregate the Indian barrios and claim them as their own.

CHAPTER THREE

THE FALL OF THE TWO REPUBLICS

THE displacement of Indians by castas in Santiago's peripheral barrios was perhaps the most far-reaching consequence of mestizaje, a process at once so gradual and so much a part of the dynamic of everyday life in the capital from the conquest forward that Spanish administrators were powerless to stop it.

Official views of mestizaje in the 1520s were exclusively defined by large numbers of unions between conquering Spaniards, overwhelmingly male and in the prime of life, and Indian women. The resulting mestizo population, though numerous and unprovided for by the framers of the two republics, was largely accommodated by both the *república de los españoles* (Spanish republic) and the *república de los indios* (Indian republic). Mestizas, and legitimate children of both sexes, were generally absorbed by the Spanish sector; the illegitimate (especially boys), who represented the vast majority of early mestizo children, tended to assume the lowly status of their mothers; the rest, an insignificant minority, found doors to both republics closed.

While the creation of the mestizo put added, unexpected strain on the two republics, the Spanish introduction of African slaves (mostly male), *negros criollos* (American-born black slaves), and a few *libertados* (black freedmen)—and their subsequent mixing with Indians, mestizos, and Spaniards in the decades before 1550—rendered the Spanish social model irrelevant. Most mulattoes (defined in Spanish Guatemala as those of both African-Spanish and African-Indian descent)[1] were blocked from passage into either republic, due to racial prejudice, to a lack of phenotypical similarities with either the dominant Spaniards or majority Indians, and to their special role, often resented, as the traders and brokers of the Spanish colonial economy.[2] As such, they became the primary agents of a new sociodemographic reality, progenitors of a casta population neither republic could absorb.

Ironically, African slaves served no practical function that the Indians could not have served as well. They were instead a status symbol in sixteenth-century Santiago, a way for Spanish vecinos to distinguish themselves from other vecinos able to afford only Indian slaves (before 1550) or servants. Concentrated eventually in a small number of highly productive agricultural estates, most slaves began life in Guatemala attached to the largest and richest households in Santiago's Spanish core, where they lived with "fifty, seventy, and even more individuals": Spanish vecinos, their wives, children, and relatives (mostly male); *paniaguados* (hangers-on), usually unmarried male Spaniards; Indian slaves, mostly female; and Indian naborías, again mostly female.[3] All ate, worked, and slept under the same roof, regardless of status or race.

Formal and informal unions between the groups, and the mestizos and mulattoes who were their offspring, produced a whole class of castas who lived with and served the Spanish vecinos under slave (in the case of some mulattoes), *criado* (servant), contract, or independent status. So numerous were these unions that the Spanish quarter essentially filled to capacity in the decades after Indian emancipation and began to spill its overflow population into the barrios. There and only there could free blacks and castas afford to live and own property while continuing to serve their Spanish employers or striking out on their own. Crown planners, despite a genuine and humane interest in preserving the all-Indian character of the república de los indios, had unwittingly invited its destruction by making no other provision for them.

The subsequent increase in barrio sexual contacts (in and out of wedlock) between Indians and the newly displaced free blacks and castas intensified with the arrival in the capital of a large but difficult to measure number of casta immigrants,[4] drawn there from other parts of the audiencia, New Spain, and distant points of the Spanish empire by news of Santiago's early growth and economic opportunity.[5] Strengthened as a force for desegregation and mestizaje by plebeian and déclassé Spanish immigrants who lacked the necessary family ties or wealth to own property in Santiago's core, these latest arrivals in the barrios, together with those displaced from Spanish Santiago, were the major outside stimulus in transforming the purely Indian neighborhoods into multiracial communities. Their offspring and generations of castas to come completed the transformation, effectively destroying the república de los indios from within.

Santiago's post-1600 cabildo officials were largely indifferent to the rapid pace of mestizaje. Manifesting none of the racial hatred that prompted their counterparts in Manila, the capital of the Spanish Philippines, virtually to quarantine the Chinese merchant community, prohibit Chinese residence within the Spanish city, and, in 1608, impose "grave penalties" on Chinese found even sleeping in Spanish houses, they were loath to retard a process that was both a direct consequence of their rapacity for servants and easily exploitable labor and the source of casta replacements for a declining Indian work force.[6] Besides, segregation had been implemented in Santiago de Guatemala and throughout Spanish America, not so much out of fear and hatred for any one group, but to protect the Indians from the alleged harmful effects of contact with castas, blacks, and Spaniards. Once the racial purity of the all-Indian communities had been compromised, local Spanish officials lacked any reason, let alone the burning ones that for centuries motivated Spanish colonists in the Philippines to persecute the Chinese, to continue a failed social policy on the Indians' behalf.[7]

Spanish indifference to the plight of the república de los indios did not, of course, extend to the república de los españoles, which experienced no appreciable residential desegregation (based on property ownership, not the exclusion of non-Spaniards) at any point in the city's history. Land values in the highly coveted blocks around the plaza mayor were simply too high for independent Indians (and other non-Spanish) to own or lease property there,[8] though a number of free mulattoes appear to have amassed sufficient wealth by the late seventeenth century to build houses on the fringes of the Spanish core.[9] Here in the republic of Spaniards, residential expansion was the order of the day, and with it a degree of displacement for the Indians (and castas) whose neighborhoods were "gentrified" as the Spanish core grew, by 1680, to roughly five blocks in every direction of the plaza mayor.[10]

Growth was hardly uniform. While low, damp topography appears to have discouraged the Spanish from settling even three blocks south of the plaza mayor,[11] they occupied considerably more than five blocks to its north and northeast, possibly forcing out, among others, some Indian residents of the Barrio de Santo Domingo, where a cluster of wealthy Genoese, Portuguese, and Spanish-born merchants had taken hold around the Dominican convent by the early decades of the seventeenth century.[12] Santiago's low-priced residential ring swelled in turn, but to a far greater degree than the Spanish core. As the urban poor, primarily casta but also Spanish, grew in numbers, they occupied previously unsettled areas, sometimes even infringing on the lands of nearby Indian settlements.[13]

Spanish vecinos seeking agricultural acreage on the perimeter of the city posed no less of a threat to the Indians, in that their acquisitions, positioned between barrio and pueblo, intruded upon both. In the Barrio de Santa Lucía (known also as the Barrio del Espíritu Santo) during the late 1730s and early 1740s, for example, solares newly ceded to the poor (mainly non-Spanish) quickly fell into the hands of wealthy Spaniards, who appear to have combined two or more plots into one parcel, presumably with the approval of city officials, and then used them to pasture their livestock.[14]

Given such Spanish contributions to the breakdown of the racial and physical integrity of the republic of Indians, it comes as no surprise that Santiago's cabildo largely ignored long-standing Crown bans on casta and Spanish residence in the barrios.[15] More surprising perhaps is that Spanish disregard for the Laws of the Indies extended into the upper echelons of the audiencia; in 1711 officials of the Barrio de San Antonio reported that one of their tributaries had received eight pesos for his solar from none other than the oidor Don Pedro de Ozaeta y Oro.[16] Generally, however, the audiencia was the Indian's best hope for enforcing the laws against barrio desegregation, as it did in 1626 in response to a petition from a group of former Indian cabildo officials of the Barrio de San Francisco.

The root of San Francisco's problem, petitioners charged, was that many of its Indian inhabitants had fled the barrio to avoid tribute and public-works obligations. To raise cash before leaving, they said, most of these Indian "vagabonds" had sold their solares to outsiders (primarily non-Indians), winning the necessary license to do so from the city's alcalde ordinario by falsely telling him both that they had secured other housing and that the sale was essential to their well-being.[17]

The consequences were dire, according to petitioners: the barrio's Indian population had lost its numerical dominance as a result of the influx of Spaniards, blacks, mulattoes, and mestizos, and the remaining Indians could no longer maintain the peace. Furthermore, they told the audiencia, the intruders' trade and commercial ventures—the clandestine manufacture and sale of liquor, for example—marred the tranquillity of their tiny community and served to siphon off funds Indians had set aside for tribute. Barrio "intruders," a probable reference to casta spouses of tribute-paying Indian women, had even gone so far as to restrain San Francisco's cabildo officials from collecting tribute, they charged.

To remedy these problems, the complainants urged the audiencia to void all sales of Indian solares to barrio outsiders and to grant a royal order with which they might both force the return of the *ausentes* (absent tributaries) and require them to build houses on their solares. The complainants asked also that the city's *escribanos públicos y escribanos reales* (public and royal notaries) be instructed to write no sales agreement violating these restrictions. Without such bans, they warned, barrio tributary rolls would swiftly become too depleted to assure the payments on which the Crown depended.[18]

As if to dramatize the urgency of their situation, the complainants noted in a postscript to their petition that Isabel Martín, an Indian widow, would on that very day be negotiating an illegal sale, trying, in fact, to sell a solar not legally hers but one ceded to her by the barrio because of her tributary status. Would not the audiencia, the petitioners pleaded, immediately order the city's alcalde ordinario to prohibit the sale?

The audiencia responded with dispatch, demanding issuance of a proclamation in San Francisco and in the city at large that no Indian be allowed to sell his or her house, solar, or maize plot to any Spaniard, mestizo, mulatto, or black. At the direction of President Don Antonio Peraza de Ayala (better known as the Conde de la Gomera), the audiencia in addition voided all previous sales, even if sanctioned by the city's alcalde, and canceled, for the time being, the pending sale by the widow Martín.[19]

Yet the inflow of Spaniards and *ladinos* (castas who, by 1700, after nearly two centuries of mestizaje, had become the dominant phenotype in Santiago de Guatemala; racially indistinguishable from each other, all could lay claim to some Spanish heritage, if only cultural) into the barrios continued at such a rate that officials there were forced in 1682 to petition the audiencia once again.[20] This time, leaders of the Barrio de San Antonio asked President Francisco de Saraza y Arce to decide the fate of Juan Velázquez, an Indian tributary who had been absent from the barrio for four months before being jailed for selling his house and solar to Nicholás de Abarca, a casta or Spaniard who lived in the adjoining non-Indian barrio of San Sebastián.[21] They urged the president to force Velázquez to return the fourteen pesos gained in the sale (so as to nullify the deal and thus keep his name on their tributary rolls) and to do everything necessary to stop any other "ladino person" from intruding upon San Antonio.[22]

Barrio leaders reminded Saraza that he had examined their solares and lands just two years before in an attempt to assess fairly the terrazgo that each of the barrio's tributaries would be required to pay their landlord, the Royal University of San Carlos. They noted that, to help guarantee payment, Saraza had then effectively prohibited Spaniards, mestizos, mulattoes, and blacks from living among the Indians by forbidding Indians to sell their solares to others. They noted, too, that Saraza had at the same time empowered San Antonio's officials to gather up their ausentes and command that they reside in the barrio.

Although San Antonio's officials clearly believed that the sale represented an intolerable ladino intrusion into their barrio, Velázquez and his mother (also a tributary of San Antonio and probably a widow) claimed in a December 1682 counterpetition that the transaction had been necessitated by serious economic difficulties. They pointed out that they owned a solar and house elsewhere in the city (having inherited the solar and house in question) and asked the audiencia to intercede on their behalf to prevent the alcalde of the barrio from harassing them, since Velázquez's mother, the actual owner of the solar, had always paid and would continue to pay the Royal University of San Carlos its due. Velázquez was evidently soon freed from jail, but the record provides no evidence of how or even whether the civil case was resolved.[23]

It seems likely that, although Spanish and Indian justices voided or aborted numerous such sales, most went uncontested, apparently because permission of the city's alcalde ordinario was so easily obtained. Furthermore, as countless sales contracts indicate, sellers had little trouble in rounding up sufficient Indian witnesses to testify that the transaction satisfied the requirement of being essential to the seller's well-being.[24]

What the historical record does not show, unfortunately, is how many sales were challenged, and, as in the Velázquez incident, whether the challenges succeeded. The trend, in any case, was toward greater penetration of the Indian barrios by castas and, to a lesser extent, free blacks and Spaniards.

ESCAPE FROM TRIBUTARY STATUS

The desegregation of the barrios owed as much to the frailty of these communities as to the strength of the castas—a fact not lost on Santiago de Guatemala's Indian or Spanish officials. Though the Crown mandated that no more than five years pass between *padrones* (tributary censuses) to ensure that tribute and labor obligations were in line with current population figures, thirty years became the norm when barrio tributary numbers plummeted. As a consequence, barrio leaders forced the remaining Indians to fulfill not only their own tribute obligations but those of their dead and missing peers, thereby spurring the Indian exodus and aggravating free-black and casta residential pressures on the barrios. Tributary rolls were then further depleted as Indians entered into formal and informal unions with the newcomers, creating new generations of castas who, by virtue of their higher status, were generally deemed off-limits to Indian alcaldes looking to meet their labor and tribute quotas.

Acutely aware that imprisonment awaited them if they failed to make up any tribute or labor shortfall, some nominees to cabildo offices actually fled the barrios.[25] Most Indian officials, however, remained behind. Powerless to attack such broad, primary sources of tributary attrition as epidemic disease and mestizaje, many hired barrio outsiders to perform repartimiento de indios duties. Some raised cash by selling community properties vacated by the countless tributaries who had either defaulted on their leases or succumbed to disease; with castas and other non-Indians the usual buyers, these officials merely passed on the problem of mestizaje-induced tributary attrition to their successors. Most, like those from San Francisco and San Antonio who fought to stop Indians from selling barrio properties to free blacks and castas, focused their attention on discouraging other Indians from trying to escape the hardships of tributary status.

Flight, the most common form of escape, was hardly peculiar to urbanized Indians, though the percentage of ausentes appears to have been higher in Santiago's barrios and peripheral small towns than in the Indian pueblos of the Valley of

Guatemala. Exceptions were to be found, however, among rural communities subject to unusual casta and Spanish pressures on land, harvests, and labor services.[26] Mixco, situated east of Santiago on the principal route to Petapa and the fertile southern reaches of the audiencia, is one such example. The harsh labor demands upon its poor-Spanish, casta, and Indian inhabitants were commensurate with its critical importance as a supplier of the muleteers and beasts of burden essential to moving products from distant provinces to markets in the capital. Flight was apparently no less common in San Juan Amatitlán, a large Indian town east of Santiago on the shores of Lake Amatitlán. Charged with regularly supplying fish and crabs to Santiago's Spanish population, the Indian inhabitants of Amatitlán suffered routine labor pressures compounded by land and labor shortages attendant upon its being surrounded by sugar estates.[27]

Ausentes, including those born in and around Santiago de Guatemala, found the capital's barrios and nearby towns much to their liking because these areas were sufficiently well populated to conceal them. And for those who wished to leave the city altogether, the capital afforded greater access to information about making a living elsewhere. No such opportunity for news or anonymity existed in Guatemala's more isolated pueblos and villages. Virtually all of the population there was Indian and had little or no contact with outsiders. They spoke strictly an Indian tongue, frequently a dialect peculiar to one or a small group of nearby towns. They all dressed in clothes of the same style, color, and design.[28] Thus an ausente in the countryside would have found it difficult to secrete himself anyplace but in his birthplace, precisely where Indian tribute collectors for his town (the local gobernador or alcaldes) lived and would look first. His only real alternative was to melt into the populace of either the ladino and Spanish towns and cities or the Spanish-owned haciendas and indigo *obrajes* (plantations) in the lowlands south and east of Santiago.[29]

When many of their tributaries decided to pursue just such a course, taking positions in the service of Spaniards both in Santiago and elsewhere in the audiencia, the alcalde and regidor of the Parcialidad de los Utatlecas de Jocotenango sought and got from Spanish authorities a *despacho* (order) allowing parcialidad officials to collect and bring back the ausentes while at the same time forcing them to remain in their home communities and pay tribute. The 1686 request targeted those Indians who spoke Castilian and were thus thought to be ladinos,[30] and it noted that they had tried to avoid tribute on the grounds that they were actually *laboríos* (independent Indians or naborías; also a reference to free blacks and free mulattoes, all of whom paid a higher laborío tribute than the Indian tributary but were freed from the dreaded repartimiento duties and lowly status), having "marched as soldiers in various [militia] companies."[31]

The claim to laborío status by the absent Utatlecas is curious in that Indian tributaries were barred from membership in the militia, although in times of emergency and manpower shortages the ban must have been lifted.[32] Heredity, moreover, not personal achievement, generally determined one's suitability for laborío status in legal proceedings, although many clearly achieved this condition without inheriting it from their parents. Whatever the extent of these exceptions, it is doubtful that Utatleca officials were as successful in finding and bringing back the ausentes as they had been in winning the despacho mandating their return.[33]

At times, complaints by Indian officials reveal in somewhat greater detail both how ausentes disguised themselves and how barrio and pueblo officials coped with tributary attrition. In 1738 the cabildo members and principales of San Felipe de Jesús, a pueblo on the capital's northern edge, observed that, while some of their ausentes resided in other towns, many more had fled to the nearby capital, where they were reported to be living in various houses (presumably Spanish) and wearing the *capotes y mantelinas* (short cloaks for men and women, respectively) common to ladinos and Spaniards.

The town's leaders claimed that their ausentes neither recognized San Felipe as their home pueblo nor paid their fair share of tribute. Some, they charged, were willing to pay the Crown only four reales annually (less than half an individual's full tribute payment), others nothing at all. Absenteeism was so rife that previous officeholders had been imprisoned for their failure to collect *rezagos* (outstanding tribute obligations) and the cabildo had been forced to hire Indians from outside the pueblo to meet Spanish repartimiento quotas for a variety of public-works projects in the capital.[34] Like their counterparts from the Parcialidad de los Utatlecas de Jocotenango, San Felipe's officials sought to force their stray tributaries to return home and fulfill their obligations.[35]

Labor shortages were no less common in the city's barrios. The cura doctrinero of the Mercedarian *doctrina* (parochial jurisdiction) of San Antonio (consisting of the barrios of La Merced, San Antonio, Santiago, San Gerónimo, and Espíritu Santo) reported in 1697, for example, that absenteeism had so reduced the Indian tributary population to which he ministered that Indian officials from each of his five communities would have failed to fill Crown- and church-imposed labor quotas had they not paid parish outsiders to take the places of the missing.[36] Labor shortages due to absenteeism had also dealt a blow to the doctrina's churches, the Mercedarian friar complained: most were devoid of ornament and in dire need of repair.

Caught, thus, between recalcitrant tributaries and dunning Spanish clerics and civil officials, Indian leaders tried to lessen the squeeze by occasionally adding to their padrones those who were exempt from Indian tributary status (though not always tributary status itself). In one such episode in 1682, La Merced's alcalde seized a chance to register the sons of a local Indian woman, Tomasa de Espinosa, and mulatto man, Blas de Monzón, as Indian tributaries while their father was away.[37] Particularly vulnerable because none had been properly certified as a laborío, the three Monzóns—Blas, Marcos, and Juan—were at the heart of a dispute that seems to have produced little in the way of litigation until 1696, when the corregidor of the valley, charged with conducting a new padrón that year, was instructed by the audiencia to register not just Indian tributaries but those who claimed to be exempt from Indian tribute by virtue of their laborío status.

Evidently designed to verify the legitimacy of previous exemptions and to aid in the collection of the laborío tribute from Santiago de Guatemala's growing laborío population, the new padrón was also intended to ensure that Indians who had left their barrios for nearby communities would continue to pay tribute and fulfill their work duties and that their children would be listed on home-barrio tributary rolls when they reached the statutory tributary-paying age of sixteen.[38] The padrón was thus something more than a concession to Merced officials who had complained bitterly that the Monzóns and others like them had claimed laborío status in such large numbers that hiring outsiders had become the only way that they and other barrio leaders could meet such community commitments as manning rondas within the city.[39] Spanish officials were obviously just as eager to close loopholes in the tribute system as their proxies in La Merced.

Puzzled as to whether to classify the Monzóns as tributaries or laboríos, the corregidor consulted the fiscal of the audiencia, who ruled that the three were laboríos, on account of a 1682 edict by the audiencia ordering them to pay the laborío tribute.[40] The ruling went against the advice of Fray Manuel de Aldana, who warned the alcalde ordinario against ignoring the "law of the belly" (by which offspring assumed the status of their mothers; not rigorously applied, except to slave women) and granting the offspring of *any* Indian woman laborío status, for fear the Crown would suffer a drastic loss of tributaries.[41]

Although the fiscal conceded that the *Recopilación*, in keeping with the law of the belly, stated that "children of free blacks or slaves born by Indian women in marriage should pay tribute like other Indians, even though it is claimed that they are not [Indians], nor [do] their fathers pay tribute,"[42] he based his decision instead on another precedent in the *Recopilación* requiring that "mulattoes pay said tribute [the laborío tribute, the exact amount of which was to be decided in each jurisdiction]."[43]

The two passages were not inconsistent, the fiscal argued, for he had not excused the Monzóns from tribute but simply confirmed that their tributary status, that of laborío, was distinct from that of Indian tributary. Accordingly, the fiscal urged the audiencia to strike the names of Blas, Marcos, and Juan Monzón from the new padrón and reversed his decision to register all other laboríos. The full audiencia concurred on 28 November 1697.[44] By 9 December, after the fiscal had examined the 1682 despacho excusing the Monzóns from Indian tributary status, the audiencia ceded them a new despacho reconfirming the original decision. And on 1 June 1699 the audiencia affirmed yet again the laborío status of Blas, Marcos, and Juan Monzón.

Still, tribute collectors for La Merced proved a stubborn, even desperate lot. The Monzóns' lawyer complained in a mid-1700 petition that barrio officials were continuing to collect his clients' laborío tributes despite a law assigning that duty to a Royal Treasury official. Moreover, barrio officials had attempted to subject the Monzóns to the nontribute obligations that fell on Indian tributaries, an indication all three remained on barrio tributary rolls despite the audiencia's despacho prohibiting it. As if the existing evidence in defense of his clients' claim to laborío status were insufficient, the Monzóns' lawyer pointed out that two of the three brothers, Juan and Marcos, had served for many years in the infantry company of the Barrio de Santo Domingo and indeed fought the enemies of the Crown when called upon.

The fiscal ruled in response that, since the laborío tribute was distinct and independent of the tributes for which the Indian alcaldes were responsible, it should, under the Laws of the Indies, be collected by a Royal Treasury official.[45] The decision removed the Monzóns (and other laboríos) from the Indian tributary padrón, effectively halting their harassment by Indian officials. The audiencia approved the fiscal's decision in full on 18 June 1700, four days before acceding to a final plea from the Monzóns' by-now wary attorney that it issue a supporting decree taking the brothers off the Indian padrón and declaring them to be laboríos.

Indian officials in La Merced had struggled off and on for nearly twenty years to retain the Monzóns as tributaries.[46]

Although their authority was weakened by the apparent removal of the Monzóns and an indeterminate number of other laboríos from the barrio's padrón, they may have found some consolation in the fact that laboríos continued to be registered here and elsewhere in the capital. Inclusion of these inscribed laboríos appears to have provided Indian leaders with the leverage to ensure a slightly broader distribution of labor and tribute burdens among barrio residents.

Sometimes the struggle for tributaries saw Indian officials from one jurisdiction square off against those from another. On 6 April 1698, in the thick of the Monzón case, Merced alcalde Marcos de San León complained to the Crown that a certain María Dominica had left La Merced with her children and the two children of María Dionisia for the contiguous pueblo of Jocotenango, where officials had quickly asserted the right to put Dominica on their padrón. The dispute apparently arose because the president of the audiencia had issued La Merced a decree supporting its claims to Dominica and the children and then decided they belonged to Jocotenango, presumably within the Parcialidad de los Guatimaltecas. Forced to appeal directly to the Crown for resolution of the matter, San León asked that the tributaries in question be made to return to the barrio in which they were natives and parishioners. Whether or not the audiencia made a "just" decision, as the Crown instructed, is unknown. What *is* known is that, of the two disputants, only a strong, populous Indian town like Jocotenango could have withstood the loss of even a handful of current and future tributaries.[47]

Frequently, litigation over tributary status centered on complex issues of lineage. In one illustrative case that ran from January 1696 to December 1702, Juan de Cárdenas took on Indian justices from the barrios of Santiago and San Gerónimo for registering his daughter, Catalina de Cárdenas, as a tributary. The dispute arose as Catalina, born 25 November 1681, approached tributary age, then intensified in 1697 when she turned sixteen and was included for the first time in a padrón completed that year. The justices lodged the standard complaint that the decline in Indian tributaries impaired their ability to meet future labor obligations. Escaping tribute through false testimony or the intervention of outsiders had become so common, they insisted, that royal tribute collection was in jeopardy.

Presenting three Spanish vecinos from San Gerónimo as witnesses to substantiate their claim, the justices argued that because Catalina's mother, Juana de Cárdenas, was a tributary, Catalina must be too.[48] Adding credence to their claim was the Spanish witnesses' account that Juana's father was a former alcalde of San Gerónimo, her three legitimate brothers longtime tribute payers there, and her mother a cofradía oficial in San Gerónimo's church. Noting that both mother and daughter were married to mulattoes, they sought specifically to make each pay tribute as if she were a widow, like all female tributaries married to castas. Barrio officials even charged that Catalina, who married the mulatto Francisco Gaitán in 1697, had done so purely to attain the higher "widow" status and thereby avoid the more onerous duties of an Indian tributary.

Further complicating matters was the status of Catalina's father. Identified as a free mulatto by San Gerónimo's leaders, probably because they sought to subject him and his offspring to the laborío, Juan presented ample evidence to show he was in fact a mestizo.[49] Three witnesses testified on his behalf that he had never paid the laborío tribute, a fairly good indication of the sincerity of his claim, since mestizos, not mulattoes, were exempt from tribute of any kind. Of the three witnesses, two, both Spaniards, affirmed that Juan's mother was a mestiza. The third, a free black, asserted that both of Juan's parents were mestizos. Such arguments over status help explain why "ladino" came to describe all castas. Precise racial categorization, at best a speculative art in Spanish America, was made useless by widespread mestizaje among the castas.

Unconcerned by Catalina's maternal descent, the audiencia was understandably reluctant to classify Juan as a mestizo: freeing him and his children from all tributary burdens in this manner would have opened the way for mulattoes and other castas to seek mestizo status. It chose instead to issue a narrow ruling based on legal precedent, as it had in the Monzón case. Citing a 1 January 1681 audiencia decree declaring that Catalina's paternal grandmother, Juana María de Cárdenas, was the natural daughter of a Spanish *hombre noble* (nobleman) and thus *reservada* (exempt), along with her descendants, from paying tribute of any kind, the audiencia decided in favor of Catalina in mid-January 1702.[50] The audiencia reaffirmed its decree on 11 December that year, ordering the justices of San Gerónimo to cease collecting tribute from father and daughter.

Litigation over social classification was as apt to bear witness to the desperation of individuals as it was to demonstrate the plight of barrio officials. In 1700 Gregoria de Mendoza alleged that, although her Indian husband was reserved from tributary status due to his advanced age (over the male statutory age of fifty-five), she had nevertheless been improperly registered in the barrio's padrón as paying tribute for him. In seeking to have her name stricken from the rolls, Mendoza noted that she, like her parents, was free of Indian *and* laborío tributes, indeed had been all her life. Pointing to her upbringing from about the age of seven in the domestic service of Doña Juana de Súñiga,[51] a Spanish vecina of Santiago, Mendoza noted as well that she was now a member of the ladino-Spanish San Sebastián Parish. The parish priest, she added, could testify that she regularly attended his church and received the sacraments there.

The fiscal of the audiencia ordered that certified copies of Mendoza's baptismal and marriage *partidas* (entries) from San Sebastián be entered into evidence, along with the relevant partida from San Gerónimo's padrón. The baptismal entry, from the register of "Baptisms of Blacks, Mulattoes, and Naborios," dated 27 November 1663, showed that Mendoza had been classified from birth as a naboría. Similarly, the marriage entry, dated 31 January 1696, identified her as an "india naboría."

With such hard evidence against the plaintiff, it is doubtful the audiencia ruled in her favor.[52] Gregoria de Mendoza may indeed have been "free" of tributes, the likely result, not of an exemption, but of an official failure to count her (and other such children who departed the barrios at a very young age for service in Spanish houses) as a naboría when she reached the statutory tribute-paying age of sixteen. She may have been married to an Indian reserved from tribute, but his status was not transferable to her. One has little reason to doubt she was a member in good standing of a non-Indian parish, but this, too, had no bearing on her status. Classified as an Indian naboría from birth, Mendoza was, for all practical purposes, forever consigned to that status.[53] Her only possible consolation was that she had managed to elude San Gerónimo's census takers for two decades.

Two distinct forms of escape from tributary status have been illustrated above. One could be described as cultural mestizaje, the other as biological mestizaje. Marked by flight from tributary payment and public-works duties, mestizaje in its cultural form typically saw Indians leave home barrios for the relative anonymity of ladino and poor-Spanish neighborhoods, where they tried to disguise themselves by speaking Castilian and adopting the dress of the urban castas. Many such ausentes took cultural mestizaje a step further: the Utatlecas from Jocotenango, for example, who sought laborío status on the basis of military service when home-parcialidad officials tried to force the group's return in 1686; and Gregoria de Mendoza, who cited active membership in a non-Indian parish (among other factors) when barrio census takers sought to make her pay the laborío tribute and perhaps even return to the alien culture of her birth.

But Indian tributaries need not have escaped their home barrios to improve their lot in life. Men could stake a legitimate claim to laborío status by joining a militia company. Women could ensure by marrying a casta that their duties as "widows" would be somewhat less burdensome than those assigned the average tributary. Neither case was uncommon, though each occurred far less frequently than incidents of desertion, few of which are documented.

Biological mestizaje was less direct yet more pervasive than its cultural counterpart. Whereas most acts of cultural mestizaje were voluntary, the thousands born into casta status, Catalina de Cárdenas among them, were the beneficiaries of circumstances beyond their control. Formal unions with free castas and Spaniards generally exempted the offspring of Indian women from tributary status but provided no such benefit for the women themselves, who retained the status of their birth. For them, one possible means of escape was to petition for reserved status at an early age and pay off their lifetime tributary debt; the other was to attain reserved age (fifty for women). Few were unfortunate enough to live that long.

BARRIO TRANSFORMATION

The impact of mestizaje in both its forms so changed Santiago de Guatemala's peripheral communities that "Indian barrio" fast became a contradiction in terms. When the Dominican friars sought permission in 1664 to build a new convent in Santa Cruz, a neighborhood then under their care, the barrio's population consisted of Indians, mestizos, and mulattoes.[54] A hundred years earlier its sole inhabitants were the Utatleca merchants who had originally settled there; a hundred years later, in the 1760s, Santa Cruz had practically lost its Indian identity.[55]

Above Santa Cruz and the Franciscan monastery lay the northern extension of San Francisco, a large part of which came to be known by at least the late seventeenth century as the Barrio de Chipilapa. Then synonymous with free mulattoes and free blacks, Chipilapa in fact had the highest, or at least the most visible, concentration of these groups in the capital.[56] Evidence of the desegregation of Chipilapa is seen in the unified Indian and casta opposition to a proposal by a barrio mulatto, Diego de Cháves, to close an alley that abutted his house, since it was a gathering place for vagabonds and the site of "many offenses to God." Cháves's neighbors approved of his plan, but San Francisco's Indian alcalde, an unspecified number of Indian tributaries, and fifteen ladino inhabitants of Chipilapa opposed it, claiming that the alley provided vital access to both community drinking water (from the Pensativo River and the fountain of the Concepción Convent) and the local church.[57]

The Indian petitioners appear, by process of elimination,

to have been residents of the barrio's parcialidad of Guatimaltecas, since San Francisco's Mexicano community was settled in lands south of the Franciscan monastery.[58] Casta penetration of the Guatimalteca community, combined with aspects of cultural mestizaje among its members, was so pervasive as to result in the parcialidad's near-total disappearance by the mid-eighteenth century.[59]

North of Chipilapa, on the northeastern edge of the city, the Barrio de la Candelaria (formerly Santo Domingo) was reported in the late seventeenth century to have included a number of *gente ladina* (ladino) residents—mestizos, mulattoes, blacks—as well as some Spaniards among its Indian members.[60] And along both sides of the *camino real* (road) that passed through Jocotenango, numerous castas and poor Spaniards settled among that community's Indian tributaries. With their arrival came disputes over the ownership of solares and the clandestine sale of liquor to the Indians. But the parcialidades of Jocotenango had such relatively large and vibrant populations that they were able to withstand the influx of castas and Spaniards.[61] Size gave strength to Jocotenango's community structure, which may in turn have blunted the impact of Hispanicization and reduced the likelihood of marriage or informal unions between its Indian and ladino inhabitants.

While Jocotenango largely weathered the casta invasion, the small barrios perched on Santiago's west and northwest edges proved to be too frail. One observer noted in 1681 that in La Merced, Santiago, San Gerónimo, and Espíritu Santo, where castas and Spaniards once lived interspersed among Indians, Indians now lived interspersed among castas and Spaniards.[62] By the time of Santiago de Guatemala's destruction by earthquakes in 1773, all of the capital's peripheral communities had been similarly transformed. Mestizaje, prompted and then ever accelerated by the ladino and poor-Spanish takeover, was the primary source of that transformation.

MEASURING INDIAN BARRIO DECAY

The gradual disappearance of Indian tributaries in Santiago de Guatemala's peripheral barrios is a story in two parts. The first, from the barrios' establishment (ca. 1550) until 1585, continued a trend begun at conquest: epidemic disease caused steep and rapid tributary declines from which few Indian communities fully recovered, despite brief periods of population stabilization and even growth between the attacks. During the second, from 1650 to 1773, mestizaje continually affected the Indian population as epidemics had intermittently affected it in the years before 1600. Between 1585 and 1650 Santiago's Indians appear to have enjoyed a degree of demographic stability.

While the Berkeley School of historical demography (Woodrow Borah, Sherburne F. Cook, and Lesley Byrd Simpson) has convincingly demonstrated the extent of the demographic catastrophe that struck central Mexico in the sixteenth century, Guatemalan tributary records for this period are so incomplete that undertaking as definitive a study for colonial Guatemala would be impossible.[63] Nevertheless, thanks to the pioneering work of Murdo MacLeod and a number of researchers following in his footsteps, a clearer, multiregional picture has emerged, suggesting that population decline in colonial Guatemala indeed reached the proportions of the Mexican tragedy.[64] The reader must be cautioned, however, that generalizations based on the available data for sixteenth-century Guatemala are necessarily provisional and that much remains to be done on Guatemalan colonial demographic history.

The earliest existing *tasación* (tributary count) for the Audiencia of Guatemala was not undertaken until 1549.[65] Even then, Santiago and its environs were omitted from the count since virtually all of the Indians of the valleys of Panchoy and Almolonga had just been freed or were still enslaved. Not until the mid-1570s, in fact, did the audiencia first compile Indian tributary figures for the valleys' milpas and some of Santiago's barrios, fully a decade after these communities began paying tribute.[66] The contemporary scholar is thus afforded only a handful of population figures and estimates for the 1550–81 period (see table 1).

These data were collected under various circumstances by persons with different criteria for determining who would be counted. (Some listed "married Indians"; some, "tributaries";

Table 1: Indian Population of the Valley of the City, 1548–1581

Date	Population Size	Remarks
1550	3,000–5,000 freed slaves	Estimate of slaves freed in and around Santiago (appears not to include naborías)
1560	5,000–6,000 married Indians	Estimate of those in and around Santiago who did not yet pay tribute to anyone
1567	1,654–1,669 tributaries	Reference to residents of the corregimiento of the valley (lower figure due to correction for 15 individuals exempt [reservados] from tributary status, deceased, or absent)
1571–72	4,025 tributaries	Number reflects pressure to raise revenues for the Crown and thus count those lawfully exempt from tributary status
1574	2,663 married tributaries	Probably accurate
1581	2,300 married tributaries	Probably accurate

Sources: William L. Sherman, personal communication (January 1972) for 1548–50; Audiencia al Rey (Santiago: 30 June 1560), AGI, Guatemala 9; Cuentas de 1567 and 1572, AGI, Contaduría 967; Audiencia al Rey (Santiago: 13 September 1574), AGI, Guatemala 10; and AGI, Pat. 183, ramo 1, for 1581.

some, "married tributaries.") One apparent result of the confusion is that whole groups were excluded from the totals: the majority of Tlaxcaltecas, Zapotecas, Mixtecas, and Mexicanos who joined Alvarado in the conquest, for instance, especially those who later settled in Almolonga (Ciudad Vieja) and claimed an exemption from tribute payment for themselves and their descendants;[67] and the naborías, both those without formal or informal ties to a particular barrio and those who were settled by the Dominicans (along with newly freed Indian slaves) in the Barrio de Santo Domingo in 1549.[68]

Given the unreliability of population figures for the 1550–72 period, no certain trend is discernible;[69] numerous reports of high Indian mortality caused by hunger, sickness, and epidemic suggest, however, that the valley's indigenous population was then in sharp decline.[70] Tributary totals for both 1574 and 1581 appear to be more reliable, in large part because the 14 percent decline in Indian tributaries (from 2,663 tributaries to 2,300 tributaries) over this seven-year period is supported by population losses reported for a number of Santiago's barrios and milpas in the tasación of 1581.

Table 2, which uses tributarios enteros figures from the 1581 tasación and subsequent censuses as the basis for the following conclusions about general tributary decline, shows that seventeen of nineteen urban barrios and milpas in the valley around Santiago (sixteenth-century data exist for no other Indian communities there) suffered population declines between 1575 and 1581; one showed population growth, another remained unchanged. The net population loss for the nineteen amounted to 13 percent, a figure consistent with the 14 percent loss shown in table 1. Hunger and epidemic were the major causes of the decline, but Indian flight from tribute and labor obligations also played a key role.[71]

Tributary decline between 1575 and 1581 was far more pronounced in the capital's barrios than in its surrounding milpas. In the three barrios closest to the Spanish core—Espíritu Santo, La Merced, and San Francisco—tributary totals fell 20 percent on average, while population in the sample of rural settlements declined by 11 percent. Although Spanish labor demands weighed more heavily on the nearby barrios' artisans and domestic servants than on the more distant milpas' macehuales and other Indian residents,[72] the drop is perhaps best attributed to disease, which struck hardest in the crowded barrios because few there enjoyed sanitary conditions or access to potable water.[73]

It is thus no coincidence that Santiago's tributary population reached its sixteenth-century nadir in the decade after the great pandemic of 1576–77.[74] The six Lake Quinizilapa towns (southwest of the capital), by contrast, reached their population nadir between 1600 and 1630.[75]

	Number of Tributaries				
Barrio/Milpa	ca. 1575	ca. 1581	1638	1684	1754
Espíritu Santo	44	33	52	est. 37 }	est. 49[a]
La Merced	55	45	52	37 }	
San Francisco[b]	111	89½	89	52	5
Subtotal	210	167½	193	126	54
		(−20%)	(+15%)	(−35%)	(−57%)
Jocotenango (Guatimaltecas)	290	275½	426	694 }	1,025
Jocotenango (Utatlecas)	156	156	212	320 }	
San Felipe	59	53½	76	180	141
Santa Isabel	24	18	33	47	47½
San Cristóbal	77	74	85	120	143½
(el Bajo & el Alto)	—	—	—	—	—
San Juan Gascón	12	10	18	9	24½
San Gaspar Vivar (Mixtecas)	16	(?)	(38)[c]	48	41½
San Lucas Cabrera	16	13	15	14½	7
San Mateo M.A.	46	44½	80	53	20
San Miguel M.A.	31	20½	25	6	14½
San Andrés Deán	31	26	28	19	9½
San Bartolomé Becerra	24	16	8	9	8
Santa Catalina Bobadilla	24	11	31	30	48½
San Andrés Ceballos	30	20	22	25½	29½
Santiago Zamora	37	44[d]	51	131	199½
San Lorenzo Monroy	64	49	41	108	138½
Subtotal	937	831	1,151	1,814	1,898
		(−11%)	(+38.5%)	(+58%)	(+5%)
Total	1,147	998.5	1,344	1,940	1,952
		(−13%)	(+35%)	(+44%)	(+1%)

[a] Two-barrio population.
[b] Both parcialidades.
[c] This estimate not included in subtotal and total for 1638.
[d] Plus one widow.

Sources: "Razón de las tasaciones . . . [1582]," AGI, Guatemala 10; "Relación del proceso . . . [1638]," AGI, Guatemala 70; AGCA, A3 2724 39046; AGCA, A3 824 15.207; and AGCA, A3 1616 26.578.

While a comparison of 1581 and 1638 tributary figures shows population gains across the board for Santiago and its environs, growth was uneven: the tributary population of the rural sample increased by 38.5 percent; Espíritu Santo, La Merced, and San Francisco, by contrast, experienced a tributary growth rate of just 15 percent.[76] While difficult to substantiate, most of the gain in both sectors seems to have been the result of natural increase, not of Indian migration into the valley of the city.

Tributary numbers show an increase for 1638 despite a series of epidemics (described as pestilence) that struck the city and its environs between 1585 and 1632; evidently, the absence of severe droughts or grain shortages over this forty-seven-year period softened the damage to Indian tributary rolls.[77] The slow growth in tributary counts for Espíritu Santo, La Merced, and San Francisco from 1581 to 1638 suggests that an additional factor, mestizaje, was by now visibly at work. These barrios, like all Indian communities, were normally able to add to their tributary populations only through the birth of children to Indian couples who were both tributaries of the same corporate community. They were certain to experience a slower rate of tributary growth than their rural counterparts, due to the increasing frequency of Indian exogamy.[78]

Tributary figures for the rural and urban sectors diverged dramatically for the first time between 1638 and 1684. While the rural milpas and towns surveyed in table 2 experienced a 58 percent gain in tributaries over 1638 levels, the three Indian barrios suffered a 35 percent loss over the same period.[79] Casta residential pressure on the barrios intensified, no doubt, increasing the likelihood of Indian intermarriage and mestizaje. In addition, local epidemics there continued to take their toll, and the growing Hispanicization of Santiago's tributaries spurred barrio Indians to escape their lowly status.[80]

Whereas the vast majority of rural settlements in this survey recorded population gains from 1581 to 1638, the 58 percent tributary growth rate registered here from 1638 to 1684 was largely restricted to the more populous towns. A number of the smaller settlements that showed tributary losses in the latter period, especially those closest to Santiago, seem certain to have felt demographic pressures akin to those of the city's Indian barrios.

From 1684 to 1754 the pace of tributary decline in the three urban communities quickened to 57 percent. At the same time, tributary growth continued in the rural sample, but at a rate of just 5 percent, a sharp drop from the 58 percent rise of the previous period. Spanish and free-casta penetration of the república de los indios, combined with mestizaje and Indian successes in avoiding tributary status, seems to have intensified in Santiago's peripheral barrios during the late seventeenth and early eighteenth centuries, then spread to a number of small, contiguous milpas. Such small outlying Indian towns as San Lucas Cabrera, San Andrés Deán, San Bartolomé Becerra, and even the more populous settlement of San Felipe all suffered declines in tributary population between the 1680s and the mid-eighteenth century.

A major factor behind the rural sample's sharp drop in tributary growth was that the two parcialidades of Jocotenango saw their tributary population rise by just 1 percent from 1684 to 1754, in sharp contrast to the 63 percent rate of growth Jocotenango achieved during the 1638–84 period. Despite its sizable Indian population and strong communal institutions, even Jocotenango showed symptoms of decay.[81]

Complete counts of tributarios enteros for *all* of Santiago's Indian barrios—conducted for the years 1638, 1670–84, and 1754 (as shown in table 3) and again used as a measure of total tributary decline—suggest that Espíritu Santo, La Merced, and San Francisco experienced deeper tributary losses than the barrios as a whole. Tributary decline throughout the city from 1638 to 1684 amounted to 12 percent, roughly a third of the drop Espíritu Santo, La Merced, and San Francisco suffered over the same period (see table 3). Similarly, while tributary totals throughout Santiago declined by 35 percent between 1684 and 1754, Espíritu Santo, La Merced, and their neighboring barrios (San Antonio, San Gerónimo, and Santiago), combined with San Francisco, sustained a decline of 51 percent.

Table 3: Indian Barrio Tributary Population: 1638, 1670–1684, 1754

Barrio	1638	1670–84	1754
Espíritu Santo	52	(37)[a]	
La Merced	52	37	94
San Antonio	50	(35)[a]	
San Gerónimo and Santiago	45	32	
San Francisco	89	52	5
Santa Cruz	27	27 (?)	11
Subtotal	315	220 (−30%)	110 (−50%)
Santo Domingo	201	213	162
Santo Domingo de los Hortelanos	58	70	57
Subtotal	259	283 (+9%)	219 (−23%)
Total	574	503 (−12%)	329 (−35%)

[a] As these estimated tributary population figures are critical in calculating population change they are included in subtotal and total for 1670–1684.
Sources: "Relación del proceso . . . [1638]," AGI, Guatemala 70; AGCA, A3 2724 39.046; AGCA, A3 824 15.207; and AGCA, A3 1616 26.578.

Such discrepancies are almost totally reduced by removing from these calculations tributary totals for the capital's two least typical barrios: the large, more populous Barrio de Santo Domingo (Candelaria) and the less urbanized Barrio de Santo Domingo de los Hortelanos, whose tributary populations together declined by about 23 percent from 1684 to 1754 after showing gains in the previous census period.[82] Tributary decline for the remaining barrios then rises to 30 percent for the 1638–84 period, and to a punishing 50 percent for the seven decades ending in 1754. Declines persisted at these levels in the period between the 1754 tasación and the destruction of the capital two decades later, as the basic causes of the drop not only remained but appear to have intensified.

SAN FRANCISCO: A CASE STUDY

The Barrio de San Francisco, founded near the convent of that name around 1550, was divided into two parcialidades, one of

Mexicanos (actually Tlaxcaltecas), the other of Guatimaltecas. Although in the sixteenth and seventeenth centuries its tributary population was smaller than that of Santo Domingo and of either of Jocotenango's two parcialidades, San Francisco was more populous than Santa Cruz, Espíritu Santo, San Gerónimo, San Antonio, Santiago, and La Merced. Fairly average, thus, in population size, San Francisco is also suited for study because it alone among Santiago de Guatemala's Indian barrios provides the researcher with a continuous series of tributary counts from 1575 to 1754, including two detailed barrio censuses for the final half-century of that period. What follows is less an analysis of why the Indian population of this barrio declined than an attempt to trace that decline and to show in somewhat greater detail the intricacies of the tributary system.

In 1581 the two parcialidades of San Francisco numbered eighty-nine and a half tributarios enteros (see table 4), down 19 percent from 1575 levels as the result of a violent epidemic that swept through New Spain and Guatemala in the late 1570s.[83] Like a number of other barrios, San Francisco showed signs of a minor demographic recovery by 1595, when the number of tributarios enteros in the barrio climbed to ninety-three.[84] The recovery had lost momentum by 1638, however, as the number of tributarios enteros fell by 4 percent to eighty-nine.[85] Indian emigration from the barrio was certainly one reason for the drop: San Francisco's cabildo complained as early as 1626 of the number of tributaries who lived as "vagabonds," selling their solares and houses to Spaniards and castas and avoiding their tribute obligations to the barrio's alcaldes.[86]

In the mid-1660s San Francisco's alcalde and Indian escribano, the master saddler José de Salvatierra and tailor Juan de Vilches, respectively, were accused, prosecuted, and convicted of blackmailing a number of mulatto and mestizo women of the barrio. The two barrio officials had threatened to expose the women to the audiencia in a bogus padrón of "scandalous" casta women unless they paid a "fee" ranging from one to ten pesos.[87] While Salvatierra and Vilches may have been moti-

Table 4: Tributario Entero Population of the Barrio of
San Francisco, 1575–1754

Year	Guatimaltecas	Mexicanos	Barrio Total
ca. 1575	—	—	111
ca. 1581	—	—	89½ (−19)
1595	—	—	93 (+4)
1638	33	56	89 (−4)
ca. 1684	27 (−18)	24½ (−56)	51½ (−42)
1716	8 (−70)	9 (−63)	17 (−67)
1735	3 (−63)	6 (−33)	9 (−47)
1754	—	—	est. 7½ (−17)

Sources: "Razón de las tasaciones . . . [1582]," AGI, Guatemala 10; Cuentas de 1595, AGI, Contaduría 969; "Relación del proceso . . . [Santiago: 13 May 1641]," AGI, Guatemala 70; AGCA, A1 2816 40.856; AGCA, A3 1252 21.698; AGCA, A3 2324 34.313; and AGCA, A3 1616 26.578.
Note: Figures in parentheses are percentages.

vated by personal greed, it seems more likely their scheme represented a desperate attempt to avoid jail by filling the gap between an out-of-date, inflated tributary count and a dwindling number of tributaries from whom they could actually collect.

Indeed, census figures for 1684 seem to bear this out, as San Francisco suffered a 42 percent tributary loss (from eighty-nine to fifty-one and a half tributarios enteros) in the nearly five decades after the 1638 tasación,[88] the first tasación to provide a breakdown for the barrio's two parcialidades.[89] Although the parcialidad of Guatimaltecas showed an 18 percent decline (from thirty-three to twenty-seven tributarios enteros) between 1638 and 1684, the parcialidad of Mexicanos suffered an almost catastrophic loss of 56 percent (from fifty-six to twenty-four and a half tributarios enteros) over the same period. Why were the Mexicanos affected so disproportionately? As the descendants of Alvarado's allies in the conquest, they may have retained greater privileges and become more Hispanicized than the Guatimaltecas, and thus found it easier to escape from tributary status.

While the next padrón for San Francisco was not completed until 1716, the barrio's general decay was again apparent as early as 1695, when the Indians there petitioned for and received permission to sell a piece of a solar (or small corral) so they might rebuild their church. According to several Spaniards who testified in favor of the sale, San Francisco contained only a few poor tributaries and lacked any other means to finance the renovation.[90] The barrio's cabildo building (which also housed a jail) was by then in a similar state of disrepair, its tile roof having collapsed some time before. In May 1716, perhaps under the leadership of newly inaugurated alcaldes and regidores, the people of San Francisco set out to raise the funds to rebuild the abandoned structure. Requesting that the audiencia act quickly to approve their financing scheme before the invierno reduced their adobe cabildo building to a "dirty solar and shelter for evildoers," they were apparently given the go-ahead for the project, albeit with different funding.[91] Whether or not the Indians obtained the necessary lumber, nails, and lime and, as intended, finished the project with their own labor is unknown. Large parts of the city were seriously damaged when an earthquake struck in September of the following year.[92]

By the padrón of 1716 the population decline of San Francisco's two parcialidades had intensified. The Guatimaltecas suffered a loss of 70 percent over 1684 levels (from twenty-seven to eight tributarios enteros), the Mexicanos a drop of 63 percent (from twenty-four and a half to nine tributarios enteros) during the same period.[93] Each parcialidad, moreover, retained just one lone *casado tributario entero* (married entire tributary, that is, a husband and wife from the same parcialidad, barrio, or other tribute-collecting jurisdiction). Such evidence underscores the demographic devastation of a century and a half of Indian unions with mestizos, free and enslaved mulattoes and blacks, and even Spaniards.[94] It suggests also the frequency with which San Francisco's inhabitants married outsiders of similar ethnolinguistic background. Numerous Mexicanos from the barrio, for example, wed Mexicanos from Almolonga (Ciudad Vieja).[95]

A detailed look at the 1716 population count reveals the extent of San Francisco's population decay and dim prospects for recovery. In addition to the one casado tributario entero in their parcialidad, the Guatimaltecas that year included three men and three women married to Indians in other communities, two men and one woman married to mestizos, one woman married to a mulatto, and two men married to laborías.[96] Five unmarried women and one single man rounded out the 1716 count. Under the prorated system devised by Spanish authorities, these nineteen tributaries were counted as eight tributarios enteros plus one unmarried woman.[97]

Similarly, the parcialidad of Mexicanos included one casado tributario entero and three men and three women married to Indians from other communities. While none of the Mexicanos was listed in the 1716 padrón as being married to a casta, four men and three women had spouses who paid the laborío.[98] Six other Mexicanos—one widower, two single men, and three single women—brought the parcialidad's total tributary population in 1716 to twenty-one or nine tributarios enteros.[99]

Of the twenty-six married tributaries in San Francisco (both men and women), only four, the two tributarios enteros, were potential parents of children who would *automatically* become tributaries of the barrio upon reaching the statutory age of sixteen. And of the twelve barrio natives married to Indian outsiders, only the six women and their offspring were listed by name and age in the padrón, a sure indication the children of the six men would be inscribed as tributaries, not in San Francisco, but in their mothers' home jurisdictions, assuming, of course, they were inscribed at all. Generally raised in the communities of their fathers, many of these children lived beyond the reach of the very Indian officials who were assigned to register them and to collect tribute from them.

Among barrio women who married naboríos, mulattoes (including slaves), or mestizos, the women alone were inscribed on San Francisco's padrón, along with the names and ages of their children—proof that desperate barrio officials would try to use the law of the belly to cast as wide a tributary net as possible, despite apparent exemptions from Indian tributary status for all of these children.[100] By contrast, when barrio men married naborías, mestizas, or mulatas, the names and ages of their spouses and children were omitted.[101] Any hopes for the demographic revival of San Francisco after 1716 thus rested with the barrio's two casados tributarios enteros; the three single Mexicano women, ages twenty, twenty-one, and thirty;[102] and the five single Guatimalteca women, ages fifteen to twenty-eight.[103]

Although the padrón of 1716 relieved the barrio's remaining Indians of paying tribute for those who had died or fled since the previous census, relief was short-lived. Bartolomé de la Cruz, alcalde of what he termed the "barrio of the Mexicanos of the Señor San Francisco," told the audiencia in 1726 of his inability to collect the barrio's annual tribute from eleven ausentes despite "having gone out personally to various pueblos and places to look for [them] at the cost of spending what I earn with my sweat and labor."[104] (De la Cruz failed to mention that two of the eleven were found to be absent in 1716 and had probably been struck from the padrón.) De la Cruz presented as well a list of nine tributaries who had died since the 1716 census; seven of the nine were women, which dealt a critical blow to the barrio's slim chances for regeneration.[105]

Making matters worse, de la Cruz reported, a few Indians had retired their lifetime tributary debt in one lump sum and been granted reserved status. One of the two was a mother of nine children and the wife of an Indian from neighboring Santa Cruz. The other, Blas Rodríguez, an ex-alcalde of San Francisco who had married a Spaniard,[106] presumably sought to narrow the social gulf between himself and his new wife by escaping all tributary obligations, including the mounting burdens of officeholding.[107]

Citing a total of twenty-one absent, dead, or reserved in San Francisco since the 1716 padrón, de la Cruz asked the audiencia to amend the barrio's tributary rolls, a request that fell on deaf ears, perhaps because a number of young Indians had reached tribute age during this ten-year period. Not until 1735, in fact, nine years after de la Cruz broached the subject, did the audiencia finally respond to San Francisco's calls for a new padrón.[108] By then, however, the demographic destruction of the barrio was nearly complete.

With just three tributarios enteros (actually two and a half tributarios enteros plus two unmarried women) in 1735—two men and one woman married to Indians from other communities, one Indian male married to a laboría, one widow, three single women, and no casados tributarios enteros[109]—the parcialidad of Guatimaltecas was now so insignificant as to rate no more than an addendum to the Mexicano partidas. San Francisco, accordingly, had come to be governed by one alcalde (instead of the original two, one from each parcialidad), a Mexicano assisted by a regidor (probably a Guatimalteca).[110]

Census takers that year found the Mexicanos little better off, counting six tributarios enteros plus one widow—one man and two women married to tributaries from other communities, two men married to laborías, one man married to a mulata, two men and one woman married to mestizos, two single men, two widows, and two unmarried women.[111] Thus, in the course of one generation, from the padrón of 1716 to the padrón of 1735, San Francisco's tributario population declined by 47 percent (from seventeen to nine tributarios enteros).

A comparison of San Francisco's age pyramids for 1716 and 1735 (see figure 1), based on *total* Indian population, demonstrates both the relatively small number of persons in the lower age brackets and the continuing decline of this group. Here, as one can quickly see, "pyramid" is something of a misnomer. By contrast, the age pyramid for the Indian pueblo of San Juan del Obispo in 1755 illustrates how a demographically strong and stable community should look. Note the relatively large numbers of young at its base and the progressively declining numbers as the population ages.[112]

By 1754 San Francisco's Indian population had dropped to an estimated seven and a half tributarios enteros.[113] A year later a report on the number of Indian male children attending schools throughout the city failed even to mention the boys from San Francisco because they were so few.[114] Without trib-

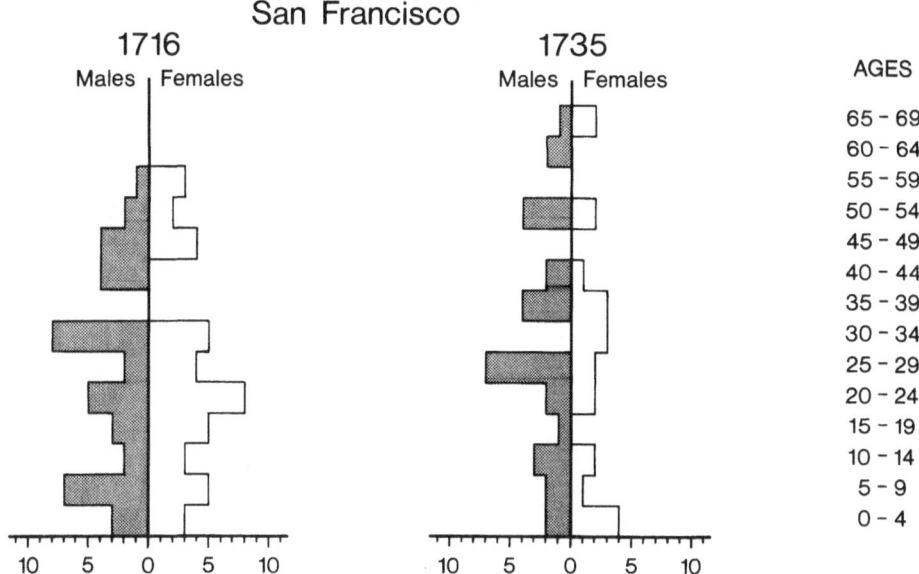

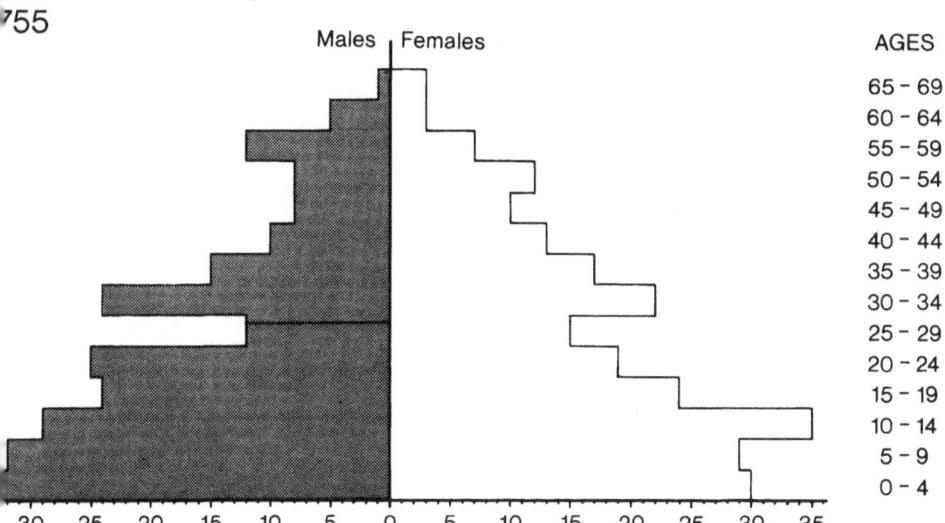

FIGURE 1. Comparison of Age Pyramids: San Francisco, 1716 and 1735; San Juan del Obispo, 1755.
Sources: AGCA, A3 1252 21.698 (1716); AGCA, A3 2324 34.313 (1735); and AGCA, A3 947 17.685 (1755).

utary counts for the 1754–73 period, Indian population decline can only be hypothesized. Given previous census patterns, however, the crowded multiracial blocks of San Francisco seem likely to have lost tributaries at a faster rate than the city's less central barrios. Mestizaje and Hispanicization were as infectious in San Francisco's last decades as pestilence and disease in its first.

CHAPTER FOUR

CASTA ORIGINS AND GROWTH

SANTIAGO de Guatemala's Indian tributaries are frequent subjects of the historical record, in good part because the Spanish kept track of their numbers in order to exact their tribute and labor. This is less true for the city's black and mulatto slaves, mestizos, and laboríos, whose special tribute, due partly to their mobility, was consistently undercollected, despite Spanish attempts to account for all naboríos, free blacks, and free mulattoes (see appendix 7). Thus this chapter introduces each of these segments of the city's *gente ordinaria* (an ecclesiastical term used in parish registers for "common people") and attempts to assess their relative numerical importance. It provides a similar evaluation of Santiago's Spaniards, given their pivotal role in casta creation and growth, and concludes with an attempt to project total population in the capital during the few decades for which data can be obtained about the size of all groups save the clergy.[1]

Little-explored parish archives are key sources in this analysis because comprehensive census data are unavailable (see appendixes 1 and 3 for marriage and baptismal data, respectively). Not before 1740, in fact, was a citywide population count conducted. All slaves and Indians, as well as many castas, were omitted; mestizo and free mulatto males *were* accounted for, but with an acknowledgment that many of their numbers had been overlooked.² A second and final census of Santiago was conducted at the behest of Archbishop Cortés y Larraz in 1768–70.³ Who was included in this parish-by-parish head count is uncertain; no less troublesome is the absence of subtotals by socioracial group.⁴ Consequently, population change over even three short decades cannot be measured accurately.

Parish archives, fortunately, reveal much about the distribution and relative size of elite and nonelite groups, both in the core of the colonial capital and on its periphery. Of the four parishes (see map 5), the Sagrario was the first, dating to the founding of Santiago in Almolonga in the late 1520s;⁵ administered from the cathedral of Santiago de Guatemala, it was gradually reduced in size as new parishes, all with their own territorial jurisdictions, were established. The parish of San Sebastián was founded about 1582, some forty years after the move to Panchoy;⁶ the earliest extant baptismal register there was dated 1594, which suggests that San Sebastián began to function as a parish church at that time. First envisioned in the 1590s, the city's third parish, Los Remedios, was finally carved out of the Sagrario in 1641;⁷ it occupied the southeastern sector of the city, serving neighborhoods around the hermitage of Los Remedios. The fourth and last parish, the Candelaria, was founded in 1750; its creation splintered the Barrio de Santo Domingo, whose hermitage had been known as Nuestra Señora de la Candelaria, from San Sebastián.⁸

How reliable are parish registers for the study of Latin American demographic history? The archbishop of Mexico noted in 1815 that parishioners had long been free to define their own racial status since priests recorded whatever parishioners told them.⁹ Baptismal and matrimonial entries were used, accordingly, only to prove a birth or marriage had occurred, not as proof of race in a court of law, where other forms of evidence were required.¹⁰ The historian Richard Konetzke, citing three prelates' *informes* (reports) to this effect, thus warns that such racial identifications are no more valid for the contemporary analyst than they were for the colonial oidor.¹¹

Parish-register reliability is also in doubt because accuracy so depended on each priest's recording every baptism,

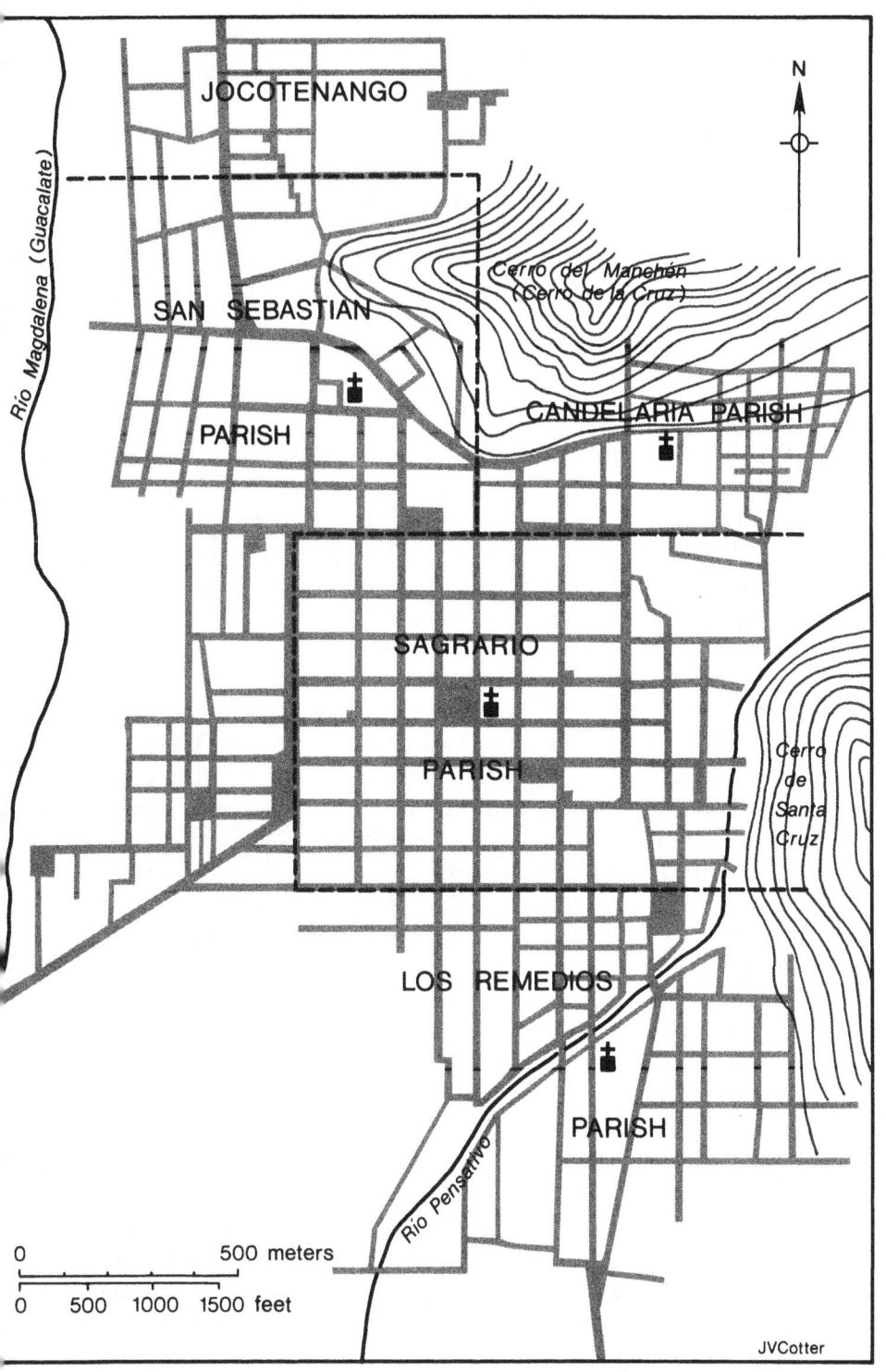

MAP 5. Parish boundaries in Santiago, ca. 1770. Sources: AGCA, A1 2124 15.091; Cortés y Larraz, *Descripción geográfico-moral*, 1:21–34; and AGI, Contaduría 983A for 1641 limits of Los Remedios Parish. Urban grid based on a map by V. L. Annis.

marriage, and burial; some padres, quite simply, were more meticulous than others.[12] But sacerdotal efficiency was also a product of parish geography and natural events. Rural priests were more likely to be lax in their recordkeeping than urban priests whose proximity to the diocese meant that they toiled under the watchful eye of church officials. The registers for a parish comprised of a central church and a number of outlying *visitas* (subordinate jurisdictions) may have been less accurate than those in parishes where the sacraments were administered at a single church. Deaths from such catastrophes as floods and droughts, earthquakes and epidemics, may at times have been so numerous that many (especially infant deaths) went unrecorded in the rush to bury the dead.

While these factors affected the quality and completeness of parish registers generally, one can only surmise how registers were kept in the four parishes of Santiago de Guatemala. At least the closeness of the city's parishes to ecclesiastical authorities must have promoted some degree of accuracy.[13] Less encouraging, however, is that, while extant records ordinarily provided coverage of all baptized or married Spaniards, blacks, castas, and naborías, separate registers maintained for the Spanish appear during catastrophes to have received far more attention than those for gente ordinaria.[14] Hence it is likely, for example, that some gente ordinaria marriages went unrecorded in the aftermath of a massive earthquake in September 1717, when unwed couples, fearing further divine retribution should they continue to live in sin, flocked to local churches (or temporary shrines if their churches had been destroyed) to be married.[15] Fortunately for the historical demographer, such occasions present infrequent, mild threats to reliability.

But what of the gente ordinaria who were neither baptized nor formally married? Legitimate and illegitimate children alike seem to have been christened with few exceptions, due to the strength of Roman Catholicism and the importance of baptismal rites to the faithful. And baptismal figures for the three oldest parishes in Santiago support the hypothesis that high illegitimacy ratios (illegitimate to legitimate births)[16] were related to high levels of gente ordinaria dependence.[17] Thus it can be seen in the central Sagrario, the parish with the largest slave and dependent casta population, that the illegitimacy ratio for gente ordinaria fell below 50 percent during only one decade on record (1690s). By contrast, illegitimacy ratios in the more peripheral parishes of San Sebastián and Los Remedios, where independent castas came increasingly to settle, were consistently below 50 percent from the 1680s forward.

One can infer, then, that church-sanctioned marriages in the Sagrario represented less than half of all gente ordinaria unions in all but one decade and that marriages involving gente ordinaria in Los Remedios and San Sebastián constituted a majority of all unions beginning in the 1680s,[18] assuming, as does the following analysis, that formal and informal unions produced similar numbers of children.[19] This means that marriage totals for gente ordinaria are drawn, at most, from slightly more than half of the total gente ordinaria population of the city. Since separate illegitimacy ratios, moreover, are unavailable for any constituent group of gente ordinaria except slaves, few of whom married in the church, the scholar cannot know when the sample for a particular group is even less typical. But as inadequate as total marriage figures may be, they are, in the absence of comprehensive and periodic census data, the sole available evidence with which to estimate the relative size of each segment of Santiago de Guatemala's diverse gente ordinaria population over the course of the capital's history.

THE AFRICAN INFLUENCE

African slaves, who had been included in the conquest party Alvarado led into Guatemala in early 1524,[20] came to be regularly introduced in the audiencia some two decades later, probably in response to the pending abolition of Indian slavery.[21] The first shipload of slaves was transported to Guatemala via Santo Domingo in 1543; on board were 150 *piezas de Indias* (young adult male slaves meeting certain specifications as to size and physical condition;[22] other slaves were defined for commercial purposes as parts of piezas de Indias).²³ In the years before the 1580s, when the Portuguese finally won the African slave concession from the Spanish Crown, the slave trade was a small-scale, largely ad hoc affair conducted by prominent Spaniards, including Alvarado and Francisco de los Cobos, secretary to Charles V.²⁴

Under a system of slave *asientos* (contracts), the Crown specified the number of African slaves to be delivered to Caribbean ports in Honduras, points of entry for slaves throughout Central America. An asiento agreement signed in 1601, for example, notes that 200 slaves were to be sent to Honduras each year. Another, signed in 1674, stipulates that 700 slaves be distributed among the ports of Havana, Veracruz and Campeche (in New Spain), and Honduras.²⁵ Still another, signed a year later, shows that 400 slaves were to be sent each year to Campeche and Honduras. What portion of the two latter totals went to Honduras is unclear, but it was probably about 200 slaves annually.

Guatemala's demand for slaves evidently exceeded Crown allotments. On 18 March 1671 Santiago's cabildo complained to the king that the provinces of the audiencia required 500 slaves a year for four successive years, two or three times the number called for under contract.²⁶ It seems doubtful, however, that even annual asiento projections of 200 slaves were met during much of the seventeenth and eighteenth centuries. Evidence suggests the importation of slaves dropped sharply between 1635 and 1690, for instance, in conjunction with a decline in Central American exports.²⁷

Because the contracts were not always filled, asiento figures by themselves are somewhat unreliable as a measure of the number of African slaves who entered Central America. More useful, perhaps, are Royal Treasury records showing how much *asentistas* (slave contractors) paid in "royal rights" for the slave concession in eight of the years between 1613 and 1628.²⁸ Notations for 1613 and 1615 show in addition how many piezas one Portuguese asentista delivered, so it is possible to fix the Royal Treasury's levy at 110 tostones per pieza, and to calculate, in turn, the number of legal slave imports into Central America during the years for which records of

Table 5: Estimates of "Piezas de Indias" Imported into Central America, 1613–1628, Based on Payment of Royal Rights

Year	Royal Rights Paid	Piezas	Asentista
1613	15,000 tostones	136	Juan Gómes
1615	14,459 tostones	132	Juan Gómes
1618	12,846 tostones	(118)	Duarte de Melo "slaves from Angola"
1624	12,183 tostones	(111)	"armasón de Domingo Ximón"
1625	4,169 tostones, 2 reales	(38)	"armasón de Domingo Ximón"
1626	16,423 tostones, 8 maravedís	(150)	"armasón de Domingo Ximón"
1627	5,090 tostones	(46)	"armasón de Domingo Ximón"
1628	24,622 tostones, 3 reales	(224)	"armasón de Domingo Ximón"

Sources: AGCA, A1 2876 26.539, fols. 229 and 233; "Oficiales reales de la Caja de Guatemala al Rey" (Santiago: 4 April 1618), AGI, Guatemala 45; and "Relación sacada por los jueces oficiales . . . desde principio del año de 1624 hasta fin de [16]28," AGI, Contaduría 973.
Note: Figures in parentheses are estimates.

derechos de negros (slave taxes) are the sole remaining documentation (see table 5).[29]

On average, then, 119 piezas were legally imported into Central America annually during the eight years for which data are available. When one takes into account Africans smuggled into Caribbean ports to avoid asiento rights and duties and expands pieza numbers to encompass actual numbers of slaves, estimates of 150 slave imports annually during the early decades of the seventeenth century (derived from asiento totals) appear to be close to the mark.[30] Unfortunately, such data for other periods are even more incomplete, and little is known about how many slaves went to the mining centers in Honduras, how many to the indigo obrajes in Sonsonate (El Salvador), and how many to the sugar estates and cattle *haciendas* (ranches) of the highland valleys and lowlands south and east of Santiago de Guatemala. More certain is that only a small percentage of the *bozales* (newly arrived African slaves) were placed in the households and clerical institutions of the capital, even if they were brought there to be sold or exchanged, because the Spanish seem to have preferred the most Hispanicized slaves for domestic service.[31]

In addition to the African slaves introduced through the Caribbean ports of Honduras, others were brought overland to Santiago from New Spain, Panama, Cartagena, and distant parts of the Audiencia of Guatemala. In 1605 a Spanish vecino of Guatemala, Jacome Lopes Corso, bought an eighteen-year-old black slave (described as being "between bozal and ladino") from a vecino of Villa de la Trinidad (in present-day El Salvador) who had personally transported the young man and others from the Kingdom of Angola to Cartagena and then on to Guatemala.[32] In 1613 Manuel de Solís sold an Angolan slave he had brought to Santiago, apparently from Mexico City, in a large shipment of male and female Angolans.[33]

Although the asiento system accounted for few slave imports into Guatemala from 1635 to 1699, baptismal records from Santiago suggest that small numbers of adult bozales continued to be bought and sold by the city's Spanish vecinos during this period. Baptismal records for the period from 1700 to 1769 indicate that adult African slaves were purchased in far greater numbers than had been the case during the latter two-thirds of the seventeenth century, but not so much as to make a sizable demographic dent in a city whose total population then numbered over 30,000.[34] Between 1710 and 1719, for example, a decade that experienced a greater influx of African-born slaves into the Spanish households of the Sagrario Parish than any other decade of the eighteenth century, baptismal records suggest that no more than ten slaves on average were imported annually. How many American-born mulatto and black slaves were settled in Santiago by their Spanish masters over this period is unknown.[35]

MULATTO AND BLACK SLAVES: A COMPARISON

While a lack of documentation makes it impossible either to present total slave import figures for Santiago and its *comarca* (district or region) or to estimate accurately the size of the city's total slave population at any specific point during its history, marriage records from the principal parishes of the

Table 6: Corrected Total Marriages by Socioracial Groups, 1570s–1760s

	Black Slave	Mulatto Slave	Free Black	Free Mulatto	Indian (naboría)	Mestizo	Spanish
1570s	—	—	—	—	—	—	(77)
1580s	—	—	—	—	—	—	174
1590s	(67)	(15)	(9)	(20)	(120)	(31)	(295)
1600s	97	18	1	42	122	24	(323)
1610s	100	19	9	59	117	41	(336)
1620s	(100)	(25)	(12)	(85)	(110)	30	(376)
1630s	(100)	(30)	(15)	(110)	(100)	66	(362)
1640s	(100)	(35)	(18)	(135)	(95)	38	(440)
1650s	99	41	22	157	87	93	(420)
1660s	55	51	17	149	69	81	(450)
1670s	81	64	35	266	137	154	(440)
1680s	61	137	29	449	201	266	492
1690s	40	89	23	391	242	264	453
1700s	18	52	12	327	190	215	340
1710s	24	63	21	461	213	353	414
1720s	13	31	21	517	273	405	375
1730s	26	38	15	669	242	462	467
1740s	21	29	16	661	188	474	403
1750s	14	16	9	747	185	527	473
1760s	5	9	14	653	224	478	335

Source: Marriage registers, appendix 1.
Note: Figures in parentheses have been adjusted to compensate for incomplete or missing data.

city at least provide some indication of the relative importance of Santiago's black and mulatto slave populations. It would be a mistake, however, to place too much emphasis on the accuracy of decennial slave marriage figures as an indicator of total slave population, since consensual unions and illegitimacy appear to have run high among this group. Between 1670 and 1749 black and mulatto slave decennial illegitimacy ratios in the Sagrario Parish fluctuated between 72 percent and 86 percent in every decade except the 1680s, when they fell to 61 percent. Only in the decades of the 1750s and 1760s did the Sagrario's black slave illegitimacy ratio fall below 70 percent again.[36] Such high rates of illegitimacy suggest that only 20–30 percent of Santiago's slaves were formally married during the greater part of the seventeenth and eighteenth centuries.[37]

These caveats aside, Santiago's black slave population (as measured by the total of recorded black slave marriages) reached its greatest size between the late sixteenth century and 1690, then began a steady decline that continued at least until 1769. The city's mulatto slave population appears to have reached its greatest size between 1660 and 1720, at which point it, too, began to decline (see table 6 for decennial data on recorded marriages, used throughout this chapter as a measure of the size of Santiago's various socioracial groups).

The sharp drop in African slave imports during much of the seventeenth century partly accounts for this decline, not just because it cut the number of potential black progenitors but because it may have prompted the reassignment of many urban slaves to ranches and sugar estates when the supply of bozales ran out.[38] A more significant factor, however, is that Spanish slave owners in Guatemala, unlike those in New Spain and Peru,[39] were apparently loath to use violence or even more subtle forms of coercion to block a slave from taking a spouse of his or her own choosing,[40] despite a vested interest in having slaves marry other slaves to ensure that the offspring of such unions were born into slavery (and became their personal property if they owned the mother).[41] Of the 801 black slaves and 702 mulatto slaves married in Santiago between 1593 and 1769, 56 percent of the black slaves and 80 percent of the mulatto slaves took spouses of free status (see appendix 1 for these and subsequent marriage data comparing parishes and identifying the socioracial identity of marriage partners).

During the period from 1593 to 1769, 84 percent of all black slave marriages recorded in Santiago occurred in the Sagrario Parish, whose boundaries closely coincided with the city's Spanish residential core. By comparison, the more multiracial San Sebastián Parish recorded only 15 percent of all black slave marriages, and the even more heterogeneous parishes of Los Remedios and the Candelaria recorded a combined total of less than 1 percent. Clearly, most black slaves who married in Santiago either resided within the Spanish households of the Sagrario or belonged to Spaniards who later put them to work on their haciendas or indigo obrajes.

It is noteworthy that among the three oldest parishes in Santiago de Guatemala (Sagrario, San Sebastián, and Los Remedios) only in the Sagrario did the number of black slaves who married (675) outnumber the number of mulatto slaves who married (523) between 1593 and 1769. In San Sebastián 119 black slaves were married between 1626 and 1769, compared with 151 mulatto slaves over the same period. In Los Remedios only 6 black slave marriages took place between 1674 and 1769, against 27 mulatto slave marriages for that period. Such figures suggest a two-sided maxim: the older the parish, the greater the percentage of black slave marriages; the newer the parish, the greater the percentage of mulatto slave unions.[42] They also suggest that over time slave ownership spread to Spaniards (and those of Spanish descent) who lived outside the city's central core, partly as the result of a gradual Spanish exodus from the Sagrario.

Decennial marriage totals for the capital as a whole show that mulatto slaves came to outnumber black slaves in Santiago during the second half of the seventeenth century. Two forms of migration, both involving selection, were important in this transformation. The first saw a reversal in slave-buying patterns: whereas 88 percent of a sample of 112 slaves sold in

Santiago between 1568 and 1644 were black, 68 percent of a sample of 95 slaves sold during the 1682–1703 period were mulatto.[43] The second is suggested by evidence that Spaniards who lived in the city and owned rural estates may have brought their mulatto slaves to the city to work and, at the same time, reassigned urban black slaves to their labores, haciendas, and estancias.[44] That Santiago's mulatto slaves came to outnumber its black slaves by the dawn of the eighteenth century, however, had less to do with Spanish preference for the mulatto phenotype than it did with the birth into slavery of relatively large numbers of mulattoes, the decline in African slave imports, and the migration to the city of mulatto slaves through purchase and exchange. Mulatto slaves filled slots once occupied by black slaves simply because there were fewer and fewer black slaves to go around.

Many of the mulatto slaves sold in Santiago were identified as the sons and daughters of mulatto and black slave women who belonged to the seller. Since the fathers of these children were not mentioned in connection with their sale, it would appear that most were the illegitimate offspring of unions between their black or mulatto slave mothers and male slaves and servants (mulattoes, Indians, mestizos, and poor Spaniards) who formed a part of the same or a neighboring Spanish household.[45] An indeterminate number of others were fathered by their Spanish owner, his relatives, or his paniaguados.[46]

Slave manumissions appear to have increased in Santiago during the course of the seventeenth century, especially among mulattoes, in large part because their fathers often treated them as kin *and* possessed the economic means to free them.[47] (Freeing a slave when one already owned his mother was of course achieved at no immediate cost.) The father of a mulatto slave, whether the mother was an enslaved mulatto or black, was a Spaniard, mestizo, Indian, mulatto, or black of free or slave status; imagine how quickly a more privileged individual among this diverse group might have acted to free his offspring (legitimate or not) upon discovering that the child not only diverged greatly from the black phenotype but bore an uncanny resemblance to himself. By contrast, the father of a black slave born of a black slave mother could only have been a black of either free or slave status; no other potential fathers, save mulatto slaves and Indians as compared with free blacks, were thought to be more dependent and consequently less able to free their children.

Higher manumission rates for mulatto slaves indicate as well that the social distance between mulatto slaves and both castas and Spaniards was narrower than that for black slaves.[48] But such matters of relative status are difficult to resolve in a multiracial society, particularly a colonial society whose lower levels were composed of different racial groups such as Indians and blacks, one free and the other enslaved. Complicating human relations in Spanish America was the elite's widespread belief that Amerindians lacked the physical strength and stamina of Africans. Thus, while slaves were not accorded even the tenuous free status of the Indians, they were not otherwise deemed inferior.[49]

FREE BLACKS AND MULATTOES

Given intense mestizaje, post-1630 declines in African slave imports, and relatively low rates of manumission for black slaves, it comes as no surprise that *negros libres* (free blacks) were Santiago de Guatemala's tiniest minority.[50] Free blacks, moreover, appear to have accounted for only a small percentage of even the city's total free population of African descent at any point in the city's history, with the possible exception of the second half of the sixteenth century, a period for which nearly all records are lost. Exhibiting a pattern of population growth and decline that corresponds roughly to that for black and mulatto slaves, Santiago's free black community (as measured by total free black marriages) began to increase in numbers in the early decades of the seventeenth century, reaching its zenith in the 1670s and then gradually declining.[51]

The distribution of free black marriages among Santiago's four parishes also closely resembles that of the city's black and mulatto slave populations. The Sagrario recorded the majority of total free black marriages, 66 percent, followed by San Sebastián, with 26 percent. The other two parishes, Los Re-

Table 7: Population of Santiago de Guatemala
("the city and its barrios"), ca. 1740

Group	Number	Comments
Free Mulattoes	2,750	Appears to refer only to adult males and not to women and children[a]
Spaniards	2,240	Includes "both big and little children" (only about 500 were "persons of known quality" or more or less pure Spanish ancestry)
Mestizos	1,810	Apparently does not include women or children[a]

[a] That the free mulatto and mestizo totals include neither women nor children is in agreement with the views of Sidney David Markman, "The Non-Spanish Labor Force," 189.
Source: AGCA, A1 210 5002, fols. 5–5v. Also published (with errors) as the "Relación geográfica del Valle de Goathemala por Guillermo Martínez de Pereda—1740."

medios and the Candelaria, together accounted for less than 10 percent of all free black marriages. These figures suggest that a considerable number of free blacks resided within Santiago's Spanish households and shops as either criados or salaried employees. The fact that so many free blacks who married in Santiago were in one way or another dependent on the dominant Spanish may also indicate that a number were *libertados* (freedmen, or the free children of slaves) who chose to continue living with their former masters after being manumitted.[52] Other free blacks in the Sagrario lived independently in the Chipilapa, a neighborhood situated on the eastern edge of the parish known, after the mid-seventeenth century, for its heavy concentration of free blacks and mulattoes.[53] It would appear that a higher percentage of these individuals, and those who inhabited other multiracial barrios on the capital's periphery, married than did free blacks who remained in a condition of servitude in the Spanish core.

Free mulattoes, by contrast with the city's small free black population, came to be Santiago's largest single socioracial and status group by at least the second quarter of the eighteenth century; population figures presented in table 7 are by no means complete, but they give some idea of the size of Santiago's free mulatto population as compared with its mestizo and Spanish groups around that time.[54]

Unlike the free black community in Santiago, the city's free mulatto population, as measured by total recorded marriages, grew steadily throughout the seventeenth century and first seven decades of the eighteenth century. No other group in the city came close to matching this record, with the exception of mestizos, whose rate of growth compares favorably with that of the mulattoes but whose decennial marriage totals do not.

The only sharp drop in total free mulatto marriages occurred between 1690 and 1710, when the city fell prey to a series of smallpox and measles epidemics that killed many more Indians and poor castas than Spaniards, at least in the Sagrario.[55] Many of the dead may well have been of (or soon to reach) marriageable age.[56] Perhaps the decline in free mulatto marriages during this period can also be attributed to the absence of large numbers of free mulatto males in their teens and twenties, sent in the 1690s to conquer the Lake Petén Itzá Maya and other Indian groups.[57] Perhaps, too, with the conquest complete, many of these young troops chose to settle in areas they attacked or passed through. Whatever the cause, population declines were severe. In San Sebastián, for example, the number of parishioners dropped 22 percent in two years (from 4,937 in 1697 to 3,848 in 1699).[58] But free mulattoes showed astonishing resilience in the decades after 1710, more than making up for their earlier population losses.

A parish-by-parish comparison of free mulatto marriages shows that the city's free mulatto population was concentrated in the Sagrario for much of the seventeenth century. Not until the 1730s and 1740s did San Sebastián (with thirty-seven and fifty-nine free mulatto marriages, respectively) match the Sagrario's free mulatto marriage totals of well over a century before (forty-two and fifty-nine free mulatto marriages, respectively, during the 1610s and 1620s).[59] By 1750 San Sebastián had overtaken the Sagrario as the parish with the largest free mulatto population in the city. The population gap between the two widened in the next two decades as free mulatto numbers expanded in San Sebastián and contracted in the Sagrario. This pattern is all the more striking given the creation of the Candelaria out of San Sebastián in the mid-1750s, in that the establishment of a fourth parish in the capital removed free mulattoes from San Sebastián's parish registers.[60] The free mulatto population of Los Remedios also expanded rapidly, though on a smaller scale than that of San Sebastián, especially after 1740.

Most mulattoes, as parish baptismal figures indicate, were born illegitimate, at least in the years before 1700. Many, of course, were the children of black or mulatto slave women and thus depended for their freedom on their fathers, who seem to have favored manumitting female mulatto slaves above all others.[61] Of a sample of twenty-five documented manumissions in Santiago during the second half of the seventeenth century,[62] twenty-one involved mulattoes, fourteen (or 67 percent) of whom were mulatas.[63] Some of the twenty-one were probably the children or concubines of those granting or purchasing their freedom, though notarial registers make no mention of whether this was in fact the case.[64] What remains important here, despite so small a sample, is that Spanish appreciation for the mulatto (as compared with the black) phenotype may have precipitated greater sexual contact between Spaniards and female mulatto slaves, which led in turn to a higher mulatto birth rate and increased manumissions of adult female mulatto slaves and their female offspring.[65]

Though it is impossible to estimate the number of mulattoes born into slavery who later passed via manumission into the free mulatto category, it would appear that greater numbers of mulattoes, both legitimate and illegitimate, were actually born free, brought into the world by Indian and free casta women and fathered by black and mulatto slaves.[66] This occurred, remarkably, despite the fact that female slaves greatly outnumbered male slaves in the large Spanish households of the city by the late seventeenth century, if not before.

Yet unions (formal and informal, endogamous and exogamous) between free mulattoes and *nonslaves* appear to have accounted for the largest number of free mulatto births in Santiago, thanks in part to the vagaries of Spanish racial classification.[67] Because African ancestry was given undue negative importance in the tangle of racial roots common to any society with a high degree of miscegenation, mulattoes were defined as those with even the slightest African heritage. Thus, while many of the numerous offspring of free mulatto exogamous unions had so little African ancestry as to justify calling them mulattoes, they were nevertheless considered so in Spanish Guatemala, thereby swelling mulatto ranks and stigmatizing one large segment of Spanish colonial society.[68]

But classification as a free mulatto was not without its benefits, as any slave or Indian tributary could have attested. Whereas Spanish views about the sanctity of private property ensured that *all* children of slave mothers were themselves deemed slaves until manumitted, the offspring of free mulatto fathers and Indian tributary mothers, especially if legitimate, were far less susceptible to the law of the belly. These children tended instead to assume the higher status of their fathers and were accordingly exempted from the harsh repartimiento de indios duties imposed upon tributaries.[69] That they, at least potentially, remained subject to the laborío tribute when they reached the age of sixteen, however, must have prompted the light-skinned among them to identify themselves as mestizos —apparently with considerable success, since the laborío tribute was collected irregularly.[70]

After about 1670 mestizaje appears to have so blurred the lines of phenotypical distinction between free mulattoes and mestizos that members of both groups came to be lumped together as ladinos.[71] Although parish priests and their assistants may have continued to ask parishioners to differentiate between the two, they increasingly omitted racial designations from parish registers altogether.[72] Treasury and judicial officials, however, enjoyed no such luxury. Compelled to continue using race as the basis for determining who paid the laborío tribute and who did not, even the most capricious tribute collector or judge must have lamented the loss of clarity in matters of genealogy.

INDIAN NABORÍAS

Santiago's Indian naborías, unlike its tributaries, were exempt from repartimiento de indios obligations and unattached by birth to the capital's Indian barrios and parcialidades. Though a hapless few, often the illegitimate children of tributary mothers and naboría fathers, were nevertheless accounted for in Indian tributary tax and ecclesiastical records, most naborías made their way into one or more of the city's burial, baptismal, or matrimonial registers reserved for gente ordinaria, a reflection of their gradual integration into the nontributary, Hispanicized segment of Santiago's population.[73]

The relatively even distribution of naboría marriages between the Sagrario and San Sebastián during the early and mid-seventeenth century suggests that each parish then held roughly half of the city's total naboría population, a pattern perhaps best attributed to the naboría's low cost as a domestic servant. While slaves represented a major investment, and wages for urbanized, adult free blacks and mulattoes were prohibitive for all except the elite, Indian naborías willing or required to work as domestics for room and board plus a pittance were in continuous supply. The average poor Spanish or well-off casta family, in ample evidence throughout Santiago by 1650, could easily have afforded one or more.

To what degree the presence of tributaries on Sagrario and San Sebastián parish registers (despite efforts by Crown and church alike to segregate them) helped accentuate this pattern is unknown; but it is clear that total tributary marriages were not in excess of those for naborías. Barrio Indians most apt to have been misidentified as naborías were those who enjoyed close and frequent contact with blacks, castas, and Spaniards within inner-city households and Spanish workshops and stores. The women among them tended to be employed in domestic capacities, their male counterparts in commerce, agriculture, and the artisan trades.[74]

Naborías brought up or born into servant status in the city's Spanish households fell into three categories: (1) hereditary servants, specifically those whose mothers *and* fathers were naborías, those whose mothers alone were naborías (since the law of the belly was occasionally applied, particularly to the illegitimate), and those with naboría fathers and nonslave mothers; (2) Indian orphans, or Indian infants left by destitute mothers at Spanish doors in the hope the families within would raise them; and (3) Indian children, mostly females from nearby barrios and towns and even from afar, who were contracted to serve a particular Spaniard for a stipulated number of years. Procurement of the latter was a relatively simple matter for the many Spanish vecinos who held one or more Indian towns in encomienda, owned labores or cattle haciendas on which whole Indian populations depended, or, as corregidores and other local officials, oversaw Indian community affairs.[75]

No less important a component of the naboría population were first-generation migrants to the capital, tributaries who sought, if not in their own generation then in the next, to break their bonds to native communities and thereby avoid tribute and numerous other tax, labor, church, and community obligations. A tiny percentage of these individuals were allowed to reside and work in the capital, provided they fulfilled pledges to continue paying tribute in their home jurisdictions. This Spanish-sanctioned arrangement frustrated and angered the alcaldes of the highland Indian towns, who were understandably opposed to any edict that would loosen their grip on tributaries and make it harder to provide laborers for work details and collect tribute.[76] The vast majority of migrant tributaries, however, came illegally to the city, seeking anonymity and a new, less inclement life. It was these Indians who were most likely to try to melt into the urban Hispanic world by speaking Castilian, adopting ladino dress, even joining a militia company, all in an attempt to make plausible their assertions of naboría status.[77]

Prior to about 1600, hereditary servants and migrant tributaries together represented an almost exclusively *dependent* naboría class exposed daily to Spaniard and casta alike (they generally served the former and worked, ate, and slept with the latter). By the second quarter of the seventeenth century (if not earlier), however, they began leaving Spanish households, stores, and workshops in ever greater numbers for lives as *independent*, self-employed artisans. For many urbanized Indians, this may well have been the first step toward passage, in one generation or more, into the mestizo segment. The naboría in this instance was not unlike the free mulatto trying to pass as a mestizo. While either scenario may seem improbable to the modern observer, phenotypical diversity and widespread illegitimacy made this rise in status possible, in large part because many legitimate mestizos looked quite Indian *and* few could be expected to prove their true socioracial identities. Thus other factors came to the fore—language skills, place of residence, wealth, reputation, dress, expertise, connections. The better these attributes, the better the chance of finding a spouse of higher status and ensuring that at least one's children enjoyed a greater degree of privilege.

While it is possible through tribute tax records to estimate the size of the city's tributary population, it is difficult to do the same for its Indian naborías.[78] Judging from the number of naboría marriages in the city, one can state only that the naboría community grew rapidly in the latter decades of the seventeenth century and, though it showed no discernible pattern of growth or decline in the eighteenth, appears to have been most numerous in the 1720s and more numerous at any point between 1700 and 1769 than between 1600 and 1699.

This latter finding suggests that naboría migration to the city increased during the late seventeenth and eighteenth centuries in response to the gradual decline in Santiago's slave and Indian tributary populations. While naborías, free mulattoes, and mestizos had once competed for the menial positions held by slaves and tributaries, the slow but general upward mobility of free mulattoes and mestizos must have left numerous low-paying slots uncontested, and thus made worthwhile the Indian exodus to the capital from Santiago's peripheral barrios and comarca, as well as from New Spain (especially Oaxaca) and the other Indian regions of Spanish Central America.[79]

How severe was the flood of new arrivals? This is impossible to answer, but it is noteworthy that Indian alcaldes throughout the valley were most vocal about their loss of tributaries between roughly 1680 and 1740, a period during which naboría marriages were at or near their peak. In the large lake town of San Juan Amatitlán, for example, Indian rulers complained in 1716 that more than a third of their 280 missing tributaries had fled to the capital. And just north of Santiago, in San Felipe de Jesús, principales spoke in 1738 of the large numbers of ausentes who had abandoned their pueblo for the anonymity of the city.[80]

Such accounts, helpful in explaining the rapid growth of Santiago's naboría community, also underline the obvious point that one community's tributaries, or at least their children, were another's naborías. In effect, naborías were living proof of both Spanish failure and flexibility—failure to halt the massive flight of tributaries from indigenous Indian communities and to collect their tribute, flexibility to stand aside as the naboría class expanded, inexorably, to accommodate new members.

MESTIZOS

Mestizos were the first group of mixed descent in Guatemala to develop in significant numbers. Unlike Indians and those of mixed African descent, they were never systematically enslaved or required to pay tribute, no doubt because they enjoyed such close ties with Spaniards. In fact, many of the first mestizos, not just the legitimate offspring of Spanish fathers and tributary or naboría mothers but also the illegitimate children of such unions who were later recognized by their fathers, were allowed to pass into Spanish ranks during the conquest and immediate postconquest periods.

A late 1540s list of 47 needy conquistadores (46 of whom were or had been married) reveals that the group fathered a total of 110 legitimate children; 18 among these conquistadores begat an additional 30 children whom they referred to as *hijos naturales* (natural offspring) or did not specifically identify as legitimate.[81] This suggests a ratio of three legitimate children to every one illegitimate child recognized by a Spanish vecino father in pre-1550 Spanish Guatemala.[82] But what of the illegitimate mestizo children *not* recognized by their fathers, the illegitimate children born during the middle and late decades of the sixteenth century?[83]

Many, to be sure, were assimilated by the Indian communities of their mothers. Increasing numbers of these young children, however, were rejected by both Spanish and Indian society and reared or abandoned by partially Hispanicized Indian mothers who could not easily find marriage partners in either group. They tended to congregate in towns and Spanish urban centers like Santiago and, as such, became a matter of major concern in both Guatemala and Spain, a vivid and constant reminder of the dismal failure of Spanish social policy.[84]

As early as 1548 Bishop Marroquín sought to have the Crown set aside an encomienda that would be used to support and educate the city's mestizo girls until they reached marriageable age and to teach trades to the boys, so as to forestall their "very great corruption."[85] The Crown responded in 1552, ordering that a *colegio* (boarding school) for orphaned mestizo boys and girls be erected in Santiago, but the project was not completed until the early 1590s,[86] by which point its original objectives had been subverted. No provision was made for the education and training of mestizo boys: the new Colegio de Doncellas (maidens) housed only girls and served as a women's prison. By the eighteenth century, if not earlier, function and name were finally aligned. The colegio became formally known as the Casa de Recogidas (house of detention). There among the orphaned mestizas, civil and ecclesiastical officials regularly deposited women accused or convicted of criminal activities.[87]

Orphaned mestizo boys, meanwhile, were either neglected or put to work. At least twice in 1553 the Crown's recommendation that they be apprenticed to tradesmen in Spain fell on deaf ears.[88] Over a century later, in February 1687, Santiago's *síndico general* (city attorney) complained in a petition to the cabildo of the "great abundance" of orphans wandering the city without trades or religious training. As a result, the cabildo authorized its alcaldes ordinarios to seek audiencia permission to round up the street urchins and indenture them to

Spanish vecinos.[89] This practice actually dated to the late sixteenth century, when the city's alcalde ordinario began placing orphaned children in the employ of Spaniards in accordance with his duties as the *padre de menores* (father of minors).[90]

While mestizo orphans may have seemed more numerous from a Spanish perspective than they were in fact, this much pitied and abused group was hardly representative of Santiago's mestizo community as a whole. The misfortune of becoming an orphan, after all, fell more heavily on illegitimate children, who needed to lose only one parent to become orphans, in contrast to most legitimate mestizos, who would have had to lose two; and roughly half the mestizos in the city by the latter decades of the seventeenth century appear to have escaped this stigma.[91] That a slightly higher percentage of mestizos appears to have been born illegitimate in the prosperous Sagrario than in either San Sebastián or Los Remedios suggests that the relatively wider socioeconomic gap between Spaniards and castas there impeded intermarriage and encouraged informal unions instead.

Yet, as table 6 demonstrates, Santiago's parishes as a whole registered phenomenal increases in mestizo marriages during the course of the seventeenth and eighteenth centuries. The only group to marry in consistently greater numbers during this period were the city's free mulattoes, though both groups experienced similarly sharp declines in total marriages from 1690 to 1709. After 1710 decennial mestizo marriage totals exceeded those for the previous period in every decade except the 1760s. The Sagrario exceeded San Sebastián in total mestizo marriages in each of the three decades between 1650 and 1679 (incomplete data make prior comparisons impossible), a reasonably good indication that most mestizos were initially attached to large Spanish households there, probably in some form of dependent status. In the four decades thereafter (1680–1719), total mestizo unions were roughly the same in each parish: mestizo unions rose in both, but at a far faster rate in San Sebastián. This redistribution, which points to a decreasing mestizo dependence on Santiago's elite Spanish community, coincided with growing mestizaje in the capital, the creation of the ladino, and rising legitimacy percentages among Santiago's gente ordinaria, especially in San Sebastián and Los Remedios. After 1720 the mestizo population shift from old parish to new, due to population decline in the Sagrario and population growth elsewhere, seems to have intensified, as mestizo marriages in the Sagrario declined decade after decade and those in San Sebastián and Los Remedios increased.[92]

Total mestizo marriages for the period from 1593 to 1669 seem inordinately low, given the major mestizo presence in Santiago by 1600. Could this be associated with missing parish registers?[93] Probably not. Mestizo decennial totals remain low for the 1650s and 1660s, decades during which marriage registers *are* extant, and it is doubtful, were data available for the preceding decades, that mestizo marriage totals would have surpassed those at mid-century and thus appreciably raised decennial totals. A more likely explanation for the apparent discrepancy is that the city's mestizos continued to be absorbed upward by the Spanish segment and downward by rural and urban Indian communities during this period, much as they had been throughout the sixteenth century. A mestizo, remember, was by definition of mixed Spanish-Indian descent, with the father almost always Spanish and the mother Indian; the socioracial abyss between the two inhibited formal unions yet encouraged informal unions and a high rate of illegitimacy. Mestizo boys, lacking recognition from their Spanish fathers, tended to adopt their mothers' culture, to remain Indian in either a Hispanic-urban setting or their mothers' native towns.[94] Mestizo girls followed a similar route, but the more Hispanicized among them, thanks to a constant shortage of creole and Spanish women, probably enjoyed greater opportunities to pass, by marriage, into a subordinate layer of Spanish society, an option largely unavailable to mestizo men.[95]

Such passing may have served to depress mestizo decennial marriage totals throughout the seventeenth and eighteenth centuries as well. While total free mulatto unions exceeded 650 in every decade between 1730 and 1769, total mestizo marriages topped 500 only once during this period. But passing was not the sole reason mestizo marriage totals seem artificially low. Among others were the considerable confusion over where to draw the socioracial line between mestizos and poor Spaniards, the increasing use of the term "ladino" for mestizos, mulattoes, and their admixtures, and, as seen in various eighteenth-century notarial documents, a growing failure to record race altogether. In short, decennial marriage totals for mestizos might have been closer to those for free mulattoes if a number of mestizos had not passed into other groups, been misidentified, or simply gone unidentified altogether.[96]

SPANIARDS

Santiago's crown and city officials regularly conducted censuses of Spanish vecinos during the sixteenth and seventeenth centuries, but, as table 8 indicates, precision was not their strong suit.[97] While any one of these estimates by itself is thus unreliable, population trends are nonetheless clear. From 1529, beginning in Santiago in Almolonga, to 1675–85 the capital's Spanish community appears to have exhibited a pattern of slow population growth followed by stability. Santiago in Almolonga apparently housed between 100 and 200 vecinos during its brief and turbulent existence. By 1562, about two decades after the Spanish had relocated in Panchoy, the number of vecinos had jumped to between 200 and 500, a sure sign that Spaniards were finally putting down roots. In the next three-quarters of a century the number of Spanish vecinos continued to climb, reaching 1,000 by 1620. With one exception, 1623, when the total was rounded off at 800 Spanish vecinos, this figure remained stable until the next to last decade of the seventeenth century.

Murdo MacLeod has found that a number of the region's small urban centers actually lost Spanish vecinos beginning in the 1570s.[98] In the face of the dramatic drop in the region's Indian population, which in turn resulted in a drop in encomienda income and basic foodstuffs,[99] many (even a majority in some locales) of their Spanish inhabitants migrated to the countryside in an attempt to achieve a degree of self-sufficiency and a livelihood in agricultural pursuits.[100] Santiago became

Table 8: The Spanish Population of Santiago de Guatemala, 1529–1770

Year	Number (unit)	Comments and Source
1529	150[a] (vecinos)	*Libro viejo*, 104
1531	100 (vecinos)	Sherman, "Indian Slavery," 89
ca. 1549	100[b] (vecinos)	There were many more Spaniards in the city without vecino status. Cabildo de Santiago a la Corona (Santiago: 30 April 1549), AGI, Guatemala 41, as cited by Sherman, "Indian Slavery and the Cerrato Reforms," 31, n. 22
1562	200–500[c] (vecinos)	Estimates made in the testimony of different witnesses in "Probanzas de Juan de Guevara y Juan de León, escribanos" (Santiago: 16 November 1562), AGI, Guatemala 111
ca. 1565–75[d]	500 (vecinos)	Juan López de Velasco estimated that 70 of this number were encomenderos, while the rest were

[a] In legal terms, a vecino was an adult Spanish male formally admitted to citizenship in a Spanish settlement. Evidence of individual admission to vecino status in Guatemala is to be found scattered through the *Libro viejo* and the later extant cabildo records. But as Woodrow Borah has pointed out, "in practice it was applied to any adult male Spanish settler of such position that he would have been eligible for citizenship in a Spanish town, for many Spanish settled in Indian towns and villages where they could have no citizenship." While Borah was referring to colonial Mexico, there is no reason to suppose that the situation was markedly different in Guatemala. See *New Spain's Century of Depression*, 6. Borah arrived at a multiplier of six to determine the total Spanish population from the number of vecinos. That high a factor was needed to take into account all women and children, as well as those dependent Spaniards who were not considered eligible for vecino status. The numerous clerical population (secular and regular) was not included in these calculations. Application of this formula to the number of vecinos of Santiago en Almolonga in 1529 might be unwise, as conquistadores may have predominated in the settlement. But applying it to the total of 500 vecinos in ca. 1570, we arrive at a Spanish population of 3,000 plus an undetermined number of clergy.

[b] In 1552 Bishop Marroquín wrote to the Crown: "La gente natural crece mucho, la castellana poco." El obispo Marroquín a la Corona (Santiago: 29 March 1552), AGI, Guatemala 156.

[c] In 1563 it was estimated that the city "no tiene arriba de 300 vecinos." Antonio de Rosales, Real Contador, a la Corona (Santiago: February 1, 1563), AGI, Guatemala 45.

[d] Estimate of the date of López de Velasco's figure is based on MacLeod, *Spanish Central America*, 218, fig. 15. A less well known figure for the same period (ca. 1573–78) is 227 vecinos (including 77 encomenderos), found in "Relación de los vecinos y encomenderos que hay en la governación de Guatemala sacada de un libro que tiene el presidente Villalobos. Da noticia del país, clima y pueblos que tienen los cinco obispados de dicha gobernación." AGI, Indiferente General 1528. Most of the vecino totals in this latter relación are lower than López de Velasco's figures.

1585	700 (vecinos)	"pobladores y tratantes." *Geografía y descripción universal*, 145. Found on a folio attached to a *relación* entitled "Los encomenderos que ay en la ciudad de guatemala y que es día de oy poseien las encomiendas son los siguientes" (1585), AGI, Guatemala 966. William Sherman, personal communication (1974)
ca. 1594	more than 500[e] (vecinos)	Juan de Pineda wrote that the city "tendrá más de 500 vecinos." "Descripción de la Provincia de Guatemala por Juan de Pineda, año 1594," in *Relaciones históricas y geográficas*, 465 (may have been written earlier than 1594)
ca. 1620	1,000 (vecinos)	Figures rounded off such as this one are open to suspicion. See Antonio Vázquez de Espinosa, *Compendium and Description*, cited in MacLeod, *Spanish Central America*, 218, fig. 15
1623	800[f] (vecinos)	Bishop Fray Juan de Zapata estimated that the city "no tendrá mas que 800 vecinos." El obispo Fr. Juan Zapata a la Corona (Santiago: 7 October 1622), AGI, Guatemala 42

[e] One observer noted that the city (apparently as a whole) had grown four times between 1570 and 1600. The reestablishment of the audiencia in Santiago in January 1570 was seen as a cause for the rapid growth, but it was noted that other Spanish settlements had grown with an increase in interprovincial commerce and trade. While Solórzano testified to the growth of the city, he claimed that it numbered about 500 vecinos in 1600; he appeared to have suggested that for every vecino there were about five children, brothers, and relatives. This calculation agrees exactly with Woodrow Borah's (see note a, this table). See also Pedro de Solórzano a la Corona (Santiago: 6 May 1600), AGI, Guatemala 59, fols. 1–2.

[f] Some months later, in June 1623, the bishop noted that no other Spanish settlement (of which there were 14) in the Audiencia of Guatemala had more than 150 vecinos. Bishop Fr. Juan de Zapata a la Corona (Santiago: 5 June 1623), AGI, Guatemala 156. But this statement and the bishop's estimate of 800 for Santiago de Guatemala are contradicted by the data for ca. 1620 from Vázquez de Espinosa, presented above for Santiago and for other Spanish settlements in MacLeod, *Spanish Central America*, 218, fig. 15. MacLeod lists five ca. 1620 Spanish population centers besides Santiago that had 200 or more vecinos.

1657–59	1,000g (vecinos)	MacLeod, *Spanish Central America*, 218, fig. 15 (this figure is apparently based on Juan Díez de la Calle)
1675–85	1,000h (vecinos)	MacLeod, *Spanish Central America*, 218, fig. 15
ca. 1740	2,240 (total population)	This total included "both big and little children," but only about 500 of that number were "persons of known quality" ("pure" Spanish). Thus about 22 percent (or 500) were Spanish and 78 percent of mixed descent. AGCA, A1 210 5002, fols. 5–5v
1768	3,000–3,500 (total)	This is a tentative estimate based on Cortés y Larraz, *Descripción geográfico-moral*, 1:23–30, as well as a combination of other sources

g On 19 February 1641 the cabildo asked the audiencia to permit the repartimiento of Indians for both public works and the construction of private houses. It noted that the number of people and vecinos was increasing in the city each day. Pardo, *Efemérides*, 55.

h The cronista D. Francisco Antonio Fuentes y Guzmán made a very high ca. 1690 estimate of 6,000 vecinos and 60,000 inhabitants, figures that included all ages and elements of the city's population, even those who entered the city for reasons of trade and commerce. *Recordación florida*, 1:151. Future careful study of parish padrones (a source Fuentes y Guzmán claimed to have used, along with alcabala and Barlovento records) may demonstrate that the city's Spanish population was larger in the late seventeenth century than it was in the eighteenth century.

the permanent seat of the audiencia in early 1570, which appears to have helped it avert such population losses.[101] Equally instrumental was the capital's position as Guatemala's (and the rest of Spanish Central America's) preeminent ecclesiastical, commercial, and administrative center.

Although the effects of depopulation were devastating in highland Guatemala, this area lost a smaller percentage of its Indian population during the epidemics of the second half of the sixteenth century than did the coastal and other lower-lying sections of Spanish Central America.[102] This meant that those of Santiago's Spanish vecinos who held nearby highland Indian towns in encomienda were better able to maintain tribute income than their counterparts in lowland urban centers and were thus encouraged to remain in the capital.[103] Besides, encomenderos represented a smaller percentage of Santiago's total Spanish population than they did in the lowland Spanish centers.[104] Having been less dependent on encomiendas in the first place, Santiago suffered fewer Spanish population losses than those cities and towns whose failed encomenderos had little choice but to move on.

In Santiago at least, Spaniards could, as a hedge against declining encomienda income, obtain land grants for wheat and cattle estancias in the immediate comarca of the city, then try their hands at commerce (buying and selling cattle or wheat).[105] A *labor de panllevar* (wheat farm), for example, often assured its Spanish owner a secure and inexpensive source of wheat, not to mention additional income. Hence, while some Spaniards left Santiago for good in the early seventeenth century to oversee such agricultural enterprises, numerous others remained in the capital, leaving the daily management of their rural estates to a relative or Indian *mayordomo* (foreman).[106]

The growth (pre-1620) and subsequent stability (1620-90) of Santiago's Spanish community were also a product of the influx of peninsular Spaniards in the Guatemalan capital. Indeed, the arrival of this mercantile elite, beginning as early as 1575 and continuing through the early nineteenth century, could very well have obscured the fact that the exodus of old creole families was as widespread in the capital as it was in the audiencia's lesser cities. In effect, a large percentage of Spaniards may have left Santiago before 1690, but the capital suffered no net losses in Spanish population due to what historian Stephen Webre considers the "constant and frequent" flow of Spanish peninsular newcomers into Guatemala.[107]

Webre's pioneering work on Santiago's elite suggests, contrary to the traditional view, that old creole families dominated neither the Guatemalan economy nor the capital's cabildo. While they controlled land ownership, to be sure, a growing scarcity of capital and markets rendered that land of little value, too common a commodity to "confer dominion over the local economy."[108] As for cabildo membership, Webre finds that the merchants "probably enjoyed access to office and favor out of all proportion to their numbers in local Spanish society."[109] Power, in any case, lay largely outside the cabildo by the late seventeenth century, according to Webre. Seats on the cabildo often went vacant because merchant families, using their political and commercial ties to Spain, established more effective channels through which to wield their influence.

Such power was enhanced by the fact that, while practically no individual of mixed descent climbed above the lower rungs of Spanish society,[110] peninsular Spaniards, in addition to Portuguese, Corsican, Genoese, Sicilian, and Canary Island mercantilists,[111] readily gained entry into the local elite, provided they had the proper credentials, especially money.[112] Peninsulares and creoles alike benefited from the arrangement, the former (mostly males) winning instant status by marrying into old creole families, the latter quickly revitalizing their flagging economic standing by marrying daughters to well-capitalized, well-connected peninsulares.[113]

However invigorating this process was for some creole families, the socioeconomic and political decline of their class was both gradual and irreversible; with each new generation, Webre argues, they became increasingly marginal, weakened by the new elite. By 1740 their numerical decline was evident as well. No longer could the arrival of privileged newcomers compensate for (and thus disguise) continued Spanish creole migration to the countryside.[114] Wheat labores and cattle estancias, once temporary residences for their owners, may have increasingly become permanent residences during the late seventeenth and eighteenth centuries,[115] as evidence of Spanish-ladino population growth in such regional agricultural trade centers as San Juan Amatitlán, San Juan Sacatepéquez, San Martín Jilotepeque, and Petapa would seem to suggest.[116] At the same time, due to possible Spanish migration from the capital, Spanish peninsular immigration, and natural increase, Spanish populations in diverse regions of eastern and southern Guatemala were growing in number.[117]

How severe was the Spanish population decline? Were one, for the sake of comparison, to take the 1675–85 estimate of 1,000 vecinos and multiply it by six to produce a conservative measure of Spanish men, women, and children then in the city,[118] it would be plain that Santiago's Spanish population suffered a serious drop in population by 1740, when census takers put the total for this group at 2,240 (see table 8). While the lack of precision in both this exercise and the 1740 census makes a 63 percent decline wholly improbable, the trend, at least, is obvious.[119]

No Spanish population totals are known to exist for the period from the 1740 census to the city's destruction in 1773. The 1768 figure of 3,000–3,500 (see table 8) is an estimate based on the assumption that Santiago's total Spanish population then accounted for about 10 percent of the city's estimated total population.[120] While Spanish of "known quality," a euphemism for European-born Spaniards and "pure" creoles, amounted to 500 persons (or 22 percent of the Spanish population total) in the 1740 relación, increased miscegenation and continued passing into the Spanish segment may well have worked to lower both total (below 500) and percentage (below 15 percent) by the early 1770s.[121] A considerably higher estimate comes from a longtime resident of Santiago who stated in 1773 that "of every twenty persons who inhabit the city nineteen and a half are poor and common people"— Indians, blacks, castas, and Spanish of mixed descent.[122] If one can assume that the other 2½ percent of the city's total population constituted the Spanish elite, they would have numbered between 750 and 875 persons. Suffice it to say that the actual total probably fell somewhere between the two rough estimates.

TOTAL POPULATION

Parish baptismal and marriage registers are too scattered to reconstruct Santiago's pre-1590 population patterns fully.[123] While the capital's gente ordinaria and Spanish population can be projected for the ensuing century and a half, reasonably accurate counts of Santiago's tributarios enteros exist for only the 1650s, 1680s, and 1750s. Hence the following estimates of total population are limited to these three decades.

Table 9: Estimated Population of Santiago de Guatemala: 1590s, 1650s, 1680s, and 1750s

Groups	1590s	1650s	1680s	1750s
Total gente ordinaria	13,720	21,717	24,620	25,041
Total Spanish	3,675	5,600	5,740	5,516
Total clergy est.	—	500	750	1,000
Indian (inner barrios)	—	2,300	2,000	1,300
Indian (four outer settlements)[a]	—	3,300	5,800	5,400
Total Indian	—	5,600[b]	7,800	6,700
Total est. population	—	33,400[c]	38,900[c]	38,300[c]

[a] Jocotenango (parcialidades of Guatimaltecas and Utatlecas), San Felipe, Santa Isabel, and San Cristóbal (both el Alto and el Bajo).
[b] From ca. 1638 data.
[c] Rounded to nearest hundred.

Santiago de Guatemala achieved an estimated population size of over 38,000 by the late seventeenth century but failed to grow further (see table 9). The 1750s number, also over 38,000, roughly corresponds with a reconstruction of Archbishop Cortés y Larraz's ecclesiastical census of 1768–70 (see table 10). Based on separate data, both suggest that well over 30,000 people lived in or around Santiago de Guatemala during its waning years as capital of the audiencia.[124]

The Indian tributary population of Santiago's inner barrios declined from an estimated 2,300 persons in the 1650s to an estimated 1,300 persons in the 1750s. But the decline is obscured when inner-barrio tributary totals are combined with those of the capital's outer Indian settlements, Jocotenango (parcialidades of Guatimaltecas and Utatlecas), San Felipe, Santa Isabel, and San Cristóbal (el Alto and el Bajo). All four experienced population growth.

Clearly the most important subplot in the sociodemographic history of Santiago de Guatemala is the dramatic rise of the gente ordinaria. As decennial marriage patterns suggest,

Table 10: Santiago de Guatemala: Total Population, ca. 1770, Estimated by Cortés y Larraz

Parish	Families	Males	Females	Adults	Children	Total Persons	Clergy and Others (added)	Adjusted Parish Totals
Sagrario	1,338	3,159	5,478	8,637	2,200	10,837	2,750[a]	13,587
San Sebastián	—	—	—	4,646 (?)	—	4,646	5,000[b]	9,646
Los Remedios	337	—	—	—	—	1,603	300[c]	1,903
Candelaria								
Ladinos	290	630	821	1,451	377	1,828	50[d]	1,878
Indios	202	—	—	714	212	926	—	926
Total	2,167	3,789	6,299	15,448	2,789	19,840	8,100	27,940[e]

[a] It appears that Spanish troops quartered in the palace of the president of the audiencia, inhabitants of the palace, parish clerics who lived within the parish, and tributary Indians who resided on the outskirts of the Sagrario were omitted from the 10,837 total. Servant residents of the president's palace and parish religious institutions were also apparently omitted. To compensate, 2,750 individuals have been added to parish totals. The Convent of Nuestra Señora de la Concepción alone had a population of 955 in 1729 Annis, *Architecture of Antigua Guatemala*, 165. See also AGCA, A1 211 for ca. 1740 data on the city's clerical population. Regarding the Franciscan monastery, see *Informe a la Audiencia sobre las limosnas para aceites y vinos a los franciscanos* (1728–32), unclassified document, AHA-SM.

[b] This sizable addition to parish totals seems justified given Cortés y Larraz's distrust of the parish priest. He suspected that the priest had deliberately understated the population so he could underreport the parish's annual rents and pocket the difference. The archbishop estimated the parish's population at 8,000, a figure that appears too low when San Sebastián's decennial baptismal and marriage totals are compared with those of the allegedly more populous Sagrario. The number added is 1,646 above Cortés y Larraz's estimate. Among other religious institutions, this parish contained the monasteries of the Mercedarians and the Recollects. Annis, *Architecture of Antigua Guatemala*, 87, 102–4.

[c] Included here are estimates of the staff and patients of the convent, hospital, and beaterio of Belém as well as the dwindling Indian population of the Barrio of Santa Cruz. The total of 1,603 given by the parish priest included men, women, and children. The priest reported that 73 persons had died since a recent padrón but he failed to take into account recent births. Baptismal records for the decade of the 1760s show that over 100 children were baptized annually in Los Remedios Parish. See "Testimonio . . . ," AGI, Guatemala 948; and Cortés y Larraz, *Descripción geográfico-moral*, 1:26–27.

[d] Candelaria was the only parish in Santiago in which the parishioners were divided by sociorracial groups. "Testimonio . . . ," AGI, Guatemala 948. The added number (50) of persons in the parish took into consideration the inhabitants and staff of the parish church, several hermitages, and the Beaterio de Santa Rosa and the Beaterio de Indias. See Cortés y Larraz, *Descripción geográfico-moral*, 1:28–29.

[e] If the Indian towns contiguous to the city and within the parishes listed in this table were included, the total would exceed 32,000.

Source: Cortés y Larraz, *Descripción geográfico-moral*, 1:21–34. Found in the AGI, Guatemala 948, vols. 1 and 2, this legajo also contains a third volume, "Testimonio de las cartas respuestas . . . [ca. 1770]," of the original letters used by Cortés y Larraz.

however, population growth for this group was restricted, especially after the late seventeenth century, to free mulattoes and mestizos and, to a lesser extent, Indian naborías (see table 6). Thus, at least among Santiago's nonelites, it would seem that a gradual democratization took place. Independent castas and Indians became ascendant as the capital's most dependent social groups, black and mulatto slaves and Indian tributaries, went into eclipse.

CHAPTER FIVE

MARRIAGE

DECENNIAL marriage figures, used in the previous chapter to estimate the relative size of Santiago's various socioracial groups over time, can also be used to calculate the incidence of marriage both within and between these groups. While tentativeness characterized the earlier results, given the lack of corroborative census data, one can say here with some certainty that parish marriage totals do not exaggerate the degree to which interracial union and mestizaje occurred in Santiago de Guatemala. Indeed, were it possible to determine rates of informal interracial union, one would probably find that the available statistics on exogamous marriage actually understate the degree of mestizaje.

Perhaps the most straightforward and accurate measure of intermarriage was developed by Charles Tilly for his study of the Vendée.[1] Beginning with simple percentages of endogamous marriage (the proportion of each group marrying within the same group), Tilly quickly found these lacking because, while they made it simple to calculate the incidence of exogamy, they neither controlled for group size nor showed the choice of partner when an individual married outside his or her own group.[2] To remedy the two problems, he devised a single index to exogamy that "compares the actual number of pairings of a given type with the 'expected' number—the 'expectation' being that choice will be independent of occupational class [socioracial grouping for purposes of this study], and therefore that the chances of an individual X's marrying a Y are exactly proportional to the fraction of the total population who are Ys, just as the chances of an X's marrying another X are proportional to the fraction of the total population who are Xs." An index of 50, according to Tilly, "means that there were exactly the expected number of marriages of the given type; the higher the index, the greater the surplus over the expected number."[3] (See appendix 2 for application of the Tilly formula.)

The Intermarriage Index, as Tilly called it, provides a single standard of comparison for every conceivable sort of union, enabling the scholar to rank each by its prevalence or strength in the population as a whole. Thus, while Tilly was able to demonstrate which of the major occupational classes in his study displayed the "strongest tendency" to marry others like them, and which of two classes, say, had the stronger marriage ties with a third, his index allows for similar comparisons among some two dozen possible socioracial marriage combinations in Santiago de Guatemala. It affords the opportunity, for example, to assay the strength of free mulatto–mestizo unions relative to free mulatto–mulatto slave unions, thereby establishing to what degree free mulattoes were upwardly mobile. By the same token, it pinpoints, with surprising results, which of Santiago's various socioracial groups formed the strongest intramarriage ties and thus tended to be most insular.[4]

Besides adapting Tilly's study of occupational classes to socioracial groups, this study also broadens the period under review. Tilly dealt only with marriages recorded over a five-year period (1780–84) in eighteen French communities; here for the first time *all* the marriage records of one Spanish American colonial city's parishes are traced over eighteen decennial periods, from 1593 to 1769.[5] All subsequent references to the eighteen periods apply to these years and not the roughly fifty years before or five years after, for which data are insufficient.

Tables 11–17, compiled solely from extant data (see "Introduction" to the appendixes), show both decennial changes in composite index scores and the number of those who married from given socioracial groups in given decades. They are the basis for the following exposition of marriage trends, presented, with minimal repetition, from the perspective of each of Santiago's socioracial groups. Although no attempt is made to extrapolate for missing data, scores based on marriage samples in which the number of persons from *either* marrying group is smaller than ten tend, as Tilly warned, to be astronomical; these are marked with an asterisk and omitted from the discussion for their unreliability. While scores based on marriage samples of under thirty persons can skew results, these are neither marked nor omitted from discussion, for they are not necessarily suspect. As for marriage patterns in Santiago's various parishes, these are evaluated wherever composite figures tell only part of the story (see appendix 2 for parish Tilly indices and appendix 1 for the marriage data on which they are based).

BLACK SLAVE MARRIAGE

Displaying unusually high percentages of exogamy over the entire course of this study, black slaves forged their strongest intermarriage ties with free blacks, doing so in each of seven decades from 1650 to 1719 and again in the 1730s and 1750s (see appendix 1). They established their next closest marital ties with mulatto slaves. During the 1720s and 1740s, in fact, black slave ties with mulatto slaves were stronger than their ties with any other group. By 1750–59 there were so few black and mulatto slaves (as measured by the number of those from either group who married) that no formal unions between the two were recorded. Marriage indices between black slaves and both mulatto slaves and free blacks exceeded expected levels with few exceptions from 1593 to 1769, a finding fully consistent with the lack of social distance among the three.[6]

Although black slave marriage ties with both free mulattoes and Indian naborías were somewhat weaker than those already cited, black slave–free mulatto indices during much of the 1593–1769 period show higher than expected marriage bonds between the two groups, bonds that prior to 1710 were actually weaker than those between black slaves and Indian naborías.

Table 11: Black Slave Marriage Indices: Santiago de Guatemala, 1593–1769

	BS–BS	BS–MS	BS–FB	BS–FM	BS–I	BS–ME	BS–SP	BS–O + U	Total BS Marriages
1593–99	738	0	121*	97	217	0	4	0	47
1600–09	322	23	0	147	145	0	0	0	97
1610–19	490	143	303*	77	93	11	2	0	100
1620–29	1112	175	0	63	142	32	0	0	38
1630–39	2160	0	936*	0	421	43	0	0	13
1640–49	968	195	423*	126	112	0	0	0	49
1650–59	694	93	312	92	114	49	2	763	99
1660–69	476	257	428	166	169	126	0	0	55
1670–79	564	178	543	71	148	58	0	1268	81
1680–89	624	216	218	71	147	32	0	2111	61
1690–99	0	208	403	119	102	82	7	0	40
1700–09	1912	441	478	88	121	27	0	0	18
1710–19	874	416	749	125	49	15	0	0	24
1720–29	0	1267	936	76	36	49	0	0	13
1730–39	6736	307	389	52	0	25	0	0	26
1740–49	5816	468	0	62	0	0	34	6785	21
1750–59	9362	0	1213*	102	0	0	0	0	14
1760–69	10608*	0	0	0	0	111*	0	26520*	5

* Based on insufficient number of marriages; see text.
BS = black slave; MS = mulatto slave; FB = free black; FM = free mulatto; I = Indian naboría; ME = mestizo; SP = Spanish; O + U = others and unidentified; C = castizo.

Thereafter, black slave–naboría marital ties sharply declined as black slave–free mulatto marriage continued at a moderately higher than expected rate through the 1750s.[7] One explanation for the divergence is that Santiago's naboría population, which probably began suffering net losses in the 1730s despite new arrivals,[8] became a relatively less significant element in the city's multiracial Spanish households as the urban free mulatto population expanded rapidly. Notwithstanding increased opportunities to wed nonslaves, small numbers of free mulattoes who continued to attach themselves to the households of Spanish vecinos married the black slaves with whom they were quartered.[9]

Black slave marital ties with mestizos were weaker than any considered above, and, not surprisingly, marriages between black slaves and Spaniards were rare indeed.[10] Black slave–mestizo marriage appears to have occurred at higher than expected levels during much of the second half of the seventeenth century, but declined to lower than expected levels after 1700. The far lower than expected black slave–Spanish marriage indices support the obvious conclusion that greater social distance between two groups lessens the likelihood of marital ties. While the decline in black slave–Indian intermarriage can be attributed to a lack of residential proximity, lower than expected rates of marriage between Spaniards and black slaves cannot be similarly explained, since the vast majority of urban slaves lived under the same roof as their Spanish masters. Status, in short, proved far more critical than geography.

MULATTO SLAVE MARRIAGE

Less numerous than their black counterparts, Santiago's mulatto slaves show weaker intramarriage indices than black slaves in all but two decades from 1620 to 1769.[11] Rarely marrying outside the Sagrario,[12] they stood a better chance of wedding persons of free status than did black slaves,[13] though Tilly indices suggest that their strongest marriage ties were with other mulatto slaves and black slaves, in that order.

Mulatto slaves forged their next strongest marital ties

Table 12: Mulatto Slave Marriage Indices: Santiago de Guatemala, 1593–1769

	MS–MS	MS–BS	MS–FB	MS–FM	MS–I	MS–ME	MS–SP	MS–O + U	Total MS Marriages
1593–99	0	0	0	570*	305*	0	0	0	4
1600–09	246	23	0	211	145	276	11	0	18
1610–19	754	143	0	121	102	117	0	0	19
1620–29	0	175	0	325	92	332	0	0	22
1630–39	0	0	0	0	730*	111*	0	0	5
1640–49	0	195	1596*	238	120	168	0	0	13
1650–59	180	93	167	199	85	178	5	1841	41
1660–69	184	257	0	295	114	77	7	0	51
1670–79	352	178	46	187	70	63	4	1605	64
1680–89	178	216	97	144	80	60	2	940	137
1690–99	282	208	181	135	92	68	6	1390	89
1700–09	534	441	331	134	73	46	6	1987	52
1710–19	444	416	190	117	75	62	0	1997	63
1720–29	1064	1267	196	96	45	71	0	0	31
1730–39	630	307	0	119	33	86	9	0	38
1740–49	1356	468	307	126	52	21	0	4914	29
1750–59	1194	0	0	154	0	18	0	9556	16
1760–69	3274*	0	0	90*	0	62*	0	14733*	9

* Based on insufficient number of marriages; see text.
Note: See table 11 for abbreviations.

with free mulattoes. These ties were most solid prior to 1670, at which point they weakened severely, but not so much as to fall below significantly higher than expected levels during the next century. The ensuing gradual decline in the mulatto slave–free mulatto marital index through 1729 is perhaps best traced to widening opportunities for free mulattoes to take nonslave spouses. (A rise in the index after 1739 is deceptive, due to the decline in mulatto slave marriages.)

Mulatto slave marital ties with Indian naborías were consistently weaker than those with free mulattoes, in good part because both groups suffered population declines. The mulatto slave–Indian naboría marriage index, while remaining higher than expected, began to weaken during the second half of the seventeenth century. By 1720 marriages between the two groups fell below expected levels, remaining there, with one minor decennial exception, through 1769. Mulatto slave–free black marital relations, erratic because Santiago's free black population was so small, were negligible until 1680, when they rose to higher than expected levels for only the second time. Notwithstanding the 1730s, they continued at higher than expected levels through 1749. Inversely, the mulatto slave–mestizo marriage index was at its strongest prior to 1660, at which point it fell sharply, but not until the 1740s did it ever fall significantly below expected levels.

Remarkably, mulatto slave marriages to mestizos, greater than expected in twelve of the eighteen decennial periods under review, were also greater than those to both naborías and free blacks in six of those periods. While mulatto slaves, finally, were far more likely to marry mestizos than were black slaves, neither stood much of a chance of marrying a Spaniard.[14]

FREE BLACK MARRIAGE

During the seventeenth century Santiago de Guatemala's free blacks appear to have enjoyed a higher percentage of exogamous marriage than any other socioracial group, slave or free, in the city (see appendix 1). The size of the free black population in Santiago best explains this phenomenon (no more than thirty-five free black marriages were recorded in *any* decade), but it should also be noted that slave manumissions, which served to replenish the group from time to time, were of decreasing importance as black slave numbers dwindled throughout this period.

Both because so few free blacks married formally prior to the mid-seventeenth century and because free black marriage data from the Sagrario are unavailable for the years 1620–49, the marriage patterns of this group are unclear prior to that date.[15] What little information we have, however, suggests that free blacks regularly married free mulattoes and black slaves before the 1650s, when free blacks for the first time married in adequate numbers to give some degree of accuracy to Tilly indices.

The period from 1650 to 1769 saw free blacks form stronger, more consistent marriage ties with black slaves than with any other group; in four of the ten decennial periods for which we have sufficient data, in fact, marriage ties between free blacks and black slaves were more significant than those among free blacks. Free blacks were next most likely to marry mulatto slaves and free mulattoes, respectively. Their marital ties with mulatto slaves were strongest during the period of that group's greatest numerical strength (ca. 1650–1729); marriage between the two, like that between free blacks and free mulattoes, was otherwise weak and irregular, though generally above expected levels.

Free black marriage ties were weakest with the three groups of Hispano-Indian descent (Spaniards, Indian naborías, and mestizos). Not surprisingly, free blacks show consistently lower than expected marriage ties with the dominant Spanish population throughout the entire period of this study, and no marriage pattern between these two socially distant groups is therefore discernible. Although Indian naborías enjoyed higher than expected bonds of marriage with both black and mulatto slaves, the same did not hold true for their marriage relations with free blacks. Only in 1690–1719 and 1760–69 did free black–naboría marriage rise above expected levels;[16] in the latter period free black ties with naborías were stronger than those with any group, a somewhat questionable finding given such

Table 13: Free Black Marriage Indices: Santiago de Guatemala, 1593–1769

	FB–FB	FB–BS	FB–MS	FB–FM	FB–I	FB–ME	FB–SP	FB–O + U	Total FB Marriages
1593–99	0	121*	0	1140*	136*	0	0	0	6
1600–09	0	0	0	948*	0	0	0	0	1
1610–19	0	303*	0	171*	86*	0	26*	0	9
1620–29	0	0	0	264*	0	406*	0	12166*	3
1630–39	0	936*	0	329*	304*	0	0	0	3
1640–49	0	423*	1596*	0	0	0	0	0	2
1650–59	624	312	167	153	0	37	0	3432	22
1660–69	2768	428	0	95	0	58	22	4706*	17
1670–79	504	543	46	99	21	76	0	2934	35
1680–89	306	218	97	129	44	67	18	4441	29
1690–99	468	403	181	83	111	20	24	5378	23
1700–09	0	478	331	105	91	40	0	8608	12
1710–19	570	749	190	104	56	34	29	5990	21
1720–29	0	936	196	165	22	45	0	0	21
1730–39	1350	389	0	166	0	44	0	0	15
1740–49	3340	0	307	94	47	56	22	0	16
1750–59	11324*	1213*	0	45*	0	97*	0	0	9
1760–69	0	0	0	102	127	20	0	9471	14

* Based on insufficient number of marriages; see text.
Note: See table 11 for abbreviations.

low numbers of free black marriages. Of the three non-African groups, mestizos were most apt to take free black partners, but only in 1660–89 and 1740–49 does the measure of this bond surpass the expected level.

Free blacks in the Sagrario fashioned stronger marital ties with all socioracial groups (save free mulattoes) than their counterparts in San Sebastián (see appendix 2). The large, multiracial Spanish households in which they generally lived provided a wide choice of partners, whereas the more humble circumstances of most of San Sebastián's Spanish parishioners meant that free black servants were few in number and had a smaller and less diverse pool of potential partners from which to choose. Accordingly, while the social gulf between the Sagrario's free blacks and mestizos might seem to have precluded all marital ties between the two, their common bond of dependent servant status actually brought them together. The free blacks of San Sebastián and Los Remedios, by contrast, had less regular contact with mestizos, since, while some mestizos there were dependent servants, others lived a humble but independent existence. Faced, thus, with the usual social barriers to finding non-African marriage partners, most who married outside their group took free mulatto spouses.[17]

FREE MULATTO MARRIAGE

A century of rapid growth in Santiago de Guatemala's free mulatto population from the 1650s forward appears not to have been the result of rising rates of endogamy. Although free mulatto intramarriage exceeded expected levels during this period, surpassing exogamous links in all of the post-1650 decennial periods, group endogamy declined as the total number of free mulattoes who married soared. The true magnitude of this inverse relationship may in fact have been obscured by the absorption of successive generations of free mulattoes by the capital's ladino (free mulatto–mestizo mixtures), mestizo, and lower-class Spanish populations.

Free mulattoes nevertheless formed their strongest exogamous ties with mulatto slaves, doing so in eleven of the eighteen decennial periods between 1593 and 1769. That this rela-

Table 14: Free Mulatto Marriage Indices: Santiago de Guatemala, 1593-1769

	FM-FM	FM-BS	FM-MS	FM-FB	FM-I	FM-ME	FM-SP	FM-O + U	Total FM Marriages
1593-99	4	97	570*	1140*	163	207	0	0	15
1600-09	452	147	211	948*	54	158	0	947*	42
1610-19	392	77	121	171*	79	244	16	0	59
1620-29	482	63	325	264*	162	185	4	0	46
1630-39	854	0	0	329*	25	209	4	986	37
1640-49	610	126	238	0	93	147	3	619*	67
1650-59	350	92	199	153	83	124	17	481	157
1660-69	446	166	295	95	86	113	10	537*	149
1670-79	360	71	187	99	65	120	7	386	266
1680-89	241	71	144	129	51	99	11	287	449
1690-99	284	119	135	83	48	103	12	316	391
1700-09	326	88	134	105	47	76	15	316	327
1710-19	248	125	117	104	41	79	32	273	461
1720-29	226	76	96	165	59	83	22	247	517
1730-39	206	52	119	166	65	83	30	227	675
1740-49	180	62	126	94	47	88	33	216	661
1750-59	174	102	154	45*	49	83	40	205	747
1760-69	172	0	90*	102	41	81	45	203	653

* Based on insufficient number of marriages; see text.
Note: See table 11 for abbreviations.

tionship was far more solid than that between free mulattoes and black slaves can be attributed to the relative social proximity of the two. In the social hierarchy of mature, post-1650 Guatemalan slave society, mulatto slaves held privileged positions, black slaves menial ones; hence the former were more desirable spouses, at least to free mulattoes.[18]

Free mulatto marriage bonds with *both* slave groups were strongest in the decades prior to 1670. Thereafter, these relationships weakened, though without dropping below expected levels. It may be no accident that this drop roughly coincided with the rapid growth of the ladino population and higher percentages of legitimacy in gente ordinaria baptisms.[19] Such phenomena were contemporaneous with the rise of a sizable independent free mulatto population in the peripheral barrios of the city.[20] Free mulatto–black slave marriage was far stronger in the Sagrario than in San Sebastián. This pattern, repeated for free mulatto–mulatto slave marriage, albeit with lower marriage scores, persisted despite declines in the number of free mulatto–black slave unions in the city at large.

As free mulatto marriage ties with slaves weakened, free mulatto–free black marriage gained strength, continuing at higher than expected levels through the 1760s. If Santiago's free mulattoes were moving up socially in the late seventeenth and eighteenth centuries, why would they continue to maintain higher than expected marital ties with free blacks, much less mulatto and black slaves? Largely due to the vagaries of classification: because so many free mulattoes were classified as ladinos, marriage indices fail to reflect the extent of free mulatto social mobility. No less plausible an explanation is that individuals properly classified as free mulattoes represented a broad socioeconomic and racial spectrum, ranging from those of privilege—a *maestro mayor de arquitectura* (chief architect) and militia captain, for example—to those without—a dark-complexioned shoemaker from the Barrio de San Sebastián, say, who was recruited for dangerous military duty at a tropical river fort.[21]

Lucía de Ibarra surely belonged in this latter category. Manumitted in 1707 along with her mother by the *alférez* (commandant of the city's militia units) Don Francisco Javier de Ibarra, a regidor of the cabildo of Ciudad Real in Chiapas, Lucía de Ibarra successfully sought an *amparo* (official decree of support) in January 1709 because she feared some official or private individual, "seeing me poor and helpless," would reenslave her.[22] At the other extreme was Felipe de Fuentes y Alvarado, son of the free black María de Alvarado and Captain Don Francisco de Fuentes y Guzmán, a prominent encomendero, alcalde ordinario of the city many times, and father of the *cronista* (chronicler) Don Francisco Antonio de Fuentes y Guzmán. Felipe, apparently born illegitimate around 1640, was raised in the Fuentes y Guzmán household by his mother, probably a servant. Apprenticed by his father at an early age, he became a master saddler but made his mark in the military, rising from alférez (1667) to captain (1671) to *sargento mayor* (sergeant major) of all of Guatemala's free pardo militia (1674). No less indicative of his stature was his late 1679 or early 1680 petition to allow his legitimate sons to enter the universities of San Carlos (Guatemala) and Mexico, then open solely to Spanish men. Although the Crown's response to his plea is unknown, Fuentes y Alvarado's case demonstrates what a young and ambitious free mulatto with prominent ancestry (and at least some support from his natural father) could achieve despite his illegitimacy.[23]

Fuentes y Alvarado had much in his favor: Spanish parentage, economic standing, probably light skin. Low socioeconomic standing and dark skin, by contrast, compounded the curse of illegitimacy (often so unjustly ascribed to mulattoes), sharply limiting opportunities for many of Spanish Guatemala's free mulattoes.[24] Thus the more humble, darker free mulattoes, essentially those of Afro-Indian descent, tended to marry slaves and free blacks and were limited in their social mobility. Free mulattoes of Spanish-mestizo descent were more likely to wed social equals or superiors and to make names for themselves in the artisan and building trades and in the pardo militia. These were the free mulattoes who clambered up the social ladder in Santiago's final century.

Free mulatto–Indian marriage bonds were strongest in the

late sixteenth century and the early and middle decades of the seventeenth century.[25] They remained moderately above expected levels through the 1680s (except for the 1630s), then persisted below expected levels in the ensuing eighty years (except for the 1720s and 1730s). This pattern differed greatly from that of late eighteenth-century León, in the Bajío region of New Spain. There, and in León's surrounding pueblos, Indian and free mulatto inhabitants were, according to David Brading and Cynthia Wu, "on the point of coalescence": roughly a third of all Indian men who married took mulatto wives from 1782 to 1785; nearly half (44.2 percent) did so in 1792–93. "After two centuries of cohabitation," the two researchers conclude, "there still existed two separate groups in society, the one composed of Indians, mulattoes and a few mestizos, and the other Spaniards and most mestizos."[26]

Free mulatto–Indian marriage patterns in Santiago de Guatemala suggest no such amalgamation or bifurcation. Though it is beyond doubt that formal and informal black-Indian and mulatto-Indian unions contributed to the rapid growth of Santiago's free mulatto population, especially during the city's first century and a half, its free mulattoes began by the late seventeenth or early eighteenth century to enjoy wider marital opportunities than their counterparts in the Bajío.

Perhaps this is best illustrated in San Sebastián Parish (see appendix 2), where free mulatto–Indian naboría marital ties did no better than hover above expected levels after the 1680s, and indeed fell significantly below expected levels in half of the subsequent decennial periods. Such results may be anticipated, given the presence in the parish of upwardly mobile free mulattoes, few of whom were likely to think of Indians, even urbanized naborías, as suitable marriage partners. But similar findings in the Sagrario come as more of a surprise. There strong, consistent marital relations between free mulattoes and naborías might be predicted in light of a common dependence on Spanish patrons. Specifically, one might presume that free mulatto criados (as well as a number of newly manumitted, mostly female, former slaves) would commonly choose spouses from among the naborías with whom they continued to live and work.[27] While early seventeenth-century marriage indices for the Sagrario confirm this, post-1669 figures do not, falling below expected levels in three of the subsequent decades and rising only slightly above those levels in the other parishes (see appendix 2). By the eighteenth century free mulattoes were indeed moving up the social ladder in the Guatemalan capital.

Free mulatto–mestizo marriage indices also bear this out. At their highest prior to the 1630s, when they dropped by more than 25 percent over the previous decennial period, the Tilly scores for free mulatto–mestizo marriage declined slowly thereafter, reaching their low point by 1719 before climbing slightly and then steadying (see appendix 2). Free mulatto–mestizo marriage appears to have been strongest in the Sagrario prior to the 1630s, at which point San Sebastián took the lead. By the 1740s, and continuing through the 1760s, free mulatto–mestizo marriage showed new strength in the Sagrario; the decline in the slave and free black populations of the Sagrario apparently led free mulattoes there to select spouses from outside their traditional pool. Rarely during the period from 1650 to 1769 did free mulatto–mestizo marriage indices fall below free mulatto–Indian indices or expected levels in either the city at large or any of its four parishes.[28]

The appearance of the castizo (defined in the nomenclature of New Spain as the offspring of a mestizo man and a Spanish woman) in Santiago's parish registers during the early eighteenth century provides evidence of the kind of racial amalgamation Brading and Wu describe. The social standing of the castizo (between mestizo and Spaniard) is suggested by the fact that the offspring of a castizo woman and a Spanish man was classified a Spaniard.[29] The social standing of free mulattoes is suggested in turn by their marital ties with the castizo. First documented in the late 1720s, marriage between the two accounted for sixty-four recorded unions by the 1760s: thirty-seven in San Sebastián, fifteen in the Sagrario, seven in Los Remedios, and five in the Candelaria.[30]

Free mulatto–Spanish marriage was concentrated in San Sebastián and, to a lesser degree, Los Remedios and the Candelaria. Unlike the Sagrario, the three outlying, more homogenous parishes often housed poor Spaniards of mixed ancestry;[31] they thus provided successful free mulattoes with some chance to marry their social superiors.[32] Not until late in the city's history, however, did free mulatto–Spanish marriage ties exceed expected levels in any parish. In San Sebastián, for example, indices began to rise in the 1730s, finally edging above expected levels in the 1760s (see appendix 2). In Los Remedios free mulatto–Spanish marriage surpassed expected levels in the 1750s, as it did in the Candelaria. Marital relations between free mulattoes and Spaniards in the Sagrario, however, peaked in the 1710s at well below expected levels and weakened thereafter. The social abyss between free mulattoes and the Sagrario's European Spanish or wealthy American Spanish was simply too great to make marriage between the two more commonplace, even for the most resourceful or upwardly mobile free mulatto.

Though composite free mulatto–Spanish marital indices for Santiago's four parishes never climbed above expected levels, it is nonetheless significant that marital bonds between the two continued to strengthen after the turn of the eighteenth century. Such increases at least hint at a slight closing of the gap between the two distinct segments, at some erosion in the economic disparity and distrust that marked their relations. Although free mulattoes and Spaniards (especially free mulatas and Spanish men) had long entered into informal unions, intermarriage of the two became more regular only with the gradual transformation of each group.

For the free mulattoes this came about through the filling of vital niches in local and long-distance commerce, the artisan and building trades, the pardo militia, and cabildo-controlled institutions. Improved economic standing, combined with greater independence for those mulattoes who escaped from criado status in Spanish households, thus contributed greatly to the transformation. So, too, did formal and informal mixing with persons of Hispano-Indian descent, which resulted in increasing numbers of free mulattoes coming to resemble the phenotype most prized by Spanish Guatemalan urban society.

At the same time, the racial composition of the Spanish segment was slowly altered by the infiltration of its lower strata by castizos, mestizos, and free mulattoes.[33] A high percentage of free mulatto–Spanish marriages between 1710 and 1769 in fact represented free mulatto unions with these "new Spaniards."[34]

But free mulatto–Spanish marital ties, especially in the peripheral barrios and parishes of Santiago de Guatemala, illustrate only one aspect of a growing free mulatto mobility. The broad contrast between pre-1650 free mulatto exogamous marriage patterns and those of the eighteenth century demonstrates convincingly that sizable numbers of free mulattoes were able to improve their lot in Spanish American urban society.

INDIAN NABORÍA MARRIAGE

Nontributary Indians show the highest intramarriage index of any socioracial group in Santiago de Guatemala.[35] At its strongest from 1620 to 1669, this index declined thereafter, probably in conjunction with the rise of the city's free mulatto and mestizo populations, whose growth may have offered growing numbers of naborías the chance, through marriage, to shed their status or at least to better the lot of their children.[36] In none of the decades under review, however, did naboría intramarriage fail to exceed by huge margins either expected levels or any measure of naboría exogamy.

Ten of the eighteen decennial periods between 1593 and 1769 saw naborías forge their strongest exogamous ties with mestizos. In none of the eighteen, moreover, did Indian naboría–mestizo marriage fail to surpass expected levels, though eighteenth-century indices were considerably weaker than those for the previous century, due largely to the increasing upward mobility of the city's mestizo population, as demonstrated by eighteenth-century rises in mestizo-Spanish marital indices. San Sebastián registered the strongest naboría-mestizo marital ties in the city (see appendix 2). Marriage ties between naborías and mestizos in the Sagrario were weaker than those in San Sebastián, suggesting that the dependent status they shared played little part in uniting them.

Table 15: Indian Naboría Marriage Indices: Santiago de Guatemala, 1593–1769

	I-I	I-BS	I-MS	I-FB	I-FM	I-ME	I-SP	I-O + U	Total I Marriages
1593–99	426	217	305*	136*	163	74	0	0	84
1600–09	272	145	145	0	54	163	2	0	122
1610–19	398	93	102	86*	79	123	2	0	117
1620–29	626	142	92	0	162	135	3	0	54
1630–39	776	421	730*	304*	25	138	0	913	40
1640–49	562	112	120	0	93	288	0	783*	53
1650–59	738	114	85	0	83	149	4	0	87
1660–69	1076	169	114	0	86	172	0	1159*	69
1670–79	590	148	70	21	65	141	3	750*	137
1680–89	554	147	80	44	51	104	3	0	201
1690–99	490	102	92	111	48	108	1	511	242
1700–09	606	121	73	91	47	89	3	544	190
1710–19	594	49	75	56	41	82	14	591	213
1720–29	404	36	45	22	59	82	11	468	273
1730–39	426	0	33	0	65	99	11	627	242
1740–49	524	0	52	47	47	98	11	758	188
1750–59	438	0	0	0	49	113	17	826	185
1760–69	396	0	0	127	41	98	21	592	224

* Based on insufficient number of marriages; see text.
Note: See table 11 for abbreviations.

In five of the remaining eight decennial periods (1593–99, 1630s, 1670s, 1680s, and 1700s) naborías formed their strongest exogamous ties with black slaves. These ties peaked in the late sixteenth and early seventeenth centuries before declining gradually, falling below expected levels for the first time in the 1710s. Indian naboría–mulatto slave marital patterns showed a similar pattern, but in the eighteenth century failed to collapse to the degree of naboría–black slave marriage relations.[37]

Indian naboría–free black marriage indices were highly erratic, fluctuating above and below the expected level, while Indian marital ties with free mulattoes showed their greatest strength in the early and middle decades of the seventeenth century, only to hover around the expected level after about 1680; these bonds were strongest in the Sagrario, somewhat weaker in San Sebastián, and weakest and most inconsistent in Los Remedios.[38] Indian marriage ties with both black and mulatto slaves were generally stronger and more durable than they were with either free blacks or free mulattoes.

Naboría unions with slaves were most often characterized by Indian women marrying slave men; Indian marriages with the groups of free color, by contrast, seem to have involved more equal numbers of Indian men and women. The predominance of Indian women in naboría-slave unions stemmed from a number of factors: Indian females outnumbered Indian males in Spanish households; female slaves, especially mulatas, were often the informal concubines of Spanish household members and thus virtually off limits to slaves as prospective brides; and, perhaps most important, male slaves apparently tried to avoid marrying other slaves so their offspring might be born free, choosing instead to take low-status Indian criadas as mates.[39]

Indian naboría males avoided marriage to slave women for the same reason. But because the status of one's offspring was no such consideration in Indian unions with free blacks and mulattoes, Indian men must have found free blacks and mulatas especially attractive mates. Unfortunately, so, too, did many free casta and poor-Spanish men, giving rise to a competition that the Indian could not often win. Although Indian women appear to have had even less chance of marrying free blacks or mulattoes, the diversity of racial mixtures within Guatemala's free black and mulatto groups nonetheless worked to the naboría's advantage. Some free blacks and mulattoes, especially those of Afro-Indian descent, considered them to be perfectly suitable marriage partners.

Far lower than expected Indian naboría–Spanish marriage indices must be attributed to the social gulf between the two, a gulf nearly as great as that between Spaniard and slave. Yet the gradual but unspectacular rise in the index after 1710 is probably due to the acceptance of persons of mixed descent into the Spanish lower strata. Not since the immediate postconquest period had Spaniards and Indians enjoyed so close a formal marital relationship. Improved marriage ties, however, were confined to the Sagrario and San Sebastián; in Los Remedios, Indian-Spanish marriage diminished after 1719, perhaps as a result of an apparent decline in the Spanish population there.

Naboría intermarriage, more broadly, is difficult to assess. Uncertainties about who was and who was not an "indio ladino" (the notarial term for naboría) were compounded by indeterminate levels of Indian migration into and out of Spanish American colonial cities and the absorption of newly urbanized Indians into the mestizo category. Interestingly, this fluidity, though specific to the naboría, was at least in evidence within the black slave pool, to which African slaves were regularly introduced and from which others escaped through flight or manumission. Of course the immigration of African slaves to Santiago de Guatemala was not as constant, as strong, or as voluntary as the influx of Indians. Similarly, slaves lucky enough to win freedom were hard pressed to shed the "black" or "mulatto" label, while recently urbanized or Hispanicized Indians could pass into the mestizo group in one generation because the distinctions separating the two were more cultural than racial.[40]

MESTIZO MARRIAGE

Mestizo intramarriage indices, like those for free mulattoes, peaked in the early and middle decades of the seventeenth century and then began gradually to decline, though without dropping below expected levels of mestizo exogamy. Until the 1710s, moreover, intramarriage indices for mestizos exceeded those for free mulattoes; thereafter, the reverse was true.[41] That mestizo endogamy fell as the number of mestizo marriages rose suggests, as did a similar inversion for free mulattoes, that intramarriage played a declining role in the growth of Santiago's mestizo population. Bolstering this view are late seventeenth- and eighteenth-century increases in total mestizo marriages with free mulattoes and, to a lesser degree, with Indians and Spaniards.

Mestizo intramarriage in both the Sagrario and San Sebastián fell sharply in the 1710s, though not so much as to push composite intramarriage figures below expected levels; comparable figures for Los Remedios, while stronger and less variable, also weakened around the turn of the century (in the 1690s). One concomitant of these declines throughout the city was a rise in mestizo-Spanish marriage indices. Speculation that the strengthening mestizo-Spanish marriage relationship (detailed below) was also one cause of these declines is supported by evidence from all three parishes that mestizo–free mulatto and mestizo-Indian indices, while consistently higher than both expected levels and measures of mestizo-Spanish marriage, were then either unchanged or declining (see appendix 2).[42]

Nonetheless, mestizos forged their strongest intermarriage ties with Indians, doing so in every post-1660 decade save the 1720s, or in ten of the eighteen decennial periods under study.[43] Much of the strength of this relationship can be attributed to the entry it provided to mestizo ranks;[44] mestizo-Indian marriage in fact contributed heavily to the growth of Santiago's mestizo population, despite the passing of numerous mestizos into poor Spanish, castizo, and even elite Spanish groups. Post-1670 measures of mestizo marriage with Indians were generally stronger in San Sebastián and Los Remedios than in the Sagrario, probably because Indians there faced less competition from mulatto slaves and free blacks in finding mestizo marriage partners; in Los Remedios, by contrast, rising mestizo-Spanish indices show that marital challenges fre-

Table 16: Mestizo Marriage Indices: Santiago de Guatemala, 1593-1769

	ME-ME	ME-BS	ME-MS	ME-FB	ME-FM	ME-I	ME-SP	ME-O + U	Total ME Marriages
1593-99	1838	0	0	0	207	74	23	0	22
1600-09	552	0	276	0	158	163	9	0	24
1610-19	486	11	117	0	244	123	11	1107*	41
1620-29	648	32	332	406*	185	135	0	1217*	30
1630-39	352	43	111*	0	209	138	11	553	66
1640-49	690	0	168	0	147	288	5	0	38
1650-59	420	49	178	37	124	149	21	812	93
1660-69	854	126	77	58	113	172	9	988*	81
1670-79	424	58	63	76	120	141	15	667	154
1680-89	302	32	60	67	99	104	19	484	266
1690-99	294	82	68	20	103	108	17	469	264
1700-09	424	27	46	40	76	89	25	480	215
1710-19	238	15	62	34	79	82	48	356	353
1720-29	174	49	71	45	83	82	52	315	405
1730-39	182	25	86	44	83	99	42	329	462
1740-49	152	0	21	56	88	98	40	301	474
1750-59	124	0	18	97*	83	113	51	290	527
1760-69	140	111*	62*	20	81	98	46	277	478

* Based on insufficient number of marriages; see text.
Note: See table 11 for abbreviations.

quently came from above (see appendix 2). Citywide declines in mestizo-Indian indices after 1700 seem consistent with reduced mestizo dependence on Spanish patrons, the rise of the castizo, and absorption of mestizos into the city's Spanish population. Increased mestizo mobility, in sum, made Indians increasingly less attractive spouses.

Mestizo–free mulatto marriage indices exceeded all other measures of mestizo exogamy in three of the decades from 1590 to 1659. Never far behind measures of composite mestizo-Indian marriage thereafter, these indices showed similar parish characteristics as well, generally registering greater strength in the more egalitarian San Sebastián and Los Remedios than in the more elite Sagrario, again because the latter's sizable mulatto slave and free black populations may have presented stiff competition for free mulattoes (and Indians) seeking mestizo marriage partners. Both the size of Santiago's free mulatto and mestizo populations and the sustained strength of their marital bonds lead one to conclude that this relationship was of key importance in the growth of a sizable ladino population in the capital.[45] As the mestizo population absorbed free mulattoes through both formal and informal unions, the term "ladino" was increasingly used to categorize mestizos, mulattoes, and their admixtures, "due to the difficulty of separating one from the other because of the close connections that existed between the two castas."[46]

Of the four pre-1660 decades in which mestizo–free mulatto marriage indices failed to exceed all other measures of mestizo exogamy (the 1600s, 1620s, 1640s, and 1650s), all but the 1640s saw mestizos build their strongest exogamous bonds with mulatto slaves. Largely concentrated in the Sagrario and San Sebastián, these ties in the Sagrario remained above expected levels through the 1750s but did so in San Sebastián only through the late seventeenth century.[47] The greater long-term strength of mestizo–mulatto slave marriage in the Sagrario, combined with evidence that mestizo-Spanish marital ties were weaker there than elsewhere in the capital, suggests that the Sagrario's mestizo inhabitants retained a relatively dependent status, due most probably to their dark complexion, impoverishment, and low level of Hispanicization (see appendix 2). As such, they were more likely to marry mulatto slaves than were the independent mestizo traders or artisans of the peripheral parishes. Unlike their richer, lighter-skinned counterparts, they were by the same token effectively barred from marrying creoles and new Spaniards.

Mestizo marriage to blacks, both free and enslaved, was especially weak. Whereas mestizo–mulatto slave marriage indices bettered expected levels in twelve of eighteen decades under study, mestizo–free black marriage rose above expected levels in just four decades, mestizo–black slave unions in just three. Occurring primarily in the Sagrario, black-mestizo unions favored free blacks over black slaves. Thus, while measures of mestizo–black slave marriage only briefly exceeded expected levels in the Sagrario, mestizo–free black marriage indices for the parish remained above the expected level during most of the period from 1650 to 1759. Clearly, typical Sagrario mestizos took free black (or mulatto slave) spouses with far greater consistency than did their more independent and affluent counterparts in San Sebastián or Los Remedios (see appendix 2).

Both mestizo endogamy and marriage with other non-elites declined as mestizo-Spanish marriage rose. While this post-1700 phenomenon was something less than dramatic, it reflects a narrowing of the social distance between mestizo and Spaniard. Close relations between the two were not strictly an eighteenth-century phenomenon, of course. Mestizos had married into the Spanish population in considerable numbers in the sixteenth century. They had presumed themselves to be and were accepted as Spaniards. They had been absorbed by conquistador and humble Spanish artisan families alike. By contrast, the mestizos who married Santiago's eighteenth-century Spanish inhabitants appear to have married into poor Spanish families, many of whom were themselves of mixed descent. Living for the most part in the peripheral parishes of the capital and making their living as artisans and traders, they achieved a modicum of economic independence and loosened the bonds that had bound them to Spaniards as servants and orphans.

Mestizo-Spanish marriage indices closely resemble measures of Spanish–free mulatto marriage in that both remained below the expected level before 1700. But while Spanish–free mulatto marriage indices subsequently rose only gradually and never reached the expected level, except in the outlying parishes, post-1710 measures of mestizo-Spanish marriage rose above the expected level in two decades and remained only slightly below it in the other four. The failure of mestizo-Spanish marital ties to grow even more sharply can be attributed to the passing of numerous mestizos, castizos, and ladinos into the lower segments of the Spanish population, a process by which mestizo ranks came to include a residue of persons of mixed descent who did not match the Spanish phenotype and cultural attributes and were thus less able to penetrate Spanish ranks.

Mestizo-Spanish marriage bonds first climbed above the expected level in Los Remedios, reaching that mark by the final decade of the seventeenth century, two decades before doing so in San Sebastián (see appendix 2). Holding above the expected level through the 1740s, marital relations between the two declined in the 1750s and 1760s, probably because the Spanish population of the parish dwindled. In San Sebastián, by contrast, mestizo-Spanish marriage indices, far lower than expected through the 1700s, climbed sharply the following decade to just above the expected level, where they remained (in all but two decades) until 1769. Despite the sharp increase, comparison of the two parish indices shows a stronger mestizo-Spanish marriage relationship in Los Remedios than in San Sebastían. This finding suggests not so much that there were significant socioeconomic differences between mestizos in the two parishes, but that San Sebastián's Spaniards enjoyed a somewhat more privileged status than Spaniards in Los Remedios.

Indeed, were all of Santiago de Guatemala's parishes placed on a continuum based on the socioeconomic standing, power, and racial purity of their Spanish inhabitants, surely the parishioners of the Sagrario would have been the richest, most powerful, and purest, with those from Los Remedios closest to the opposite pole, and the parishioners of San Sebastián and the Candelaria somewhere in between. With mestizo status in roughly opposite proportions, it is easy to see why mestizo-Spanish marriage registered its greatest strength in Los Remedios, waned in San Sebastián, and dropped to its weakest levels in the Sagrario.

In the seventeenth century at least, mestizo-Spanish marital indices from the Sagrario were on a par with those of San Sebastián. But as the mestizo-Spanish marriage index climbed sharply to a new plateau above the expected level in San Sebastián early in the eighteenth century, similar indices for the Sagrario peaked well below the expected level and then remained there through the 1760s. Posting only a minor increase in mestizo-Spanish marriage, the Sagrario proved stubbornly resistant to the factors that brought rises in mestizo-Spanish intermarriage elsewhere in the Guatemalan capital. For the typical mestizo and Spaniard who resided in the Sagrario, the socioeconomic gap between the two proved to be unbridgeable.

SPANISH MARRIAGE

Second in strength only to that for Indian naborías, Spanish intramarriage indices peaked in the 1700s and then declined, a pattern consistent with evidence of increased Spanish marriage to nonelites during this period.[48] Not unexpectedly, comparison of Spanish intramarriage in Santiago's two principal parishes reveals sharper eighteenth-century declines in San Sebastián than in the Sagrario, though indices for both remained well above expected levels.

Considered previously from the perspective of the nonelites and hence best described here in summary, Spanish intermarriage varied greatly by group, parish, and period. Thus those of lowest status in Santiago—black and mulatto slaves, free blacks, Indian naborías—rarely married Spaniards anywhere in the city at any point in its history. Outside the Sagrario, by contrast, in the multiracial peripheral parishes of San Sebastián and Los Remedios, marital bonds between Spaniards and upwardly mobile mestizos and free mulattoes gained considerable strength around the turn of the eighteenth century, despite obvious socioracial differences and economic

Table 17: Spanish Marriage Indices: Santiago de Guatemala, 1590-1769

	SP-SP	SP-BS	SP-MS	SP-FB	SP-FM	SP-I	SP-ME	SP-O + U	Total SP Marriages
1590-99	324	4	0	0	0	0	23	0	206
1600-09	406	0	11	0	0	2	9	0	193
1610-19	442	2	0	26*	16	2	11	0	196
1620-29	318	0	0	0	4	3	0	162*	226
1630-39	290	0	0	0	4	0	11	0	245
1640-49	338	0	0	0	3	0	5	171*	242
1650-59	358	2	5	0	17	4	21	194	390
1660-69	380	0	7	22	10	0	9	190*	422
1670-79	450	0	4	0	7	3	15	238	432
1680-89	462	0	2	18	11	3	19	262	492
1690-99	482	7	6	24	12	1	17	273	453
1700-09	520	0	6	0	15	3	25	304	340
1710-19	420	0	0	29	32	14	48	304	414
1720-29	460	0	0	0	22	11	52	341	375
1730-39	432	0	9	0	30	11	42	325	467
1740-49	392	34	0	22	33	11	40	354	403
1750-59	326	0	0	0	40	17	51	323	473
1760-69	392	0	0	0	45	21	46	396	335

* Based on insufficient number of marriages; see text.
Note: See table 11 for abbreviations.

disparities between Spaniards and castas. At the same time, Spaniards, like mestizos, came increasingly to marry castizos (who only appeared in parish registers as an identifiable socioracial type after 1720), ladinos, and other persons of mixed descent who often went unidentified in parish registers.[49]

Using Spanish intermarriage indices generally as a measure of "marital proximity" to Spaniards offers valuable insight into changes in Santiago's socioracial stratification after 1650.[50] It has already been established that Spanish marital relations with African slaves, free blacks, and Indian naborías remained unchanged and far lower than expected, though each of these groups changed in size. The gradual eighteenth-century rise toward the expected level in free casta marriage to Spaniards also suggests that they of all the nonelites saw the greatest improvement in their marital relations with Spaniards. But while it might have been anticipated that mestizos would enjoy relatively close marital ties with the dominant segment, the most striking variation in marital proximity was the growth of the free mulatto–Spanish relationship, not in the central and more prestigious Sagrario, but in the less stratified peripheral parishes of San Sebastián, Los Remedios, and the Candelaria.

It is somehow fitting that those having the weakest marriage relationship with Santiago de Guatemala's nonelites—the predominantly European Spanish of the Sagrario—were also the most apprehensive about being outnumbered and overrun by the city's multiracial poor. For what they did not (and could not) realize was that intermarriage and race mixture, besides falling far short of creating a single socioracial source of opposition, actually encouraged competition among the various nonelite groups and thereby diverted their attention from a potentially far more productive (yet deadly) competition with the dominant segment. Upward mobility, in effect, pacified each of the nonelites, serving as a vital ingredient in the mortar that held Spanish Guatemalan urban society together. Without it, a small Spanish minority would have been unable to rule the capital and its comarca for over two centuries.

PLATES

PLATE 1. *Conquest and Reduction of Guatemala.* This late sixteenth-century painting is a highly idealized depiction of the conquest and settlement of Guatemala. Museo de América, Madrid. Reproduced with permission of Index, Barcelona.

PLATE 2. *War of Guatemala and Its Provinces.* Note Spaniard (Pedro de Alvarado?) on horseback, cotton-armored Tlaxcalan troops at rear left, and Kaqchikel warriors under attack on right. From Diego Muñoz Camargo, "Historia de Tlaxcala" manuscript in Special Collections Department, University of Glasgow Library, Scotland. Photograph courtesy of Photo Archive, CIRMA, La Antigua Guatemala.

El Yllmo. Sr. Mtro. Dn. Fransisco Marroquin, natural de las Montañas de O-
viedo Cura de Santiago de Guatem.ª primer Obpo. que gobernó esta Sta. Ygles
por renuncia del R.P. Fr. Domingo Betanzos del orn. de Sto. Domingo: Fue electo
18. de Diziembre de 1533: La erigió, y fundó en virtud de Bula del Sr. Paulo
II de la misma fecha por Septiembre de 1541. gobernó hasta 18 de Abril de
1563. que fallecio, se sepultó en la Sta. Yglesia Catedral.

PLATE 3. Portrait of Francisco Marroquín, first bishop of Guatemala. After Alvarado's death in 1541, he directed resettlement of some of the conquistador's emancipated Indian slaves in Jocotenango. Courtesy of Palacio Arzobispal. Iconographic Gallery of Bishops and Archbishops of Santiago de Guatemala, Cathedral of Guatemala, Guatemala City.

PLATE 4. Antigua (formerly Santiago de Guatemala), looking southward from Cerro de la Cruz, photographed by Eadweard Muybridge in 1876. Multiarched Palace of the Captains General is directly below peak of Agua volcano, and Convent of La Merced is in right foreground. Courtesy of the Boston Athenaeum.

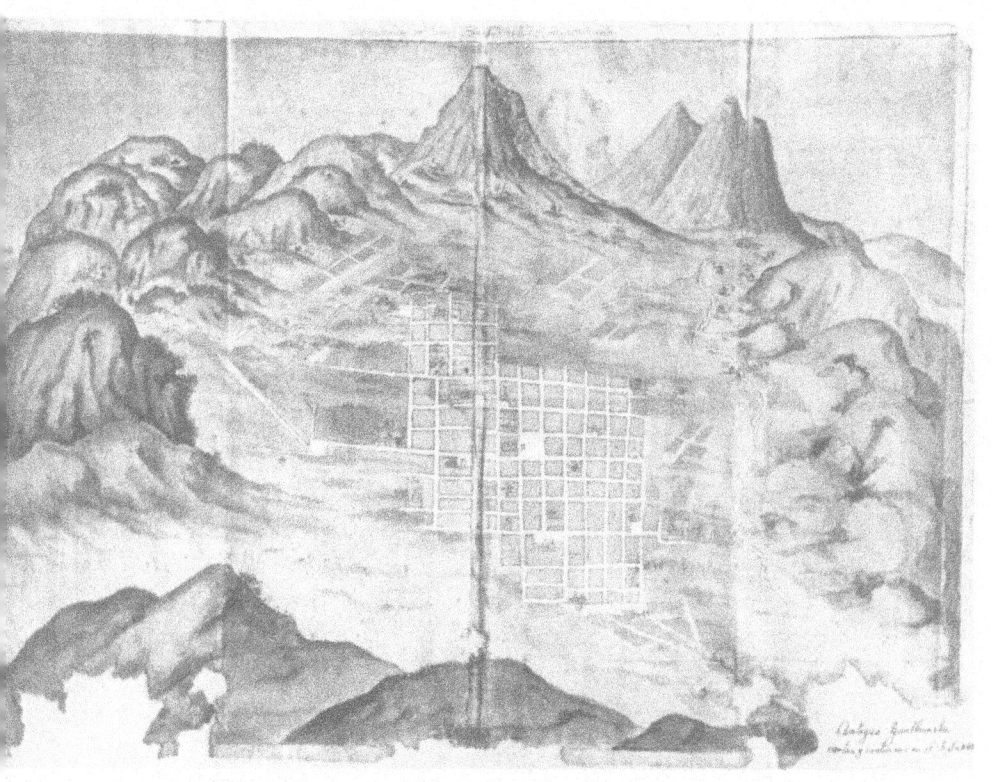

PLATE 5. Early eighteenth-century map of Santiago de Guatemala looking southward, showing street layout and numerous religious institutions in the city and surrounding towns. Photograph courtesy of Photo Archive, CIRMA, La Antigua Guatemala.

PLATE 6. Fuentes y Guzmán's map of the "City of Guatemala," looking southward, showing location of principal urban churches and monasteries and churches in surrounding towns, ca. 1690. From Francisco Antonio de Fuentes y Guzmán, "Recordación florida" manuscript. Published with permission of the Patrimonio Nacional, Biblioteca del Palacio Real, Madrid.

PLATE 7. Colonial period cabildo building in Antigua, on northeast corner of central plaza, with oxcarts on edge of market and market stall in plaza, photographed by Eadweard Muybridge in 1876. Indian (ceramics?) vendors carry wooden cargo racks. Courtesy of the Boston Athenaeum.

PLATE 8. Painting of market in central plaza with cathedral under construction, Santiago de Guatemala, ca. 1678, looking eastward. Compare with Muybridge's photograph of same market, two centuries later (pl. 9). Foreground of painting by Antonio Ramírez Montúfar. Private collection, Cuernavaca, Morelos, Mexico. Published with permission of owner. Photograph

PLATE 9. Antigua market, photographed by Eadweard Muybridge in 1876. View is to the southwest, with Agua volcano at left, Fuego volcano at right, and multiarched Palace of the Captains General on far side of central plaza. Compare with 1678 depiction of market (pl. 8). Courtesy of the Boston Athenaeum.

PLATE 10. Indian cabildo members of Santa María de Jesús in foreground, photographed by Eadweard Muybridge in 1876. Cane and wattle and daub (*bajareque*) structures with thatched roofs appear in background. Courtesy of the Boston Athenaeum.

PLATE 11. Church of Santa María de Jesús with Indians and non-Indians, photographed by Eadweard Muybridge in 1876. Courtesy of the Boston Athenaeum.

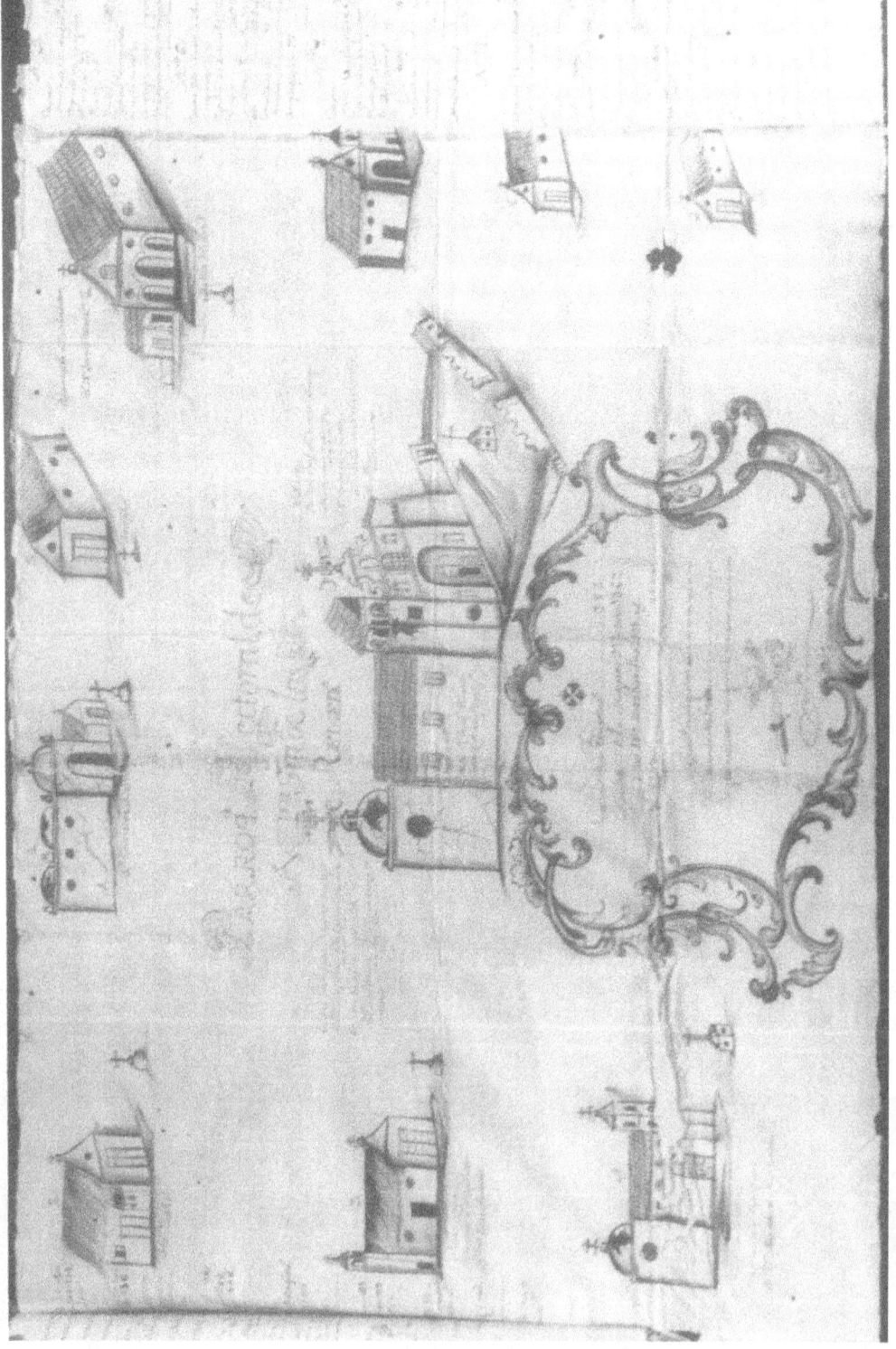

PLATE 13. Parish church of Los Remedios, 1782. Detail from a painting on paper. Earthquakes of 1773 probably caused cracks and other damage to the church. Courtesy of the Archivo Histórico Arquidiocesano "Francisco de Paula García Peláez," Guatemala City.

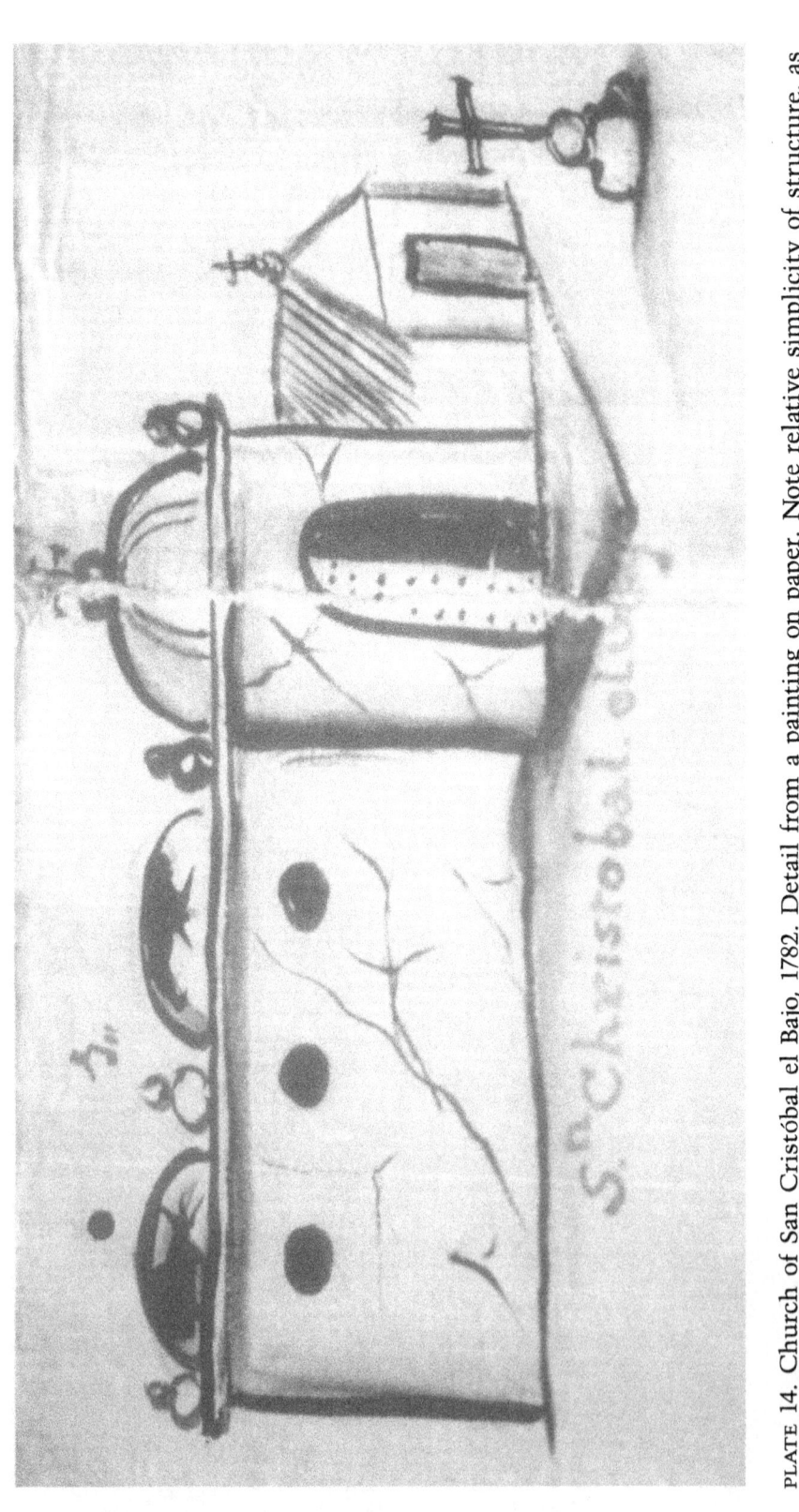

PLATE 14. Church of San Cristóbal el Bajo, 1782. Detail from a painting on paper. Note relative simplicity of structure, as compared with Los Remedios Parish church, and many cracks in walls, probably from 1773 earthquakes. Courtesy of the Archivo Histórico Arquidiocesano "Francisco de Paula García Peláez," Guatemala City.

CHAPTER SIX

SUPPLYING THE CITY: THE CASTA ECONOMIC REVOLUTION

THE gradual displacement of Indians by castas was no less evident in the capital's market supply system than in its barrios. Indeed, the process by which the city's official economy proved so inadequate and inhospitable as to push many castas into a black market in domestic goods bore a remarkable resemblance to the way in which Santiago's Spanish households filled to capacity and then spilled their casta overflow into the barrios. This is not to suggest that most castas contravened government regulations and monopolies designed to ensure the capital a stable source of food and supplies and its Spanish creole merchants a hefty profit, only that castas became increasingly engaged in illegal aspects of Santiago's complex market system as they grew in numbers.

Such activity was hardly evident around 1550, of course. Then the city's supply routes were traveled almost solely by Indians—tamemes bearing tributary items (chickens and grain, primarily) for their encomenderos or for Spanish officials, as well as traders and vendors from the towns and villages in the surrounding piedmont, valleys, and sierra, most of whom lived within a half-day of the capital by foot or on horseback.[1] What these Indians sold or carried usually depended on their habitat.[2] Thus those who lived in the *tierra templada* (temperate zone) of Panchoy and the surrounding valleys delivered maize, wheat, vegetables, and fruit to the city. Those who lived in the nearby piedmont were major suppliers of cacao, as well as salt, fish, and other products from the *tierra caliente* (hot zone) of the contiguous Pacific coastal plain. And those who lived in the highland *tierra fría* (cold zone) transported timber, ice, firewood, charcoal, and grain. Lacking any special resource or preconquest skill (mat and basket weaving, for example, or pottery making), other Indians became the purveyors of various Spanish-introduced products (pork lard and butter, among others) or were trained as cart builders, bakers, or butchers.[3]

Acting primarily as vendors and buyers for Spanish masters or employers, urban tributaries and naborías (both barrio residents and house servants to the Spanish) enjoyed the most direct contact with the rural traders, largely because many had some command of Spanish and could serve as *regatones* (intermediaries) in commercial relations between their superiors and the traders, virtually none of whom spoke any language other than their maternal tongue (K'iche', Kaqchikel, Poqomam, and others) or some Nahuatl. While some Spanish servants or poor relatives of Spanish vecinos and first-generation mestizos also performed these roles, and a few black and mulatto slaves were put to menial work or made agents of the Spanish,[4] virtually all of the participants in this mid-sixteenth-century rural-urban network were Indian.[5]

Beginning as early as the late sixteenth century, the socioracial composition of market participants began to change. Free blacks and castas, recent products of manumission and race mixture, started making their commercial presence felt, not just in the public plazas and tiendas where business was conducted in the city, but in the region's outlying trading and agricultural towns and on the Spanish-owned wheat farms and sugar estates. Many were petty traders filling legitimate slots once occupied by Indians, but an increasing number were independent traders who had turned to the black market because Spanish economic and political monopolies blocked them from pursuing legitimate avenues of trade and commerce and because the number of slots for artisans and low-level municipal officials had failed to keep pace with the rapid growth of the free casta population.

Joined by Hispanicized Indians and poor Spaniards, the free blacks and castas usually penetrated the market system by stopping Indian traders as they made their way to the city and either stealing their goods outright or coercing them to sell their cargo at low prices. These strong-arm tactics not only deprived Indian traders of a higher return on their merchandise but contravened audiencia and cabildo legislation meant to regulate the supply and distribution of various goods and to protect revenue-producing government monopolies. This new class of predominantly casta regatones would in turn sell or resell their newly acquired goods at a profit in the capital, thereby raising prices and the ire of Spanish officials.

Beginning as early as the late sixteenth century, Santiago's cabildo issued repeated decrees prohibiting blacks, Indians, Spaniards, and especially free castas from leaving the city to intercept traders bringing food to its central market.[6] No product, moreover, appears to have been exempt from Spanish measures to stop regatón interference in relations between producer-vendors and buyers. Cattle and sheep were to be delivered on the hoof to the city's *matadero* (slaughterhouse) solely by persons contracted to do so. Maize, wheat, and *frijoles* (beans) were to be delivered only to designated buyers in the plaza mayor and sold at fair prices to both *panaderos* (bread bakers) and the populace at large to avoid hoarding and excessive profits in periods of scarcity. Even trade in common, inexpensive goods such as garden vegetables, flowers, wood, charcoal, and sacate was regulated, though the regatones seem to have ignored them in favor of products that brought a good price on the legal market or were in sufficient demand on the black market to be worth the risk of imprisonment by Spanish authorities. These higher-priced goods included maize, wheat, and meat, as well as sugar, tobacco, eggs, poultry, meat byproducts, cotton thread, cloth dyestuffs, and clothing.[7]

The rapid growth of the black market, despite frequent attempts by Spanish officials to put the regatones out of business, serves as testimony to the traders' ability both to provide top-quality goods unavailable through legal channels and to create, albeit unwittingly, a silent but highly supportive clientele. No less important a factor in the black market's growth was Spanish connivance, not to mention outright participation. Economic opportunities outside government-regulated trade and either church or government service were limited for Santiago's Spanish vecinos, and the black market provided a measure of economic safety for those fighting to maintain their tenuous social standing.[8] But it was not just marginal Spaniards, in danger of slipping socially, who engaged in the illicit trade. Many prominent vecinos, including cabildo and audiencia officials, saw in the black market a way to augment their wealth.

While such activity assured a continuous flow of luxury goods for the powerful and served as a hedge against social disgrace for the middle-level Spaniards, it was the lifeblood for many free castas, Indians, and poor Spaniards. Their illicit role in the distribution and sale of wheat, maize, poultry and meat, and liquor is the primary focus below.

WHEAT

In the early decades after the city's founding, the great bulk of Santiago's wheat was supplied by tributary towns within its jurisdiction. While a sizable crop was planted by Indians on their own land, much was also grown nearby, in fields owned or claimed by Spanish encomenderos. In both cases, tributaries were obliged to plant, weed, and harvest the wheat. Plowing the land and threshing the harvested crop were most often left to the encomenderos.[9]

Indian production of wheat fell sharply after the mid-sixteenth century, due in part to a sharp decline in the Indian population and to a reduction in individual encomiendas.[10] No less a factor, however, was the expanding Spanish role in wheat farming throughout the Valley of Guatemala.[11] To ensure themselves control of wheat production and hence the ability to set prices, Spanish *labradores* (farmers) not only waylaid Indian traders bringing wheat to sell in the capital but actually prevented Indians from planting wheat on their own land.[12]

Indians, obviously, were not prevented from providing the

labor necessary to produce the Spanish wheat as cultivation spread throughout the Valley of Guatemala during the late sixteenth and seventeenth centuries. Under the repartimiento labor system, which persisted in Guatemala until the end of the colonial regime, one-quarter of the tributary population of a given Indian town was assigned on a rotating basis to work on nearby labores, often for as many as forty-nine weeks annually. Such practices differed significantly from those in New Spain, where no more than one-tenth the population (and usually far less) of any Indian town was ever pressed into fieldwork, and where agricultural repartimiento was abandoned, at least in the Valley of Mexico, in the early 1630s.[13]

With control of wheat cultivation in the Valley of Guatemala largely in Spanish hands by the late sixteenth century, many labradores found it easy to hoard their harvests despite numerous cabildo prohibitions against the practice.[14] Writing in the 1630s, Friar Thomas Gage noted that some "rich monopolists from the city" used wheat *trojes* (granaries) in the sierra town of San Lucas Sacatepéquez, where the cold, dry climate afforded spoil-free storage for up to three years. According to Gage, they were waiting for "their best opportunity to bring [the stored wheat] out to sale, at the rate of their own will and pleasure,"[15] a charge suggesting that the large hoarders of wheat operated with the knowledge and cooperation of Santiago's cabildo, even that labradores and cabildo members were often one and the same.[16] Fortunately, while hoarding drove up prices by cutting supplies,[17] wheat shortages were rarely so severe as to cause widespread starvation.[18]

As the largest wheat-consuming center between Sonsonate (in present-day El Salvador) and Ciudad Real de Chiapas (in present-day Mexico), Santiago drew on the harvest of a region stretching as far west as Quezaltenango and Totonicapán and as far east as Jalapa and San Luis Jilotepeque.[19] City and audiencia officials were forced to institute measures ensuring that wheat from this vast region flowed into Santiago and would not be exported elsewhere until all of the capital's food needs were met.[20] In February 1705, for example, in an attempt to stop would-be smugglers from seeking a higher price for their wheat in Chiapas and points beyond, the audiencia ordered the alcaldes mayores of Quezaltenango and Totonicapán to inspect all wheat cargoes passing through the town of San Miguel Totonicapán and, if necessary, redirect them to Santiago.[21] Compelled to identify themselves and the intended buyers of their wheat, the transporters turned out to be mostly Indian *cargadores* (bearers) from either the western highlands or the large towns along the capital's western artery (Sololá, Tecpán Guatemala), but also included a Spanish panadero from Santiago and free mulatto and ladino *arrieros* (muleteers) from Mixco, Santiago, and Quezaltenango. Unlike those who made a living intercepting city-bound traders, these free mulatto and ladino regatones, as well as many Indian muleteers, generally received the Crown's approbation for linking the capital to its most distant producers.[22]

Ground into flour upon delivery in the capital, wheat in the sixteenth century was a widely available staple, in part because only the Spanish peninsulares and creoles desired it. Even then, however, the Spanish elite found the manufacture and sale of bread to be a worthwhile, if meager, source of additional income. Despite laws to the contrary, no less than five Spanish alcaldes ordinarios put their servants and slaves to work between 1589 and 1598 baking bread in their houses and selling it in Santiago's public plaza.[23] By the mid-seventeenth century wheat shortages had become common, in small part because, though bread consumption was (and would continue to be) concentrated in Santiago's Spanish core and immediate barrios, the Hispanicized casta population began buying bread in ever greater numbers. At the same time, commercial baking in Santiago fell increasingly to free mulatto and poor Spanish *panaderas* (female bread bakers) who lived in the peripheral barrios of the city and sold their bread there, in a departure from late sixteenth-century patterns, and in the plaza mayor.[24]

In the early 1690s the cabildo began hearing complaints that many castas with little baking experience were joining the ranks of the panaderos to capitalize on the high price of bread. Scarce wheat supplies, of course, meant higher wheat prices as well, leading numerous panaderos to cut their dough with corn flour or to bake loaves underweight by audiencia standards.[25] In addition, panaderos seeking lower-cost wheat would themselves go outside Santiago or send their employees to buy it directly from Indian, ladino, and Spanish wheat producers. These panaderos were no different from the regatones, or so the argument went, and they only encouraged producers to raise their prices further.[26]

To help eliminate these problems, the audiencia renewed its ban against the regatones and ordered each panadero to stamp his or her loaves with a distinctive mark.[27] But such measures had no positive impact, particularly as long as the city's wheat supply remained low, an even more common occurrence in the late seventeenth and eighteenth centuries than it had been previously; on the contrary, regulation often had the unintended effect of making bread a more precious commodity, either because growing numbers of panaderos no longer found it profitable to continue in their profession or because they sold their bread clandestinely to avoid audiencia-imposed controls.

MAIZE

From the conquest forward, maize was most commonly supplied to the Spanish as tribute. Each year Indian towns in Santiago's comarca were obligated either to deliver a fixed number of fanegas of the crop or to plant a specific number of fanegas of seed, which, when harvested, would go to the Crown or to individual encomenderos, depending upon who held the town in encomienda.[28] Like other foodstuffs, the harvest would then pass into general consumption at public auctions administered by Royal Treasury officials.[29]

While bread consumption was somewhat unusual beyond the boundaries of Santiago's most Hispanicized barrios, maize, especially in the form of tortillas, knew no such territorial limits. It was in fact the primary staple for at least two-thirds of Santiago's population, including Indian residents of the peripheral barrios, Indian servants and African slaves attached to Spanish households, less Hispanicized and poorer free castas, and the most destitute Spaniards. Commonly far more plentiful than wheat in colonial Guatemala, maize was also cheaper and less subject to wild fluctuations in price.[30] In seventeenth-century central Mexico, by contrast, the high incidence of drought and the competition among a number of large urban centers for a limited maize harvest combined to prompt steep price hikes and food riots the likes of which Santiago never experienced.[31]

Maize paid as tribute by Indian towns in the Valley of Guatemala frequently fell short of filling Santiago's needs, so the Indians there grew additional supplies for sale in the capital. Most was transported by Indian cargadores from the valleys to the north, northwest, and northeast of the capital and thus passed through Jocotenango,[32] where regatones gathered daily, buying the crop in bulk from the city-bound vendors and later reselling it at a profit in Santiago's plaza mayor.[33] Though at first most of the regatones were either Indian residents of the city's barrios and adjoining towns or black slaves acting as proxies for their Spanish masters, free castas came to dominate the illicit trade in maize.

To bypass Spanish and Indian officials stationed at the *garita* (customs station) in Jocotenango, the urban regatones began intercepting maize cargoes in the countryside, using unguarded secondary routes to enter the city.[34] Spanish officials countered with measures of their own.[35] In January 1697 they ordered the Indian alcaldes of towns at the two busiest entrances to Santiago to lie in ambush every night to arrest any regatón on the way to rendezvous with the rural traders.[36] But such measures provided no more than temporary relief, and *regatonería* (reselling) persisted well into the eighteenth century, with the rural Indian traders its most frequent victims.[37]

POULTRY AND MEAT

Indians throughout Santiago's comarca regularly supplied chickens and eggs to the city, selling them in the streets and public plazas and using them to pay tribute or land rent to Spanish landowners or religious institutions. Indians from Jocotenango and the Barrio de la Candelaria were required to work for the Spanish as *porqueros* (pork dealers and butchers) and *mantequeros* (lard makers and dealers). Purchasing pigs in the comarca, they slaughtered the animals at their houses, then sold the meat and lard directly to the public.[38] All tended to travel singly and were regularly victimized by regatones acting on their own or on orders from a Spanish vecino or official.[39] Membership in a *gremio* (guild) seems to have afforded the porqueros and mantequeros little protection.

Though scarce and costly, mutton, by contrast, was rarely mentioned as a target of regatón interference. The record shows that few tried to sell it illegally and that the illicit rustling and slaughter of sheep in the Valley of Guatemala were no more than minor irritants.[40] The supply network for mutton was apparently simple enough that the Spanish had little trouble preventing free-casta entrepreneurs from gaining a foothold. Responsibility for assuring the city an adequate mutton supply was annually auctioned off to the highest bidder, who as *obligado* (contractual meat supplier) for the next year was required to supply sheep to the city's matadero at a predetermined price.[41]

Beef presented quite a different story. So broad and complex was the network for its sale and distribution, despite nominal Spanish control, that attempts to protect official monopolies governing every aspect of beef production from pasture to butcher shop proved futile. As early as the 1550s the cabildo faced difficulties in finding a single obligado willing and able to contract for Santiago's beef supply. At these times, during periods of drought resulting in poor harvests and a lack of pasturage, the cabildo was forced to apportion the obligation among the city's principal *hacendados* (ranchers) and cattle traders, thereby increasing the chances for graft. By 1650 the soaring popularity and decreasing cost of beef had outstripped the ability of the city's central *carnicería* (butcher shop) to process it. As a result, cattle slaughtered in the matadero were hauled in carts to various barrio carnicerías, increasing the potential for free casta interference and making ordinances regulating the quality and sale of beef difficult to enforce.[42]

Attenuated or not, the city's official supply network for beef encouraged obligados to sell their best cattle to black-market butchers on the outskirts of Santiago or to conduct their own clandestine slaughtering operations.[43] Often only the poorest specimens reached the matadero because delivery there required payment of an *alcabala* (sales tax), alms giving, and a number of ancillary fees, not to mention receiving a lower price for one's herd.[44]

The matadero was itself a reliable source of black-market beef. Besides selling cattle on the hoof, the obligados peddled quarters of beef from the slaughterhouse with the connivance of the official in charge. In addition, Spaniards obligated to supply beef to comarca towns or the city's monasteries would arrange for the matadero to slaughter more cattle than called for under contract, then sell the excess to black-market vendors.[45]

While most of the cattle slaughtered appear to have been the legitimate property of the cattle traders and Spanish hacendados with whom they dealt, the illegal network of butchers and vendors made cattle rustling a small but viable enterprise.[46] Dominant among the rustlers were free castas who brought their stolen cattle to the outskirts of Santiago for slaughter and sold the meat to regular black-market street vendors who in turn hawked it as fresh beef or *carne salada* (salted beef). Also serving as conduits for the street vendors were barrio carnicerías.[47] One Spanish official charged in the mid-1750s that street peddlers won preferred service from the *fieles* (overseers, especially of carnicerías) in return for their regular patronage;[48] another claimed that vendors obtained the best service and meat by bribing the fieles.[49]

Indian women vendors were given the chance to quit the black market in 1681, when the audiencia granted them permission to sell beef in the city's central plaza. The ruling apparently opened the way for an even larger number of *mulatas revendedoras* (female mulatto peddlers, especially of beef) to operate legally, provided they, like the Indian women, purchased their meat solely from Santiago's official obligado and used a balance and weights to ensure that no customer was cheated.

Fearing that competition from the women would reduce

city revenues from the beef monopoly, the cabildo appealed unsuccessfully to the audiencia to reverse its decision, presumably because a recent investigation revealed that the women were in fact shortchanging buyers.[50] Not until some two decades later, however, did the cabildo prevail, finally persuading the audiencia to outlaw all revendedora sales in the capital and to prohibit obligados from selling live cattle or beef quarters to them.[51] The 20 October 1699 decision was handed down some thirty-three months after city officials jailed a group of mulatas revendedoras for buying beef from a former obligado (purchases from other than the officially designated obligado of the moment were declared illegal because they threatened the city's monopoly) and for failing to use scales.

The castas revendedoras (the majority of whom were identified as mulatas) appear to have constituted an informal hereditary gremio in Santiago. In January 1715 twelve of its members sought licenses to sell fresh and *adobado* (pickled) loins of beef in Santiago's public plaza.[52] Tradition, they contended —the fact that they, their mothers, grandmothers, and *their* mothers and grandmothers had practiced this trade[53]—dictated that they receive official sanction, a privilege for which they claimed they were willing to pay, if only to alleviate cabildo fears of diminished revenues from the official monopoly.[54] The petitioners in addition cited the humanity of their regatonería. Noting that the minimum allowable meat purchase in the carnicerías was then six and a half pounds (one-half real), the twelve women argued that they alone put beef within reach of the poor by buying it in bulk from the carnicerías and reselling it in small, affordable quantities.[55]

The mulatas' petition was swiftly denied, their practice of buying and reselling meat ruled illegal.[56] Soon thereafter, though all known revendedoras had been personally notified of the ban, local alguaciles caught four of the vendors again selling beef in the plaza mayor. Abandoning their baskets of meat for refuge in the nearby cathedral, three made good their escape. The fourth was apprehended and given a public whipping as a warning to her compatriots. Undeterred, the revendedoras returned to the plaza within the week.[57]

The regularity of official complaints about illegal beef and cattle sales and declining matadero revenues confirms that Spanish authorities met with little success in breaking up the vast black-market network of casta and Indian revendedoras, butchers, rustlers, cattle traders, Spanish hacendados, and city officials, many of them free mulattoes and mestizos posted to the city's matadero and carnicerías.[58] But the beef-consuming public did as much if not more to perpetuate this network, turning en masse to the black market, despite the relatively high cost of beef,[59] because the official monopoly was plagued by quality and supply problems, unsanitary conditions, unethical weighing practices, bribery, and long waits.[60] In short, producers and consumers alike had too much at stake in the black market for the audiencia, much less the cabildo, to shut it down.

WINE AND SPIRITS

Knowing which alcoholic beverage a person customarily drank was as good a way to identify economic and socioracial status in Spanish Guatemala as knowing whether he or she regularly ate bread or tortillas. Most Spaniards drank wine and other spirits imported from Spain and, by the late sixteenth century, Peru.[61] Most Indians and castas drank cheap local concoctions distilled from maize and sugar.

This simple rule of thumb was far from foolproof, of course. Despite Spanish legislation prohibiting wine sales to Indians, restricting licenses for *pulperías* (small grocery stores legally permitted to sell wine) and taverns, and barring drinking establishments from the barrios, wine was sold regularly to Indians throughout the city and its comarca, either by Spanish tavern keepers directly or through the Indian traders they supplied.[62] Clearly the effort to protect Indians from alcohol's corrupting influence was weakened by those who enjoyed the profits.

Spanish altruism, furthermore, seems to have waxed and waned with the economic cycle and concerns about public order. In years when license revenues were found wanting or the city was relatively calm, more than a dozen individuals (including a few free mulattoes and mestizos in the late seventeenth and early eighteenth centuries) were allowed to open pulperías and taverns in the barrios.[63] When public drunkenness and brawls dominated the Spanish consciousness, however, the cabildo moved to limit tavern and pulpería ownership to Spaniards and to shut down barrio bars and wine stores, relying instead on license fees from the twelve to sixteen taverns in Santiago's Spanish core.[64]

Largely blocked from owning either taverns or pulperías, the free castas (along with some déclassé Spaniards and Indians) made a living by illegally producing and selling *chicha* (a local alcoholic drink made from maize fermented in either sugar water or fruit juice and brown sugar) and other liquors.[65] Although complete documentation about the incidence of bootlegging and illegal liquor consumption in Santiago is unavailable to the historian, as it is for most clandestine activity, the historical record makes repeated mention of efforts to crack down on the chicha trade as a result of its ill effects on public order, wine sales, and, after the mid-1750s, official sales of *aguardiente de caña* (sugarcane brandy).[66] Such evidence at least suggests that production and consumption of clandestine liquor among Santiago's nonelite were widespread.[67] No less suggestive of this conclusion is the high frequency of alcoholism, assault, and murder in the capital, the victims (and perpetrators) of which were almost exclusively Indian, free casta, and poor-Spanish residents of the outlying barrios.[68] Consequently, while the production and sale of clandestine chicha and other liquors provided a livelihood for a sizable number of free castas and other nonelites, it brought death and injury to many, many more.

Unique, then, for its destructive power, free casta bootlegging otherwise fit the pattern of clandestine roles that numerous nonelites were forced to play when they found their path was blocked by Spanish monopolies and insufficient legitimate job opportunities.[69] Spanish authorities, furthermore, met with as much success in curtailing the manufacture and sale of chicha as they did in stopping the black market in such commodities as maize, wheat, and beef, both because trade in each provided a means of support for so many free castas (and, to a lesser extent, Indians and Spaniards) and because officially sanctioned supply and distribution networks were so inadequate. In the final analysis, however, the castas could never have transformed Santiago's market supply system had it not been for the concurrent decline of the city's tributary population. Replacement of Indians by free mulattoes and mestizos may well have been the most important change in the course of Santiago's history.

CHAPTER SEVEN

CONCLUSION

SEVERAL students of Latin American colonial history have sought to bring order to the vast array of changes societies there experienced as a result of miscegenation and socioeconomic change. The Dutch historian-sociologist Harry Hoetink, for one, coined the terms "segmented society" and "homogenous society" to describe two stages of sociodemographic development, and Colin Palmer introduced "multiracial society" to describe a stage between Hoetink's two types. Here I have traced the evolution of Santiago de Guatemala from its sixteenth-century origins as a segmented society into a mid-seventeenth century multiracial society and, by the mid-eighteenth century, the incipient stages of a homogeneous society.[1]

Hoetink defines a segmented society as one that "*at its moment of origin* consists of at least two groups of people of different races and culture, each having its own social institutions and social structure; each of these groups . . . having its own rank in the social structure; and society as a whole being governed by one of the segments."[2] Santiago, ca. 1549, consisted of a central core of Spanish households and church and Crown institutions ringed by barrios populated by newly emancipated Indians. Indian and Spanish alike possessed separate religious institutions, languages, governing bodies. Power emanated from the core.

Only in its early years did Santiago conform to the Hoetink model. As a direct result of miscegenation, which began in the Spanish households before emancipation, Santiago gradually evolved into a plural or a multiracial society.[3] Early postconquest generations, while easily assimilated by the community of either a Spanish or Indian parent, belied the pretense of racial separation. Subsequent miscegenation, accelerated and complicated by the forced introduction of African slaves, produced no such easy social arrangement. Beginning in the second half of the sixteenth century unassimilated mestizos were joined by an ever increasing number of persons of mixed Afro-Indian and Afro-Spanish descent who, unlike the mestizos, were rarely able to pass into the two segments that constituted early colonial Guatemalan society.

The peripheral barrios bore the brunt of the change. There the same biological and social factors that altered the socioracial composition of households in the Spanish core produced a chain of events that led to Indian flight and the influx of castas and Spaniards. The end result was the decay of the once autonomous Indian barrios and the rise of multiracial neighborhoods in their place.

Thus, by 1750, Santiago was becoming what Hoetink calls a homogeneous society, one "characterized by the absence of racial factors that, with others, *determine social structure*, and also by the existence of one basic pattern of culture which is interwoven with a single institutional system."[4] Santiago, remember, was evolving toward this third level; it had yet to get there. At the very least, the gradual disintegration of the barrios and associated Indian institutions (cabildos and related aspects of self-rule, as well as chapels), coupled with ongoing miscegenation, ensured that urban core and periphery became more similar in socioracial composition.

Nevertheless, the continual influx into Santiago of significant numbers of migrant Indians (labeled naborías) and Spaniards (especially peninsulares) constantly reinforced the lowest and highest strata of urban society.[5] It would be a mistake, however, to assume that this reinforcement had the same impact on the Indian and Spanish groups. While immigrant peninsular Spaniards did join the Spanish elite, individual Indian immigrants did not become community members and tributaries of Santiago's weakened Indian barrios. Rather, these Indian migrants stood somewhere between these communities and the gente ordinaria. In effect, the Indian and Spanish-elite segments maintained their distinctiveness while only the burgeoning "middle strata" of mixed descent became increasingly homogenized in both socioracial and cultural terms.[6]

As Santiago, the hub of the region's economic and political system, evolved away from a segmented society, the Indian towns of the Valley of Guatemala retained many of the characteristics of a distinct racial and cultural segment. Indeed, numerous towns preserved their overwhelming indigenous majorities and cultural integrity to a degree that the capital's Indian barrios and adjacent pueblos could not.[7] By contrast, other, larger pueblos northeast and east of Santiago became either trade centers within the Spanish-dominated regional trade system or supply and distribution centers for Spanish wheat farms and sugar estates. Their gradual demographic and socioeconomic transformation was thereby assured.[8]

SOCIAL MOBILITY

For Hoetink, the most important factor distinguishing one segmented society from another is "the degree of intersegmentary social mobility." He defines three types of segmented societies based on this criterion:

(1) the type in which there is no (group) mobility between the segments (for example, the Deep South of the United States);
(2) the type in which rise is only possible half-way towards the social position of the dominant segment on the basis of physical characteristics (for example, the British, French, and Dutch parts of the Caribbean);
(3) the type in which maximum social rise is possible by degrees: a group with racial characteristics of the lowest can, through biological mingling, attain an intermediate social position in society, and a group with racially mixed characteristics can attain the dominant social position on the basis of its culture heritage (for example, Brazil and Spanish-speaking parts of the Caribbean).[9]

Hoetink further defines his three types of segmented societies:

> In the first type no group with an intermediate social position is recognized. In the second and third types such a group is recognized on the basis of its racial characteristics. In societies of types 1 and 2 the socially dominant group is distinguished by its racial characteristics, which are those of the originally dominant segment; in societies of type 3 the socially dominant group contains individuals with the racial characteristics of the originally dominant segments as well as those with mixed racial characteristics.[10]

How does the analysis of Santiago's evolution conform with Hoetink's typology?

By around 1750 the society found in Santiago de Guatemala contained elements of Hoetink's types 2 and 3. The city, however, fit neither type exactly. While the dominant socioracial segment of colonial Guatemala included Spaniards of mixed parentage as well as those of more or less pure European descent, the former found niches in only the lower echelons of society and did not gain positions of high authority or prestige.

The most likely exception to this limitation on passing into the Spanish segment probably occurred during the decades immediately after the Spanish conquest of Guatemala, when Spaniards married Indian women or fathered mestizos they recognized as legitimate offspring. These mestizos or their immediate descendants probably achieved positions of civil and ecclesiastical authority, but their successes have gone unrecorded, in large part because the dominant segment sought to perpetuate a myth of racial purity.

Lacking the benefit of influential conquistador fathers, those who passed into the Spanish segment as a result of generations of race mixture appear to have landed only in the lowest ranks of that segment. Far more numerous than their predecessors, these new Spaniards found it harder to join the ranks of the Spanish elite in seventeenth- and eighteenth-century colonial society than had been the case during the immediate postconquest period. Similarly, Spanish immigration to Guatemala in the late sixteenth century (and continuing after 1800 and beyond) had the effect of replenishing elite ranks, making unnecessary the admittance of those of humble background or questionable racial appearance.[11]

Nevertheless, persons of mixed descent (like the type 3 individuals above) passed into Santiago's dominant social group in all of the colonial centuries. In the mid-sixteenth century mestizo women were accepted as full members of the Spanish segment because they and Spanish women were so few. By the early seventeenth century, as the Spanish creole population grew, Spanish women appear to have outnumbered eligible Spanish males, despite the creation of convents (which inducted young women who might have otherwise married Spaniards) and the immigration of peninsular males into Guatemala.[12] With members of the elite less likely to choose marriage partners outside their group, those of questionable socioracial background were so few as to become unidentifiable within the elite. In the broad or less precisely defined sense of Hoetink's "dominant social group," those of mixed descent opened the doors of the Spanish group in the late seventeenth and eighteenth centuries, but rarely did they get beyond the threshold.

HOMOGENEITY AND HETEROGENEITY IN SANTIAGO DE GUATEMALA

While all socioracial and status groups were represented in the city's core and periphery by the early seventeenth century, non-Spanish groups who lived and worked in the center of the city were very different from those who resided in the outlying neighborhoods. Spaniards in the urban core were most often merchants, owners of rural agricultural estates, encomenderos, master craftsmen, and government officials. Members of the elite, they generally sought black, casta, or Indian live-in servants and slaves.

In the surrounding barrios, in stark contrast, the socioeconomic distance between free castas, Hispanicized Indians, and Spaniards (mostly poor) was often minimal. Households typically consisted of a one- or two-parent family with, perhaps, some relatives. Servants, except for criados and Indian girls and young women from surrounding towns, were a rarity.

This is not to deny that striking inequalities also existed here. Spanish master craftsmen in the barrios almost always had casta apprentices; casta artisans employed few apprentices.[13] Water supplies were adequate in outlying barrios thickly settled with Spaniards; in barrios where Indians and castas lived, water supplies were inadequate or nonexistent.[14] Despite such evidence of status distinctions and discrimination against subordinate groups, the multiracial peripheral barrios of Santiago came to be more homogeneous in their socioeconomic structure than was possible in the city's core.

By the early or mid-eighteenth century castas (including ladinos), free blacks, urban Indians, and poor Spaniards constituted a multiracial urban *plebe común* (commoners) or "laboring poor," living together as neighbors, spouses, in-laws, employees, and employers, attending the same churches, even sending their children to some of the same schools.[15] They drank, celebrated, and mourned together, endured low wages and high food prices together. They lived in humble houses, paid mortgage interest on their solares and houses to the same monasteries and city council, suffered from the same diseases, died together. All barrio dwellers, especially new Spaniards, must have realized that their existence was in many ways inferior to that of the Spanish creole and peninsular elite of Santiago's core. Dependent groups in the Spanish core (excluding bozales), as well as the poor Hispanicized population of mixed descent living in the towns and rural estates of the comarca, must have come to the same realization.

The homogenization of the multiracial laboring poor in the barrios produced no serious threats to Santiago's existing social order at any point in the city's history. Spanish authorities attempted to control the plebe by patrolling the streets, maintaining adequate food supplies, and trying unsuccessfully to control liquor consumption. Do these measures alone tell the whole story? Probably not. Socioracial stratification within the plebe itself, measured by the degree of access to jobs, potable water, housing, and other measures of economic status, generated competition between both individuals and subgroups (castizos and mestizos, for example) and made one's status all-important. The quest for personal advancement in the Spanish-dominated colonial status system subverted any desire to act collectively to bring about reform, let alone overthrow the elite. Had that quest of the nonelites *not* served as an escape valve and a source of social stability, the Spanish would have done well to create it. Instead, they lived in fear of an uprising by either the urban plebe or the rural Maya majorities.[16]

Yet a degree of harmony, or at least a tolerance of the status quo, was maintained between the subordinate groups and the Spanish elite. Personal relations between the elite and nonelite, especially the formation of ritual kinship ties of *compadrazgo* (relationship between godparents and parents of a child) and hierarchical patron-client systems, could well be essential elements in any explanation of the durability and longevity of Spanish Guatemalan society.[17]

HOMOGENEITY: STILLBORN IN GUATEMALA

In spite of this apparent harmony between elite and nonelite, Hoetink's "homogeneous society" was restricted to population pockets in Santiago's outlying, multiracial barrios and in the extensive regions to the east and south of the capital. It never fully evolved in either Santiago's Spanish core or the vast areas of Indian Guatemala that, lacking the natural resources to attract Spaniards and ladinos, were immune to the socioracial homogenization and socioeconomic changes described in this study.

Guatemala has failed even in the nineteenth and twentieth centuries to evolve into a homogeneous society. While the reasons for this are too complicated and numerous to examine here, they nevertheless deserve careful consideration if Guatemala is to survive as a society without the deep ethnic divisions that in recent times have prompted what some might describe as selective genocide against the Indian majority by the agro-industrial elite and their sometime military allies.[18] An important but still unanswered question is whether the majority of poor ladinos will continue to go along with these repressive policies or will look beyond ethnic distinctions and prejudices to see that the key to a more just and tranquil life may be in forging a new democratic majority with the Maya.

If Guatemala had required the continual importation of large numbers of African slaves in the late colonial and early national periods to provide labor for, say, an expanding sugar industry, it is doubtful that the socioracial lines of the middle sector (first castas, later ladinos) would have become so blurred. Under these circumstances, a more differentiated caste system would have developed, and groups of African descent, more numerous and thus more visible, might today be the object of discrimination, as they are elsewhere in the Americas. Because forced African immigration dropped to a trickle in the early seventeenth century and never again increased, miscegenation and Hispanicization transformed Santiago and the rest of Guatemala east and south of the capital into what MacLeod calls the "Ladino East." By contrast, in MacLeod's "Indian West"—the areas north and west of Santiago where few Spaniards, African slaves, free castas, and ladinos lived because economic opportunities were so scarce there—Indian society remains intact despite ongoing revolutionary struggle, massacres, general hardship, and widespread dislocation.[19]

Even at the nadir of Indian depopulation (due primarily to epidemic disease), native peoples have always outnumbered ladinos and Spaniards in the Indian highlands.[20] Indian population recovery, beginning in the seventeenth century and continuing, with minor setbacks, to the present, has allowed the solid Maya majority north and west of Antigua Guatemala (the former Santiago de Guatemala) to protect their cultural heritage and assert their rights. In spite of predictions by non-Indian anthropologists and Guatemalan intellectuals and bureaucrats, modernization and a university education have not led inevitably to the ladinoization of the Maya.

Today a growing number of educated, articulate spokespersons for Guatemala's Maya majority are openly hostile to any talk or program that promotes their assimilation into ladino Guatemala.[21] Ironically, just as the Maya have voiced anti-assimilation sentiments, members of Guatemala's European/white elite have objected to being labeled "ladinos," along with other non-Indians, in national censuses and other statistics. While the elite may themselves not want to be assimilated, they seem to favor the assimilation (or even, in some cases, the elimination) of the Indian. For the white elite, of course, the problem of self-identity is largely a question of status and semantics, while for the Indian majority it is a far more vital question of physical and cultural survival.[22] It is thus that the three-tier socioracial society of mid-eighteenth-century Santiago (Indian, ladino, Spaniard) persists in a modified form in contemporary Guatemala.[23]

CLASSIFICATION AND ASSIMILATION IN COMPARATIVE PERSPECTIVE

Socioracial classification varied throughout Spanish America. Even within the confines of southern Mesoamerica, patterns Chance and Taylor encountered in the city of Antequera (now Oaxaca) differ greatly from those found in Santiago.

One of the most significant of these lay in the creation of intermediate groups to accommodate persons who could no longer be easily identified as belonging to one casta group or another. In Santiago, as a result of miscegenation, intermarriage, upward mobility, and gradual assimilation, "ladino" came to describe those of unclear socioracial descent. Because ladino was a secular term deemed inappropriate for Santiago's marriage registers, increasing numbers of ladinos went unidentified as to racial status (see table 18, particularly the growth in post-1720 marriages). Similarly, those who could pass as Spaniards (because they looked Spanish and were affluent) came to be so labeled, though most were barred from admission into the elite.

"Creole," used to describe American-born Spaniards (as contrasted with peninsular Spaniards) in Antequera, was a term rarely found in Santiago's parish registers. Antequera, moreover, lacked an all-inclusive, sub-Spanish category of the importance or size of Santiago's ladino group, and fewer there than in Santiago went without a racial label in the marriage registers. According to Chance and Taylor, "the most probable explanation for the small size of the casta population is the assimilation of large numbers of mestizos, castizos, and mulattoes into the creole group."[24]

Table 18: Marriages of Others and Unidentified: Santiago de Guatemala, 1650–1769

	O+U-BS	O+U-MS	O+U-FB	O+U-FM/C*	O+U-I/C*	O+U-ME/C*	O+U-SP/C*	Total O+U Marriages/C*
1650–59	1	1	1	4	0	3	2	12
1660–69	0	0	1	3	1	1	1	7
1670–79	1	3	2	8	6	1	2	23
1680–89	2	3	1	16	0	4	15	41
1690–99	0	2	2	17	3	2	14	40
1700–09	0	4	2	31	6	8	12	63
1710–19	0	3	1	23	3	14	12	56
1720–29	0	0	0	17/ 2	5	12/ 3	18/ 2	52/ 7
1730–39	0	0	0	36/ 9	8	19/11	27/ 7	90/27
1740–49	2	1	0	59/14	12/1	41/10	56/14	171/39
1750–59	0	2	0	59/14	10/4	41/14	49/19	161/51
1760–69	2	2	3	57/25	10	28/ 6	28/19	130/50
Total	8	21	13	330	64	174	236	846

* Castizo marriages as a subtotal of O + U marriages to other groups.
Note: See table 11 for abbreviations.

Used to describe the children of Spanish-mestizo unions, "castizo" first appeared in Antequera's parish registers in the 1690s but did not surface in Santiago until the 1720s. Given available documentation, it is difficult to state that socioracial homogenization developed more quickly in Antequera than it did in Santiago, though this may well have been the case. From a careful reading of Chance and Taylor it appears, however, that Antequera's black and mulatto groups were never as numerous as they were in Santiago. Nevertheless, while "pardo" and *"morisco"* (quadroon) were introduced into Antequera's parish registers in the mid-eighteenth century, they rarely appeared in Santiago's marriage registers.

In Antequera, Chance and Taylor believe, the Spanish elite used "castizo," "morisco," and "pardo" to protect their "powerbase and social status from the threat of dilution."[25] One must doubt the practicality, however, of creating subcategories to divert and contain those who would otherwise have been deemed Spaniards. In Antequera and Santiago alike, the related processes of intermarriage, miscegenation (in and out of marriage), and assimilation were endemic if not unstoppable, even if anyone had ever tried.

Were sociodemographic patterns in Antequera and Santiago typical of those elsewhere in Mesoamerica and Central America? Patricia Seed finds "relatively little incidence of interracial marriage" in Mexico during the first two colonial centuries.[26] Mostly illegitimate, castas were few in number until about 1650, when they "began to grow and increasingly participate in legitimate marriage," according to Seed.[27] Neither of Seed's assertions necessarily contradicts evidence of significant casta populations in both Antequera and Santiago, since her frame of reference is Mexico as a whole. In both Oaxaca and Guatemala, Spaniards and persons of mixed ancestry were dwarfed in numbers by the majority Indian population.

Indian population dominance, concentrated in the highlands of Mesoamerica, faded gradually in the ladino areas east and south of Santiago and in the rest of lower Spanish Central America, due to the more lasting impact of Indian depopulation and mestizaje. Looking at seven censuses from 1777 to 1812 for a number of towns in Costa Rica, the only country in southeastern Central America for which even scattered figures on mestizaje and intermarriage exist, Lowell Gudmundson finds that a majority of Afro–Costa Rican women in all but one town had their children out of wedlock. Many Afro–Costa Rican men, for economic reasons, also remained single. The Afro–Costa Rican population assimilated so quickly into the general population in part because most of its women resided in towns, where mestizaje was most likely, and because most of its men worked in the relative isolation of the rural sector.[28] Unlike Indians in Oaxaca and highland Guatemala, who remained an overwhelming majority, the indigenous population of Costa Rica's Central Valley had all but disappeared by the late seventeenth century.[29]

By the eighteenth century castas formed a majority of Costa Rica's urban and rural work force and total population, while the indigenous population filled the rural niche in Oaxaca and most of highland Guatemala. A fairly even distribution of castas, the absence of a sizable Indian population, a slowdown in African slave imports, and a decline in the immigration of peninsular Spaniards all speeded the assimilation of castas in Costa Rica. A similar pattern prevailed in most of Spanish Central America, except at higher altitudes, including parts of Guatemala's Ladino East, where a number of concentrations of Indians survived, and Santiago itself, situated on the frontier between Ladino East and Indian West.

Population data for selected cities in New Spain and Spanish Central America (see table 19), from the 1750s in the case of Santiago to the 1790s and ca. 1800 for the others, demonstrate contrasting patterns of urban ethnic composition. One important feature that differentiates Puebla and Antequera from Santiago—and Santiago, in turn, from the smaller urban centers of El Salvador, Nicaragua, and Costa Rica—is the relative importance of castas (ladinos), Indians, and Spaniards as a percentage of total urban population. In absolute numbers, the largest urban casta populations are in Puebla and Santiago, but the number of castas as a percentage of total urban population

City	Year	Spaniards	Mestizos	Mixed Castas	Mulattoes	Indians	Unidentified	Total
Puebla	1791	18,369 (25.7)	13,358 (18.7)	12,670 (17.8)	2,930 (4.1)	24,039 (33.7)		71,366
Antequera	1792	6,955 (38.6)	3,316 (18.4)		2,514 (14.0)	5,018 (27.9)	205 (1.1)	18,008
				5,830 (32.4)				
				28,958 (40.6)				
Quezaltenango	1800	464 (4.2)		5,536 (50.3)		5,000 (45.5)		11,000
Santiago de Guatemala	1750s	6,500 (17.0)		25,000 (65.4)		6,700 (17.5)		38,200
San Salvador	1800	614 (5.1)		10,860 (90.0)		585 (4.9)		12,059
San Miguel	1800	239 (4.3)		5,300 (95.7)				5,539
San Vicente	1800	218 (5.3)		3,869 (94.7)				4,087
Sonsonate	1800	441 (12.9)		2,795 (81.7)		185 (5.4)		3,421
Granada	1800	863 (10.5)		5,675 (68.9)		1,695 (20.6)		8,233
León	1800	1,061 (14.0)		6,366 (84.1)		144 (1.9)		7,571
Cartago	1800	632 (7.6)		7,705 (92.4)				8,337
San José	1800	1,976 (23.7)		6,350 (76.3)				8,326

Source: Chance, *Race and Class*, 156, table 15; Thomson, *Puebla de los Angeles*, 62–63; and van Oss, "Central America's Autarkic Colonial Cities," 43, table 2.
Note: Figures in parentheses are percentages.

generally increases from northwest to southeast. Given sizable Indian populations in Mesoamerica, Indian numbers as a percentage of total urban population generally decline as one travels from Puebla to Cartago and San José (Costa Rica).

Spaniards, too, were more significant in absolute numbers and as a percentage of total urban population in highland Mexican and Guatemalan cities than in the cities to the southeast. Unfortunately, data for Santiago predate by almost fifty years the data for the other cities included in table 19. In that fifty-year period patterns of miscegenation and assimilation already underway by 1750 would have accelerated in Santiago (and, after 1775, in the new capital), as they did elsewhere.

Both geographically and ethnically Santiago de Guatemala straddled the frontier between two Mesoamerican cities (Puebla and Antequera) with large Spanish and Indian populations and eight Central American cities (listed below Santiago in table 19) where the Spanish and Indian populations were smaller.[30] Of these cities, only Santiago and San Salvador had Spanish and Indian populations of similar size. What distinguishes Santiago from its neighbor, however, is that San Salvador's Spanish and Indian populations each represented only 5 percent of that city's total inhabitants, while each of these groups made up fully 17 percent of Santiago's population.

Casta population size (relative to numbers of Indians and Spaniards) distinguishes Santiago from all other cities in table 19. While approximately 32–41 percent of the population of the two Mesoamerican cities was casta, and castas represented over 80 percent of total population in six of the eight Central American cities, they constituted 65.4 percent of Santiago's population. In short, Santiago was less ethnically balanced than Puebla or Antequera, but more diverse than the overwhelmingly casta or ladino Central American cities. Santiago's population was almost two-thirds casta, but its hinterland consisted of some sixty, mainly Maya towns. Its urban-rural composition was thus more similar to, say, Antequera, with its large surrounding Indian population, than to the Central American cities and comarcas, where such differences were less striking. Highland Guatemala's large and resilient Indian population was a key variable in the evolution of that society's urban history before and after 1773.[31]

This date is pivotal in the urban history of Guatemala, because in July and December of that year destructive earthquakes struck Santiago, leading audiencia officials to abandon the capital and demand that much of its population move east to the Valley of La Ermita, the present-day site of Guatemala City.[32] The move was symbolic for the ethnic history of Guatemala in that it relocated the source of Spanish power from the Indian West to the Ladino East. Not only were the direction and focus of Spanish-ladino economic and political interests forever changed, but the transformation and even destruction of Indian Guatemala were delayed and probably averted.

APPENDIXES

INTRODUCTION

SEPARATE parish records were kept in Santiago de Guatemala for Spaniards, Indians, and a group that included blacks, mulattoes, mestizos, and naborías (the latter four representing the gente ordinaria). While this system of recordkeeping is perhaps the best illustration of Spanish success at maintaining racial separation, it, too, ultimately failed, in direct proportion to the degree of race mixture each of Santiago's four parishes experienced over time.

The most Spanish of the city's parishes, the Sagrario, kept the most segregated registers. Separate baptismal, marriage, and burial registers were maintained there for both Spaniards and gente ordinaria. San Sebastián, second only to the Sagrario in the size of its Spanish population, maintained separate baptismal and marriage registers for Spaniards and gente ordinaria, but recorded all parishioner burials in a single register.

The dualistic (tripartite, if one takes Indian registers into account) system of parish recordkeeping broke down in Los Remedios and the Candelaria, where each parish kept registers of baptisms, marriages, and burials without regard to race. In the Candelaria, moreover, all non-Indian parishioners were lumped together as ladinos. Clearly, segregated registers were deemed unnecessary in parishes with sparse Spanish populations. Church officials may also have considered the socioeconomic standing and racial purity of a parish's Spaniards when deciding how to organize registers in a new parish.

Inhabitants of Santiago's Indian barrios often had their own hermitages or attended special Indian chapels attached to monasteries that ministered to their communities. Their records, most of which are now lost, were kept separately, probably either in barrio hermitages or within the various monasteries. The sole surviving records are a few short runs of marriages included in the parish registers of San Sebastián and Los Remedios (thanks, apparently, to a clerical error or the lack of a suitable separate register). Accordingly, these have been omitted from this study.

SAGRARIO

The oldest baptismal register for Santiago de Guatemala is for Spaniards of the Sagrario. Its entries begin in January 1577 and end in 1608. Pre-1577 registers for the Sagrario may have been stored in the Archivo Histórico Arquidiocesano (AHA) in the early 1970s, but for reasons unknown I was neither told of them nor shown them. The next known Spanish baptismal register for this parish begins in 1612. From that date baptismal records continue without interruption through the entire period of this study. No separate baptismal records for gente ordinaria in the Sagrario Parish are available for the pre-1639 period, but they run continuously thereafter.

Spanish marriage registers for the Sagrario run from 1577 to 1773 with the exception of 1640–48 (two 1645 marriages *are* recorded). Marriage registers for the Sagrario's gente ordinaria begin in 1593 and run without interruption through 1624. Though marriage data for gente ordinaria are lost for 1625–48, there is a complete run from 1649 through the end of the colonial period.

Spanish burial registers run without interruption from 1631; gente ordinaria burial registers begin in 1632 and likewise run without interruption through the period of this study.

SAN SEBASTIÁN

The oldest extant parish register in the Parish of San Sebastián contains baptisms of gente ordinaria beginning in 1594. Gente ordinaria baptisms run without interruption from that date through the entire life of Santiago de Guatemala. Spanish baptismal records for the Parish of San Sebastián are lost for the pre-1639 period. They run from 1639 to 1700, are missing for 1701–40, and then run continuously from 1741 through the end of this study. As with baptismal records, marriage registers for gente ordinaria begin in 1626 and run without interruption from that date forward. Those for Spaniards begin in 1637 and run uninterrupted through the period of this study.

Pre-1643 burial registers are missing; a complete run exists for the remainder of the city's lifespan.

LOS REMEDIOS

Here registers were kept in common for all parishioners. Baptismal registers begin in May 1641 and run without interruption through June 1714. A fifth baptismal register, covering the period from July 1714 through December 1751, has been lost. Except for possible under-recording of baptisms for some months in the late 1760s, the remaining baptismal registers are complete from 1752 through the end of 1776. While the number of Spanish baptisms is difficult to assess because they were combined with gente ordinaria baptisms in parish registers, it appears that the Spanish population of Los Remedios was negligible from 1641 to 1660 and from 1752 to 1776. Spanish baptisms do not even begin to appear until after 1660 and are few after 1752. Spanish and gente ordinaria marriages were recorded together in Los Remedios in a series of registers that are extant from 1674 and run without interruption until 25 April 1777. As in the case of marriages, all burials in Los Remedios are kept in one series of registers. The first extant burial entry dates from November 1676. The registers run without interruption from that date until June 1764. After 1764 folios are missing for a part of each year or for the entire year in the cases of 1767–68 and 1771–72.

NUESTRA SEÑORA DE LA CANDELARIA

Created in 1750, just twenty-three years before Santiago's destruction, the Candelaria kept three categories of registers (baptisms, marriages, and burials) in common. None appears to be missing.

APPENDIX 1

MARRIAGE TABLES: SANTIAGO DE GUATEMALA, 1577–1769

BEGINNING with total marriages by decade, both in the parishes and in the city as a whole, this appendix also provides composite marriage figures for each socioracial group—black slaves, mulatto slaves, free blacks, free mulattoes, Indian naborías, mestizos, and Spaniards, in that order. Marriage figures for each sociracial group are then broken down by parish. One caveat: marriage totals are based on available data.

Abbreviations: BS = black slave; MS = mulatto slave; FB = free black; FM = free mulatto; I = Indian naboría; ME = mestizo; SP = Spaniard; O + U = others and unidentified (those who fit in none of the above categories); and C = castizo.

Total Marriages by Decade: Santiago, 1577–1769

	Sagrario	San Sebastián	Los Remedios	Candelaria	Composite
1577–79	(23)				(23)
1580–89	(174)				(174)
1590–99	(342)				(342)
1600–09	398				(398)
1610–19	454				(454)
1620–29	(326)	(39)			(365)
1630–39	(195)	(170)			(365)
1640–49	(48)	367			(415)
1650–59	416	339			(755)
1660–69	430	370			(800)
1670–79	516	449	(62)		(1,027)
1680–89	600	562	126		1,288
1690–99	554	549	134		1,237
1700–09	451	489	93		1,033
1710–19	571	562	125		1,258
1720–29	536	615	126		1,277
1730–39	651	728	139		1,518
1740–49	545	717	163		1,425
1750–59	466	841	172	50	1,529
1760–69	288	748	141	149	1,326
Total	7,984	7,545	1,281	199	17,009

Note: Parentheses indicate data are missing or incomplete. In most cases the decennial parish and composite marriage totals are slightly larger than the combined group subtotals (see app. 4 below), since a number of marriages are included in which the race of neither partner could be determined.

Black Slave Marriages: Santiago, 1593–1769

	BS–BS	BS–MS	BS–FB	BS–FM	BS–I	BS–ME	BS–SP	BS–O+U	TOTAL
1593–99	18	0	1	2	25	0	1	0	47
1600–09	38	1	0	15	43	0	0	0	97
1610–19	54	6	4	10	24	1	1	0	100
1620–29	22	4	0	3	8	1	0	0	38
1630–39	5	0	1	0	6	1	0	0	13
1640–49	28	3	1	10	7	0	0	0	49
1650–59	45	5	9	19	13	6	1	1	99
1660–69	9	9	5	17	8	7	0	0	55
1670–79	18	9	15	15	16	7	0	1	81
1680–89	9	14	3	15	14	4	0	2	61
1690–99	0	6	3	15	8	7	1	0	40
1700–09	3	4	1	5	4	1	0	0	18
1710–19	2	5	3	11	2	1	0	0	24
1720–29	0	4	2	4	1	2	0	0	13
1730–39	15	2	1	6	0	2	0	0	26
1740–49	9	2	0	6	0	0	2	2	21
1750–59	6	0	1	7	0	0	0	0	14
1760–69	1	0	0	0	0	2	0	2	5

Mulatto Slave Marriages: Santiago, 1593–1769

	MS–MS	MS–BS	MS–FB	MS–FM	MS–I	MS–ME	MS–SP	MS–O + U	TOTAL
1593–99	0	0	0	1	3	0	0	0	4
1600–09	1	1	0	4	8	3	1	0	18
1610–19	3	6	0	3	5	2	0	0	19
1620–29	0	4	0	9	3	6	0	0	22
1630–39	0	0	0	0	4	1	0	0	5
1640–49	0	3	1	5	2	2	0	0	13
1650–59	2	5	2	17	4	9	1	1	41
1660–69	3	9	0	28	5	4	2	0	51
1670–79	7	9	1	31	6	6	1	3	64
1680–89	13	14	3	69	17	17	1	3	137
1690–99	9	6	3	38	16	13	2	2	89
1700–09	7	4	2	22	7	5	1	4	52
1710–19	7	5	2	27	8	11	0	3	63
1720–29	4	4	1	12	3	7	0	0	31
1730–39	3	2	0	20	2	10	1	0	38
1740–49	4	2	1	17	2	2	0	1	29
1750–59	1	0	0	12	0	1	0	2	16
1760–69	1	0	0	4	0	2	0	2	9

Free Black Marriages: Santiago, 1593–1769

	FB–FB	FB–BS	FB–MS	FB–FM	FB–I	FB–ME	FB–SP	FB–O + U	TOTAL
1593–99	0	1	0	3	2	0	0	0	6
1600–09	0	0	0	1	0	0	0	0	1
1610–19	0	4	0	2	2	0	1	0	9
1620–29	0	0	0	1	0	1	0	1	3
1630–39	0	1	0	1	1	0	0	0	3
1640–49	0	1	1	0	0	0	0	0	2
1650–59	2	9	2	7	0	1	0	1	22
1660–69	5	5	0	3	0	1	2	1	17
1670–79	3	15	1	9	1	4	0	2	35
1680–89	1	3	3	13	2	4	2	1	29
1690–99	1	3	3	6	5	1	2	2	23
1700–09	0	1	2	4	2	1	0	2	12
1710–19	1	3	2	8	2	2	2	1	21
1720–29	0	2	1	14	1	3	0	0	21
1730–39	1	1	0	11	0	2	0	0	15
1740–49	3	0	1	7	1	3	1	0	16
1750–59	3	1	0	2	0	3	0	0	9
1760–69	0	0	0	7	3	1	0	3	14

Free Mulatto Marriages: Santiago, 1593–1769

	FM-FM	FM-BS	FM-MS	FM-FB	FM-I	FM-ME	FM-SP	FM-O + U/C[a]	TOTAL
1593–99	1	2	1	3	6	2	0	0	15
1600–09	10	15	4	1	7	4	0	1	42
1610–19	15	10	3	2	12	13	4	0	59
1620–29	14	3	9	1	11	7	1	0	46
1630–39	16	0	0	1	1	14	1	4	37
1640–49	33	10	5	0	8	9	1	1	67
1650–59	57	19	17	7	15	24	14	4	157
1660–69	62	17	28	3	11	17	8	3	149
1670–79	124	15	31	9	23	48	8	8	266
1680–89	189	15	69	13	36	92	19	16	449
1690–99	175	15	38	6	37	86	17	17	391
1700–09	169	5	22	4	28	52	16	31	327
1710–19	210	11	27	8	32	102	48	23	461
1720–29	236	4	12	14	65	136	33	17/ 2	517
1730–39	303	6	20	11	69	169	61	36/ 9	675
1740–49	275	6	17	7	41	194	62	59/14	661
1750–59	317	7	12	2	44	214	92	59/14	747
1760–69	275	0	4	7	45	191	74	57/25	653

[a] FM–C unions included in FM–O + U totals.

Indian Marriages: Santiago, 1593–1769

	I-I	I-BS	I-MS	I-FB	I-FM	I-ME	I-SP	I-O + U/C[a]	TOTAL
1593–99	44	25	3	2	6	4	0	0	84
1600–09	51	43	8	0	7	12	1	0	122
1610–19	60	24	5	2	12	13	1	0	117
1620–29	25	8	3	0	11	6	1	0	54
1630–39	17	6	4	1	1	10	0	1	40
1640–49	19	7	2	0	8	14	0	3	53
1650–59	37	13	4	0	15	16	2	0	87
1660–69	32	8	5	0	11	12	0	1	69
1670–79	54	16	6	1	23	29	2	6	137
1680–89	87	14	17	2	36	43	2	0	201
1690–99	116	8	16	5	37	56	1	3	242
1700–09	106	4	7	2	28	35	2	6	190
1710–19	107	2	8	2	32	49	10	3	213
1720–29	118	1	3	1	65	71	9	5	273
1730–39	82	0	2	0	69	73	8	8	242
1740–49	65	0	2	1	41	61	6	12/1	188
1750–59	49	0	0	0	44	72	10	10/4	185
1760–69	75	0	0	3	45	79	12	10	224

[a] I-C unions included in I-O + U totals.

Mestizo Marriages: Santiago, 1593–1769

	ME–ME	ME–BS	ME–MS	ME–FB	ME–FM	ME–I	ME–SP	ME–O + U/C[a]	TOTAL
1593–99	13	0	0	0	2	4	3	0	22
1600–09	4	0	3	0	4	12	1	0	24
1610–19	9	1	2	0	13	13	2	1	41
1620–29	8	1	6	1	7	6	0	1	30
1630–39	21	1	1	0	14	10	5	14	66
1640–49	12	0	2	0	9	14	1	0	38
1650–59	24	6	9	1	24	16	10	3	93
1660–69	35	7	4	1	17	12	4	1	81
1670–79	49	7	6	4	48	29	10	1	154
1680–89	83	4	17	4	92	43	19	4	266
1690–99	83	7	13	1	86	56	16	2	264
1700–09	95	1	5	1	52	35	18	8	215
1710–19	118	1	11	2	102	49	56	14	353
1720–29	112	2	7	3	136	71	62	12/ 3	405
1730–39	128	2	10	2	169	73	59	19/11	462
1740–49	120	0	2	3	194	61	53	41/10	474
1750–59	113	0	1	3	214	72	83	41/14	527
1760–69	120	2	2	1	191	79	55	28/ 6	478

[a] ME–C unions included in ME–O + U totals.

Spanish Marriages: Santiago, 1577–1769

	SP–SP	SP–BS	SP–MS	SP–FB	SP–FM	SP–I	SP–ME	SP–O + U/C[a]	TOTAL
1577–79	23	0	0	0	0	0	0	0	23
1580–89	170	0	0	0	1	3	0	0	174
1590–99	202	1	0	0	0	0	3	0	206
1600–09	190	0	1	0	0	1	1	0	193
1610–19	187	1	0	1	4	1	2	0	196
1620–29	223	0	0	0	1	1	0	1	226
1630–39	239	0	0	0	1	0	5	0	245
1640–49	239	0	0	0	1	0	1	1	242
1650–59	360	1	1	0	14	2	10	2	390
1660–69	405	0	2	2	8	0	4	1	422
1670–79	409	0	1	0	8	2	10	2	432
1680–89	434	0	1	2	19	2	19	15	492
1690–99	400	1	2	2	17	1	16	14	453
1700–09	291	0	1	0	16	2	18	12	340
1710–19	286	0	0	2	48	10	56	12	414
1720–29	253	0	0	0	33	9	62	18/ 2	375
1730–39	311	0	1	0	61	8	59	27/ 7	467
1740–49	223	2	0	1	62	6	53	56/14	403
1750–59	239	0	0	0	92	10	83	49/19	473
1760–69	166	0	0	0	74	12	55	28/19	335

[a] SP–C unions included in SP–O + U totals.

Black Slave Marriages: Sagrario, 1593–1769

	BS–BS	BS–MS	BS–FB	BS–FM	BS–I	BS–ME	BS–SP	BS–O+U	TOTAL
1593–99	18	0	1	2	25	0	1	0	47
1600–09	38	1	0	15	43	0	0	0	97
1610–19	54	6	4	10	24	1	1	0	100
1620–29	19	4	0	3	7	1	0	0	34
1630–39	—	—	—	—	—	—	—	—	—
1640–49	3	1	0	3	2	0	0	0	9
1650–59	35	5	7	16	12	5	1	1	82
1660–69	8	9	5	16	8	7	0	0	53
1670–79	18	8	13	9	12	7	0	1	68
1680–89	7	11	2	15	12	2	0	2	51
1690–99	0	6	3	10	6	7	1	0	33
1700–09	3	4	1	5	4	1	0	0	18
1710–19	2	5	3	8	2	1	0	0	21
1720–29	0	4	2	4	1	0	0	0	11
1730–39	12	0	1	5	0	2	0	0	20
1740–49	6	2	0	6	0	0	1	1	16
1750–59	6	0	1	4	0	0	0	0	11
1760–69	1	0	0	0	0	2	0	1	4

Mulatto Slave Marriages: Sagrario, 1593–1769

	MS–MS	MS–BS	MS–FB	MS–FM	MS–I	MS–ME	MS–SP	MS–O+U	TOTAL
1593–99	0	0	0	1	3	0	0	0	4
1600–09	1	1	0	4	8	3	1	0	18
1610–19	3	6	0	3	5	2	0	0	19
1620–29	0	4	0	7	2	6	0	0	19
1630–39	—	—	—	—	—	—	—	—	—
1640–49	0	1	0	1	0	0	0	0	2
1650–59	2	5	1	13	4	9	1	1	36
1660–69	3	9	0	21	5	3	2	0	43
1670–79	7	8	1	18	5	5	1	3	48
1680–89	9	11	2	42	12	12	1	3	92
1690–99	8	6	2	25	13	9	1	1	65
1700–09	5	4	1	18	5	5	1	1[a]	40
1710–19	4	5	2	18	7	7	0	1	44
1720–29	4	4	1	7	3	6	0	0	25
1730–39	3	0	0	13	2	9	0	0	27
1740–49	4	2	1	13	2	1	0	1	24
1750–59	1	0	0	8	0	1	0	1	11
1760–69	1	0	0	3	0	1	0	1	6

[a] Juan Anderson, a native of Scotland, married a mulatto slave named Marzela de Ygero in 1706. Made legitimate by the marriage, years after her birth, their daughter married a Spaniard in 1710.

Free Black Marriages: Sagrario, 1593–1769

	FB-FB	FB-BS	FB-MS	FB-FM	FB-I	FB-ME	FB-SP	FB-O+U	TOTAL
1593–99	0	1	0	3	2	0	0	0	6
1600–09	0	0	0	1	0	0	0	0	1
1610–19	0	4	0	2	2	0	1	0	9
1620–29	0	0	0	0	0	1	0	1[a]	2
1630–39	—	—	—	—	—	—	—	—	—
1640–49	0	0	0	0	0	0	0	0	0
1650–59	1	7	1	4	0	0	0	1	14
1660–69	0	5	0	3	0	1[b]	2	1	12
1670–79	0	13	1	3	1	3	0	1[c]	22
1680–89	1	2	2	8	1	2	1	0	17
1690–99	1	3	2	5	4	1	2	2	20
1700–09	1	1	1	1	1	1	0	0	6
1710–19	1	3	2	5	2	2	1	1	17
1720–29	0	2	1	9	1	3	0	0	16
1730–39	1	1	0	6	0	1	0	0	9
1740–49	3	0	1	2	1	1	0	0	8
1750–59	2	1	0	2	0	2	0	0	7
1760–69	0	0	0	1	1	0	0	2	4

[a] A Frenchman married a free black woman in 1621.
[b] Found in the Spanish marriage register for the Sagrario, September 1667.
[c] A woman married a *chino* (a man of possible Filipino-Chinese descent) who was a native of Mexico City, in 1677.

Free Mulatto Marriages: Sagrario, 1593–1769

	FM–FM	FM–BS	FM–MS	FM–FB	FM–I	FM–ME	FM–SP	FB–O + U/C[a]	TOTAL
1593–99	1	2	1	3	6	2	0	0	15
1600–09	10	15	4	1	7	4	0	1[b]	42
1610–19	15	10	3	2	12	13	4	0	59
1620–29	8	3	7	0	8	6	1	0	33
1630–39	—	—	—	—	—	—	—	—	—
1640–49	2	3	1	0	1	1	0	0	8
1650–59	31	16	13	4	10	17	7	1[c]	99
1660–69	39	16	21	3	8	11	4	2	104
1670–79	66	9	18	3	11	26	3	4	140
1680–89	95	15	42	8	19	33	5	6	223
1690–99	88	10	25	5	18	30	3	6	185
1700–09	78	5	18	1	11	25	7	10	155
1710–19	108	8	18	5	13	44	23	15	234
1720–29	106	4	7	9	28	64	19	4	241
1730–39	150	5	13	6	29	74	20	19/5	316
1740–49	112	6	13	2	16	67	16	27/6	259
1750–59	127	4	8	2	6	71	24	11[d]/2	253
1760–69	56	0	3	1	8	30	6	15/2	119

[a] FM–C unions included in FM–O + U totals.
[b] A Portuguese man married a free mulatto woman on 24 June 1600, two days before his death. Found in the Spanish register.
[c] Bartolomé Gutiérrez, a free mulatto, married María de Ayala, the natural daughter of Don Andrés de Ayala, in 1651.
[d] Includes Antonio Día, a Naples native who in 1754 married the free mulatto María Santos Mijangos in the Chipilapa, where they both resided.

Indian Marriages: Sagrario, 1593–1769

	I-I	I-BS	I-MS	I-FB	I-FM	I-ME	I-SP	I-O + U	TOTAL
1593–99	44	25	3	2	6	4	0	0	84
1600–09	51	43	8	0	7	12	1	0	122
1610–19	60	24	5	2	12	13	1	0	117
1620–29	16	7	2	0	8	4	1	0	38
1630–39	—	—	—	—	—	—	—	—	—
1640–49	2	2	0	0	1	1	0	0	6
1650–59	14	12	4	0	10	13	1	0	54
1660–69	17	8	5	0	8	9	0	1	48
1670–79	33	12	5	1	11	14	0	4	80
1680–89	38	12	12	1	19	17	0	1[a]	100
1690–99	48	6	13	4	18	16	0	1	106
1700–09	42	4	5	1	11	13	1	0	77
1710–19	43	2	7	2	13	19	2	1	89
1720–29	41	1	3	1	28	22	2	5	103
1730–39	36	0	2	0	29	27	0	5	99
1740–49	18	0	2	1	16	10	2	5	54
1750–59	14	0	0	0	6	8	2	2	32
1760–69	12	0	0	1	8	5	2	5	33

[a] Juan Lorenzo (John Lawrence?), an English native of Jamaica, married an Indian widow in 1686.

Mestizo Marriages: Sagrario, 1593–1769

	ME–ME	ME–BS	ME–MS	ME–FB	ME–FM	ME–I	ME–SP	ME–O + U/C[a]	TOTAL
1593–99	13	0	0	0	2	4	3	0	22
1600–09	4	0	3	0	4	12	1	0	24
1610–19	9	1	2	0	13	13	2	1	41
1620–29	5	1	6	1	6	4	0	0	23
1630–39	0	0	0	0	0	0	2	0	2
1640–49	2	0	0	0	1	1	0	0	4
1650–59	18	5	9	0	17	13	8	2	72
1660–69	26	7	3	1[b]	11	9	2	1	60
1670–79	27	7	5	3	26	14	4	0	86
1680–89	41	2	12	2	33	17	5	2	114
1690–99	46	7	9	1	30	16	2	0	111
1700–09	45	1	5	1	25	13	11	2	103
1710–19	53	1	7	2	44	19	18	10	154
1720–29	37	0	6	3	64	22	17	2/1	151
1730–39	39	2	9	1	74	27	17	8/6	177
1740–49	37	0	1	1	67	10	7	8/1	131
1750–59	18	0	1	2	71	8	12	5/2	117
1760–69	8	2	1	0	30	5	4	9/1	59

[a] ME–C unions included in ME–O + U totals.
[b] Found in the Spanish register, September 1667.

Spanish Marriages: Sagrario, 1577–1769

	SP–SP	SP–BS	SP–MS	SP–FB	SP–FM	SP–I	SP–ME	SP–O + U/C[a]	TOTAL
1577–79	23	0	0	0	0	0	0	0	23
1580–89	170	0	0	0	1	3	0	0	174
1590–99	202	1	0	0	0	0	3	0	206
1600–09	190	0	1	0	0	1	1	0	193
1610–19	187[b]	1	0	1	4	1	2	0	196
1620–29	223	0	0	0	1	1	0	1	226
1630–39	193	0	0	0	0	0	2	0	195
1640–49	29	0	0	0	0	0	0	0	29
1650–59	172	1	1	0	7	1	8	1	191
1660–69	191	0	2	2	4	0	2	0	201
1670–79	191	0	1	0	3	0	4	0	199
1680–89	176	0	1	1	5	0	5	0	188
1690–99	158	1	1	2	3	0	2	2	169
1700–09	137	0	1	0	7	1	11	1	158
1710–19	126	0	0	1	23	2	18	3	173
1720–29	123	0	0	0	19	2	17	5	166
1730–39	147	0	0	0	20	0	17	9/2	193
1740–49	117	1	0	0	16	2	7	11/4	154
1750–59	111	0	0	0	24	2	12	12/8	161
1760–69	60	0	0	0	6	2	4	5/3	77

[a] SP–C unions included in SP–O + U totals.
[b] Includes one 1610 marriage between an Italian man and a Spanish woman.

Black Slave Marriages: San Sebastián, 1626–1769

	BS–BS	BS–MS	BS–FB	BS–FM	BS–I	BS–ME	BS–SP	BS–O+U	TOTAL
1626–29	3	0	0	0	1	0	0	0	4
1630–39	5	0	1[a]	0	6	1	0	0	13
1640–49	25	2	1	7	5	0	0	0	40
1650–59	10	0	2	3	1	1	0	0	17
1660–69	1	0	0	1	0	0	0	0	2
1670–79	0	1	2	5	4	0	0	0	12
1680–89	2	3	1	0	2	2	0	0	10
1690–99	0	0	0	2	2	0	0	0	4
1700–09	0	0	0	0	0	0	0	0	0
1710–19	0	0	0	3	0	0	0	0	3
1720–29	0	0	0	0	0	1	0	0	1
1730–39	3	2	0	1	0	0	0	0	6
1740–49	3	0	0	0	0	0	1[b]	1	5
1750–59	0	0	0	2	0	0	0	0	2
1760–69	0	0	0	0	0	0	0	0	0

[a] In 1631, a male black slave belonging to Isabela de Céspedes married Catalina Marcías, a free black and criada of Doña Francisca de Cáceres of San Sebastián.
[b] Francisco Antonio de Uribe, a black slave from Guinea who belonged to Candelaria vecina Juana Manuela Romero, married the Spanish widow Juana de Estrada in 1744.

Mulatto Slave Marriages: San Sebastián, 1626–1769

	MS–MS	MS–BS	MS–FB	MS–FM	MS–I	MS–ME	MS–SP	MS–O+U	TOTAL
1626–29	0	0	0	2	1	0	0	0	3
1630–39	0	0	0	0	4	1	0	0	5
1640–49	0	2	1	4	2	2	0	0	11
1650–59	0	0	1	4	0	0	0	0	5
1660–69	0	0	0	7	0	1	0	0	8
1670–79	0	1	0	12	1	1	0	0	15
1680–89	4	3	0	24	4	4	0	0	39
1690–99	1	0	1	8	3	2	1	0	16
1700–09	2	0	1	2	2	0	0	2	9
1710–19	2	0	0	8	1	4	0	3	18
1720–29	0	0	0	5	0	0	0	0	5
1730–39	0	2	0	6	0	1	1	0	10
1740–49	0	0	0	1	0	0	0	0	1
1750–59	0	0	0	3	0	0	0	1	4
1760–69	0	0	0	1	0	1	0	0	2

Free Black Marriages: San Sebastián, 1626–1769

	FB–FB	FB–BS	FB–MS	FB–FM	FB–I	FB–ME	FB–SP	FB–O + U	TOTAL
1626–29	0	0	0	1	0	0	0	0	1
1630–39	0	1	0	1	1	0	0	0	3
1640–49	0	1	1	0	0	0	0	0	2
1650–59	1	2	1	3	0	1	0	0	8
1660–69	5	0	0	0	0	0	0	0	5
1670–79	3	2	0	5	0	1	0	0	11
1680–89	0	1	1	4	1	2	0	0	9
1690–99	0	0	0	0	1	0	0	1	2
1700–09	0	0	1	2	1	0	0	2	6
1710–19	0	0	0	2	0	0	1	0	3
1720–29	0	0	0	1	0	0	0	0	1
1730–39	0	0	0	3	0	1	0	0	4
1740–49	0	0	0	3	0	2	1	0	6
1750–59	1	0	0	0	0	0	0	0	1
1760–69	0	0	0	4	2	0	0	0	6

Free Mulatto Marriages: San Sebastián, 1626-1769

	FM-FM	FM-BS	FM-MS	FM-FB	FM-I	FM-ME	FM-SP	FM-O + U/C[a]	TOTAL
1626-29	6	0	2	1	3	1	0	0	13
1630-39	16	0	0	1	1	14	1	4	37
1640-49	31	7	4	0	7	8	1	1	59
1650-59	26	3	4	3	5	7	7	4	59
1660-69	23	1	7	0	3	6	4	0	44
1670-79	46	5	12	5	10	15	5	1	99
1680-89	77	0	24	4	15	46	10	5	181
1690-99	70	2	8	0	14	45	10	4	153
1700-09	70	0	2	2	16	18	4	16	128
1710-19	83	3	8	2	9	42	22	6	175
1720-29	107	0	5	1	34	53	13	10/ 1	223
1730-39	129	1	6	3	32	75	38	11/ 4	295
1740-49	117	0	1	3	16	102	41	22/ 6	302
1750-59	143	2	3	0	29	104	59	37/ 9	377
1760-69	137	0	1	4	26	121	56	24/17	369

[a] FM–C unions included in FM–O + U totals.

Indian Marriages: San Sebastián, 1626–1769

	I-I	I-BS	I-MS	I-FB	I-FM	I-ME	I-SP	I-O + U/C[a]	TOTAL
1626–29	9	1	1	0	3	2	0	0	16
1630–39	17	6	4	1	1	10	0	1	40
1640–49	17	5	2	0	7	13	0	3	47
1650–59	23	1	0	0	5	3	1	0	33
1660–69	15	0	0	0	3	3	0	0	21
1670–79	18	4	1	1	10	12	0	0	45
1680–89	42	2	4	1	15	22	2	0	88
1690–99	57	2	3	1	14	34	0	1	112
1700–09	59	0	2	0	16	19	1	4	102
1710–19	58	0	1	0	9	23	7	1	99
1720–29	67	0	0	0	34	42	7	0	150
1730–39	41	0	0	0	32	41	8	2	124
1740–49	42	0	0	0	16	47	4	7/1	116
1750–59	27	0	0	0	29	42	8	7/3	113
1760–69	58	0	0	2	26	59	6	3	154

[a] I-C unions included in I-O + U totals.

Mestizo Marriages: San Sebastián, 1626–1769

	ME–ME	ME–BS	ME–MS	ME–FB	ME–FM	ME–I	ME–SP	ME–O + U/C[a]	TOTAL
1626–29	3	0	0	0	1	2	0	1	7
1630–39	21	1	1	0	14	10	3	14	64
1640–49	10	0	2	0	8	13	1	0	34
1650–59	6	1	0	1	7	3	2	1	21
1660–69	9	0	1	0	6	3	2	0	21
1670–79	16	0	1	1	15	12	4	1	50
1680–89	32	2	4	2	46	22	11	0	119
1690–99	30	0	2	0	45	34	8	0	119
1700–09	43	0	0	0	18	19	2	4	86
1710–19	45	0	4	0	42	23	31	2	147
1720–29	61	1	0	0	53	42	40	2/2	199
1730–39	71	0	1	1	75	41	35	6/2	230
1740–49	60	0	0	2	102	47	41	26/8	278
1750–59	69	0	0	0	104	42	65	29/9	309
1760–69	72	0	1	0	121	59	48	10/4	311

[a] ME–C unions included in ME–O + U totals.

Spanish Marriages: San Sebastián, 1626–1769

	SP–SP	SP–BS	SP–MS	SP–FB	SP–FM	SP–I	SP–ME	SP–O + U/C[a]	TOTAL
1626–29[b]	—	—	—	—	—	—	—	—	—
1630–39[b]	46	0	0	0	1	0	3	0	50
1640–49	210	0	0	0	1	0	1	1	213
1650–59	188	0	0	0	7	1	2	1	199
1660–69	204	0	0	0	4	0	2	1	211
1670–79	207	0	0	0	5	0	4	0	216
1680–89	238	0	1	0	10	2	11	0	261
1690–99	225	0	0	0	10	0	8	0	244
1700–09	143	0	0	1	4	1	2	0	150
1710–19	142	0	0	0	22	7	31	6	209
1720–29	122	0	0	0	13	7	40	8/ 1	190
1730–39	149	0	1	0	38	8	35	15/ 5	246
1740–49	99	1	0	1	41	4	41	41/ 8	228
1750–59	119	0	0	0	59	8	65	31/10	282
1760–69	92	0	0	0	56	6	48	22/16	224

[a] SP–C unions included in SP–O + U totals.
[b] Spanish marriage data are missing for the years 1626–1638.

Black Slave Marriages: Los Remedios, 1674–1769

	BS-BS	BS-MS	BS-FB	BS-FM	BS-I	BS-ME	BS-SP	BS-O+U	TOTAL
1674–79	0	0	0	1	0	0	0	0	1
1680–89	0	0	0	0	0	0	0	0	0
1690–99	0	0	0	3	0	0	0	0	3
1700–09	0	0	0	0	0	0	0	0	0
1710–19	0	0	0	0	0	0	0	0	0
1720–29	0	0	0	0	0	1	0	0	1
1730–39	0	0	0	0	0	0	0	0	0
1740–49	0	0	0	0	0	0	0	0	0
1750–59	0	0	0	1	0	0	0	0	1
1760–69	0	0	0	0	0	0	0	0	0

Mulatto Slave Marriages: Los Remedios, 1674–1769

	MS–MS	MS–BS	MS–FB	MS–FM	MS–I	MS–ME	MS–SP	MS–O+U	TOTAL
1674–79	0	0	0	1	0	0	0	0	1
1680–89	0	0	1	3	1	1	0	0	6
1690–99	0	0	0	5	0	2	0	1	8
1700–09	0	0	0	2	0	0	0	1	3
1710–19	1	0	0	1	0	0	0	0	2
1720–29	0	0	0	0	0	1	0	0	1
1730–39	0	0	0	1	0	0	0	0	1
1740–49	0	0	0	3	0	1	0	0	4
1750–59	0	0	0	1	0	0	0	0	1
1760–69	0	0	0	0	0	0	0	0	0

Free Black Marriages: Los Remedios, 1674–1769

	FB–FB	FB–BS	FB–MS	FB–FM	FB–I	FB–ME	FB–SP	FB–O + U	TOTAL
1674–79	0	0	0	1	0	0	0	1	2
1680–89	0	0	1	1	0	0	1	0	3
1690–99	0	0	0	1	0	0	0	0	1
1700–09	0	0	0	1	0	0	0	0	1
1710–19	0	0	0	1	0	0	0	0	1
1720–29	0	0	0	4	0	0	0	0	4
1730–39	0	0	0	2	0	0	0	0	2
1740–49	0	0	0	2	0	0	0	0	2
1750–59	0	0	0	0	0	0	0	0	0
1760–69	0	0	0	1	0	1	0	1[a]	3

[a] Miguel de la Carrera, a free black native of Guinea, married Manuela de la Fuente (born legitimate) in 1762.

Free Mulatto Marriages: Los Remedios, 1674–1769

	FM–FM	FM–BS	FM–MS	FM–FB	FM–I	FM–ME	FM–SP	FM–O + U/C[a]	TOTAL
1674–79	12	1	1	1	2	7	0	3	27
1680–89	17	0	3	1	2	13	4	5	45
1690–99	17	3	5	1	5	11	4	7	53
1700–09	21	0	2	1	1	9	5	5	44
1710–19	19	0	1	1	9	16	3	2	51
1720–29	23	0	0	4	3	19	1	3/1	53
1730–39	24	0	1	2	8	20	3	6	64
1740–49	46	0	3	2	9	25	5	10[b]/2	100
1750–59	43	1	1	0	7	33	5	9/2	99
1760–69	39	0	0	1	8	21	1	13/2	83

[a] FM–C unions included in FM–O + U total.
[b] Don Juan Barrera, a native of Nice in the Condado of Savoy, married the legitimate free mulatto Gabriela de Paz in 1743.

Indian Marriages: Los Remedios, 1674–1769

	I-I	I-BS	I-MS	I-FB	I-FM	I-ME	I-SP	I-O + U	TOTAL
1674–79	3	0	0	0	2	3	2	2	12
1680–89	7	0	1	0	2	4	0	0	14
1690–99	11	0	0	0	5	6	1	1	24
1700–09	5	0	0	0	1	3	0	2	11
1710–19	6	0	0	0	9	7	1	1[a]	24
1720–29	10	0	0	0	3	7	0	0	20
1730–39	5	0	0	0	8	5	0	1	19
1740–49	5	0	0	0	9	4	0	0	18
1750–59	8	0	0	0	7	16	0	1	32
1760–69	5	0	0	0	8	6	0	2	21

[a] Matías de la Cruz, an Indian tributary from San Gerónimo, married Beatriz de los Reyes, the legitimate daughter of a free mulatto father and mestizo mother, in 1718. As an infant, Cruz had been *expuesto en la puerta* of María Candelaria, also a San Gerónimo tributary.

Mestizo Marriages: Los Remedios, 1674–1769

	ME–ME	ME–BS	ME–MS	ME–FB	ME–FM	ME–I	ME–SP	ME–O + U/C[a]	TOTAL
1674–79	6	0	0	0	7	3	2	0	18
1680–89	10	0	1	0	13	4	3	2	33
1690–99	7	0	2[b]	0	11	6	6	2	34
1700–09	7	0	0	0	9	3	5	2	26
1710–19	20	0	0	0	16	7	7	2	52
1720–29	14	1	1	0	19	7	5	8/1	55
1730–39	18	0	0	0	20	5	7	5/3	55
1740–49	23	0	1	0	25	4	5	7/1	65
1750–59	19	0	0	0	33	16	2	6/3	76
1760–69	17	0	0	1	21	6	0	9/1	54

[a] ME–C unions included in ME–O + U totals.
[b] Antonio de Valdez, a slave of the Archicofradía del Santísimo Sacramento (who had been born out of wedlock), married the mestiza Antonia Bernarda Hernández in 1692.

Spanish Marriages: Los Remedios, 1674–1769

	SP–SP	SP–BS	SP–MS	SP–FB	SP–FM	SP–I	SP–ME	SP–O + U/C[a]	TOTAL
1674–79	11[b]	0	0	0	0	2	2	2[c]	17
1680–89	20	0	0	1	4	0	3	15	43
1690–99	17	0	0	0	4	1	6	12	40
1700–09	11	0	0	0	5	0	5	11	32
1710–19	18	0	0	0	3	1	7	3	32
1720–29	8	0	0	0	1	0	5	5/1	19
1730–39	15	0	0	0	3	0	7	3	28
1740–49	7	0	0	0	5	0	5	4[d]/2	21
1750–59	4	0	0	0	5	0	2	3	14
1760–69	0	0	0	0	1	0	0	1	2

[a] SP–C unions included in SP–O + U totals.
[b] A Portuguese married a Spanish woman in 1676.
[c] A Frenchman married Leonor Bernal, not identified as to race, in 1676.
[d] A Frenchman married a Spaniard in 1740.

Black Slave Marriages: Candelaria, 1757–1769

	BS–BS	BS–MS	BS–FB	BS–FM	BS–I	BS–ME	BS–SP	BS–O + U	TOTAL
1757–59	0	0	0	0	0	0	0	0	0
1760–69	0	0	0	0	0	0	0	1	1

Mulatto Slave Marriages: Candelaria, 1757–1769

	MS–MS	MS–BS	MS–FB	MS–FM	MS–I	MS–ME	MS–SP	MS–O + U	TOTAL
1757–59	0	0	0	0	0	0	0	0	0
1760–69	0	0	0	0	0	0	0	1	1

Free Black Marriages: Candelaria, 1757–1769

	FB–FB	FB–BS	FB–MS	FB–FM	FB–I	FB–ME	FB–SP	FB–O + U	TOTAL
1757–59	0	0	0	0	0	1	0	0	1
1760–69	0	0	0	1	0	0	0	0	1

Free Mulatto Marriages: Candelaria, 1757–1769

	FM–FM	FM–BS	FM–MS	FM–FB	FM–I	FM–ME	FM–SP	FM–O + U/C[a]	TOTAL
1757–59	4	0	0	0	2	6	4	2/1	18
1760–69	43	0	0	1	3	19	11	5/4	82

[a] FM–C unions included in FM–O + U totals.

Indian Marriages: Candelaria, 1757–1769

	I-I	I-BS	I-MS	I-FB	I-FM	I-ME	I-SP	I-O + U	TOTAL
1757–59	0	0	0	0	2	6	0	0	8
1760–69	0	0	0	0	3	9	4	0	16

Mestizo Marriages: Candelaria, 1757–1769

	ME-ME	ME-BS	ME-MS	ME-FB	ME-FM	ME-I	ME-SP	ME-O + U	TOTAL
1757–59	7	0	0	1	6	6	4	1	25
1760–69	23	0	0	0	19	9	3	0	54

Spanish Marriages: Candelaria, 1757–1769

	SP-SP	SP-BS	SP-MS	SP-FB	SP-FM	SP-I	SP-ME	SP-O + U/C[a]	TOTAL
1757–59	5	0	0	0	4	0	4	3/1	16
1760–69	14	0	0	0	11	4	3	0	32

[a] SP–C union included in SP–O + U total.

APPENDIX 2

MARRIAGE INDICES

CHARLES Tilly's Intermarriage Index (explained at length in chapter 5) provides a single standard of comparison for every conceivable sort of union, enabling the scholar to rank each by its prevalence or strength in the population as a whole. How are Tilly indices derived? From values found in appendix 1, using the following formula:

$$\frac{100 \times \text{number of marriages between groups } X \text{ and } Y \quad \times \quad \text{total number of marriages in decennial sample}}{\text{number of persons marrying group } X \quad \times \quad \text{number of persons marrying in group } Y}$$

For the intermarriage of, say, free mulattoes and mestizos in Santiago as a whole from 1680 to 1689, multiply 100 × 92 (the number of free mulatto-mestizo marriages in that decade, available in either "Free Mulatto Marriages" or "Mestizo Marriages") × 1,288 (the number of marriages for all groups in that decade, available in "Total Marriages by Decade"). Divide the result by 266 (the number of mestizo marriages in 1680–89, available in "Mestizo Marriages") × 449 (the number of free mulatto marriages for that decade, found in "Free Mulatto Marriages"). Thus from 1680 to 1689 in Santiago as a whole mestizo–free mulatto unions would receive a score of 99: 100 × 92 × 1,288 / 266 × 449 = 99.

One would use the same formula to derive a Tilly score for, say, mulatto slave–mestizo unions in the Sagrario during the 1680s. Multiply 100 × 12 (the number of mulatto slave–mestizo marriages in the

Sagrario during that decade, available in either "Mulato Slave Marriages" or "Mestizo Marriages") × 600 (the number of Sagrario marriages for all groups in 1680–89, available in "Total Marriages by Decade"). Divide the result by 114 (the number of mestizo marriages in 1680–89, available in "Mestizo Marriages: Sagrario") × 92 (the number of mulatto slave marriages for that decade, found in "Mulatto Slave Marriages: Sagrario"). For the period from 1680 to 1689 in the Sagrario, then, mulatto slave–mestizo unions receive a score of 69: 100 × 12 × 600 / 114 × 92 = 69.

To calculate a Tilly score for the intramarriage of, for example, free mulattoes during the 1680s throughout Santiago's four parishes, use the following formula:

$$\frac{100 \times \text{number of marriages in group } X \times \text{total number of marriages in decennial sample}}{\text{number of persons marrying in group } X^2} \times 2$$

Multiply 100 × 189 (the number of free mulatto intramarriages in Santiago during the 1680s, available in "Free Mulatto Marriages") × 1,288 (the number of marriages for all groups in that decade, available in "Total Marriages by Decade"). Divide the result by the square of 449 (the number of free mulatto marriages in Santiago during the 1680s, found in "Free Mulatto Marriages"). Then multiply that result × 2. The Tilly score for 1680s free mulatto intramarriage in Santiago is 241: $(100 \times 189 \times 1{,}288 / 449^2) \times 2 = 241$ (as reflected in table 14).

Tilly indices for the city at large are found in chapter 5, tables 11–17. Parish Tilly indices, based on available data as explained in the "Introduction" to the appendixes, follow here.ABbreviations are the same as those for appendix 1, with one addition: an asterisk indicates a Tilly score is based on insufficient evidence; as pointed out in chapter 5, a sample of 10 or fewer marriages tends to produce what Tilly called "astronomical" results.

Abbreviations: BS = black slave; MS = mulatto slave; FB = free black; FM = free mulatto; I = Indian naboría; ME = mestizo; SP = Spaniard; O + U = others and unidentified (those who fit in none of the above categories); and C = castizo.

Black Slave Marriage Indices: Sagrario, 1593–1769

	BS–BS	BS–MS	BS–FB	BS–FM	BS–I	BS–ME	BS–SP	BS–O + U	Total BS Marriages
1593–99	738	0	121*	97	217	0	4	0	47
1600–09	322	23	0	147	145	0	0	0	97
1610–19	490	143	303*	77	93	11	2	0	100
1620–29	642	121	0	52	106	25	0	0	34
1630–39	—	—	—	—	—	—	—	—	—
1640–49	356*	266*	0	200*	178*	0	0	0	9
1650–59	434	70	254	82	113	35	3	507*	82
1660–69	244	170	338	125	135	95	0	0	53
1670–79	402	126	448	49	114	62	0	759	68
1680–89	322	141	138	79	141	21	0	1176	51
1690–99	0	155	252	91	95	106	10	0	33
1700–09	836	251	418*	81	130	24	0	0	18
1710–19	518	309	480	93	61	18	0	0	21
1720–29	0	780	609	81	47	0	0	0	11
1730–39	3906	0	362*	52	0	37	0	0	20
1740–49	2554	284	0	79	0	0	22	3406	16
1750–59	4620	0	605*	67	0	0	0	0	11
1760–69	3600*	0	0	0	0	244*	0	7200*	4

Mulatto Slave Marriage Indices: Sagrario, 1593–1769

	MS–MS	MS–BS	MS–FB	MS–FM	MS–I	MS–ME	MS–SP	MS–O + U	Total MS Marriages
1593–99	0	0	0	570*	305*	0	0	0	4
1600–09	246	23	0	211	145	276	11	0	18
1610–19	754	143	0	121	102	117	0	0	19
1620–29	0	121	0	218	54	268	0	0	19
1630–39	—	—	—	—	—	—	—	—	—
1640–49	0	266*	0	300*	0	0	0	0	2
1650–59	128	70	83	152	86	144	6	1156*	36
1660–69	140	170	0	202	104	50	10	0	43
1670–79	314	126	49	138	67	63	5	358	48
1680–89	128	141	65	123	78	69	3	652	92
1690–99	210	155	85	115	105	69	5	852	65
1700–09	282	251	188*	131	73	55	7	1128	40
1710–19	236	309	153	100	102	59	0	1298	44
1720–29	686	780	134	62	62	85	0	0	25
1730–39	536	0	0	99	49	123	0	0	27
1740–49	756	284	284*	114	84	17	0	2271	24
1750–59	770	0	0	134	0	249	0	4236	11
1760–69	1600*	0	0	121*	0	81*	0	4800*	6

Free Black Marriage Indices: Sagrario, 1593–1769

	FB–FB	FB–BS	FB–MS	FB–FM	FB–I	FB–ME	FB–SP	FB–O + U	Total FB Marriages
1593–99	0	121*	0	1140*	136*	0	0	0	6
1600–09	0	0	0	948*	0	0	0	0	1
1610–19	0	303*	0	171*	86*	0	26*	0	9
1620–29	0	0	0	0	0	424*	0	9750*	2
1630–39	—	—	—	—	—	—	—	—	—
1640–49	—	—	—	—	—	—	—	—	—
1650–59	424	254	83	120	0	0	0	2971*	14
1660–69	0	338	0	103	0	60	36	3583*	12
1670–79	0	448	49	50	29	82	0	2345	22
1680–89	416	138	65	127	35	62	19	0	17
1690–99	278	252	85	75	105	25	33	2770	20
1700–09	2506*	418*	188*	48*	98*	73*	0	0	6
1710–19	396	480	153	72	75	44	19	3359	17
1720–29	0	609	134	125	33	67	0	0	16
1730–39	1608*	362*	0	137*	0	41*	0	0	9
1740–49	5110*	0	284*	53*	126*	52*	0	0	8
1750–59	3804*	605*	0	53*	0	114*	0	0	7
1760–69	0	0	0	61*	218*	0	0	7200*	4

Free Mulatto Marriage Indices: Sagrario, 1593–1769

	FM-FM	FM-BS	FM-MS	FM-FB	FM-I	FM-ME	FM-SP	FM-O + U	Total FM Marriages
1593-99	4	97	570*	1140*	163	207	0	0	15
1600-09	452	147	211	948*	54	158	0	947*	42
1610-19	392	77	121	171*	79	244	16	0	59
1620-29	286	52	218	0	124	154	6	0	33
1630-39	—	—	—	—	—	—	—	—	—
1640-49	300*	200*	300*	0	100*	150*	0	0	8
1650-59	264	82	152	120	78	99	15	420*	99
1660-69	310	125	202	103	69	76	8	413*	104
1670-79	348	49	138	50	51	111	6	369	140
1680-89	230	79	123	127	51	78	7	269	223
1690-99	284	91	115	75	51	81	5	299	185
1700-09	296	81	131	48*	42	71	13	291	155
1710-19	226	93	100	72	36	70	32	244	234
1720-29	196	81	62	125	60	94	25	222	241
1730-39	196	52	99	137*	60	86	21	206	316
1740-49	182	79	114	53*	62	108	22	210	259
1750-59	184	67	134	53*	35	112	27	184	253
1760-69	228	0	121*	61*	59	123	19	242	119

Indian Marriage Indices: Sagrario, 1593-1769

	I-I	I-BS	I-MS	I-FB	I-FM	I-ME	I-SP	I-O + U	Total I Marriages
1593-99	426	217	305*	136*	163	74	0	0	84
1600-09	272	145	145	0	54	163	2	0	122
1610-19	398	93	102	86*	79	123	2	0	117
1620-29	432	106	54	0	124	89	5	0	38
1630-39	—	—	—	—	—	—	—	—	—
1640-49	534*	178*	0	0	100*	200*	0	0	6
1650-59	400	113	86	0	78	139	4	0	54
1660-69	634	135	104	0	69	134	0	896*	48
1670-79	532	114	67	29	51	105	0	645	80
1680-89	456	141	78	35	51	89	0	600	100
1690-99	474	95	105	105	51	75	0	523	106
1700-09	638	130	73	98*	42	74	4	0	77
1710-19	620	61	102	75	36	79	7	642	89
1720-29	414	47	62	33	60	76	6	520	103
1730-39	478	0	49	0	60	100	0	658	99
1740-49	672	0	84	126*	62	77	13	1009	54
1750-59	1274	0	0	0	35	100	18	1456	32
1760-69	634	0	0	218*	59	74	23	873	33

Mestizo Marriage Indices: Sagrario, 1593–1769

	ME–ME	ME–BS	ME–MS	ME–FB	ME–FM	ME–I	ME–SP	ME–O + U	Total ME Marriages
1593–99	1838	0	0	0	207	74	23	0	22
1600–09	552	0	276	0	158	163	9	0	24
1610–19	486	11	117	0	244	123	11	1107	41
1620–29	368	25	268	424*	154	89	0	0	23
1630–39	0	0	0	0	0	0	100*	0	2
1640–49	1200*	0	0	0	150*	200*	0	0	4
1650–59	288	35	144	0	99	139	24	578*	72
1660–69	622	95	50	60	76	134	7	717*	60
1670–79	376	62	63	82	111	105	12	0	86
1680–89	378	21	69	62	78	89	14	526	114
1690–99	414	106	69	25	81	75	6	0	111
1700–09	382	24	55	73*	71	74	30	438	103
1710–19	256	18	59	44	70	79	39	371	154
1720–29	174	0	85	67	94	76	36	355	151
1730–39	162	37	123	41*	86	100	32	368	177
1740–49	236	0	17	52*	108	77	19	416	131
1750–59	122	0	249	114*	112	100	30	398	117
1760–69	132	244*	81*	0	123	74	25	488	59

Spanish Marriage Indices: Sagrario, 1590–1769

	SP-SP	SP-BS	SP-MS	SP-FB	SP-FM	SP-I	SP-ME	SP-O + U	Total SP Marriages
1590–99	324	4	0	0	0	0	23	0	206
1600–09	406	0	11	0	0	2	9	0	193
1610–19	442	2	0	26*	16	2	11	0	196
1620–29	284	0	0	0	4	4	0	144*	226
1630–39	198	0	0	0	0	0	100*	0	195
1640–49	332	0	0	0	0	0	0	0	29
1650–59	392	3	6	0	15	4	24	218*	191
1660–69	406	0	10	36	8	0	7	0	201
1670–79	498	0	5	0	6	0	12	0	199
1680–89	598	0	3	19	7	0	14	0	188
1690–99	612	10	5	33	5	0	6	328	169
1700–09	496	0	7	0	13	4	30	285	158
1710–19	480	0	0	19	32	7	39	330	173
1720–29	478	0	0	0	25	6	36	323	166
1730–39	514	0	0	0	21	0	32	337	193
1740–49	538	22	0	0	22	13	19	354	154
1750–59	400	0	0	0	27	18	30	289	161
1760–69	582	0	0	0	19	23	25	374	77

Black Slave Marriage Indices: San Sebastián, 1626–1769

	BS–BS	BS–MS	BS–FB	BS–FM	BS–I	BS–ME	BS–SP	BS–O + U	Total BS Marriages
1626–29	1462*	0	0	0	61*	0	0	0	4
1630–39	1006	0	436	0	196	20	0	0	13
1640–49	1146	167	459	109	209	0	0	0	40
1650–59	2346	0	499	101	60	95	0	0	17
1660–69	18500*	0	0	420*	0	0	0	0	2
1670–79	0	249	680	216	333	0	0	0	12
1680–89	2248*	432*	624*	0	128*	94*	0	0	10
1690–99	0	0	0	179*	245*	0	0	0	4
1700–09	0	0	0	0	0	0	0	0	0
1710–19	0	0	0	321*	0	0	0	0	3
1720–29	0	0	0	0	0	309*	0	0	1
1730–39	12132*	2426*	0	41*	0	0	0	0	6
1740–49	17208*	0	0	0	0	0	63*	14340*	5
1750–59	0	0	0	223*	0	0	0	0	2
1760–69	0	0	0	0	0	0	0	0	0

Mulatto Slave Marriage Indices: San Sebastián, 1626–1769

	MS–MS	MS–BS	MS–FB	MS–FM	MS–I	MS–ME	MS–SP	MS–O + U	Total MS Marriages
1626–29	0	0	0	200*	81*	0	0	0	3
1630–39	0	0	0	0	340*	53*	0	0	5
1640–49	0	167	1668*	226	142	196	0	0	11
1650–59	0	0	848*	460*	0	0	0	0	5
1660–69	0	0	0	736*	0	220*	0	0	8
1670–79	0	249	0	363	67	60	0	0	15
1680–89	296	432*	0	191	66	48	0	0	39
1690–99	428	0	1716*	179	92	58	14	0	16
1700–09	2414*	0	906*	85*	160*	0	0	5433*	9
1710–19	694	0	0	143	32	85	0	3122	18
1720–29	0	0	0	276*	0	0	0	0	5
1730–39	0	2426*	0	148*	0	32*	30*	0	10
1740–49	0	0	0	237*	0	0	0	0	1
1750–59	0	0	0	167*	0	0	0	21025*	4
1760–69	0	0	0	101*	0	120*	0	0	2

Free Black Marriage Indices: San Sebastián, 1626–1769

	FB–FB	FB–BS	FB–MS	FB–FM	FB–I	FB–ME	FB–SP	FB–O + U	Total FB Marriages
1626–29	0	0	0	300*	0	0	0	0	1
1630–39	0	436*	0	153*	142*	0	0	0	3
1640–49	0	459*	1668*	0	0	0	0	0	2
1650–59	1060*	499*	848*	215*	0	202*	0	0	8
1660–69	14800*	0	0	0	0	0	0	0	5
1670–79	2226	680	0	206	0	82	0	0	11
1680–89	0	624*	0	138*	71*	105*	0	6244*	9
1690–99	0	0	1716*	0	245*	0	0	0	2
1700–09	0	0	906*	127*	80*	0	0	8150*	6
1710–19	0	0	0	214*	0	0	90*	0	3
1720–29	0	0	0	276*	0	0	0	0	1
1730–39	0	0	0	185*	0	79*	0	0	4
1740–49	0	0	0	119*	0	86*	52*	0	6
1750–59	168200*	0	0	0	0	0	0	0	1
1760–69	0	0	0	135*	162*	0	0	0	6

Free Mulatto Marriage Indices: San Sebastián, 1626–1769

	FM–FM	FM–BS	FM–MS	FM–FB	FM–I	FM–ME	FM–SP	FM–O + U	Total FM Marriages
1626–29	276	0	200*	300*	56	43	0	0	13
1630–39	398	0	0	153*	11	101	9	459	37
1640–49	654	109	226	0	93	146	3	622*	59
1650–59	506	101	460*	215*	87	192	20	575*	59
1660–69	880	420*	736*	0	120	240	16	0	44
1670–79	422	216	363	206	101	136	10	454*	99
1680–89	264	0	191	138*	53	120	12	310*	181
1690–99	328	179*	179	0	45	136	15	359*	153
1700–09	418	0	85*	127*	60	80	10	382	128
1710–19	304	321*	143	214*	29	92	34	321	175
1720–29	264	0	276*	276*	63	73	19	276	223
1730–39	216	41*	148*	185*	64	80	38	247	295
1740–49	184	0	237*	119*	33	87	43	237	302
1750–59	170	223*	167*	0	57	75	47	223	377
1760–69	150	0	101*	135*	34	79	51	203	369

Indian Marriage Indices: San Sebastián, 1626–1769

	I-I	I-BS	I-MS	I-FB	I-FM	I-ME	I-SP	I-O + U	Total I Marriages
1626–29	274	61*	81*	0	56	70*	0	0	16
1630–39	362	196	340*	142*	11	66	0	425	40
1640–49	564	209	142	0	93	299	0	781*	47
1650–59	1432	60	0	0	87	147	5	0	33
1660–69	2518	0	0	0	120	252	0	0	21
1670–79	798	333	67	0	101	239	0	0	45
1680–89	610	128*	66	71*	53	118	5	0	88
1690–99	498	245*	92	245*	45	140	0	490*	112
1700–09	554	0	160*	80*	60	106	3	479	102
1710–19	666	0	32	0	29	89	19	568	99
1720–29	366	0	0	0	63	87	15	0	150
1730–39	388	0	0	0	64	105	19	587	124
1740–49	448	0	0	0	33	104	11	618	116
1750–59	356	0	0	0	57	101	21	744	113
1760–69	366	0	0	162*	34	92	13	486	154

Mestizo Marriage Indices: San Sebastián, 1626–1769

	ME–ME	ME–BS	ME–MS	ME–FB	ME–FM	ME–I	ME–SP	ME–O + U	Total ME Marriages
1626–29	478*	0	0	0	43*	70*	0	557*	7
1630–39	174	20	53*	0	101	66	16	266	64
1640–49	634	0	196	0	146	299	5	0	34
1650–59	922	95	0	202*	192	147	16	1614*	21
1660–69	1510	0	220*	0	240	252	17	0	21
1670–79	574	0	60	82	136	239	17	898*	50
1680–89	254	94*	48	105*	120	118	20	0	119
1690–99	232	0	58	0	136	140	15	0	119
1700–09	568	0	0	0	80	106	8	569	86
1710–19	234	0	85	0	92	89	57	382	147
1720–29	190	309*	0	0	73	87	65	309	199
1730–39	196	0	32*	79*	80	105	45	317	230
1740–49	112	0	0	86*	87	104	46	258	278
1750–59	122	0	0	0	75	101	63	272	309
1760–69	112	0	120*	0	79	92	52	241	311

Spanish Marriage Indices: San Sebastián, 1626–1769

	SP-SP	SP-BS	SP-MS	SP-FB	SP-FM	SP-I	SP-ME	SP-O + U	Total SP Marriages
1626–29	—	—	—	—	—	—	—	—	—
1630–39	626	0	0	0	9	0	16	0	50
1640–49	340	0	0	0	3	0	5	172*	213
1650–59	322	0	0	0	20	5	16	170*	199
1660–69	340	0	0	0	16	0	17	175*	211
1670–79	398	0	0	0	10	0	17	0	216
1680–89	392	0	0	0	12	5	20	0	261
1690–99	414	0	14	0	15	0	15	0	244
1700–09	622	0	0	0	10	3	8	0	150
1710–19	366	0	0	90*	34	19	57	269	209
1720–29	416	0	0	0	19	15	65	324	190
1730–39	358	0	30*	0	38	19	45	296	246
1740–49	274	63*	0	52*	43	11	46	314	228
1750–59	252	0	0	0	47	21	63	298	282
1760–69	274	0	0	0	51	13	52	334	224

Black Slave Marriage Indices: Los Remedios, 1674–1769

	BS–BS	BS–MS	BS–FB	BS–FM	BS–I	BS–ME	BS–SP	BS–O + U	Total BS Marriages
1674–79	0	0	0	230*	0	0	0	0	1
1680–89	0	0	0	0	0	0	0	0	0
1690–99	0	0	0	253*	0	0	0	0	3
1700–09	0	0	0	0	0	0	0	0	0
1710–19	0	0	0	0	0	0	0	0	0
1720–29	0	0	0	0	0	229*	0	0	1
1730–39	0	0	0	0	0	0	0	0	0
1740–49	0	0	0	0	0	0	0	0	0
1750–59	0	0	0	174*	0	0	0	0	1
1760–69	0	0	0	0	0	0	0	0	0

Mulatto Slave Marriage Indices: Los Remedios, 1674–1769

	MS–MS	MS–BS	MS–FB	MS–FM	MS–I	MS–ME	MS–SP	MS–O + U	Total MS Marriages
1674–79	0	0	0	230*	0	0	0	0	1
1680–89	0	0	700*	140*	150*	64*	0	0	6
1690–99	0	0	0	158*	0	99*	0	1675*	8
1700–09	0	0	0	141*	0	0	0	3100*	3
1710–19	6250*	0	0	123*	0	0	0	0	2
1720–29	0	0	0	0	0	229*	0	0	1
1730–39	0	0	0	217*	0	0	0	0	1
1740–49	0	0	0	122*	0	63*	0	0	4
1750–59	0	0	0	174*	0	0	0	0	1
1760–69	0	0	0	0	0	0	0	0	0

Free Black Marriage Indices: Los Remedios, 1674–1769

	FB–FB	FB–BS	FB–MS	FB–FM	FB–I	FB–ME	FB–SP	FB–O + U	Total FB Marriages
1674–79	0	0	0	115*	0	0	0	3100*	2
1680–89	0	0	700*	93*	0	0	98*	0	3
1690–99	0	0	0	253*	0	0	0	0	1
1700–09	0	0	0	211*	0	0	0	0	1
1710–19	0	0	0	245*	0	0	0	0	1
1720–29	0	0	0	238*	0	0	0	0	4
1730–39	0	0	0	217*	0	0	0	0	2
1740–49	0	0	0	163*	0	0	0	0	2
1750–59	0	0	0	0	0	0	0	0	0
1760–69	0	0	0	57*	0	87*	0	4700*	3

Free Mulatto Marriage Indices: Los Remedios, 1674–1769

	FM–FM	FM–BS	FM–MS	FM–FB	FM–I	FM–ME	FM–SP	FM–O + U	Total FM Marriages
1674–79	204	230*	230*	115*	38	89	0	230*	27
1680–89	212	0	140*	93*	40	110	26	280	45
1690–99	162	253*	158*	253*	53	82	25	253	53
1700–09	202	0	141*	211*	19	73	33	211	44
1710–19	182	0	123*	245*	92	75	23	245*	51
1720–29	206	0	0	238*	36	82	13	238	53
1730–39	162	0	217*	217*	91	79	23	217	64
1740–49	150	0	122*	163*	82	63	38	163	100
1750–59	150	174*	174*	0	38	75	62	174	99
1760–69	160	0	0	57*	65	66	85*	170	83

Indian Marriage Indices: Los Remedios, 1674–1769

	I-I	I-BS	I-MS	I-FB	I-FM	I-ME	I-SP	I-O + U	Total I Marriages
1674–79	258	0	0	0	38	86	61	517*	12
1680–89	900	0	150*	0	40	109	0	0	14
1690–99	512	0	0	0	53	99	14	558	24
1700–09	768	0	0	0	19	98	0	845	11
1710–19	260	0	0	0	92	70	16	521*	24
1720–29	630	0	0	0	36	80	0	0	20
1730–39	386	0	0	0	91	67	0	732	19
1740–49	504	0	0	0	82	56	0	0	18
1750–59	268	0	0	0	38	113	0	538	32
1760–69	320	0	0	0	65	75	0	671	21

Mestizo Marriage Indices: Los Remedios, 1674–1769

	ME–ME	ME–BS	ME–MS	ME–FB	ME–FM	ME–I	ME–SP	ME–O + U	Total ME Marriages
1674–79	230	0	0	0	89	86	41	0	18
1680–89	232	0	64*	0	110	109	27	382	33
1690–99	162	0	99*	0	82	99	59	394	34
1700–09	192	0	0	0	73	98	56	358	26
1710–19	184	0	0	0	75	70	53	240*	52
1720–29	116	229*	229*	0	82	80	60	229	55
1730–39	166	0	0	0	79	67	63	253	55
1740–49	178	0	63*	0	63	56	60	251	65
1750–59	114	0	0	0	75	113	32	226	76
1760–69	164	0	0	87*	66	75	0	261	54

Spanish Marriage Indices: Los Remedios, 1674–1769

	SP-SP	SP-BS	SP-MS	SP-FB	SP-FM	SP-I	SP-ME	SP-O + U	Total SP Marriages
1674–79	472	0	0	0	0	61	41	365*	17
1680–89	272	0	0	98*	26	0	27	293	43
1690–99	284	0	0	0	25	14	59	335	40
1700–09	200	0	0	0	33	0	56	291	32
1710–19	440	0	0	0	23	16	53	391*	32
1720–29	558	0	0	0	13	0	60	663	19
1730–39	532	0	0	0	23	0	63	496	28
1740–49	518	0	0	0	38	0	60	776	21
1750–59	702	0	0	0	62	0	32	1229	14
1760–69	0	0	0	0	85	0	0	7050*	2

Black Slave Marriage Indices: Candelaria, 1757-1769

	BS-BS	BS-MS	BS-FB	BS-FM	BS-I	BS-ME	BS-SP	BS-O + U	Total BS Marriages
1757-59	0	0	0	0	0	0	0	0	0
1760-69	0	0	0	0	0	0	0	14900*	1

Mulatto Slave Marriage Indices: Candelaria, 1757-1769

	MS-MS	MS-BS	MS-FB	MS-FM	MS-I	MS-ME	MS-SP	MS-O + U	Total MS Marriages
1757-59	0	0	0	0	0	0	0	0	0
1760-69	0	0	0	0	0	0	0	14900*	1

Free Black Marriage Indices: Candelaria, 1757–1769

	FB–FB	FB–BS	FB–MS	FB–FM	FB–I	FB–ME	FB–SP	FB–O + U	Total FB Marriages
1757–59	0	0	0	0	0	200*	0	0	1
1760–69	0	0	0	182*	0	0	0	0	1

Free Mulatto Marriage Indices: Candelaria, 1757–1769

	FM–FM	FM–BS	FM–MS	FM–FB	FM–I	FM–ME	FM–SP	FM–O + U	Total FM Marriages
1757–59	124	0	0	0	69	67	69	278*	18
1760–69	190	0	0	182*	34	64	62	182*	82

Indian Marriage Indices: Candelaria, 1757–1769

	I–I	I–BS	I–MS	I–FB	I–FM	I–ME	I–SP	I–O + U	Total I Marriages
1757–59	0	0	0	0	69*	150*	0	0	8
1760–69	0	0	0	0	34	155	116	0	16

Mestizo Marriage Indices: Candelaria, 1757–1769

	ME–ME	ME–BS	ME–MS	ME–FB	ME–FM	ME–I	ME–SP	ME–O + U	Total ME Marriages
1757–59	112	0	0	200*	67	150*	50	200*	25
1760–69	236	0	0	0	64	155	26	0	54

Spanish Marriage Indices: Candelaria, 1757–1769

	SP–SP	SP–BS	SP–MS	SP–FB	SP–FM	SP–I	SP–ME	SP–O + U	Total SP Marriages
1757–59	196	0	0	0	69	0	50	313*	16
1760–69	408	0	0	0	62	116	26	0	32

APPENDIX 3

GENTE ORDINARIA AND SPANISH BAPTISMS: SANTIAGO DE GUATEMALA, 1640–1769

SANTIAGO de Guatemala's baptismal data are presented below in four tables: the first includes the entire city; the second, Sagrario Parish; the third, San Sebastián Parish; and the fourth, Los Remedios Parish. The periods covered in each table vary according to the data available. The first table also includes baptisms from Candelaria Parish. The Candelaria baptisms are included in the gente ordinaria city totals as all non-Indians baptized in that parish were entered as ladinos (see "Introduction" to the appendixes). Throughout these four tables decennial legitimate and illegitimate percentages are rounded off so that totals equal 100 percent.

Gente Ordinaria and Spanish Baptisms: Santiago, 1640–1769

	Gente Ordinaria					Spanish				
	Total Baptisms	Legitimate		Illegitimate		Total Baptisms	Legitimate		Illegitimate	
		Total	Percentage	Total	Percentage		Total	Percentage	Total	Percentage
1640–49	2,425	564	23	1,861	77	1,620	967	60	653	40
1650–59	2,765	728	26	2,037	74	1,650	1,032	63	618	37
1660–69	3,244	866	27	2,378	73	1,775	1,062	60	713	40
1670–79	3,303	1,140	35	2,163	65	1,830	1,166	64	664	36
1680–89	3,540	1,686	48	1,854	52	1,740	1,225	70	515	30
1690–99	3,823	2,151	56	1,672	44	1,839	1,324	72	515	28
1700–09	4,437	2,480	56	1,957	44	1,989	1,439	72	550	28
1710–19	5,165	2,831	55	2,334	45	1,829	1,216	66	613	34
1720–29	7,083	3,834	54	3,249	46	1,532	1,037	68	495	32
1730–39	8,553	4,382	51	4,171	49	1,432	1,023	71	409	29
1740–49	8,379	4,598	55	3,781	45	1,240	785	63	455	37
1750–59	8,009	4,649	58	3,360	42	1,182	835	71	347	29
1760–69	8,469	4,844	57	3,625	43	1,243	926	74	317	26

Note: Based on available data. See "Introduction" to the appendixes for details.

Gente Ordinaria and Spanish Baptisms: Sagrario, 1630–1772

	Total Baptisms	Gente Ordinaria					Spanish				
		Legitimate		Illegitimate		Total Baptisms	Legitimate		Illegitimate	
		Total	Percentage	Total	Percentage		Total	Percentage	Total	Percentage
1630–39	183	0	0	183	100	—	—	—	—	—
1640–49	1,406	227	16	1,179	84	84	52	62	32	38
1650–59	1,622	369	23	1,253	77	773	527	68	246	32
1660–69	1,806	326	18	1,480	82	712	431	61	281	39
1670–79	1,699	439	26	1,260	74	840	557	66	283	34
1680–89	1,689	700	41	989	59	760	526	69	234	31
1690–99	1,466	748	51	718	49	667	444	67	223	33
1700–09	1,722	779	45	943	55	726	519	71	207	29
1710–19	2,205	1,002	45	1,203	55	744	432	58	312	42
1720–29	3,163	1,353	43	1,810	57	621	369	59	252	41
1730–39	3,810	1,676	44	2,134	56	694	481	69	213	31
1740–49	3,345	1,595	48	1,750	52	673	417	62	256	38
1750–59	3,133	1,540	49	1,593	51	711	478	67	233	33
1760–69	3,069	1,475	48	1,594	52	792	573	72	219	28
1770–72	1,626	694	43	932	57	142	108	76	34	24

Gente Ordinaria and Spanish Baptisms: San Sebastián, 1594–1773

	Gente Ordinaria					Spanish				
	Total Baptisms	Legitimate Total	Percentage	Illegitimate Total	Percentage	Total Baptisms	Legitimate Total	Percentage	Illegitimate Total	Percentage
1594–99	209	127	61	82	39	—	—	—	—	—
1600–09	324	146	45	178	55	—	—	—	—	—
1610–19	419	178	42	241	58	—	—	—	—	—
1620–29	427	162	38	265	62	—	—	—	—	—
1630–39	596	254	43	342	57	54	24	44	30	56
1640–49	805	248	31	557	69	780	447	57	333	43
1650–59	887	291	33	596	67	877	505	58	372	42
1660–69	1,050	377	36	673	64	982	576	59	406	41
1670–79	1,143	488	43	655	57	970	604	62	366	38
1680–89	1,286	690	54	596	46	966	688	71	278	29
1690–99	1,689	1,017	60	672	40	1,055	798	76	257	24
1700–09	2,003	1,284	64	719	36	118	87	74	31	26
1710–19	2,230	1,399	63	831	37	—	—	—	—	—
1720–29	3,170	2,038	64	1,132	36	—	—	—	—	—
1730–39	3,863	2,246	58	1,617	42	—	—	—	—	—
1740–49	4,234	2,531	60	1,703	40	489	319	65	170	35
1750–59	4,055	2,627	65	1,428	35	461	348	75	113	25
1760–69	1,666	1,055	63	611	37	438	342	78	96	22
1770–73	1,819	1,114	61	705	39	73	52	71	21	29

Gente Ordinaria and Spanish Baptisms: Los Remedios, 1641–1776

	Gente Ordinaria					Spanish				
	Total Baptisms	Legitimate Total	Percentage	Illegitimate Total	Percentage	Total Baptisms	Legitimate Total	Percentage	Illegitimate Total	Percentage
1641–49	196	81	41	115	59	—	—	—	—	—
1650–59	256	68	27	188	73	—	—	—	—	—
1660–69	388	163	42	225	58	81	55	68	26	32
1670–79	461	213	46	248	54	20	5	25	15	75
1680–89	565	296	52	269	48	14	11	79	3	21
1690–99	668	386	58	282	42	117	82	70	35	30
1700–09	712	417	59	295	41	83	50	60	33	40
1710–19	316	172	54	144	46	45	20	44	25	56
1720–29	—	—	—	—	—	—	—	—	—	—
1730–39	—	—	—	—	—	—	—	—	—	—
1740–49	—	—	—	—	—	—	—	—	—	—
1750–59	545	321	59	224	41	8	7	87	1	13
1760–69	1,045	604	58	441	42	13	11	85	2	15
1770–76	672	405	60	267	40	1	0	0	1	100

APPENDIX 4

POPULATION

ESTIMATES of total population in chapter 4, table 9, are based on corrected total marriage figures for Santiago's various socioracial groups, as presented in table 6. By themselves these decennial group totals show only relative changes and suggest that certain groups were larger than others. Used with estimates of average annual marriage rates per thousand population in conjunction with actual illegitimacy ratios, however, they form the basis of estimated population totals for the 1590s, 1650s, 1680s, and 1750s.

Marriage rates per thousand for all known populations range from about seven to fourteen per thousand of total population, according to both Daniel Scott Smith (in June 1974, when he was with the Family History Summer Institute at Chicago's Newberry Library) and D. E. C. Eversley (author of the 1965 work "A Survey of Population in an Area of Worcestershire from 1660 to 1850 on the Basis of Parish Registers").

A low marriage rate of seven per thousand has been assigned to black slaves due to their low social standing in Spanish Guatemala. Also contributing to this low marriage rate are the cultural disadvantages bozales suffered in urban Hispanic society and the disproportionate number of males among imported slaves.

Mulatto slaves have been assigned a marriage rate of eight per thousand, a notch higher than that for black slaves because they enjoyed a relatively wider range of economic and marriage opportunities. The mulatto's lighter pigmentation, combined with a higher degree of acculturation to Hispanic culture, made such opportunities possible. Although free blacks did not directly suffer the indignities of slavery (unless previously enslaved), they lacked social standing in Santiago. Accordingly, they, too, have been given a marriage rate of eight per thousand.

Free mulattoes enjoyed considerable economic opportunities. In addition, they had a better chance to marry members of all socioracial groups (including Spaniards) than any other non-Spanish group except mestizos. They have thus been assigned a marriage rate of eleven per thousand.

Indians counted in parish registers were primarily those who either had escaped from tributary status by migrating to Santiago's Spanish core and working as servants and artisans or had been born into naboría status and raised among Spaniards. While they did not suffer from the stigma of slavery, the fact that many were females under the marriageable age suggests that they merit a lower marriage rate than that for a group with more balanced age and sex distributions. Naborías, therefore, have been given a marriage rate of seven per thousand.

Mestizos, by contrast, were a group with more balanced age and sex distributions and the highest social status of any of the non-Spanish socioracial groups found in Spanish Guatemalan society. While they, like free mulattoes, were often reputed to be illegitimate, evidence from Santiago suggests that a majority, not just those who passed into Spanish ranks, married. Like free mulattoes, they have been assigned a marriage rate of eleven per thousand.

The dominant Spanish, who were not as free of the burden of illegitimacy as might be suspected, seem to have had a higher marriage rate than any of the six groups just considered. They have been given a marriage rate of twelve per thousand.

To determine group size in given decades, the average annual number of marriages for each group (from table 6) was multiplied by 100, with the product being divided by that group's marriage rate per thousand. To illustrate, the 1590s estimate (rounded) of 960 black slaves was determined by multiplying 67 black slave marriages by 100 and dividing that number by 7, the marriage rate per thousand for black slaves. Total numbers of married gente ordinaria have been similarly calculated for the 1590s, 1650s, 1680s, and 1750s.

But this procedure only accounts for those who married, a minority in Santiago de Guatemala. To calculate the remainder of Santiago's population, numbers of married gente ordinaria were multiplied by ratios of illegitimate to legitimate baptisms, all of which are based on data in appendix 3, except for the 1590s ratio, which was conservatively set at a level roughly 10 percent higher than that for the 1650s, since illegitimacy declined progressively among the gente ordinaria after 1650.

The total estimated gente ordinaria population for the four decades in question was determined, finally, by adding decennial estimates of legitimate and illegitimate gente ordinaria. Total Spanish population was determined in the same fashion. Clergy numbers were estimated. Indian tributary numbers are based on tributary records, which show that severe Indian population losses in Santiago were obscured by population increases in Santiago's outer settlements.

Abbreviations: BS = black slave; MS = mulatto slave; FB = free black; FM = free mulatto; I = Indian naborío; ME = mestizo; SP = Spaniard; O + U = others and unidentified (those who fit in none of the above categories); C = castizo; and GO = gente ordinaria.

How Santiago's Population Was Estimated: 1590s, 1650s, 1680s, 1750s

	1590s	1650s	1680s	1750s
BS	960	1,410	870	200
MS	190	510	1,710	200
FB	110	275	360	110
FM	180	1,430	4,080	6,790
I	1,710	1,240	2,870	2,640
ME	280	850	2,420	4,790
Total legitimate GO				
× multiplier	3,430 × 3.0	5,715 × 2.8	12,310 × 1.0	14,730 × 0.7
Total illegitimate GO	10,290	16,002	12,310	10,311
Total GO	**13,720**	**21,717**	**24,620**	**25,041**
Total legitimate SP				
× multiplier	2,450 × 0.5	3,500 × 0.6	4,100 × 0.4	3,940 × 0.4
Total illegitimate SP	1,225	2,100	1,640	1,576
Total SP	**3,675**	**5,600**	**5,740**	**5,516**
Clergy (est.)	—	500	750	1,000
Indian tributaries	—	5,600	7,800	6,700
Total population		**33,417**	**38,910**	**38,257**

APPENDIX 5

EPIDEMIC DISEASE IN SANTIAGO AND ENVIRONS, 1519–1769

1520 Cholera, Kaqchikel country. Bancroft, *History of Central America*, 1:621; and MacLeod, *Spanish Central America*, 98.
1521 *Viruela* (smallpox), Guatemalan highlands. Bancroft, *History of Central America*, 1:621; and Lovell, "Disease and Depopulation."
1532–34 *Sarampión* (measles), Central America. MacLeod, *Spanish Central America*, 98.
1536 Pestilence and hunger, Guatemalan highlands. Fuentes y Guzmán, *Obras históricas*, 2:271.
1545 Pestilence, Mexico. "La pestilencia que ha habido entre los indios en la Nueva España no a llegado en Guatemala y aquí y en Nicaragua plega a dios que no llegue por aca que a morir muchos menos que han muerto en México no quedaría indio por que ay muy pocos ansí aquí como en Nicaragua aunque en Guatemala ay más pero muy pocos en comparación de lo de México." Audiencia al Rey (Gracias a Dios: 31 December 1545), AGI, Guatemala 9.
1545 Pestilence and *gucumatz (cocoliztli)*, Central America. MacLeod, *Spanish Central America*, 98.
1560–61 Pestilence, Guatemala. Large numbers of Indians died in the province in 1560, due to pestilence said to be brought by Lacandón Indians. Supplies were sent because other Indians were dying of hunger. Audiencia al Rey (Santiago: 30 June 1560), AGI, Guatemala 9.

Pestilence was so widespread in February 1561 that Spanish officials were unable to collect tribute payments from the

Indians because the healthy were so busy caring for the sick. Audiencia al Rey (Santiago: 7 February 1561), AGI, Guatemala 9.

1563–65 Drought, famine, epidemic, Guatemala. President Landecho informed the king in 1563 that Indians avoided the hospital established for them, the Hospital de Santiago, because "they did not want to come to get cured." Landecho al Rey (Santiago: 3 February 1563), AGI, Guatemala 9; MacLeod, *Spanish Central America*, 99.

1571 Fear of sickness due to hunger, Guatemala and New Spain. Maize was in very short supply. Wanting to give aid to the neediest towns, the audiencia sought direction from the Crown on what action to take under similar circumstances in the future. Audiencia al Rey (Santiago: 6 September 1571), AGI, Guatemala 9.

1574 Fewer Indians, greater numbers of Spaniards each day, Guatemala. Franciscan friars complained to the king: "Los naturales son cada día menos, los españoles cada día más." "A su Magestad de los frailes menores" (Guatemala: 12 March 1574), AGI, Guatemala 169.

1576–77 Pneumonic plague, smallpox, many deaths, Central America. "La enfermedad que nro señor a permitido por estas partes a llevado muchos yndios. Creo que no fueran tantos si los corregidores y encomenderos les huvieran acudido como fuera razón." El obispo al Rey (Santiago: 25 February 1577), AGI, Guatemala 156.

"Alcanço a estas provincias la enfermedad de las viruelas que entre los indios ha sido contagiosa y general; han muerto muchos aunque los más han sido niños de poca edad y aun la enfermedad no ha pasado." Fiscal Lic. Eugenio de Salazar al Rey (Guatemala: 13 March 1577), AGI, Guatemala 10; see MacLeod, *Spanish Central America*, 98.

1582 Population diminished by three or four previous pestilences, Guatemala. "En lo que toca a morirse los indios e ir en disminución son juicios secretos de Dios que los hombres no los alcanzan y lo que este testigo ha visto en el tiempo que ha estado en estas provincias es que desde la provincia de México han venido tres o cuatro pestilencias con las cuales ha venido la tierra en grandísima disminución." Testimonio del Deán de la Catedral de Guatemala, Pedro de Lievana (8 November 1582), AGI, Guatemala 114.

1585 Severe sickness, Quezaltenango. The audiencia ordered that twenty-one pesos be paid to Corregidor Luis de Monterroso for medicines and barber Antón Moreno for helping to cure the "grande enfermedad" there. Cuentas de 1585, AGI, Contaduría 968.

1592–93 Major pestilence, Audiencia of Guatemala. The province had seen a "gran pestilencia generalmente en todo el distrito de esta real audiencia." Cuentas de 1594–96, AGI, Contaduría 969.

1600–01 General epidemic, Central America. MacLeod, *Spanish Central America*, 98.

1607–8 Pestilence or epidemic, Central America. "Enfermedad general que los naturales desta tierra an tenido demás de un año a esta parte . . . [ha] sido una peste o epidemia que con mucha brevedad en dos o tres días y algunas vezes de repente morían estos indios míseros sin que admitiese remedios no se pudiese entender la cura de ella sino acaso porque con lo que uno sanaban otros morían." Dr. Alonso Criado de Castilla a su Majestad (Guatemala: 30 November 1608), AGI, Guatemala 12; and MacLeod, *Spanish Central America*, 98.

1614 General pestilence, Santiago. The city's cabildo asked the Mercedarian Convent to organize a *rogativa* (supplication) and procession bearing images of Nuestra Señora de las Mercedes to bring an end to the "peste general." LC 10, AGCA, A1 1772 11.766, fol. 212 (Cabildo: 2 August 1614); see MacLeod, *Spanish Central America*, 99.

1623 Pestilence results in death of many children and adolescents, Guatemala. "Desde principio de agosto deste año cesó la peste general que hubo en este reyno y según la noticia que esta ciudad tiene en los pueblos de indios ay poca diminución de tributarios porque los que fallezieron en mayor número eran niños y muchachos." Cabildo al Rey (Santiago: 9 October 1623), AGI, Guatemala 967.

1631–32 Great pestilence (*tabardillo*, typhus) and many deaths, Central America. Indians and Spaniards alike died in great numbers in Santiago and the Indian towns. Antonio de Molina, *Antigua Guatemala*, 24–25; and MacLeod, *Spanish Central America*, 98. A rogativa and procession were used as appeals to end the pestilence. LC 12, AGCA, A1 1774 11.768, fol. 129 (Cabildo: 27 April 1632).

1647 Sickness and pestilence, Santiago and environs. Many Spaniards and Indians died. Little space remained in the city's churches and cathedral to bury the dead. People fled to the countryside to escape the sickness. "El año pasado huvo en esta ciudad muy grande peste y murieron más de 2000 personas y pobres por falta de médicos aprobados." Most civil and church institutions offered to pay the salary of a trained doctor if one could be found. LC 15, AGCA, A1 1777 11.771, fol. 220 (Cabildo: 17 April 1648). See Molina, *Antigua Guatemala*, 44–45; Fuentes y Guzmán, *Obras históricas*, 1:173; and MacLeod, *Spanish Central America*, 99.

1650 Pestilence, Seville. The audiencia suggested that Spanish clothing imported through the port of Santo Tomás de Castilla be opened in the countryside and left for forty days and that shipments from Veracruz be stopped altogether. But cabildo members voted unanimously not to detain clothing or passengers from Veracruz since recent letters from that port failed to mention pestilence there; besides, they reasoned, shipments from Veracruz took four months to reach Santiago, and clothing parcels were usually opened in Veracruz when they were turned over to the muleteers for transport. LC 16, AGCA, A1 1778 11.772, fols. 92v–93 (Cabildo: 20 September 1650).

1650 Gucumatz and bubonic plague, Guatemalan highlands. MacLeod, *Spanish Central America*, 99.

1659–60 Locusts, volcanic eruptions, smallpox, measles, Santiago and environs. In response to high death rates experienced since October 1659, a general religious procession was proposed by the audiencia president and approved by the bishop and the city's cabildo. LC 17, AGCA, A1 1779 11.773, fols. 237v–38. Indian towns lost so many tributaries that they appealed to the audiencia to come to their aid. Audiencia a su Majestad (Santiago: 9 August 1660), AGI, Guatemala 20. Also see Molina, *Antigua Guatemala*, 106; MacLeod, *Spanish Central America*, 99; and Don Martín Carlos a su Majestad (Guatemala: 25 July 1660), AGI, Guatemala 20, fol. 1.

1665–66 Pestilence, Santiago and the Guatemalan highlands. The cabildo proposed a procession of supplication to appeal for an end to the sickness, which had caused many deaths. LC 18, AGCA, A1 1780 11.774, fols. 113 (Cabildo: 9 July 1666) and 124–24v (Cabildo: 9 October 1666). Also see Pardo, *Efemérides*, 73; *Historia Belemítica*, 281; and MacLeod, *Spanish Central America*, 99.

1669 Sickness and drought, Santiago. Maize fields were dry because the invierno, which usually arrived by mid-May, had yet to start. A procession was conducted with the image of Nuestra Señora del Socorro, described as the "queen of the heavens." LC 18, AGCA, A1 1780 11.774, fols. 228v–29 (Cabildo: 17 May 1669).

1686–87 Pestilence (typhus and/or pneumonic plague), Santiago and Central America. Many deaths were recorded in Santiago and numerous processions planned. The epidemic lasted into 1687, when the audiencia president reported that the Royal Hospital of Santiago had only 24 beds but needed 200 to care for the sick of all classes. The epidemic was so "violent" that after "two or three months they had buried more than a tenth of the rational living beings [age of communion and above] of the city and its barrios." Those that suffered most were "poor Spaniards, gente ordinaria, mestizos, mulattoes, and innumerable Indians." Francisco Vázquez, *Crónica de la Provincia del Santísimo Nombre de Jesús de Guatemala*, 4:388. See also MacLeod, *Spanish Central America*, 98; and LC 21, AGCA, A1 1783 11.777, fols. 192–92v (Cabildo: 17 January 1687).

1693–94 Smallpox, Santiago. Due to the rise of yet another smallpox epidemic, the city's cabildo proposed processions of supplication on 18 May 1696. Pardo, *Efemérides*, 118.

1699 Pestilence, Santiago. Molina, *Antigua Guatemala*, 172.

1703 Epidemics, Santa Lucía Monterroso, known today as Santa Lucía Milpas Altas, located due east of Santiago. Tributary deaths left the town's alcalde with a tribute debt of fifty tostones, which he paid off in 1711 by selling a piece of land to a Spaniard, Captain Manuel de Lira, for sixty tostones. AGCA, A1, leg. 1, exp. 60.

1704–5 Pestilence, Guatemalan highlands. MacLeod, *Spanish Central America*, 100.

1707 Sickness, Santiago. A rogativa was arranged to beseech Nuestra Señora del Socorro for aid. LC 25, AGCA, A1 1787 11.781, fol. 35 (Cabildo: 21 January 1707).

1708 Smallpox, Santiago and the Valley of Guatemala. A rogativa and a general procession were proposed in October. The previous January, rumor of an epidemic in the Barrio de San Sebastián swept the city. Manuel de Paredes, a master blacksmith who was reportedly trying to cure the sick, was ordered by the cabildo to desist, under pain of a 100-peso fine should he ignore the warning. LC 25, AGCA, A1 1787 11.781, fols. 59 (Cabildo: January 1708) and 81–81v (Cabildo: 5 October 1708).

1709 General epidemic, Indian towns of the Valley of Guatemala. Presidente Osorio a su Majestad (Santiago: 8 March 1709), AGI, Guatemala 221.

1710–12 Rabies, Santiago. Numerous rabid dogs were the cause of "a very pestilent odor" in April 1710. Apparently as part of their labor obligations, Indians were ordered to kill the rabid dogs and bury them outside the city. The problem persisted into 1712. The record shows cabildo discussions about how to kill the infected dogs. LC 25, AGCA, A1 1787 11.781, fols. 127–27v (Cabildo: 4 April 1710) and 197 (Cabildo: 22 January 1712). See also Pardo, *Efemérides*, 137.

1710–11 Massive depopulation, Indian towns near Santiago. An unknown chronicler noted more than twenty pueblos "almost totally wiped out," some "left with thirty persons and others with less than seven or eight persons so that now they do not deserve the name of pueblos but rather depopulated towns." *Isagoge*, 290–91.

1716 Sickness, Santiago and the towns of the Valley of Guatemala. Because these areas were "infected," the cabildo suggested that the appropriate saints intercede with the "divine majesty" to bring the sickness to a halt. Pardo, *Efemérides*, 143 (23 April 1716).

1723 Smallpox, Santiago. The cabildo minutes for 19 May 1723 note high mortality in the city and its surrounding barrios due to an outbreak of the "peste de viruela." See Pardo, *Efemérides*, 154; and MacLeod, *Spanish Central America*, 100.

1724 Locust plague and sickness, Santiago and environs. To free the city's inhabitants of the locust plague and sickness, the cabildo agreed on 23 May to hold a public rogativa before the image of the Jesús Nazareno in the Convent of La Merced. Pardo, *Efemérides*, 156.

1725 Smallpox, Santiago. Supplication before the image of Nuestra Señora del Socorro was ordered by the cabildo on 24 April to bring an end to the epidemic that struck the city. Pardo, *Efemérides*, 159.

1728 Measles, Santiago and environs. The cabildo ordered a religious procession on 6 April. Pardo, *Efemérides*, 165.

1733 Smallpox, Santiago and environs. A "peste de viruelas" was reported continuing in the city and its barrios on 19 June. The cabildo called on 9 July for a procession of penitents to bring an end to the epidemic. The alcalde of the Utatlecas of Jocotenango reported in September that "there was much sickness from smallpox and many tributaries had died" in his town. AGCA, A3 2819 40.916. See also Pardo, *Efemérides*, 175; and MacLeod, *Spanish Central America*, 100.

1741 Tabardillo, Santiago and environs. On 30 May the cabildo was asked to take measures to stop the spread of the "peste de tabardillo" and deaths from "pains in the side." Pardo, *Efemérides*, 189; and MacLeod, *Spanish Central America*, 100.

1746 Tabardillo and food shortages, Santiago and environs. This typhus epidemic was made more serious by grain shortages due to low July rainfall. The cabildo gloomily forecast on 9 September that with all of these troubles there was the "threat of one of the biggest calamities and plagues with which God wishes to punish us for being violators of His divine precepts." A procession with the image of Nuestra Señora de las Mercedes was called for on 11 September. Three days later the hacendados of the surrounding region were required to supply 100,000 fanegas of maize to the poor of the city and the towns of the Valley of Guatemala. LC 32, AGCA, A1 1794 11.788, fols. 138–41.

1748 Peste de sarampión, San Pedro de las Huertas (also known as San Pedro del Tesorero). Indians of this town due south of the city blamed the large number of deaths on their heavy labor repartimiento obligations. Those who had barely recovered were forced to take their turn working on Spanish agricultural lands, which resulted in their becoming sick again and, in some cases, dying. To take account of the population decline since the 1739 census, the audiencia ordered a new count on 27 July 1748. AGCA, A2 2828 41.110.

1749 Peste de calenturas (tabardillo or typhus), Santiago. The cabildo ordered on 7 January that measures be taken to stop the spread of "calenturas." Pardo, *Efemérides*, 202.

1752 Smallpox, Santiago and its barrios. After a month-long epidemic, a religious procession was ordered by the cabildo in early February. Pardo, *Efemérides*, 206.

1761 Smallpox, Santiago and environs. By 29 May it was noted that "sickness and general epidemic" had "spread generally through this city and its circumferential barrios, bringing death especially among the poor" due to a lack of food and medicine. Accordingly, 3,000 pesos were appropriated from alcabala funds to be distributed among the city's poor: 1,000 pesos each to the Sagrario and San Sebastián, 600 pesos to Los Remedios, 400 pesos to the Candelaria. On 9 June, in response to an order by the audiencia, the cabildo agreed to require doctors to visit the poor free of charge. Doctors and surgeons were assigned specific barrios; Santiago's four apothecaries were each granted fifty pesos to pay for medicine administered to the poor. On 17 July, the three apothecaries who had actually distributed medications were each given an additional fifty pesos to continue their work. AGCA, A1 2379 18.030 (1761), and LC 37, AGCA A1 1799 11.793, fols. 158v and 167v.

This epidemic also struck towns in the valley, including San Sebastián del Tejar, located north of the city and east of Chimaltenango. In September 1761 the Indians there sought, in the absence of an obligado, to slaughter cattle and set the price at seven pounds per real. Audiencia and cabildo alike approved the request, suggesting both recognized the importance of a good diet for the maintenance of good health and the recovery of those stricken by the epidemic. LC 37, AGCA A1 1799 11.793, fol. 182v.

1769 Measles, Santiago and environs. Santiago and the Valley of Guatemala were struck by a measles epidemic that began in April and lasted four months. A procession, supplication, and *novenario* (public worship), ordered to begin on 15 May, were dedicated to the cult of San Sebastián, the patron saint of the pestilence. On 6 June 1,500 pesos were set aside for the poor of the city's parishes. LC 45, AGCA, A1 1807 11.801, fols. 35v and 40v.

Writing in San Sebastián's burial register in July, when the epidemic finally ended, a cleric noted that 250 *criaturas* (infants) had died during the epidemic, in addition to 100 criaturas who had been clandestinely buried in various city churches. APSS, caja 4, lib. 9 (note found between burial entries for 25 July and 29 July 1769).

APPENDIX 6

CASE STUDY: THE LOSS OF A TRIBUTARY DUE TO RESIDENTIAL MOBILITY

IGNACIO Sánches, a native of San Antonio and cantor in the barrio's church, petitioned the audiencia in 1716 regarding the tributary status of his wife, Josepha de la Encarnación. Sánches noted in his complaint that his wife's parents were San Francisco natives who had left that barrio to live in San Antonio, where Encarnación was born. He pointed out that he and his wife had children and a house in San Antonio and that his wife worked there as a cloth dyer.

How could it be, Sánches asked the audiencia, that the justices of San Francisco threatened to carry him and his wife off to live in San Francisco when they had no reason and no place to live there? Since the Crown let Indians live where they found it most convenient, Sánches continued, it "should stop the extortion and order that my wife's name be removed from the padrón of the Barrio of San Francisco and put here on the padrón of San Antonio since the tributes are the same and all belong to His Majesty. In that way we may pay entirely in San Antonio while meeting our other obligations, which I must carry out as a native of our pueblo."

The petition went to the audiencia around 10 December 1716. The fiscal ruled that Encarnación should pay tribute to San Antonio, the barrio where she was married, the barrio where she lived, the barrio where her children would find it hardest to hide from Indian officials and avoid padrones, as registration in San Francisco might have encouraged. He thus insisted that Encarnación's name be removed from San Francisco's padrón and added to San Antonio's and that the justices of both barrios be notified of the change. The audiencia accepted the fiscal's opinion and on 17 December 1716 issued a supporting decree. AGCA, A1 6071 54.652.

APPENDIX 7

NABORÍA AND LABORÍO TRIBUTE COLLECTION

BEGINNING in the mid-1570s, Indians not attached to a particular tributary jurisdiction or listed on a tribute padrón were supposed to begin to pay a form of tribute or capitation tax, as were free blacks, free mulattoes, and *zambos* (persons of mixed Afro-Indian descent).[1] While one would hope that administrative records for this new tribute would help in determining the size of these groups, much as Crown tabulations of Indian tributaries helped in reconstructing the Indian demographic past, no naboría tribute padrones are known to exist and extant records on the collection of the tribute are scant.[2] The available data reveal more about the difficulty of collecting the tax than they provide in the way of demographic information.

Fiscal records from 1576 to 1581 demonstrate that the city's Indian, free black, and free mulatto inhabitants were elusive. A 1577 report defined the naborías as "the Indian naborías, free blacks, and mulattoes who served in the Spanish residences." (Please note that this text, to eliminate confusion, has heretofore used "naboría" to refer only to nontributary Indians.) "Not a thing has been collected" from them, the report continued, because they lack known residences and constantly "move from one place to another."[3] This was no exaggeration. Between 1576 and 1578 nearly all naborías appear to have avoided payment for a year or more. Not until 1579 were some twenty-five gold pesos deposited in the Royal Treasury in Guatemala against laborío tribute obligations for 1576; shortly thereafter sixteen more were collected as payment for 1578. The amounts collected apparently represented only a tiny portion of the annual tax, as suggested by reports that the naborías of the city of Guatemala owed more than eighty-two gold pesos for 1581.[4] The 1581 tribute figure would have been helpful in determining the size of the city's free black and free mulatto populations had Indian naboríos not been included in the count.

Santiago's naboría population seems to have grown rapidly in the late sixteenth century. In 1593 Corregidor Baltasar de Orena collected the equivalent of 529 tostones in tribute from the "blacks and mulattoes and Indian naborías of this city of Guatemala for the year of 1592." The total, nearly twice that for 1581, suggests that the city's naboría population nearly doubled in slightly more than a decade, assuming tribute collection was as unproductive in 1581 as it was in 1592.[5]

By 1603 free black and free mulatto males eighteen years old and over were assessed an annual tribute of four tostones, single women sixteen years and over two tostones; married and single men paid the same tribute, while married women were exempt. All Indian naboría males eighteen and over were subject to an annual tribute of one tostón and dependent naboría children were exempt. All naboría men and women were required to pay tribute annually until reaching the respective ages of sixty and fifty. In addition, every naboría tributary was to pay an additional tostón for "servicio del tostón." The audiencia edict that defined the above tribute payment schedule also specified that a new naboría tributary list be drawn up within three months and that subsequent lists be made every three years.[6] There is no evidence to suggest or deny enforcement of these rulings.

By the early 1680s the "naboría tribute" had become the "laborío tribute." Apparently collected only from free blacks and free mulattoes, it now amounted to twelve reales annually for single men, twenty reales for married men, and ten reales for single women. While the naboría tribute was collected by Spaniards during the sixteenth century and, it appears, most of the seventeenth century, the mulatto captains of the pardo militia companies in the city and surrounding valley took on the task in 1681. Allegations that they and their subordinates used excessive force in tribute collection prompted the Crown to return the job to Spaniards in 1682.[7]

ABBREVIATIONS

ARCHIVES cited in the notes have been assigned the following abbreviations:

AGCA	Archivo General de Centroamérica, Guatemala City
AGI	Archivo General de Indias, Seville
AHA	Archivo Histórico Arquidiocesano "Francisco de Paula García Peláez" (formerly the Archivo Eclesiástico de Guatemala, AEG), Guatemala City
AHA-SM	Archivo Histórico Arquidiocesano—Sección Mercedaria (formerly AEG-SM), Guatemala City
APC	Archivo de la Parroquia de la Candelaria, Guatemala City
APLR	Archivo de la Parroquia de los Remedios, Guatemala City
APS	Archivo de la Parroquia del Sagrario, Guatemala City
APSS	Archivo de la Parroquia de San Sebastián, Guatemala City

NOTES

CHAPTER ONE From Conquest to Emancipation

1. Murdo J. MacLeod, *Spanish Central America*, 39–41. Maya ethnolinguistic names follow spellings approved by the Academia de las Lenguas Mayas, Guatemala City, Guatemala.
2. W. George Lovell, *Conquest and Survival*, 59.
3. Lovell, *Conquest and Survival*, 59.
4. MacLeod, *Spanish Central America*, 39–41.
5. Whether the Aztec ruler died at Indian hands for his alleged cowardly and traitorous behavior, or was killed by the Spaniards, is unclear. As Miguel León-Portilla states, "No one knows for certain how Motecuhzoma died." *The Broken Spears*, 83 (quotation), 90. On Maya linguistic diversity, see Arturo Valdés Oliva, *Lenguas indígenas de Guatemala*.
6. Eric Wolf, *Sons of the Shaking Earth*, 84–86.
7. Robert M. Carmack, *The Quiché Mayas of Utatlán*, 143.
8. Adrián Recinos, Delia Goetz, and Dionisio José Chonay, eds., *The Annals of the Cakchiquels*, 96–100.
9. *Isagoge*, 180. See also Sandra Orellana, *The Tzutuhil Mayas*, 113.
10. Jorge F. Guillemín, *Iximché*, 11. For more on the founding of Iximché, see J. Antonio Villacorta C. and Carlos A. Villacorta, *Arqueología guatemalteca*, 99–114.
11. See Stephan F. de Borhegyi, "Settlement Patterns of the Guatemalan Highlands," 73–74, for a comparison of rural and urban highland settlements.
12. See Robert M. Carmack, *Quichean Civilization*, 377, for a list of Iximché's surrounding towns. For a valuable discussion of pre-Hispanic, colonial, and postindependence town and *municipio* (municipality) evolution, see W. George Lovell and William R. Swezey, "Indian Migration and Community Formation." Indispensable to an understanding of early encomiendas is Wendy J. Kramer, "Politics of Encomienda Distribution."
13. *Isagoge*, 180. Some think the 1,200 peso figure is too conservative.

See, for example, Hubert Howe Bancroft, *History of Central America,* 1:682, n. 10.

14. Recinos, Goetz, and Chonay, *Annals of the Cakchiquels,* 124. The indigenous residents of Iximché were not alone among the Kaqchikel in seeking refuge in the mountains. This response to invasion and repression has been a typical Mayan reaction in both the 1520s and the late twentieth century. See W. George Lovell, "Surviving Conquest."

15. Recinos, Goetz, and Chonay, *Annals of the Cakchiquels,* 124–29; MacLeod, *Spanish Central America,* 43; and Bancroft, *History of Central America,* 1:678–95.

16. Recinos, Goetz, and Chonay, *Annals of the Cakchiquels,* 125–27.

17. Santiago in Almolonga was located not in Almolonga (or Ciudad Vieja, as it came to be known), but on or near the site of the village of San Miguel Escobar. Janos de Szecsy, *Santiago en Almolonga,* 15–16.

18. *Libro viejo.* See also the account of Alvarado's brother, "Testimonio sobre cómo Jorge de Alvarado fundó la ciudad de Santiago [1 December 1584]," Archivo General de Indias (AGI), Patronato, leg. 77, no. 2, ramo 2, fols. 5v–6v.

19. *Libro viejo.* See also Dan Stanislawski, "The Origin and Spread of the Grid-Pattern Town" and its sequel, "Early Spanish Town Planning in the New World." In a letter of 4 January 1542, Captain Joan de Lobera suggests that Alvarado's house occupied the high part of the plaza, with the city above it to the south. Agustín Estrada Monroy, *Datos para la historia de la iglesia en Guatemala,* 1:93.

20. Estimates of the Spanish population are based on a 5 November 1529 count by members of the city's cabildo. Santiago, they reported, had 150 vecinos, half of whom were likely to be off on military campaign at any one time. *Libro viejo,* 104. For a complete discussion of naborías, see William L. Sherman, *Forced Native Labor,* 102–11.

21. Alvarado's "Mexican auxiliaries" were Mexican, Tlaxcaltecan, Cholutecan, Zapotecan, and Mixtecan Indians.

22. James Lockhart, *Spanish Peru, 1532–1560,* 136.

23. Marroquín a su Majestad (28 February 1542), in Carmelo Sáenz de Santa María, S.J., *Marroquín,* 183. Marroquín's remark, though it came early in the year following the destruction of Santiago in Almolonga, refers to life in Almolonga and Panchoy, to which the bishop and his flock had relocated.

24. Verle L. Annis, *Architecture of Antigua Guatemala,* 3–4. Annis convincingly dispels the myth that a lake atop Agua volcano washed away the tiny settlement when a wall in the crater burst. So, too, does Jan Van de Putte, in "Phénomènes séismiques et volcaniques au Guatemala." The credibility of both suffers because they incorrectly identify the location of Santiago in Almolonga (see n. 17 above).

25. Marroquín a su Majestad (20 February 1542), in Sáenz de Santa María, *Marroquín,* 175.

26. This area was also known as the Valley of the Tiangues or Tianguis.

27. J. Joaquín Pardo, *Efemérides,* 6.

28. See Christopher H. Lutz, *Historia sociodemográfica,* 55–58, for a description of these lands. A land-distribution system instituted in 1527 was abruptly abandoned a year later when the cabildo found that some Spanish

vecinos had too much property, others none at all. Under the new system, the valley was divided into *caballerías* (600 x 1,000 paces) and *peonías* (half a caballería). Each vecino was to receive some fertile land along the banks of the Magdalena River, as well as some *monte* (woodland) and sierra (river frontage was extended for parcels containing disproportionate amounts of sierra). Distributions were based on vecino standing in the community and *servicios* (contributions) to the conquest. *Libro viejo*. See also Ernesto Chinchilla Aguilar, *El primer reparto de tierras para labranza*.

29. Antonelli, it seems, did not reach America before the second half of the sixteenth century. Carmelo Sáenz de Santa María, "Estudio preliminar," in *Obras históricas*, 1:lx, n. 174. For a contradictory but unconvincing view, based on research by Robert S. Chamberlain in the Mexican national archives, see J. Joaquín Pardo, *Miscelánea histórica*, 15.

30. Francisco Antonio de Fuentes y Guzmán, *Obras históricas*, 1:154. Fuentes y Guzmán attributes these arguments to Antonelli.

31. Most assume "milpa" refers in the Guatemalan context only to maize plots. J. Eric S. Thompson, for one, mistakenly corrects chronicler Thomas Gage for using the term to describe "little petty towns." See Thomas Gage, *Travels*, 207, n. 15.

32. Fr. Antonio de Remesal, *Historia general*, 2:44.

33. The height of the valley floor ranges from 1,500 meters (4,921 feet) to 1,550 meters (5,085 feet) above sea level. The standard geographical reference for this and related data is Francis Gall, comp., *Diccionario geográfico de Guatemala*, 1:118–38.

34. Both active volcanoes, Acatenango and Fuego lie 3,962 meters (12,998 feet) and 3,837 meters (12,588 feet) above sea level, respectively. Gall, *Diccionario geográfico de Guatemala*, 1:6 and 2:129–31.

35. Fuentes y Guzmán, *Obras históricas*, 1:94.

36. The Valley of Jocotenango, like the Valley of Almolonga, is part of the larger Valley of Panchoy.

37. A fourth route, less used than the other three, entered the Valley of Panchoy from the southeast after climbing Agua's eastern slopes (near Palín or San Cristóbal Amatitlán) and descending through Santa María de Jesús and San Juan del Obispo. Gage, *Travels*, 181.

38. One can safely assume planning was finished no later than 18 November, when Santiago's cabildo ordered all vecinos to enclose the solares they had received at the new site by the Day of San Juan (24 June) 1542.

39. Remesal, *Historia general*, 2:45. Remesal infers that solares in Santiago in Almolonga may have been distributed without regard for the status of vecinos.

40. Remesal, *Historia general*, 2:45. The two lost volumes cover the years 1530–41 and 12 September 1541–53, respectively. Complete photostatic copies were last seen in Spain at the Exposición Hispano-Americana of 1893, where they were on public display. See *Diario de Centro América* 65/3469 (3 July 1893):1. Lawrence Feldman, personal communication (4 August 1987).

41. Annis, *Architecture of Antigua Guatemala*, 4. Although Antonelli's participation is questionable at best (see n. 29, above), his plan is analyzed here, both because it is commonly accepted and because it may have been the work of others.

42. Annis, *Architecture of Antigua Guatemala*, 4. Annis believes the original plan also included a broad avenue that ran north to south along the western edge of the formal traza. Another broad avenue was to delineate the northern edge of the traza, but it may have been blocked by urban expansion.

43. This was the sole remaining corner, as the traza's southwest corner had already been reserved for the hermitage of Santa Lucía, which was dedicated on 22 November 1542. Annis, *Architecture of Antigua Guatemala*, 93–94.

44. The solar opposite the northwest corner had apparently been taken by 1542, when Bishop Marroquín intervened on behalf of the Mercedarians, persuading the conquistador and vecino Alonso Alvarez to grant them his solares in Panchoy. Remesal, *Historia general*, 1:219; and Héctor Humberto Samayoa Guevara, "Historia del establecimiento de la orden mercedaria," 35.

45. Pardo, *Efemérides*, 7. All thirteen titles are to be found in the Archivo General de Centroamérica (AGCA), A3 2863 41.694. Solar records for the 1540s and early 1550s have not survived.

46. Sáenz de Santa María, *Marroquín*, 310. The first title in which Mexía's "traza nueva" is mentioned is dated 14 July 1558. AGCA, A3 2863 41.694.

47. "Título de María Alvarez . . . [11 August 1559]," AGCA, A3 2863 41.694. Both solares, held by Juan Alvarez until his death, were Mexía grants, though one came to María de Alvarez through Padre Sebastián de Morales.

48. AGCA, A1 2313 17.165, fol. 4v. How, when, and to whom these new solares were sold is unknown.

49. *Diccionario de la lengua española*, 531. See also François Chevalier, *Land and Society in Colonial Mexico*, 253ff., for a more detailed discussion of censos.

50. William L. Sherman, "Aspects of Change," 173.

51. MacLeod, *Spanish Central America*, 103. MacLeod's conclusions are impressively documented in Kramer, "Politics of Encomienda Distribution."

52. *Libro viejo*; and "Los indios que eran esclavos . . . [1576]," AGI, Guatemala 54. On Honduran mining, see Linda Newson, *The Cost of Conquest*, 112–13. For a case study of a Spanish entrepreneur's combined use of encomienda, Indian slaves, and gold mining to achieve wealth in the early decades after the conquest, see Wendy J. Kramer, W. George Lovell, and Christopher H. Lutz, "Fire in the Mountains."

53. AGCA, A1 6943 57.812, fols. 26–29v.

54. The milpa of Santa Catarina de Barahona is another case in point. The Indians there stated that they were (or were descended from) natives of Chamelco (probably San Juan Chamelco, in Verapaz), Utatlecas (Quiché), Atitlán (Tzutuhil), Chontales (Tabasco or Oaxaca), and Pipiles (Pacific coast of Guatemala). "Los indios que eran esclavos . . . [1576]," AGI, Guatemala 54, fol. 29v; see also fols. 14, 18v, 25, and 27.

55. Sherman, "Aspects of Change," 175.

56. Sherman, "Aspects of Change," 175.

57. The audiencia tried for more than two centuries to erode the authority and territorial jurisdiction of the alcaldes ordinarios over the Valley of Guatemala. It finally won the struggle around 1750, when the Crown created two new *alcaldías mayores* (districts), Chimaltenango and Sacatepéquez-

Amatitanes, thereby limiting the cabildo's authority to up to twelve miles from Santiago in some cases and to the very edge of the city in others. For the evolution of the conflict, see Ernesto Chinchilla Aguilar, *El ayuntamiento colonial*, 159-69.

58. Royal authority was especially weak from 1563 to 1570, when the audiencia was dissolved and Guatemala fell under the jurisdiction of New Spain. MacLeod, *Spanish Central America*, 85. After 1570 the audiencia tried repeatedly to limit the authority of the city's cabildo over the Valley of Guatemala. Chinchilla Aguilar, *El ayuntamiento colonial*, 163-65.

59. Cited in Sherman, "Aspects of Change," 176.

60. Sherman, *Forced Native Labor*, 12. Sherman continues: "This is not to say that the high ideals of Spanish legislation were fully realized; indeed, life for the Indians remained that of servitude to their white masters throughout the sixteenth century and beyond. Officials who followed Cerrato were not his equal in zeal and courage, and the social patterns of the conquest society took further root."

61. MacLeod, *Spanish Central America*, 114.

62. MacLeod, *Spanish Central America*, 120.

63. MacLeod, *Spanish Central America*, 119.

64. For the ongoing debate over the rise and decline of Indian slavery in Spanish Central America, see Sherman, *Forced Native Labor*, 70-82; MacLeod, *Spanish Central America*, 50-57 and 108-13; and Linda A. Newson, *Indian Survival in Colonial Nicaragua*, 102-6, and *Cost of Conquest*, 108-11, passim.

CHAPTER TWO **Spanish Settlement of the Indian**

1. "Parcialidad" has various meanings in Spanish Guatemala. Most often it refers to a pre-Hispanic Indian lineage that came to constitute a barrio or section of a particular town, but not around Santiago de Guatemala, where Indians were forcibly resettled irrespective of ethnic origin. Among the exceptions were Alvarado's Mexican auxiliaries, in Almolonga, and the Utatlecas (K'iche') and Guatimaltecas (Kaqchikel), in Jocotenango.

2. Domingo Juarros, *Compendio*, 2:223-24; and Antonio Batres Jáuregui, *La América Central*, 2:101.

3. The following sources were widely used in compiling this settlement list: "Autos . . . Jocotenango [1685]," AGI, Escribanía de Cámara 337B; "Los indios que eran esclavos . . . [1576]," AGI, Guatemala 54; Annis, *Architecture of Antigua Guatemala*, 221-22; Juarros, *Compendio*, 2:223-24; Batres Jáuregui, *La América Central*, 2:101; Fuentes y Guzmán, *Obras históricas*, 1:367 and 369; and Archivo Histórico Arquidiocesano—Sección Mercedaria (AHA-SM), leg. 1, exp. 5, fols. 1-2.

4. Remesal, *Historia general*, 1:262-71.

5. Although all were set free, all were required to fulfill certain labor obligations, including building *tiendas* (stores), the rents for which would variously go for the marriage of both conquistadores' daughters and *huérfanas* (female orphans), as well as to the poor of the city's hospital; raising wheat to support *capellanías* (chaplaincies); and constructing, in Santiago's cathedral, a chapel dedicated to San Pedro. See Remesal, *Historia general*,

1:262–71, for a fuller description of obligations. Records for the early 1580s (as listed in this chapter, pages 24–32) show that each of 156 Utatleca tributaries was also subject to an annual terrazgo of ten reales, a monetary levy first imposed around 1550 by the College of Santo Tomás, a Dominican institution. "Razón de las tasaciones . . . [1582]," AGI, Guatemala 10.

6. Alvarado's herd numbered 1,100 head of sheep in 1538; at his death the total had grown to 4,000 head. Whether all were cared for by the Indians of San Dionisio de los Pastores is unknown. William L. Sherman, "A Conqueror's Wealth," 209, n. 33, and 213.

7. Cuentas de 1582, AGI, Contaduría 968.

8. Identified as a separate parcialidad, the Sacatecas were for reasons of tribute collection joined with the Guatimaltecas, even though the Utatlecas' tribute was collected separately. "Autos . . . Jocotenango [1685]," AGI, Escribanía de Cámara 337B, fols. 571v–72v. For a careful recent study of the eastern Kaqchikel, see Barbara E. Jones Borg, "Ethnohistory of the Sacatepéquez Cakchiquel Maya."

9. "Los indios que eran esclavos . . . [1576]," AGI, Guatemala 54, fols. 6v and 27, shows the all-encompassing nature of "Guatimalteca."

10. Each of 276 Guatimaltecas (ca. 1582) was subject to a terrazgo of ten reales, an amount first levied around 1550 by the College of Santo Tomás. "Razón de las tasaciones . . . [1582]," AGI, Guatemala 10.

11. William L. Sherman, personal communication (7 January 1972). Sherman's figure, used in conjunction with the knowledge that each of fifty vecinos (roughly half the vecino total in 1549) owned slave *cuadrillas* (gangs), indicates that each cuadrilla consisted of between sixty and one hundred slaves—divided among the vecino's rural milpa, urban household and workshops, and mines.

12. Although Cerrato's success in emancipating virtually all of the valley's slaves aroused strong opposition in most quarters, the newly freed Indians got their strongest support from the regular clergy. See William L. Sherman, "Indian Slavery in Spanish Guatemala," 125–95 (esp. 175–81), for the views of Fr. Francisco Bustamante, probably a Franciscan. See also Bustamante a su Majestad (Santiago: 22 March 1551), AGI, Guatemala 168.

13. Many former slaves *did* leave their homes at emancipation, quitting the milpas for the city (or vice versa) or returning to their native towns, as may have been the case with Indian mine workers, most of whom had relatively weak ties to the valley.

14. While the Crown had ruled in the mid-1570s that Spaniards and Indians should be exempt from terrazgos, this royal cédula remained a dead letter for the inhabitants of the valley. AGCA, A1 1513, fol. 509; and J. Joaquín Pardo, *Prontuario*, 145.

15. Landecho a su Majestad (3 February 1563), AGI, Guatemala 9, in Sherman, *Forced Native Labor*, 92, 201.

16. These petitions, or "memorials," are presented in a bilingual Nahuatl-Spanish edition by Karen Dakin and Christopher H. Lutz, eds., *Nuestro pesar, nuestra aflicción*.

17. For mention of the imposition of tributary payment, see Audiencia a su Majestad (Santiago: 30 June 1560), AGI, Guatemala 9; see also Cuentas de 1567, AGI, Contaduría 967. In 1565, for example, a tributary from a terrazgo-

paying milpa or barrio was assessed six reales, one-half fanega maize, and one gallina de castilla, to which those exempted were required to add three reales.

18. The two exceptions are the milpas of San Cristóbal and Santa Lucía Monterroso (see list "Santiago's Other Settlements").

19. Juan Maldonado de Paz a su Majestad (23 May 1614), AGI, Guatemala 62. Interestingly, tributary assessors worked in halves but not thirds or sixths. Thus a count might be expressed as, say, "fifty-two and a half tributarios enteros plus one widow" or "twelve tributarios enteros plus two women married to men reserved from tribute." Chapter 3 describes such intricacies.

20. Tributary figures in this list of barrios are from "Razón de las tasaciones . . . [1582]," AGI, Guatemala 10; Cuentas de 1596, AGI, Contaduría 969; and "Relación del proceso . . . [Santiago: 13 May 1641]," AGI, Guatemala 70.

21. See "Los indios que eran esclavos . . . [1576]," AGI, Guatemala 54, fol. 16, for the Guatimaltecas' version of their resettlement north of the Dominican monastery.

22. The increased use of "Candelaria" for the Barrio de Santo Domingo in the eighteenth century may be attributable to the transformation of that community's hermitage into a parish church (Parish of Nuestra Señora de la Candelaria). Pedro de Cortés y Larraz, *Descripción geográfico-moral*, 1:28. However, Fuentes y Guzmán, *Obras históricas*, 3:311, refers to it as the Barrio de la Candelaria as early as the late seventeenth century.

23. The Franciscans and Mercedarians appear to have escaped the fury of Spanish vecinos in founding barrios near their monasteries, apparently because they were less aggressive than the Dominicans in recruiting the former slaves.

24. AGCA, A1 2297 16.846.

25. The first available data, for 1638, show forty-five tributaries in the Barrio de San Gerónimo.

26. The first available data, for 1638, show fifty tributaries in the Barrio de San Antonio.

27. The Barrio del Espíritu Santo came to include two small milpas in seventeenth-century Spanish counts of Indian tributaries: Santa Catalina and Santa María Magdalena Analco, both located to the west of the barrio. AGCA, A3 2724 39.046 (1652–71).

28. A dispute over ownership of the Barrio de Santa Cruz erupted between Don Juan and the Utatleca immigrants in 1550. Don Juan claimed that the land was his, both because the names of the Utatlecas were not on the bill of sale and because they had failed to reimburse him for the purchase price. He sought, moreover, to force them to pay tribute to him and treat him as their *señor* (lord). The Indians of the barrio argued that Don Juan had no rights to their land or services because he had been reimbursed. Cerrato found for the Utatlecas on 5 April 1552, freeing them of any obligations to Don Juan but ordering them to reimburse him more fully. AGCA, A1 2297 16.846, fols. 3–4v. For the precise location of the lands, see AGCA, A1 2297 16.846.

29. Tributary figures cited in this list are from "Razón de las tasaciones . . . [1582]," AGI, Guatemala 10; "Los indios que eran esclavos . . . [1576]," AGI, Guatemala 54; Cuentas de 1575, AGI, Contaduría 968; and "Relación del proceso . . . [Santiago: 13 May 1641]," AGI, Guatemala 70.

30. See Batres Jáuregui, *La América Central*, 2:100–101, esp. n. 9.

31. "Los indios que eran esclavos . . . [1576]," AGI, Guatemala 54, fol. 28. No colonial chronicle or national history, however, mentions Juan de Cháves's role in founding San Antonio.
32. "Los indios que eran esclavos . . . [1576]," AGI, Guatemala 54.
33. AGCA, A1 5959 52.228 (1704).
34. Pardo, *Efemérides*, 37.
35. Fuentes y Guzmán, *Obras históricas*, 3:311.
36. "Autos . . . Jocotenango [1685]," AGI, Escribanía de Cámara 337B, fols. 230v–31v; and AGCA, A1 5329 44.902.
37. Cuentas de 1575, AGI, Contaduría 968.
38. Cuentas de 1576, AGI, Contaduría 968.
39. Fuentes y Guzmán, *Obras históricas*, 2:327, was the first to state that Gascón de Guzmán founded the milpa. Juarros, *Compendio*, 2:223, and Batres Jáuregui, *La América Central*, 2:100, later perpetuated the error. AGCA, A1 6943 57.812, fols. 26–29v, proves all three were wrong.
40. Cuentas de 1575, AGI, Contaduría 968; and "Razón de las tasaciones . . . [1582]," AGI, Guatemala 10.
41. AGCA, A3 2798 40.473.
42. AGCA, A1 5936 51.921.
43. "Los indios que eran esclavos . . . [1576]," AGI, Guatemala 54, fols. 36–38.
44. Fuentes y Guzmán, *Obras históricas*, 2:328; and AGCA, A3 2863 41.694.
45. Szecsy, *Santiago en Almolonga*; quote from Fr. Francisco Vázquez, *Crónica* 4:34.
46. The first known tributary count was made in the late seventeenth century. AGCA, A3 824 15.207 (1684).
47. AGCA, A1 6943 57.812, fols. 26–29v; and "Razón de las tasaciones . . . [1582]," AGI, Guatemala 10.
48. A contract signed 18 September 1549 confirms Castellanos's role. Fuentes y Guzmán, *Obras históricas*, 1:110. See also AGCA, A1 1571 10.215, fols. 419–52 (1700).
49. The first available data, for 1638, show a tributary population of 153 in San Pedro del Tesorero.
50. John L. Phelan, *The Kingdom of Quito*, 48; and Magnus Mörner, *La corona española*, 11, and *Race Mixture*, 45–48. For a case study of racial segregation in sixteenth-century Puebla, New Spain, see Fausto Marín-Tamayo, *La división racial*.
51. For a discussion of Spanish turpitude, see Mörner, *La corona española*, 27–36.
52. Alonso López de Zorita, *Breve y sumaria relación*, 131. The church, of course, was to be the primary civilizing agent.
53. This seems doubtful, given Spanish resettlement practices. Principales from one region would probably have been suspicious of so-called principales from other regions, especially those who claimed their status had been conferred by parents. See "Los indios que eran esclavos . . . [1576]," AGI, Guatemala 54.
54. One important caveat is that barrio Indians *did* take common Spanish surnames. In Santo Domingo, for example, the name Cháves appears

repeatedly for over two centuries. See "Los indios que eran esclavos . . . [1576]," AGI, Guatemala 54; AGCA, A1 5368 45.403 (1672), fol. 7; AGCA, A1 5368 45.389 (1675); and AGCA A1 2975 (1770). For a discussion of Indian hereditary rulers in preconquest and Spanish Guatemala, see Carmack, *Quichean Civilization*, 50 and passim, and "La estratificación quicheana prehispánica."

55. This paragraph is based on "Los indios que eran esclavos . . . [1576]," AGI, Guatemala 54; AGCA, A1 4701 40.670; Cortés y Larraz, *Descripción geográfico-moral*, vol. 1; and Annis, *Architecture of Antigua Guatemala*. In New Spain (e.g., Puebla and Mexico City), it was not uncommon to see several Indian populations represented by a single Indian cabildo. See Mörner, *La corona española*, 55; and Charles Gibson, "Rotation of Alcaldes," 215–16 and passim.

56. For the maximum size of Indian cabildos, see Gibson, "Rotation of Alcaldes," 214.

57. Not until the seventeenth century, it seems, was Jocotenango represented by a gobernador. Of the Indian communities contiguous to Santiago, Jocotenango was alone in this respect (though Indian communities elsewhere were ruled by gobernadores). "Los indios que eran esclavos . . . [1576]," AGI, Guatemala 54; and "Autos . . . Jocotenango [1685]," AGI, Escribanía de Cámara 337B.

58. For the Mexican (Calhua Mexica-Tenochtitlán) origins of the Mexicanos of Santo Domingo, see AGCA, A1 5368 45.403 (1703); for the Tlaxcaltecan origins of the Mexicanos of San Francisco, see AGCA, A1 2297 16.846. Whether or not the Sacatecas of Jocotenango were represented on the cabildo of the Parcialidad de los Guatimaltecas de Jocotenango remains unclear. Presidente Don Enrique Enríquez a su Majestad (Santiago: 17 February 1685), AGI, Guatemala 29, suggests they were, at least until the 1680s. Moreover, Spanish efforts to ensure the political participation of all major Indian groups elsewhere in the New World are well documented. In Toluca, New Spain, for example, the Indian cabildo was composed of three alcaldes so speakers of the city's three language groups (Nahuatl, Otomí, Matlatzinca) would each have a voice. Gibson, "Rotation of Alcaldes," 215.

59. This case is based almost entirely on "Autos . . . Sto. Domingo . . . [1703]," AGCA, A1 5368 45.403.

60. While it is uncertain that the Mexicanos of San Francisco also held a dominant position in their barrio, some evidence points in that direction. In 1726 Bartolomé de la Cruz, alcalde of San Francisco's Mexicanos, complained to the audiencia of difficulties in tribute collection, on account of large numbers of Mexicano and Guatimalteca absentees. De la Cruz did not say he was alcalde of first vote, but tribute collection was generally the responsibility of that official. AGCA, A3 2818 40.888 (1726). By 1735 in San Francisco, one alcalde, a Mexicano, remained. The barrio's parcialidad of Guatimaltecas apparently had too few tributaries from which to choose an alcalde. AGCA, A3 2324 34.313 (1735).

61. AGCA, A1 5368 45.403. For a full discussion of the alternativa and its broader implications, see Phelan, *Kingdom of Quito*, 267–69.

62. The friar thought Ramírez undependable because his work took him from the barrio for extended periods. De los Reyes was probably no less

concerned that Ramírez's extra-barrio contacts would have a corrupting influence on his fellow Indians.

63. De los Reyes replaced a Guatimalteca nominee for regidor mayor with another Guatimalteca. The four regidor positions were thus evenly divided between Guatimaltecas and Mexicanos, as had long been the custom, with each parcialidad having one regidor mayor and one *regidor segundo* (second regidor). AGCA, A1 5368 45.403. Nothing is known of the parcialidad affiliation of either the original candidate for alguacil mayor or his replacement.

64. AGCA, A1 5368 45.403.

65. AGCA, A1 5368 45.403. For the distribution of Pipil in preconquest and Spanish Guatemala, see Sarah W. Miles, "The Sixteenth Century Pokom-Maya," fig. 1, and "Summary of the Preconquest Ethnology," 276–87; Carmack, *Quichean Civilization*, 128, 153, 198–99, 206, 327; MacLeod, *Spanish Central America*, 33–34; and William R. Fowler, Jr., *The Evolution of the Ancient Nahua Civilizations*, 51–56.

66. AGCA, A1 5368 45.403. Whether the folio was written in "Mexicana Pipil" has never been verified. Although the Mexicanos called the document a fake, their attorney shamelessly used it as proof that his clients had helped foster the religious life of the barrio.

67. "Los indios que eran esclavos... [1576]," AGI, Guatemala 54, fol. 4v.

68. "Los indios que eran esclavos... [1576]," AGI, Guatemala 54, fol. 4v and passim; "Cartas enviadas a su Majestad [de] varios pueblos de indios... [Seville: 28 April 1573]," AGI, Guatemala 54, fols. 8ff. (Nahuatl original) and 31 (Spanish); and Dakin and Lutz, *Nuestro pesar, nuestra aflicción*.

69. "Los indios que eran esclavos... [1576]," AGI, Guatemala 54; Cuentas de 1595, AGI, Contaduría 969; AGCA, A3 824 15.207 (1684); AGCA, A3 2813 40.779 (1703); AGCA, A3 1616 26.578 (1754); and AGCA, A3 951 17.732 (1763).

70. William L. Sherman, "Tlaxcalans in Post-Conquest Guatemala," 129–32.

71. Creoles were most apt to idealize the conquest in this manner. Severo Martínez Peláez, *La patria del criollo*, 51–56.

72. AGCA, A1 5368 45.403, fols. 19–26v. This tribute exemption was reconfirmed on 1 September 1639 during the presidency of Don Alvaro Quiñónez Osorio.

73. Documentary evidence backs him up. Though the Mexicanos of Almolonga were exempt from tribute, their compatriots in Santo Domingo were not. "Los indios que eran esclavos... [1576]," AGI, Guatemala 54; Cuentas de 1595, AGI, Contaduría 969; AGCA, A3 824 15.207 (1684); AGCA, A3 2813 40.779 (1703); AGCA, A3 1616 26.578 (1754); and AGCA, A3 951 17.732 (1763).

74. AGCA, A1 5368 45.403.

75. AGCA, A1 5368 45.403.

76. AGCA, A1 5368 45.403. The curas doctrineros of the Valley of Mexico enjoyed a similar veto power during the Spanish colonial period. Charles Gibson, *The Aztecs under Spanish Rule*, 179.

77. Indeed, this discussion is based on criminal cases, most of which are to be found in AGCA, A2.

78. Mörner, *La corona española*, 148–52. Spaniards, for example, were

commonly charged and fined for selling wine to Indians. AGI, Contaduría 967, esp. Cuentas de 1565.

79. For population estimates of Spanish, Indian, and casta (including blacks and nontributary Indians) groups in Santiago, see concluding sec., chap. 4, and app. 4.

80. For a useful discussion of the causes of crime in sixteenth-century England, many of which apply to the present case, see Joel Samaha, *Law and Order*, 36–37. For urban crime in colonial Latin America and sources for additional reading, see Gabriel Haslip-Viera, "The Underclass."

81. This apparent pattern is strikingly different from that of Elizabethan Essex, where social inferiors rarely committed crimes against the possessions or persons of their superiors. Samaha, *Law and Order*, 24. Perhaps high levels of social, economic, and racial inequality in Spanish Guatemala account for the difference.

82. For a brief discussion of the role of mulatto militias in Spanish America, see Frederick P. Bowser, "Colonial Spanish America." On all militias in seventeenth-century Central America, see Stephen Webre, "Compañías de milicia." On urban militias generally, see Christon I. Archer, "Military," 201–7.

83. "Lista general de la gente miliciana de españoles . . . [1707]," AGI, Guatemala 219, fol. 6v, shows, for example, that Diego de Porres, a well-known architect in the capital, was among the many castas listed on the roster of the Spanish infantry company in the Barrio de San Francisco. See also AGCA, A2 300 6767 (1712).

84. A 1677 audiencia proposal to give mulattoes and blacks a taste of judicial power (by naming to Santiago's cabildo a mulatto regidor who would serve as their governor) was unexplainably dropped. AGCA, A1 1521 10.076, fols. 77–77v.

85. Patrol duty, considered part of Indian public-works duties in the city, probably went unpaid. The body of criminal cases in Santiago (AGCA, A2) helps illuminate how these patrols functioned. See, for example, AGCA, A2 147 2738.

86. AGCA, A2 146 2689 (1761).

87. Much has been written in recent years about Indian rebellions in Mexico and elsewhere in Latin America. Among these works are Taylor, *Drinking, Homicide, and Rebellion*, and *Riot, Rebellion, and Revolution*; Anthony McFarlane, "Riot and Rebellion in Colonial Spanish America"; and Severo Martínez Peláez, *Motines de indios*. Recently, Murdo J. MacLeod, "Indian Riots and Rebellions," has engagingly suggested that the only full-fledged Indian uprising in Central America during the first two centuries of Spanish rule was the Tzeltal Revolt of 1712–13, in highland Chiapas.

CHAPTER THREE **The Fall of the Two Republics**

1. "Sambo" and "zambo," terms often used in Spanish America to describe those of African-Indian descent, were rarely used in Santiago and its comarca.

2. See chapter 6.

3. Pilar Sanchiz Ochoa, *Los hidalgos de Guatemala*, 68. The average

household in Santiago's Spanish core contained roughly fifteen to twenty individuals; black and mulatto slaves, however, seem to have been attached only to the largest households.

4. Numerous others, including free blacks, black slaves, and Indians, were among the new arrivals in the capital, and not all came voluntarily (slaves being the prime example). But it was the castas, themselves the product of mestizaje, who appear to have been most significant in furthering barrio mestizaje.

5. Parish marriage registers are perhaps the best source on migration to the city. See "Introduction" to the appendixes for a description of their accuracy and availability.

6. *Nueva recopilación de leyes*, 2:341 (lib. 6, tít. 8, ley 18).

7. Despite Sino-Spanish economic interdependence established in the Manila galleon trade (Chinese silks and other goods in exchange for Mexican silver), Spanish troops periodically massacred Manila's Chinese inhabitants during the seventeenth and eighteenth centuries. The Spaniards enjoyed the enthusiastic support of the Filipinos in this endeavor. John L. Phelan, *The Hispanization of the Philippines*.

8. Independent Indians are defined here as those who were unattached to Spaniards as domestic servants or apprentices, had escaped their tributary obligations, and were living outside their birthplaces (see chap. 4). The disparities in property values between the peripheral barrios and the Spanish core can be appreciated by comparing the censo on a *medio solar* (small house lot, generally for Indians) and house in the Barrio de la Merced with the censo held on two houses owned by a Spaniard, apparently located between the plaza mayor and the Convent of the Concepción. While the lessee of the former paid the Mercedarians an annual interest of 4 tostones, which at the standard rate of five percent represented a principal of 80 tostones, the lessee of the latter annually paid 103 tostones (80 to the cathedral, 23 to the Mercedarians) on a principal of some 2,060 tostones. Thus the annual interest on two Spanish-owned houses exceeded the total value of the solar and house in La Merced. Censo of Gerónimo de Cháves, indio ladino en Mexicana (2 January 1615, held by the Convent of La Merced), AHA-SM, fardo 1610; and AHA-SM, leg. 2, exp. 18 (23 September 1619).

9. For core settlement patterns, see the 1679 ecclesiastical census of the Sagrario Parish: "Libro del estado de las almas . . . ," Archivo de la Parroquia del Sagrario (APS), lib. 17.

10. This estimate is based on a 1679 cabildo edict ordering all persons within a five-block radius of the central plaza to replace their straw roofs with tile (if they had not yet done so) as a precaution against fire. Referring to this radius as the "boundaries of the city," the edict suggests that the high-priced, Spanish-populated core was seen as the city, the largely casta and Indian barrios beyond as its outlying slums, where no one could be expected to afford the cost of a tile roof. AGCA, A1 5551 48.044 (1679).

11. Ladinos were not similarly deterred. By the eighteenth century, they represented a large minority, if not a majority, in the barrio of the Tortuguero (not one of the city's original barrios), whose northern edge was three or four blocks south of the plaza mayor.

12. Gage, *Travels*, 186–87. This area near the Dominican convent ap-

pears to have retained its original name, Santo Domingo. The Indian settlement of that name came to be called Barrio de la Candelaria. The new name originated with the barrio's hermitage, Nuestra Señora de la Candelaria, which became Santiago's fourth parish church in the 1750s.

13. Even Jocotenango, a contiguous settlement that proved able to resist the casta invasion, suffered some of these pressures. See "Autos . . . Jocotenango [1685]," AGI, Escribanía de Cámara 337B; Libro de Cabildo (LC) 30, AGCA, A1 1792 11.786, fol. 155 (Cabildo: 1 October 1733); AGCA, A1 4559 38.890 (1764); AGCA, A1 100 2.155 (1775); and Auto del obispo Sr. Don Fr. Pedro Pardo de Figueroa (Santiago: 8 March 1738), "Libro . . . de los feligreses difuntos . . . de S. Sebastián de Goathemala [1758–70]," Archivo de la Parroquia de San Sebastián (APSS), caja 3, lib. 5.

14. See, for example, AGCA, A1 2361 17.829, esp. fol. 121; and AGCA, A3 2457 36.061.

15. These were actually devised to protect rural Indian communities from casta and Spanish penetration, then applied in the urban setting. Mörner, *La corona española*.

16. AGCA, A1 1 56. Mention of the sale to the oidor came fifteen to twenty days after the fact, when barrio officials contested the sale of another Indian solar to a free mulatto.

17. AGCA, A1 2245 16.190, fol. 159. The necessary license for the sale of property by an Indian was defined in lib. 6, tít. 1, ley 27 of *Nueva recopilación de leyes*, cited in AGCA, A1 5954 52.146 (1695).

18. AGCA, A1 2245 16.190, fol. 159 (1626). Throughout their petition to the audiencia, as this summary shows, the Indians of San Francisco hinted that any decline in their tributary numbers would result in a drop in Crown revenues. The message was not lost on Spanish officials, under pressure from home to maintain, if not increase, royal revenues.

19. AGCA, A1 2245 16.190, fol. 159 (1626).

20. Previously, "ladino" was most often used with "Indian" (as in "indio ladino") to describe Castilian-speaking or Hispanicized Indians; also see censo document cited in n. 8, this chapter. Precisely when "ladino" came to have a socioracial meaning is unclear, but as early as the 1690s Fuentes y Guzmán referred to mestizos, mulattoes, and blacks of Barrio de la Candelaria as "gente ladina." *Obras históricas*, 1:166. A century later the term referred to persons who were neither Spanish nor Indian. Today the term is used to describe all non-Indians, much to the chagrin of Guatemalans of "pure" European descent. Writings on the term include Arturo Taracena Arriola, "Contribución"; and Martínez Peláez, *La patria del criollo*.

21. Beginning in the second half of the sixteenth century, as nearby Indian communities proved unable to accommodate casta and Spanish penetration/mestizaje, numerous castas and poor Spaniards and a small number of wealthy Spaniards began settling in the underused lands to the west of the Barrio de la Candelaria (Santo Domingo). Established gradually and informally, the Barrio de San Sebastián saw the foundation of the city's second parish (same name) in the 1590s. The similar growth and spread of non-Indian populations on the southeast and northeast peripheries of the city led to the respective founding of Santiago's third and fourth parishes, Los Remedios (1641) and the Candelaria (1750). See chapter 4.

22. The president of the audiencia suspended the sale of the solar, at least temporarily, on 16 December 1682. AGCA, A1 6939 57.717.

23. AGCA, A1 6939 57.719.

24. Evidence that this requirement was satisfied appears as early as 9 July 1559 in a property transfer from Indian tributaries in La Merced to the Spaniard Hernando de Argueta Santizo. AHA-SM, leg. 1, exp. 29. This shows that the requirement, however ineffective, was on the books soon after the Indian barrios were founded. For further examples of the sale of Indian-owned solares to non-Indians, see AGCA, A1 1 56 (1711); AGCA, A1 4119 32.628 (1673); and AGCA, A1 94 2046 (1711).

25. AGCA, A1 5368 45.389 (1675).

26. For descriptions of these towns, see Fuentes y Guzmán, *Obras históricas*; Cortés y Larraz, *Descripción geográfico-moral*, 1:46–52 and 2:202–14; and Ernesto Chinchilla Aguilar, *Historia y tradiciones*. See also Feldman, "A Tumpline Economy," 125. For a classic article on flight and other types of Mayan population movement, see Nancy M. Farriss, "Nucleation versus Dispersal."

27. Economic pressure and mestizaje, hastened by the forced importation of black African slaves to work the sugar estates, resulted in the gradual decay of the town's Indian population from the mid-sixteenth century forward.

28. Little is known about the evolution of Indian dress from the pre-Hispanic period to present-day Guatemala. There is some indication, however, that designs were quite simple in the late eighteenth and early nineteenth centuries, and that the elaborate *huipiles* (blouses) and *camisas* (shirts) commonly worn today were of the sort worn previously by cofradía members only on church festival days. Douglas Madigan, personal communication (1972). If this is true, dress may have once been less of an identifier than it has been in this century. Valuable studies on Guatemalan Indian dress include two by Lilly de Jongh Osborne: *Indian Crafts of Guatemala and El Salvador* and *Guatemala Textiles*. More recent studies on indigenous textiles and dress do not address change in the colonial period, because documentation thereon is scarce to nonexistent. See Linda Asturias de Barrios, *Comalapa*, 7; and Hilda Delgado Pang, "Guatemalan Ethnographic Textiles," 91.

29. Murdo J. MacLeod, "Ethnic Relations and Indian Society," 189–214.

30. AGCA, A3 2809 40.698. Knowledge of Spanish appears to have been necessary for any Indian wishing to escape from a town into the ladino-Spanish culture that predominated in Guatemala's capital and in its large commercial and lowland agricultural export centers.

31. It is difficult to define "laborío" in late seventeenth- and eighteenth-century Guatemala. The term is probably derived from "naboría," used in the sixteenth century to describe Indians who were independent of any Indian jurisdiction and free of Indian tributary status but not the laborío tribute, which also came to be levied against free blacks and free mulattoes in the 1580s. By 1700, it appears, persons referred to as laboríos were (1) Indian tributaries who claimed laborío status based on military service and (2) the offspring of Indian women and either naboría, free mulatto, or free black fathers. In the latter case, young men often joined the militia on reaching adulthood to help secure laborío status. For tribute collection from

free blacks, free mulattoes, and Indian naborías, see AGCA, A1 2245 16.190, fol. 182v (1585); and AGCA, A1 4538, fol. 99ff. (1603).

32. For a discussion of the Indian's limited role in the militia companies of New Spain, see Christon I. Archer, "Pardos, Indians and the Army of New Spain," esp. 245–46. See also Webre, "Compañías de milicia," 519, 525. In this discussion of late seventeenth-century Central American militias, Webre notes how exceptional it was for the town of Chiapa de los Indios to have a militia company of Indian principales.

33. AGCA, A3 2809 40.698 (1686).

34. Table 2 shows that San Felipe's tributary population declined by 22 percent from 1684 to 1754 (from 180 to 141).

35. AGCA, A3 2821 40.987. At times Indians who married outside of their barrios lived in their spouses' towns and continued to pay tribute to home jurisdictions. See AGCA, A1 1562 10.206, fol. 7, for the 1658 case of an Indian from Santo Domingo who resided with his wife in her pueblo, San Miguel Petapa. Though the practice was rare, Indians were even granted permission to reside outside home barrios. In 1607 Sebastían López, of Santo Domingo de los Hortelanos, sought and got permission from the audiencia president to move to Santo Domingo de los Oficiales (artisans), where he already had a house and relatives. Permission was granted because the two communities were deemed part of the same tributary and ecclesiastical jurisdiction. AGCA, A1 2772 24.134.

36. AGCA, A3 2811 40.727. The Mercedarian cura also remarked on the difficulties priests encountered when crossing parish lines to administer the sacraments to stray parishioners.

37. Though a crucial section of the document verifying the boys' laborío status is badly damaged, audiencia receipts show that at least two of the three boys, Marcos and Juan, paid the laborío. According to La Merced's alcalde, however, all seven Monzón children were tributaries. See AGCA, A1 1523, fols. 210v–11.

38. The padrón reflects two major points. First, that the fiscal of the audiencia, citing precedent, judged that Indian tributaries who wished to change their place of residence should not be impeded by any civil or ecclesiastical official, except when placed in *reducciones de indios* (centers of concentrated or "reduced" Indian population) or when such a move was prejudicial to the interests of an encomendero. *Nueva recopilación de leyes*, 2:192 (lib. 6, tít. 1, ley 12). See also AGCA, A3 2811 40.727. Second, that whether absent or present, all able-bodied tributaries must aid in the burdens and communal services of their barrio and doctrina, since it was unjust that all these obligations fall on those present. Listing ausentes along with the barrios in which they were living, the fiscal hoped, would help barrio officials locate them and exact their tribute and labor. AGCA, A3 2811 40.727.

39. AGCA, A3 2811 40.727.

40. Dated 6 April 1682, the decision was inscribed in a marginal note in a previous padrón, which, though now lost, was probably conducted that year. AGCA, A3 2811 40.727.

41. AGCA, A3 2811 40.727.

42. *Nueva recopilación de leyes*, lib. 6, tít. 5, ley 8.

43. *Nueva recopilación de leyes*, lib. 7, tít. 5, ley 1.
44. AGCA, A3 2811 40.727.
45. For details on laborío tribute collection, see AGCA, A1 4588, fol. 99 (1603). See also appendix 7.
46. Whether the audiencia had the last word in this decision is unknown. AGCA, A3 2811 40.727.
47. AGCA, A1 1523, fols. 208-10v.
48. Commonly cited by barrio officials and others desperate to meet Crown tribute and labor quotas, the law of the belly afforded a simple way to determine lineage and hence identify tribute payers.
49. AGCA, A3 2812 40.737.
50. Interestingly, Catalina was born illegitimate. She was thus unentitled to status as the legal granddaughter of Juana María de Cárdenas until her parents married some time after her birth. That Catalina's legitimacy was certified by the parish priest on 15 November 1696 suggests that Juan de Cárdenas was then beginning to mount a legal defense. AGCA, A3 2812 40.737. Juana María de Cárdenas was the natural daughter of the Spanish captain Don Juan Cárdenas Mazariegos and María Hernández, an Indian from the pueblo of San Lucas Sacatepéquez. Juana's change of name and connection with a Spanish family clearly helped sway the authorities in Catalina's favor.
51. Mendoza's parents evidently placed her in Súñiga's home in return for a fee. AGCA notarial registers, especially for the period between roughly 1580 and 1650, contain numerous examples of this practice. Mendoza states in her petition that she left home after being confirmed in the church. AGCA, A3 2812 40.734. This suggests she began her servitude around the age of seven. On Indian contract labor in the late sixteenth century, see Sherman, *Forced Native Labor*, 210–12.
52. The record does not show precisely how the petition was decided or why the audiencia would have allowed Indian officials to list a naboría like Mendoza on their tributary padrón, given the crucial nature of the distinction in the Monzón case.
53. Her only possible escape from naboría status was to attain reserved age (fifty).
54. Audiencia a su Majestad (Santiago: 21 August 1664), AGI, Guatemala 21. The audiencia's description is confirmed by an examination of registers of the Parish of Los Remedios (Archivo de la Parroquia de los Remedios or APLR).
55. The Barrio de Santa Cruz had between twenty-seven and twenty-nine tributarios enteros from 1596 to 1684, but only six married Indian tributaries in 1758, by which time women had been exempted from tribute payment. Of the six, one was married to an Indian woman (whose male offspring alone would become tributaries) and the remaining five were married to ladino women (whose children would not become tributaries). See Cuentas de 1596, AGI, Contaduría 969; "Relación del proceso . . . [ca. 1638]," AGI, Guatemala 70; AGCA, A3 824 15.207 (1684); and AGCA, A3 2327 34.340, fols. 4-4v (1758).
56. AGCA, A1 2364 17.879. Other documents demonstrating the large

number of castas in Chipilapa include Cuentas de 1685, AGCA, A1 2219 15.915, fol. 4; Cuentas de 1686, AGCA, A1 2219 15.915, fols. 16–17; AGCA, A1 2348 (1718); and AGCA, A1 2449 18.842 (1736).

57. AGCA, A1 2364 17.879. The source is unclear about whether or not the alley was closed.

58. AGCA, A1 2297 16.846.

59. For details of the decline of San Francisco's Indian population, see "San Francisco: A Case Study," in this chapter.

60. Fuentes y Guzmán, *Obras históricas*, 1:166. Regarding change of the barrio's name from Santo Domingo to Candelaria, see the list "The Republic of Indians: Barrios Founded ca. 1550" in chapter 2, pages 24–26.

61. For evidence of residential pressures on Jocotenango, see n. 13 above. The combined parcialidades of Jocotenango included over 1,000 tributaries between roughly 1680 and 1755. See AGCA, A3 824 15.207 (1684); and AGCA, A3 1616 26.578 (1754).

62. AGCA, A1 4019 30.956. An inventory of land rent documents for the Royal University of San Carlos reveals that in 1680 seventy-three terrazgos were held by ladinos in the Candelaria, San Sebastián, San Felipe, Jocotenango, San Antonio, San Gerónimo, and the Espíritu Santo. AGCA, A1 1965 13.346, item 39. One can gain an impression of the density of the barrios' casta (especially mulatto) population by examining criminal records, such as AGCA A2 144 2636, a case involving the murder of an Indian regidor of the Barrio de Santiago by a mulatto vecino from San Gerónimo. For evidence of numerous pardos or mulattoes having lived west of the Barrio de Santiago around the hermitage called El Chajón in the late 1760s, see AGCA, A2 148 2775. An examination of some ninety censo contracts held here by the Mercedarians suggests Spaniards and castas began penetrating these barrios before 1600. AHA-SM, legs. 1–2; and AHA-SM, fardos 1610, 1620, and 1630.

63. Members of the Berkeley School concentrated their early studies on central Mexico, both the core of the Aztec-Tenochca tribute empire and the Spanish viceroyalty of New Spain, which gave them the benefit of a long run of tributary (and tributary-related) records extending from the late Aztec period through the Spanish colonial period. See Sherburne F. Cook and Woodrow Borah, *Essays in Population History*, 1:1–72.

64. See MacLeod, *Spanish Central America*. As for the researchers who followed MacLeod, see Lovell, *Conquest and Survival*, which summarizes and cites much of the recent work by Lovell, Lutz, William R. Swezey, Elías Zamora Acosta, Thomas T. Veblen, and Robert M. Carmack. Also see Newson, *Cost of Conquest* and *Indian Survival in Colonial Nicaragua*.

65. "Las tasaciones . . . [1549]," AGI, Guatemala 128. This document details the kinds and amounts of tribute paid, encomenderos, personal service, and personal-service reforms that Cerrato instituted to relieve the Indian pueblos of many of their labor obligations to the encomenderos. It shows that tribute payments were reduced in some cases but gives no hint of severe population decline. For the tribute assessments from over forty other Indian towns, see AGCA, A3 2797 40.466 (1553). See also W. George Lovell, Christopher H. Lutz, and William R. Swezey, "The Indian Population of

Southern Guatemala." For fragments and analysis of earlier tribute assessments, see Wendy J. Kramer, W. George Lovell, and Christopher H. Lutz, "Las tasaciones de tributos."

66. "Razón de las tasaciones . . . [1582]," AGI, Guatemala 10.

67. Sherman, "Tlaxcalans in Post-Conquest Guatemala." While most or all of these Indian allies appear by the mid-eighteenth century to have lost their sixteenth-century appeals for tribute exemption, the Tlaxcaltecas (and probably the Mexicanos and Guatimaltecas as well) were at least exempted from their maize tribute, one fanega per tributary. The Indians of Ciudad Vieja, however, continued to pay a *servicio del tostón* (one-half silver peso, assessed against each full tributary) and one-half *almúd* (1/24 fanega) of maize per tributary for the defense of Granada, Nicaragua. AGCA, A3 2839 41.335. By the 1580s the Mixtecas of San Gaspar Vivar and the Mexicanos of both San Francisco (actually Tlaxcaltecas in the case of this barrio) and Santo Domingo were paying full tribute to the Crown. While the Mixtecas seem to have disappeared from tributary records, having died or melted into the surviving Mayan population, the Mexicanos of San Francisco and Santo Domingo continued to pay tribute in the mid-eighteenth century. See "Razón de las tasaciones . . . [1582]," AGI, Guatemala 10; "Los indios que eran esclavos . . . [1576]," AGI, Guatemala 54; Cuentas de 1595, AGI, Contaduría 969; and AGCA, A3 951 17.732 (1754).

68. Cabildo a Carlos V (Santiago: 15 September 1549), AGI, Guatemala 41, in Sherman, "Indian Slavery in Spanish Guatemala," 185.

69. The 1560 population figures presented in table 1, for example, apparently include all of the milpas of slaves freed a decade earlier, as well as the Indian allies from New Spain. In any case, the rough estimate of 5,000–6,000 married Indians is confirmed by Audiencia al Rey (Santiago: 30 June 1560), AGI, Guatemala 9. In 1571–72 Licenciado Valdés de Cárcamo arrived at a figure of 4,025 tributaries: 3,949 males and 76 widows. Valdés, according to numerous Indian complaints and later audiencia correspondence, counted persons under and over tributary age (younger than sixteen, older than fifty for women, fifty-five for men) as well as sick persons who should have been given reserved status. Valdés's count is thus grossly inflated and does not represent a population upswing. See "Los indios que eran esclavos . . . [1576]" and "Cartas enviadas a su Majestad [de] varios pueblos de indios . . . [Seville: 28 April 1573]," both AGI, Guatemala 54, for Indian complaints about Valdés's tasaciones. See Audiencia al Rey (Santiago: 13 September 1574), AGI, Guatemala 10, for Valdés's tributary totals and criticisms of them. See also Christopher H. Lutz, "Introducción histórica." The 1574 figure is among the most accurate early counts of the tributaries of the valley of the city. The population increase over 1567 levels suggests that the 1574 figure included the Indian allies from New Spain who had sought exemption from tribute payment but lost their appeal. Audiencia al Rey (Santiago: 13 September 1574), AGI, Guatemala 10.

70. Audiencia al Rey (Santiago: 30 June 1560), AGI, Guatemala 9; Audiencia al Rey (Santiago: 7 February 1561), AGI, Guatemala 9; and Audiencia al Rey (Santiago: 6 September 1571), AGI, Guatemala 9.

71. "Cartas enviadas a su Majestad [de] varios pueblos de indios . . .

[Seville: 28 April 1573]," AGI, Guatemala 54; and "Los indios que eran esclavos . . . [1576]," AGI, Guatemala 54.

72. For the pressures applied by the Spanish on Indian communities according to their relative proximity to Spanish population centers, see Christopher H. Lutz and W. George Lovell, "Core and Periphery in Colonial Guatemala"; and Lutz, "Introducción histórica."

73. E. A. Wrigley develops this idea in the pre–Industrial Revolution context in *Population and History*, 95–96. The late 1570s were a period of widespread epidemics and death for both Mexico and Guatemala. For a report of the *viruelas* (smallpox) epidemic of 1576–77, which hit children especially hard, see El obispo al Rey (Santiago: 25 February 1577), AGI, Guatemala 156; and Fiscal Lic. Eugenio de Salazar al Rey (Santiago: 13 March 1577), AGI, Guatemala 10. The dean of the Cathedral of Guatemala, Pedro de Lievana, noted during his tenure in Santiago that three or four pestilences in Mexico had also struck Guatemala, causing a sharp decline in population. "Información . . . [8 November 1582]," AGI, Guatemala 114. See appendix 5 and W. George Lovell, "Disease and Depopulation in Early Colonial Guatemala."

74. For the great pandemic, see MacLeod, *Spanish Central America*, 98. La Merced went from forty-five to fifty-one and a half tributarios enteros, San Francisco from eighty-nine and a half to ninety-two and a half, between 1581 and 1596. Cuentas de 1596, AGI, Contaduría 969. See table 3 for the even greater fall in the city's tributary population by the 1750s.

75. It is a tricky business, when data are scattered, to estimate when a population has reached its nadir. For one thing, the observer of such phenomena must take into account the gap between the time when a given population begins to grow (when annual births outnumber deaths) and the time when that growth results in increased numbers of tributaries (when the newborn reach the age of majority). Hence the fragmentary 1596 data (see previous note) indicate the start of population recovery some nineteen years after the 1576–77 epidemic. On the relationship between nadir and recovery, see Christopher H. Lutz, "Population History of the Parish of San Miguel Dueñas," 121–35.

76. Cuentas de 1596, AGI, Contaduría 969. For a discussion of the use of tribute counts (goods and cash required for payment) as one method of determining Indian tributary population size when actual counts are unavailable, see Cook and Borah, *Essays in Population History*, 1:19ff.

77. Epidemics of varying intensity struck the city and region in 1585 (Quezaltenango), 1592–93, 1607–8, 1614, 1623, and 1632. MacLeod, *Spanish Central America*, 99. See also appendix 5.

78. "Exogamy" as used here applies to both church-sanctioned and informal unions.

79. San Gaspar Vivar is added to the list of rural milpas in the tributary totals of 1638, 1684, and 1754. The Mixtecas lived there in the 1570s and 1580s (as well as earlier) but later disappeared.

80. See "San Francisco: A Case Study," in this chapter, for a study of population decline in the Barrio of San Francisco. A serious epidemic struck Santiago and its *comarca* (district or region) in 1647, killing more than 2,000 persons that year alone. Audiencia a su Majestad (Santiago: 21 June 1647),

AGI, Guatemala 16; and LC 15 (Cabildo: 17 April 1648), AGCA, A1 1777 11.771, fol. 220.

81. For a discussion of economic roles played by the Indians of this town, see chapter 6.

82. From the late sixteenth century onward, Santo Domingo's tributary size remained at least twice that of San Francisco, the second biggest Indian barrio in the city. Santo Domingo de los Hortelanos, while forming part of the peripheral ring of barrios around Santiago's Spanish core, appears to have been less urbanized than the others. This may have changed in the late seventeenth and eighteenth centuries, however, as free castas occupied solares along the three main routes to and from the city, one of which, Las Animas, made Santo Domingo de los Hortelanos a hub of activity.

83. "Razón de las tasaciones . . . [1582]," AGI, Guatemala 10. The document is dated 1582, but the data appear to be from 1581. The Franciscans reported around 1575 that they administered to 225 Indians (ages thirteen to fourteen and above) in the Barrio de San Francisco. "Memoria de la visita . . . ," AGI, Guatemala 169. On the *peste* (epidemic) of the late 1570s, see Lovell, "Disease and Depopulation."

84. Cuentas de 1595, AGI, Contaduría 969.

85. The Guatimaltecas numbered thirty-three tributaries, the Mexicanos fifty-six. "Relación del proceso . . . [Santiago: 13 May 1641]," AGI, Guatemala 70.

86. AGCA, A1 2245 16.190, fol. 159.

87. "Criminal, año de 1664, contra José de Salvatierra y Juan de Vilches indios alcalde y escribano del barrio de San Francisco, por haber empadronado las Mulatas y Mestizas de su propia autoridad," AGCA, A2 137 2471.

88. AGCA, A3 824 15.207. Fuentes y Guzmán writes (ca. 1690) that "the number of parishioners is 67 tributarios," a number not inconsistent with the 1684 count of fifty-one and a half tributarios enteros. *Obras históricas*, 1:358.

89. "Relación del proceso . . . [Santiago: 13 May 1641]," AGI, Guatemala 70.

90. AGCA, A1 5954 52.146.

91. The Indians sought permission from the audiencia to use 120 pesos of a terrazgo that the barrio held on the house of a Spanish vecino of the city, reasoning that the annual interest on the terrazgo (six pesos, or 5 percent of the principal) was insufficient for the planned repairs. They also asked the audiencia to rebate a quarter of their tributes, probably for a period of three years, to help defray construction costs, as Crown law specified for projects deemed to be in the public good. The audiencia decided the people of San Francisco should rebuild their cabildo from the interest on the 120 peso principal, not the principal itself, despite an estimate of 400 pesos for the job by the city's alcalde ordinario and chief master carpenter. Taking into account the cost of materials and labor (mason, carpenter, and Indian workers), the estimate appears to have ignored the Indians' claim that they themselves would provide the necessary labor. AGCA, A1 151 2959 (1716).

92. Tomás de Arana, *Relación de los estragos y ruinas*.

93. AGCA, A1 2816 40.856.

94. This conclusion is based on a complete survey of all marriage entries in the extant marriage registers of Santiago de Guatemala's four

parishes from the late sixteenth century until the 1770s. See chapters 4–5 and appendix 1.

95. Mixco, a Pokomam-speaking town east of Santiago, shows a similar pattern. A brief survey of a mid-eighteenth-century population census shows that of the vecinos of Mixco who married outsiders, 63 percent wed residents of either the Pokomam-speaking town of Santa Cruz Chinautla or the Pokomam-speaking Parish of Petapa. AGCA, A3 948 17.700 (1756); and Cortés y Larraz, *Descripción geográfico-moral*, 1:48. On Indian town intermarriage and migration, see Lawrence H. Feldman, Robert E. Brown, and Susan Garzon, "Alien Spouses in Eighteenth Century Guatemala."

96. It is unclear whether the two women who paid the laborío were either direct descendants of Indian naborías or the offspring of mulatto-Indian unions.

97. This system of counting tributarios enteros, described briefly in the text preceding the lists "The Republic of Indians, Barrios Founded ca. 1550" and "Santiago's Other Settlements," displayed a new feature in the seventeenth-century: male and female tributaries who lived outside their home barrios were assigned respective values of one-half and one-third a tributario entero. Using the 1716 count of Guatimaltecas as a model (with prorated tributario entero values in parentheses), the parcialidad contained 1 casado tributario entero (1); 3 men (1-1/2) and 3 women (1) married to Indians in other communities; 2 men (1) and 1 woman (1/3) married to mestizos; 1 woman (1/3) married to a mulatto; 2 men (1) married to laborías; 5 unmarried women (1-2/3); and 1 single man (1/2). The total of 8 1/3 tributarios enteros would have been entered on the padrón as "8 tributarios enteros plus one unmarried woman," since thirds were never included as parts of tributario entero totals.

98. One of the three women, a twenty-year-old married to either a mulatto or black slave, was not counted as a tributary because, having left the city with her husband, she was deemed an ausente. AGCA, A3 1252 21.698.

99. AGCA, A3 1252 21.698.

100. The children of tributary mothers and naborío, free mulatto, or free black fathers were subject to the laborío and hence generally freed from Indian tributary status; the children of tributary mothers and mestizo fathers were generally exempt from tributary status of any kind. "Generally" is the key word here, for barrio leaders sometimes succeeded in applying the law of the belly to those who should have been exempted from it.

101. Similarities in inscription procedures did not of course mean that the children of all such unions enjoyed the same status. See note 100 above.

102. The thirty-year-old was unlikely to marry since she suffered from an enlarged neck, most likely from a thyroid condition, a common health problem in colonial Guatemala and later periods as well.

103. Though they were *potential* mothers, the single women were unlikely to help in the regeneration of San Francisco, not only because they then lacked partners, but because many were beyond the age of formal marriage.

104. AGCA, A3 2818 40.888.

105. Six of the seven women can be identified from the tributary list of 1716. Of those six who died between 1716 and 1726, five were listed as un-

married in 1716; the other was married to an Indian laborío. AGCA, A3 2818 40.888.

106. AGCA, A3 2818 40.888.

107. To retire his tributary debt, Rodríguez was required to pay forty tostones and two and two-thirds reales to the Royal Treasury. The payment amounted to one year's tribute multiplied by sixteen, the difference between his age in 1724 (thirty-nine) and the age of tributary exemption (fifty-five). AGCA, A3 2887 42.267.

108. The 1735 tasación was conducted at the request of the barrio's alcalde, Manuel de la Trinidad. Though many barrio tributaries had died, Trinidad told the audiencia, they remained on the tasación "as if they were alive," obligating past alcaldes to pay their debts. While Indians usually assumed at least a portion of census expenses, the 1735 tasación cost the barrio nothing. Among the three sworn witnesses chosen to aid in the new tributary count was Blas Rodríguez. AGCA, A3 2324 34.313.

109. AGCA, A3 2324 34.313.
110. AGCA, A3 2324 34.313.
111. AGCA, A3 2324 34.313.

112. For a discussion of age pyramids and the age structure of populations, see Wrigley, *Population and History*, 23–26.

113. Records for the parish of San Juan del Obispo show that San Francisco contained just four and a half tributarios enteros in 1754, shortly after Indian women had been exempted from tributary status. AGCA, A3 1616 26.578. Women have been added to this total to make the 1754 figure comparable with earlier population counts. Hence the number of tributarios enteros in the barrio has been put at seven and a half.

114. By comparison, the largest of the city's Indian barrios, Santo Domingo (Candelaria), was reported to contain forty-one Indian schoolboys that year. AGCA, A1 2642 22.029.

CHAPTER FOUR Casta Origins and Growth

1. There can be little doubt that Santiago's Spanish population evolved as much as any other group in the history of the city. The volume of material testifying to that fact far exceeds such documentation for all other socioracial groups combined. This study, however, focuses on the nonelites.

2. See table 7.
3. See table 10.

4. Candelaria records, most specific as to socioracial group in this census, distinguish between Indians and ladinos. Cortés y Larraz, *Descripción geográfico-moral*, 1:28.

5. Juarros, *Compendio*, 1:147.

6. Before becoming a parish, San Sebastián had the status of an *hermita* (hermitage). After the city was struck by severe tremors in 1565, the cabildo, with the destruction of Santiago in Almolonga fresh in its mind, decided to make San Sebastián "Protector of Santiago de Guatemala" and to build the first hermita to him that year. Located north of the city, high up on the slopes of the Cerro (hill) de San Felipe (also known as Cerro del Manchén), the hermita was abandoned because getting there proved so difficult.

The new hermita was built northwest of the convent of La Merced and opened to the public in 1582. Juarros, *Compendio*, 1:147. The neighborhood around the new church came to be known as the Barrio of San Sebastián. The barrio and parish were not coterminous; parish boundaries far exceeded those of the barrio.

7. The Crown ordered the creation of the Parish of Nuestra Señora de los Remedios by elevating the hermita of that name to parish status on 29 May 1594. Pardo, *Prontuario*, 118; and AGCA, A1 1513, fol. 750. The creation of Los Remedios is put at 1641 because the earliest parish register, listing baptisms of gente ordinaria, is dated May 1641. Iglesia del Calvario, Guatemala, APLR.

8. See the first baptismal register, Parroquia de la Candelaria, Guatemala, APC.

9. Richard Konetzke, "Documentos."

10. Konetzke, "Documentos." The archbishop's statement that parish registers were not used in the courts as proof of racial status appears open to question. Since racial identification often determined an individual's social and tribute-paying status, such data would have been essential in legal disputes over ancestry. See the case of Gregoria de Mendoza, cited in this study.

11. Konetzke, "Documentos." Konetzke's other informes were from the archbishops of Cuba and Caracas. The Mexican prelate's remarks are cited here because Guatemala abuts Mexico and the two have similar social structures and institutions as a result.

12. Accuracy in registration is a comparatively recent urge. In France, for example, historical demographers have found that "registration is only really good after 1740." In England Anglican registers are similarly incomplete after the late eighteenth century, due less to poor administration than to an increase in religious sects. T. H. Hollingsworth, *Historical Demography*, 185. Comparing French and English registers with those in Spanish America is still uncommon: the latter are only beginning to be explored. A recent exception is Patricia Seed, *To Love, Honor, and Obey in Colonial Mexico*, 227–41. Seed compares Mexican and West European marriage patterns, questioning the conclusions of previous scholars of European family history that do not apply to all periods in Mexico or even Spain.

13. Parish registers, judging from folio notations, were regularly inspected by episcopal and archiepiscopal authorities. Also enhancing accuracy was the fact that the city's parishes remained compact, urban jurisdictions until 1757. Outlying Indian towns were then added to San Sebastián, Los Remedios, and the Candelaria as a result of Bourbon reforms, which sought to secularize parish (and barrio) administration to limit the power of the religious orders. Prior to the creation of Los Remedios Parish, for example, marriages performed in its hermita were recorded in the Sagrario's registers. Likewise, services performed in private chapels or convents were recorded in the registers of the parish in which each was located. See Cortés y Larraz, *Descripción geográfico-moral*, 1:32, for a date and brief description of Bourbon reforms. For details of which towns were added to which parishes, see AGCA, A3 2164 32.479 (1737); AGCA, A1 98 2111 (1772); and Lutz, *Historia sociodemográfica*, 215, n. 25. On the impact of the Bourbon reforms see Miles L. Wortman, *Government and Society*, 129–56.

14. Burial records, rarely used in this study, bear this out. In San Sebastián, for example, register notes for July 1769 state that many were interred clandestinely during a measles epidemic. See appendix 5 and APSS.

15. Remarkably, APS, APSS, and APLR marriage registers all include statements about special exceptions made to speed the marriage process. In addition, they list an unusually large number of persons who received the marriage sacrament in the days immediately following the earthquake. It is nevertheless doubtful that all who married were listed in parish registers. On "collective panic" in response to earthquakes in Santiago, see André Saint-Lu, "Movimientos sísmicos."

16. More useful than the illegitimacy ratio, according to Edward Shorter, is the illegitimacy rate, which he describes as "the number of illegitimate births per 1,000 unmarried women in the population of childbearing age." Unfortunately, census data on the number of unmarried women in Santiago de Guatemala are not easily obtained for the period under study. See "Illegitimacy," 259.

17. Changes in legitimacy and illegitimacy ratios (or rates) are extremely difficult to analyze. For a discussion of the complexities of this problem, see Peter Laslett and Karla Oosterveen, "Long-term Trends in Bastardy," 255–57.

18. While the increasing independence of the gente ordinaria in the peripheral parishes may help explain why illegitimacy ratios fell starting in the late seventeenth century, the continued predominance of wealthy Spaniards in the Sagrario may well have led unwed mothers from outlying barrios and towns to abandon unwanted children at the doors of vecinos, who then raised them as criados. If this was indeed the case, it may have raised the Sagrario's illegitimacy ratio (and lowered that of the peripheral parishes). One could test this hypothesis by determining what portion of the illegitimate in the Sagrario and San Sebastián were *hijos naturales* (natural offspring) and how many were *hijos de la iglesia* (children of the church) or *expuestos en la puerta* (left in the doorway) of a house or church. Relatively high and low percentages of hijos naturales in San Sebastián and the Sagrario, respectively, would help confirm the hypothesis.

19. David Brading and Cynthia Wu's sociodemographic study of León (New Spain) neither supports nor refutes this assumption: they found "most people married" and thus felt no need to account for the parents of the illegitimate. "Population Growth and Crisis," 6.

20. Gonzalo Aguirre Beltrán, *La población negra de México*, 8.

21. Spanish royal officials and settlers warned the Crown that dire economic consequences would ensue if Indian slavery were abolished. Sherman, "Indian Slavery in Spanish Guatemala," 136ff., and *Forced Native Labor*, 172–76. The introduction of African slaves was apparently seen as an expedient, albeit expensive, alternative.

22. See n. 26, below.

23. Pardo, *Efemérides*, 8.

24. Philip D. Curtin, *Atlantic Slave Trade*, 21–25.

25. Aguirre Beltrán, *La población negra de México*, 33, 51.

26. The royal edict in response to the procurador's request referred to 500 "piezas [de Indias]," but the cabildo asked for 500 "slaves." AGCA, A1

2208 15.768. Curtin explains the difference between the two as follows: "A pieza de India was a measure of potential labor, not of individuals. For a slave to qualify as a pieza, he had to be a young adult male meeting certain specifications as to size, physical condition, and health. The very young, the old, and females were defined for commercial purposes as functional parts of a pieza de India." *Atlantic Slave Trade*, 22. For the seventeenth- and eighteenth-century evolution of the term, see Philip D. Curtin, *Economic Change in Precolonial Africa*, 175.

27. One such piece of evidence is the asiento of 1765. Aguirre Beltrán, *La población negra de México*, 88. MacLeod, *Spanish Central America*, 298, notes a decline in slave imports during the mid-seventeenth century, a decline corroborated by Santiago's *procurador* (attorney or legal representative) in Spain, who stated in 1670 that, despite an asiento agreement with the Grillos (a Genoese banking and slave trading family), no slaves had arrived in the province since 1638. AGCA, A1 2199 15.755, fol. 50; and Pedro Tobar Cruz, "La esclavitud del negro en Guatemala," 13.

28. "Royal rights" were variously called *derechos reales, derechos de esclavos*, and *derechos de negros* (a tax assessed for each African slave imported into Spain's American colonies, set at 110 tostones in the early seventeenth century) in Royal Treasury records and reports. See Oficiales reales de la Caja de Guatemala al Rey (Santiago: 4 April 1618), AGI, Guatemala 45; and "Relación sacada por los Jueces oficiales . . . desde principio del año de 1624 hasta fin de [16]28," AGI, Contaduría 973.

29. In 1613 a Portuguese asentista, Juan Gómes, sailed his caravel *(Nuestra Señora de Nazarén)* from Angola to the port of Santo Tomás de Castilla with "136 piezas de negros y negras" aboard. Gómes was obliged to pay 15,000 silver tostones in local duties for his slave cargo, plus 1,020 tostones (30 reales per pieza) to officials in Seville. AGCA, A1 2876 26.539, fol. 229. Two years later, in February 1615, Gómes arrived in Trujillo (Honduras) with 132 "piezas" aboard his caravel. He paid 14,459 tostones in local duties and 990 tostones to officials in Seville. Eight *muleques* (African slaves under the age of five) brought for the audiencia president and his oidores were also included in the 1615 cargo. Royal rights equal to half those on "negros grandes" were to be paid for each of the muleques. AGCA, A1 2876 26.539, fol. 233.

30. Roughly 21,000 slaves were introduced into Central America during the entire period of the slave trade, with an average of 70 slaves imported annually between the 1520s and the 1820s. Curtin, *Atlantic Slave Trade*, 21–23. Curtin suggests the actual figure may be somewhat lower, but that the estimate appears to square with "qualitative impressions" and with mid-twentieth-century estimates of Central Americans of African descent. *Atlantic Slave Trade*, 47, 91. I believe the actual figure is much higher for Guatemala than modern observation would suggest, given high rates of mestizaje (which ultimately obscured African lineage) and countless seventeenth- and eighteenth-century historical references to a sizable free mulatto population. Despite the "ladinoization" of the general populace, the English traveler Henry Dunn noted the importance of mulattoes in Guatemala's population as late as the 1820s. *Guatimala*, 90, 94. Curtin wisely

avoids using a single formula for reducing piezas to slaves, since the makeup of slave cargoes varied considerably. *Atlantic Slave Trade,* 22–23.

31. See Lutz, *Historia sociodemográfica,* appendix 7; "Evolución demográfica de la población no indígena"; and "La población no española."

32. Registro de Cristóbal Aceituno de Guzmán, AGCA, A1 433 8836 (11 May 1605). The sale cost Lopes Corso 700 tostones.

33. Registro de Cristóbal Aceituno de Guzmán, AGCA, A1 2581 20.825 (9 August 1613), fol. 34. Aguirre Beltrán, *La población negra de México,* 37–38, mentions a *negrero* (slave trader) named Manuel Solís who was established in Mexico City in the 1620s. If Solís and the asentista Gómes (see n. 29, above) worked separately, it would seem that, at least in some years, the actual number of Central American slave imports may have exceeded 150.

34. See the section "Total Population," in this chapter.

35. Gente ordinaria baptismal registers for the Sagrario show that 346 adult slaves (almost all of whom were African-born bozales) were baptized there between the 1640s and 1770s. While data on the ratio of male to female slaves in Santiago are not easily obtained, 63 percent of the 346 were males. A count of slaves found in a 1679 Sagrario padrón shows, by contrast, that among persons positively identified as slaves sixteen years or older females outnumbered males 2.8 to 1. See APS, Libro de Padrones.

36. APS, Gente Ordinaria baptismal registers.

37. Of all adult slaves (eighteen years of age and older) sold in Lima between 1560 and 1650, 5.5 percent of the males and 9.5 percent of the females were married. Frederick P. Bowser, *African Slave in Colonial Peru,* 256–57. According to Bowser, bills of sale were almost always accurate regarding the marital status of slaves so as to avoid later legal problems. Among male and female slaves in the 26–35 age bracket (sold less often than younger, stronger slaves), marriage percentages rose to only 13 percent and 16.6 percent, respectively. No such accuracy is possible for Santiago's slaves.

38. The forced emigration or export of slaves through sales and barter agreements may also account for the decline. So, too, may periods of economic dislocation, when household slaves were perhaps sold or relocated with greater frequency. Determining the primacy of emigration or export would require quantitative analysis of all slave sales, purchases, and barter agreements in colonial notarial registers for Santiago. Only then would it be possible to estimate whether these contracts resulted in a net increase or decrease in the city's slave population. For an incomplete list of extant registers in the AGCA, see *Indice de los documentos,* 281ff.

39. Aguirre Beltrán suggests that slaves in New Spain usually married partners chosen by their masters. *La población negra de México,* 257. Slave owners in Peru interfered similarly. Bowser, *African Slave in Colonial Peru,* 255–67.

40. Such evidence, if it exists, might be found in Mexico City, in the Inquisition section of the Archivo General de la Nación. The Holy Office of the Inquisition in Mexico had jurisdiction over the bishopric (later an archbishopric) of Guatemala. In rare instances in Mexico, slaves petitioned the Holy Office or Ecclesiastical Court for "permission to marry over the objections of a master." Colin A. Palmer, "Negro Slavery in Mexico," 129.

41. Stiff enforcement of the law of the belly may explain why large

numbers of black and especially mulatto slave women listed in 1676-81 Sagrario padrones appear to have been unmarried. APS, Libro de Padrones.

42. The only exception to the maxim is the Candelaria, where only one black slave marriage and one mulatto slave marriage were recorded from 1757 to 1769 (when this survey stops).

43. Trends in slave sales confirm the finding that female slaves, especially mulattoes, greatly outnumbered males in the Sagrario from the late 1670s onward. APS, Libro de Padrones (1676-81). Slave-sale data are derived from the following AGCA notarial registers, listed by escribano: Luis Aceituno de Guzmán (1609-10, including entries beginning in 1568); Luis Aceituno de Guzmán (1575-76, including 1609 entries); A1 2023 (Cristóbal Aceituno de Guzmán, 1584); A1 425 8828 (Cristóbal Aceituno de Guzmán, 1588); A1 428 8831 (C. Aceituno de G., 1591); A1 430 8833 (C. Aceituno de G., 1602); A1 432 8835 (C. Aceituno de G., 1604); A1 431 8834 (C. Aceituno de G., 1605); A1 433 8836 (C. Aceituno de G., 1605-6); A1 2581 (C. Aceituno de G., 1613); A1 540 9043 (1619-20); A1 757 9250 (Pedro de Estrada, 1624-28); A1 758 9251 (P. de Estrada, 1632-37); A1 760 9253 (P. de Estrada, 1639); Sebastián Ramírez (1644); Gaspar de Gallegos (1651-52); Luis de Andino (1659-60); Francisco Muñoz (1664-66); A1 530 9033 (Benito Berdugo, 1678); Bernabé Rojel (1682); A1 1019 9512 (1684-89); A1 457 8860 (José Ignacio Agreda, 1688); Benito Berdugo (1690-92); A1 648 9141 (Sebastián Coello, 1697); Guillermo de Pineda M. (1698); and A1 653 9146 (Sebastián Coello, 1703).

44. Confirmation of this hypothesis awaits further research. It is based on surveys of many AGCA documents and Sagrario padrones dated 1676-81.

45. Other mulatto slave children put up for sale were indeed legitimate, suggesting that the father was sold before the child.

46. See, for example, AGCA, A1 648 9141, fol. 126, which tells of the sale of Nicolás, the thirteen- or fourteen-year-old son of a female slave and her owner.

47. A not atypical example is one-year-old Felipa, daughter of Sebastiana, a black slave belonging to Captain Don Antonio de Roa y Rivas. The captain freed the infant girl on 11 May 1698 "because of the love and kindness which he had for [her]." It seems likely that he was her father. AGCA, uncatalogued notarial register of Guillermo de Pineda M. (1698). For an especially insightful study of slave manumission and the variable of color, see Stuart B. Schwartz, "The Manumission of Slaves in Colonial Brazil."

48. See Bowser, "Colonial Spanish America," 28-29.

49. Mörner, *Race Mixture*, 60, suggests that the legal status of slaves was superior to none, but that they enjoyed a higher social status than Indians (not including the nobility). This study expands Mörner's social and legal hierarchy, finding that *within* the slave group mulattoes were distinctly better off than blacks, both legally and socially, as illustrated by the intermarriage patterns of the two (see chap. 5).

50. Association of the term *negro* with slave status in colonial Guatemala may have led some free blacks to identify themselves as free mulattoes when asked by local priests to state their race for the record. Santiago's parish registers, therefore, may understate free black numbers, though it is doubtful the distortion is more serious for this group than for others. See Konetzke, "Documentos"; and Mörner, *Race Mixture*, 60.

51. Early seventeenth-century increases would be more pronounced were data not missing from the Sagrario, the parish most heavily populated with black slaves, for 1625–48.

52. Other freedmen must have remained with Spanish masters in the large, multiracial households of San Sebastián. "Padrón de la Parroquia del Señor San Sebastián . . . 1699," AGI, Guatemala 160. Sadly, however, this census does not provide the rich detail on ethnic diversity and status found in APS, Libro de Padrones, covering 1676–81.

53. See the section on "Barrio Transformation," in chapter 3.

54. Note that the Spanish total was thought to be inflated by the inclusion of about 1,720 *plebe común* (commoners), "among whom abound to a high degree the feminine sex." Excluded from the relación were castas and black slaves, as well as those of "low status" who had no fixed domicile and were of unknown *calidad* (quality). See AGCA, A1 210 5.002, fols. 6–6v; or Guillermo Martínez de Pereda, "Relación geográfica del valle de Goathemala," 8.

55. MacLeod, *Spanish Central America*, 98–100, documents a number of these epidemics. See also LC 21, AGCA, A1 1783 11.777, fols. 179–79v and 192–92v, for the peste epidemic from late 1686 to early 1687; LC 25, AGCA, A1 1787 11.781, fol. 35, for "sickness in the city" in 1707; and LC 25, AGCA, A1 1787 11.781, fols. 81–81v, for smallpox in 1708. The differential mortality of both castas (gente ordinaria) and poor Spanish (those not living in the Sagrario) as compared with the Spanish of the Sagrario is apparent from a preliminary survey of burial registers in the Sagrario, San Sebastián, and Los Remedios.

56. While epidemics may have had a negative impact on marriage totals during the 1690s and 1700s, both legitimate and illegitimate gente ordinaria baptisms continued to grow over that period. The most dramatic increase in baptisms occurred among the illegitimate in the Sagrario. See appendix 3.

57. One major aim of this expedition (and others into unconquered Indian areas, such as that into the Lacandón a few years earlier) was to enslave Indians who had avoided Spanish rule. MacLeod, *Spanish Central America*, 298–300, 392. See also Grant D. Jones, "The Last Maya Frontiers of Colonial Yucatan," 71, 73, and *Maya Resistance to Spanish Rule*. Jones, personal communication (November 1988), states Spanish expeditionary forces suffered no major losses against the Itzá.

58. Obispo de Guatemala al Presidente de la Audiencia (Guatemala: 17 August 1699), Informe no. 2, AGI, Guatemala 160.

59. Free mulatto totals in the Sagrario kept pace with those in San Sebastián even though the creation of Los Remedios in 1641 shrunk the number of parishioners under the Sagrario's jurisdiction. With higher rates of gente ordinaria illegitimacy in the Sagrario than in San Sebastián, it appears also that free mulattoes were more numerous in the Sagrario than total marriage figures for that group indicate.

60. Eighty-two free mulatto marriages took place in the Candelaria during the 1760s, one fewer than in Los Remedios during that decade.

61. Females, if not *mulatto* females, were far more likely to be manumitted than males in Spanish cities throughout the New World. Of 320

manumissions in Peru between 1560 and 1650, 67 percent involved females. Moreover, 82 percent of the manumissions involved females and children while only 3 percent of the sample involved adult males ages sixteen to thirty-five. Bowser, "Colonial Spanish America," 31. Bowser does not distinguish between blacks and mulattoes.

62. Data for this sample have been collected from AGCA notarial registers (uncatalogued entries are identified only by the name of the escribano): Gaspar de Gallegos (1651); Luis de Andino (1660); A1 530 (1677–79); Bernabé Rojel (1682); A1 1019 9512 (1687–88); Benito Berdugo (1692); A1 648 (1697); and Guillermo de Pineda M. (1698). The apparent infrequency of manumissions prior to 1650 suggests that miscegenation was yet to have a major impact on Santiago.

63. While this sample is tiny and covers only fifty years, its finding of mulata predominance among those manumitted is bolstered by studies of Brazil and other areas of Spanish America. See, for example, Frederick P. Bowser, "The Free Person of Color," 331–68; Bowser, *African Slave in Colonial Peru*, 298; and Schwartz, "Manumission," 612, 616–18. Schwartz confirms this view, personal communication (June 1974).

64. Ten of the fourteen mulata manumissions were through payment and the other four were unconditional. Three of the seven mulatto males were manumitted through payment, while two were through self-purchase, one was unconditional, and one was on the condition of two years' service to the owner's wife. Of the manumitted blacks, the lone male and two of the females were freed through payment; the other female was unconditionally freed. Ages were given in only thirteen of the twenty-five cases, making no age trend easily discernible.

65. At work here is something Harry Hoetink calls "somatic norm image," an ideal racial type based upon the physical features of the dominant group in a segmented society, one that comes to be esteemed by subordinate and dominant groups alike. Thus the mulatto phenotype is deemed more desirable than the black phenotype because it embodies elements of the Spanish phenotype. *The Two Variants in Caribbean Race Relations*, 120, 185, passim. See also Bowser, "The Free Person of Color"; Bowser, *African Slave in Colonial Peru*; and Schwartz, "Manumission."

66. Even with high rates of manumission, freed mulattoes would have been a tiny group compared with the children of Indian and free casta women. Verifying this is impossible, however, without complete manumission statistics.

67. A fourth factor in the growth of the free mulatto population—the presence in Santiago of large numbers of free mulattoes in search of economic opportunity—is not addressed, only because it is so difficult to measure. Illustrative of the use of marriage registers toward this end, however, is a study by J. Nadal and E. Giralt to determine the "frequency of [French] migrants" into Catalonia in the sixteenth and seventeenth centuries. *La population catalane*, cited in Hollingsworth, *Historical Demography*, 176–77.

68. For example, an interrogatory on behalf of a Spanish woman charged the woman's accuser, a free mulata, of being a "vile and low person because, aside from being a mulatto, she gets drunk." AGCA, A1 4088 32.429. Such remarks about castas and mulattoes abound in AGCA and AGI documents. Most were written by Spanish creoles and Crown officials.

69. Nothing, of course, was automatic. In the Cárdenas case, for example (see chap. 3), Indian leaders cited the law of the belly in attempts to retain a tributary; the defendants argued that paternal descent should be the deciding factor. The law of the belly, as it turned out, was superseded by an order exempting all Cárdenas descendants from even the laborío.

70. If the disadvantages of free mulatto status outweighed the advantages, parish registers may understate Santiago's free mulatto population and overstate the number of its mestizos. It is doubtful that distortions were any more severe for this group than for others, however, given efforts by so many gente ordinaria to escape their ancestry. Questions of accuracy are further complicated by vagueness in the definition of mulatto. The working sociocracial classification system in Santiago and its comarca in no way resembled more ideal systems (see Mörner, *Race Mixture*, 56–60), because high rates of illegitimacy left so many without genealogical histories. Thus illegitimacy was a stigma, but it facilitated racial self-identification.

71. See chapter 3, n. 20 (and the text to which it relates).

72. This is borne out by late seventeenth- and early eighteenth-century increases in "Others and Unidentified" listed in group marriage tables, appendix 1, and in table 18.

73. While Indian naborías, like free blacks and mulattoes, were in theory subject to the laborío tribute, most were mobile and elusive and thus difficult to keep track of and collect from. See appendix 7.

74. See the case of Ana, an Indian woman from the Barrio de Santo Domingo, who was contracted in February 1575 to work a year for Inés Díaz and her husband, Juan Pérez de Mérida. The contract could be extended if it took longer than a year to work off a thirty-tostón loan she had "freely accepted" as part of the deal. AGCA, uncatalogued notarial register of Luis Aceituno de Guzmán, 1575–76. The household chores required of an Indian girl or woman servant might include washing clothes and cooking (making chocolate and tortillas, for example). See, for example, AGCA, A1 425 9351 (28 March 1588); and AGCA, A1 legs. 425, 428, 430, 432, and 540. All are filled with contracts regarding the entry of Indian girls and women into the service of Spanish families. For the service of Indian men and boys in houses and businesses, see AGCA, A1: 424, exps. 9367, 9378, 9382, 9399, and 9410; 429, exps. 9782, 9907, 9912, and 10.002; and 432, exps. 10.581, 10.595, and 10.809.

75. See, for example, the case of Francisca, an orphan girl from Patzicía who was signed, with the permission of the alcalde of the city, to a ten-year domestic contract by local encomenderos Doña Ana Corral and Lorenzo del Balle in September 1588. Francisca was to receive 100 tostones to help with her marriage upon completion of the contract period. AGCA, A1 425 9447.

76. Permission to migrate to the city was usually obtained after the fact. For examples of two individuals who sought and received such audiencia support against the wishes of their Indian cabildos, see AGCA, A1 6071, 54.649 (Chimaltenango: 1672) and 54.651 (Pinula: 1685). Each of the two sought the authority to remain in the service of Spaniards. In 1672 a group of nineteen tributaries from Santo Tomás Chichicastenango received permission to live in the Utatleca parcialidad of Jocotenango. Sellers of *ropa de la tierra* (Indian-made clothing) in the city's market, the Maxeños (natives of Chichicastenango) had migrated years before, settling among fellow K'iche'

speakers and marrying into the Utatleca parcialidad. They continued to pay tribute and support religious celebrations in Chichicastenango, despite their new ties in Santiago de Guatemala. The audiencia set a penalty of 100 pesos should the Indian justices of Chichicastenango try to harass them. AGCA, A1 1564 10.208, fols. 130–32v.

77. See chapter 3. In the case of Antequera (Oaxaca), John Chance notes that "it seems unlikely that a migrant would have undergone a complete identity transformation." He thus sees the city as a refuge for Indians, believes they left their towns due to push rather than pull factors, and wisely doubts rural Indians were able to become "urban Indians" or naborías quickly. *Race and Class*, 90–91.

78. Careful study of extant parish padrones would be unrewarding, since Indian children below the age of communion (roughly ages seven to eleven, legitimate and illegitimate, orphans and abandoned infants) were omitted. In any case, a preliminary survey of the first fifty households (almost all with Spanish heads) in the 1679 Sagrario padrón reveals that thirty-seven Indians of communion age or older resided therein. Twenty-nine (or 78 percent) were female. Indians may have been more prevalent earlier in the seventeenth century, prior to the rapid increase in the free casta population. APS, Libro de Padrones.

79. Less worldly Indian newcomers may have been persuaded to work for wages that urbanized or ladinoized Indians and castas would have rejected. Personal observations and informal interviews suggest that a similar pattern prevails today in Guatemala City and numerous provincial towns. For brief life histories of eighteenth-century Indian migrants to the capital, see Lutz, "Santiago de Guatemala."

80. AGCA, A1 5369 45.410 (1716); and AGCA, A3 2821 40.987 (1738).

81. While a few children of Spaniards listed as neither legitimate nor natural may well have been legitimate, they were probably offset by "y otros naturales," listed as such by four conquistadores in addition to their legitimate children. AGCA, A1 2196 15.750, fols. 158–60v. That almost all of the eighteen conquistadores listed as having "natural children" were among the first twenty of the forty-seven men on the list makes one suspect that the details about illegitimate offspring were intentionally or inadvertently omitted from the rest of the document. The actual illegitimacy ratio, therefore, may be higher.

82. There were roughly 100 Spanish vecinos in 1549, in addition to many more Spaniards without that status. Cabildo de Santiago a la Corona (Santiago: 30 April 1549), AGI, Guatemala 41, cited in Sherman, "Cerrato Reforms," 31, n. 22.

83. This question is based on Gonzalo Aguirre Beltrán's hypothesis that the legitimate offspring of Spaniard and Indian were labeled Spaniard, creole, or American and that the illegitimate offspring of these two groups were called mestizos. See *La población negra de México*, 250. Aguirre Beltrán suggests, in short, that a cultural criterion, marriage within the church, separated Spaniard from mestizo, not a biological one. For a brief discussion of Aguirre Beltrán's hypothesis and study in general, see Magnus Mörner, "El mestizaje," 133.

84. All socioracial groups in Santiago had their share of orphans, but

mestizo orphans appear to have received special attention, perhaps because the Spanish took some responsibility for the mestizo's existence.

85. El obispo Marroquín a la Corona (Guatemala: 4 February 1548), AGI, Guatemala 156, fols. 2v–3. Marroquín may have envisioned creation of a colegio when he later wrote of the need "to collect these mestizo men and women, children of those who have worked and won these parts." El obispo Marroquín a la Corona (Gracias a Dios: 1 August 1548), AGI, Guatemala 156, fols. 2–2v. Marroquín apparently favored miscegenation as a way to get better treatment for Indians. He suggested to the Crown that Spaniards, especially royal officials, be obliged to marry Indian women to achieve that end. J. Fernando Juárez y Aragón, "En el homenaje," 53, as cited by William L. Sherman, "Dissent among the Bishops," 6; Sherman notes the absence of any supporting document.

86. AGCA, A1 1511, fol. 93. The intervening years saw the Crown again issue orders to begin the project, which was to be modeled after a colegio soon to be built in Mexico City. For other cédulas regarding the colegio (dated 1553 and 1565), see Pardo, *Prontuario*, 71, 99. The audiencia expressed its interest in a letter to the Crown, stating that "in this city there is great need to collect the mestizo boy orphans and the mestizo girls." Audiencia a la Corona (Santiago: 25 May 1555), AGI, Guatemala 9.

87. For accounts of life in the colegio, also known as the Colegio de la Presentación de Nuestra Señora, see Annis, *Architecture of Antigua Guatemala*, 288–89; and J. Joaquín Pardo, Pedro Zamora Castellanos, and Luis Luján Muñoz, *Guía de la Antigua Guatemala*, 128–31. Charles Gibson suggests that formal education of mestizos began earlier in Mexico City than in Santiago, but claims that the Colegio de San Juan de Letrán played a limited role. *Aztecs under Spanish Rule*, 383.

88. A royal cédula of 17 April 1553 (Madrid) suggests that mestizo orphan boys and other "badly inclined" individuals be shipped to Seville, where city officials would place them in trades. AGCA, A1 2195 15.749, fol. 294.

89. LC 21, AGCA, A1 1783 17.777, fols. 194–94v; see also Pardo, *Efemérides*, 104. A serious epidemic in late 1686 could well have created a larger orphan population than usually existed in the city. Pardo, *Efemérides*, 104. See also appendix 5.

90. Spanish children, too, were so indentured. For two late examples, see AGCA, uncatalogued notarial registers of Benito Berdugo (contract signed 27 June 1692) and Guillermo de Pineda M. (contract signed 10 April 1698). For some unruly minors the practice was a form of punishment, but it is doubtful that this was the general intent. For Indian complaints about abuses of Indian orphans in the final third of the sixteenth century, see Lutz, "Introducción histórica." For numerous examples of contract labor in the late sixteenth century, see Sherman, *Forced Native Labor*, 208–12.

91. This finding is based on the assumption that illegitimacy ratios for gente ordinaria generally are reliable indicators of mestizo illegitimacy in particular. Parish baptismal figures demonstrate that illegitimacy ratios for gente ordinaria fell below 50 percent in both San Sebastián and Los Remedios by the latter decades of the seventeenth century, though they remained slightly above 50 percent in the Sagrario. Hence the observation that

"roughly half" the mestizo population of the city was born of married parents by the late seventeenth century. See appendix 3.

92. In Los Remedios, total mestizo marriages failed to approach levels in the city's two larger parishes, but grew steadily from the 1670s through the 1750s, only to decline inexplicably in the 1760s.

93. Data from San Sebastián are missing for the 1590s, 1600s, 1610s, and early 1620s, while from the Sagrario data are missing for the late 1620s, 1630s, and much of the 1640s. See "Introduction" to the appendixes.

94. Returning to a native settlement was especially difficult for Indian women who had learned Spanish ways, according to Licenciado Arteaga Mendola (fiscal of the audiencia). Originally taken from their towns as orphans and put under contract to Spaniards, many were rejected upon returning (and, one would assume, upon the expiration of their contracts) for having married blacks and mulattoes or serving as their concubines. Others were rejected merely for not knowing how to prepare food their Indian husbands would eat, having learned to cook in the city. Many quickly returned to the city upon seeing the comparative squalor of their native towns. Spaniards had no less difficulty giving up their Indian servants. Arteaga Mendola noted the audiencia's opposition when he asked that Indian girls raised in the service of Spaniards be returned to their *lugares* (places) upon reaching marriageable age. Perhaps because the subject was taboo, the fiscal omitted mention of Indian women's relations with Spaniards. Licenciado Arteaga Mendola a la Corona (Santiago: 16 December 1570), AGI, Guatemala 9, fol. 1v.

95. Chance, *Race and Class*, 97, documents the passage of a mestiza, born out of wedlock and later recognized by her Spanish father, into Oaxaca's local Spanish elite.

96. Additional evidence of the reluctance to identify persons by socioracial group can be found in a comparison of Mercedarian censo records from the late sixteenth, seventeenth, and mid-eighteenth centuries. Socioracial identifications are common in the earlier records, rare in the later ones. For the first two centuries, see the numerous *expedientes* (documents) in the AHA-SM, legs. 1–2, and *fardos* (bundles) for the 1610s and 1620s. For the mid-eighteenth century, see Fincas de la Antigua Guatemala del Convento de la Merced (3 bound vols.), AHA-SM.

97. The figure of roughly 100 vecinos for 1549 may well be the best estimate of the entire pre-1700 series, because the city's cabildo confirmed to the Crown that the figure did *not* include *habitantes* (Spaniards without vecino status). It seems likely that other estimates similarly excluded habitantes, but they include no explicit statement to that effect. Since there appears to be no easy way to determine Spanish nonvecino totals, discussion of population change is based solely on numbers of vecinos, or those formally admitted as citizens of the city. For a comparison of vecino and habitante in colonial Ecuador, see Phelan, *Kingdom of Quito*, 17, 49. Also see table 8, note a.

98. MacLeod, *Spanish Central America*, 217.

99. The drops in encomienda income and basic foodstuffs were accompanied by a scarcity of beef and rising prices in the cities and towns of the comarca. See Lutz, *Historia sociodemográfica*, appendix 9, for evidence of a

sharp rise in beef prices in Santiago between the 1580s and the early decades of the seventeenth century.

100. Prior to 1630 landowners favored growing indigo because it did not place them in the same "monocultural trap" posed by sugarcane or cacao production. They could raise cattle on the same lands without any danger to the xiquilite plant, from which indigo is made. MacLeod, *Spanish Central America*, 133, 218–20.

101. See table 8, note e.

102. Highland Guatemala was not alone in this respect. Other highland regions such as Chiapas and highland Honduras enjoyed similar levels of relative immunity. On Chiapas, see Peter Gerhard, *The Southeast Frontier of New Spain*, 158–60, 169–70, to compare Chiapas (highlands) and Soconusco (coastal lowlands). On highland Honduras, see Newson, *Cost of Conquest*, 4–5. Citing MacLeod, Newson notes that Indians had a better chance of survival in regions Spaniards seeking riches tended to pass over. In this regard, also see Lutz and Lovell, "Core and Periphery."

103. This is not to suggest that all of Santiago's encomenderos held encomiendas in the highlands. See, for example, MacLeod's analysis of cacao encomenderos from Santiago whose holdings were located in the rich coastal province of Izalcos. *Spanish Central America*, 80–95. The definitive work on early Guatemalan encomienda is Kramer, "Politics of Encomienda Distribution."

104. Of sixteen audiencia towns for which encomendero-vecino ratios are available, including a number of lowland population centers, only two had higher ratios than Santiago de Guatemala (which listed 77 encomenderos among its 227 vecinos, a ratio of 1:2.9). "Relación de los vecinos y encomenderos que hay en la gobernación de Guatemala sacada de un libro que tiene el presidente Villalobos . . . ," AGI, Indiferente General 1528. The relación is undated, but 1573–78 seems likely, given that these were the years of Villalobos's presidency. Specific data and ratios were kindly provided by Dr. Salvador Rodríguez Becerra, Departamento de Antropología, Universidad de Sevilla.

105. One such individual was Bernal Díaz del Castillo's son Francisco, who was listed in the Libro Becerro (a padrón for the purpose of collecting the *alcabala* [sales tax]) as a regidor of the city, encomendero, wheat-farm owner, and merchant. See AGCA, A1 1804 11.810 (the Libro Becerro), which runs from 1604 to the mid-1620s. MacLeod, *Spanish Central America*, 221, uses this document in a table showing changing occupational patterns in the city over this period. See Dorothy Jane Joba, "Santiago de los Caballeros," for a complete and highly informative analysis of the Libro Becerro.

106. An early seventeenth-century *visita* (inspection tour) of the valleys east and northeast of Santiago revealed that the vast majority of labores had Indian mayordomos. Juan Moreno's labor in the Valley of Sacatepéquez was cared for by his black slave Elena; her master, the document shows, had left his house on the property a month before. Another labor was managed by a mestizo. None was run by a free mulatto. AGCA, A1 5762 48.242 (20 November–1 December 1606). David Jickling, "Los vecinos de Santiago de Guatemala en 1604," 162, notes that Santiago's 1604 alcabala census indicates that, while some rural property owners lived *either* on their haciendas or in

cities other than Santiago, most maintained residences *both* on their haciendas and in the capital.

107. Stephen Webre, "Cabildo Membership," 132–33. For a valuable study on sixteenth-century Spanish migration between northern Extremadura and Latin America, see Ida Altman, *Emigrants and Society*.

108. Webre, "Cabildo Membership," 309.

109. Webre, "Cabildo Membership," 218.

110. Webre, "Cabildo Membership," 153.

111. Joba, "Santiago de los Caballeros," 120–39; De la Peña and López Díaz, "Comercio y poder," 469–505; and Gage, *Travels*, 186–87. The non-Spanish Europeans were generally not as seamlessly assimilated as their Spanish counterparts.

112. Joining the peninsulares, according to Webre, were other newcomers from elsewhere in America—"merchants, office holders or both, in search of opportunity." "Cabildo Membership," 218.

113. This pattern of intermarriage is quite distinct from that between creoles and peninsulares in colonial Oaxaca, where the abyss between the two was so wide that Chance called them "two distinct ethnic groups." Chance, *Race and Class*, 104.

114. Richard Morse's centrifugal-centripetal model for characterizing the movement of people *from* the colonial city and *into* the national-period Latin American city fits this elite movement to the countryside and regional towns better than it fits nonelite, especially Indian, migration to the city. See Morse, "Latin American Cities," 480–81; and Morse, "Recent Research on Latin American Urbanization," esp. 41. Actually, the movement of peoples from all sectors might best be described as a continuous movement back and forth.

115. If any single event could have prompted an exodus from capital to countryside, it would surely have been the earthquake of September 1717. While it appears that the great majority of those who fled eventually returned, some left the city for good, taking up residence in the surrounding towns and even in such faraway places as San Salvador. "Testimonio . . . sobre el lastimoso estrago y ruina . . . 1717," AGI, Guatemala 660, fols. 12v–13, 32v, and 49v–50.

116. Population increases in these four trade centers were probably due both to natural increase and to the influx of urban residents seeking a better life. For evidence of Spaniards and castas in the formerly all-Indian towns, see Mörner, "La política de segregación," 142–43, 147. On a 1678 visita to the towns of Petapa, San Juan Amatitlán, and Escuintla, President D. Fernando de Escobedo discovered that fewer Spaniards, mestizos, and mulattoes had enlisted in these towns' militia companies than actually lived there, perhaps indicating that many there were new arrivals. See Presidente de la Audiencia Don Fernando Francisco de Escobedo a la Corona (Santiago: 16 May 1678), AGI, Guatemala 26. By 1740 *all* towns in the Valley of Guatemala were reported to contain 1,320 Spaniards of all ages, 1,420 free mulatto males, and 690 mestizos. AGCA, A1 210 5002, fols. 6–6v.

117. Lutz, "Evolución demográfica" and "Población no española."

118. See table 8, notes a and e. Interestingly, the estimate of 6,000 Span-

iards comes close to estimates based on total Spanish marriages for the 1680s (5,740). See table 9.

119. The 1740 Spanish population figure seems far too low in light of decennial population estimates based on total marriages for this group. Yet the marriage-based estimate for the 1750s (5,516, as stated in appendix 4) seems far too high in light of ca. 1770 estimates (3,000–3,500), based on the notion that Spaniards then represented 10 percent of Santiago's 30,000–35,000 total population (see table 8). One would think that the *actual* decline in total Spanish population bore some resemblance to the 29 percent drop in Spanish decennial baptismal totals between the 1680s and the 1740s (see appendix 3).

120. This estimate, consistent with marriage-based figures and the census by Cortés y Larraz (see table 10), is at odds with Sidney David Markman, *Colonial Architecture of Antigua Guatemala*, 16–17, who calculates that a "total of 15,061 inhabitants is indicated as residing in Antigua and its immediate environs just prior to the earthquake [of 1773]." Annis, *Architecture of Antigua Guatemala*, 7, states that "it is not beyond reason to believe that the colonial capital may have had as many as thirty thousand inhabitants of all castes within its extended boundaries, including a substantial ecclesiastical population." Annis notes that modern Antigua "has a population of more than fifteen thousand and it must be noted that most of the heavily populated districts of the colonial period have reverted to agricultural use with a minimal population." He also states that the poor, then as now, lived in crowded conditions, and that servants and their children were numerous in the larger households.

121. "Pure" in this context was of course relative: few creoles were without at least one Indian or black ancestor. Immigration is an important variable here. Were a study of Spanish marriage registers to reveal that a larger number of peninsulares came to Santiago during the eighteenth century than is now currently believed, the 15 percent figure would need to be revised upward.

122. Padre Pedro Martínez de Molina . . . al Presidente de la Audiencia (Santiago: 17 September 1773), AGI, Guatemala 647.

123. See "Introduction" to the appendixes.

124. Jorge Luján Muñoz, "El desarrollo demográfico de la ciudad de Santiago de Guatemala," comes to similar conclusions.

CHAPTER FIVE **Marriage**

1. Charles Tilly, *The Vendée*.
2. Analyses of marriage patterns in the Spanish American context are similarly limited. See Marcello Carmagnani, "Demografia e società," a study of two seventeenth-century northern Mexican mining centers, and Brading and Wu, "Population Growth and Crisis," a study of eighteenth- and nineteenth-century León, Mexico, that only modifies Carmagnani's use of intra- and intermarriage percentages. The failure of either study to take into account the absolute number of total marriages in a given decade is particularly disconcerting. What might seem to be a significant intermarriage percentage for one racial group would be far less noteworthy if the other group married

in larger numbers and if the total number of persons of all groups marrying in that period were ignored.

Just such an argument was leveled at John B. Chance and William B. Taylor, "Estate and Class in a Colonial City," for the use of intra- and intermarriage percentages in an analysis of Oaxaca. Robert McCaa, Stuart B. Schwartz, and Arturo Grubessich claimed in 1979 that Chance and Taylor's "dependence on simple statistics (percentages) has led, we believe, to a series of unwarranted conclusions and to an emphasis on spurious relationships." The study by McCaa, Schwartz, and Grubessich added that "more probing use of statistics—specifically endogamy measures [i.e., David J. Strauss, "Measuring Endogamy"], models of statistical independence, and correlation coefficients—produces a more accurate picture of marital and occupational structures." "Race and Class in Colonial Latin America," 422-23.

In the same issue of *Comparative Studies in Society and History (CSSH)*, Chance and Taylor acknowledged the application of Strauss's "newly developed statistical method to parish marriage data" used by McCaa et al. but defended their own methodology and conclusions. "Estate and Class."

Patricia Seed and Philip F. Rust joined the fray in 1983. Charging that using Strauss was shortsighted, they recommended instead the GSK method (named for James E. Grizzle, Frank C. Starmer, and Gary G. Koch) to "test the degree of statistical significance of differences in intermarriage among racial groups." GSK, they concluded, confirms the Taylor and Chance contention that "mestizos and mulattoes had very low levels of endogamy" and did not constitute closed groups in late eighteenth-century Oaxaca. "Estate and Class in Colonial Oaxaca Revisited," 706-7.

This time *CSSH* editors included one response and one counter-response. McCaa and Schwartz wrote that they had discarded Strauss's methodology in favor of marriage propensities ("odds"), as previously developed by McCaa in "Modeling Social Interaction." These odds, they found, "support Taylor and Chance's argument about the gradual merging of Mulattoes and Mestizos (and Indians as well), but also confirm our contention that racial considerations continued to exert a substantial constraint upon nuptial choice through the end of the colonial period." "Measuring Marriage Patterns," 172.

In response, Seed and Rust, "Across the Pages with Estate and Class," questioned McCaa and Schwartz's defense of earlier arguments and methods. Whether or not one agrees with Seed and Rust, their analysis provides a brief and useful summary of a long and ongoing debate that, according to Woodrow Borah, has "generated some vivid language and perhaps some heat." "Trends in Recent Studies of Colonial Latin American Cities," 549.

Seed and McCaa have each published important articles on marriage and race (examining periods of one to three years) in Bourbon New Spain, applying some of the methodologies discussed above. See Seed, "The Social Dimensions of Race"; and McCaa, "*Calidad, Clase*, and Marriage in Colonial Mexico."

3. Tilly, *Vendée*, 94.

4. Although Tilly provides a formula for arriving at intermarriage scores, he fails to spell out the precise formula by which he derived intramarriage scores. He kindly did so, however, in subsequent correspondence with Peter Smith, then of the University of Wisconsin–Madison. Personal communication (16 April 1974).

5. What distinguishes this study of exogamous marriage patterns in colonial Spanish America from most others is that it uses parish data to divide the population into as diverse a number of status and socioracial groups as are sufficiently represented in parish records. Comparing such data from the city's four parishes, it further delineates the socioeconomic and socioracial structures and patterns of each jurisdiction.

6. Black slave–free black marriage was more erratic than black slave–mulatto slave marriage, largely because free blacks were so few in number. While Tilly indices tend to overemphasize this relationship, due to a low number of marriages, it is clear the two black groups had close, long-term marital bonds.

7. Only seven black slave–Indian marriages were recorded in Santiago between 1700 and 1769. Were they extant, the Indian doctrina registers kept by the various religious orders might reveal other such marriages.

8. The total naboría marriage figures that suggest this population decline are unsatisfactory because they say so little about Indian migration into and out of the capital, about which largely anecdotal evidence abounds. See data drawn from criminal cases, for example, in Lutz, "Santiago de Guatemala."

9. These free mulattoes were probably poor, unskilled, dependent individuals with distinctly African features and thus least able to marry into a higher status group or to pass as ladinos.

10. Six black slave–Spanish marriages were recorded in Santiago between the late sixteenth century and the 1760s. Similarly, the casta marriage register from a Mexico City parish shows one such marriage (a Spanish male–female slave union) and one castizo male–female slave union between 1646 and 1746. Edgar F. Love, "Marriage Patterns," 89. Patricia Seed, *To Love, Honor, and Obey*, cites no Spanish marriages with either black or mulatto slaves.

11. The two decennial exceptions were the 1690s and 1720s. Regarding the size of black and mulatto slave groups, see note 13.

12. That mulatto slaves (and black slaves, too) rarely married *anyone* outside the Sagrario is predictable, since the slave population there was consistently larger than that of all the city's other parishes combined. Some sixty-six mulatto slave-black slave unions were recorded in the Sagrario between 1593 and 1769, while only eight such marriages took place elsewhere, all in San Sebastián (app. 1).

13. Most mulatto slaves availed themselves of that opportunity. Of the 702 mulatto slaves married in Santiago between 1593 and 1769, 80 percent took spouses of free status, while only 56 percent of 801 black slaves did so (app. 1).

14. Mulatto slaves nonetheless stood a better chance of marrying Spaniards than black slaves. Ten mulatto slave-Spanish unions are to be found in Santiago's extant registers, against six black slave-Spanish marriages.

15. Numerous free blacks formed informal unions with the servants and slaves alongside whom they worked and lived. It would appear, for example, that a lower percentage of free blacks married formally than was true of the city's more upwardly mobile free mulatto population, even as early as the late sixteenth century. A ca. 1588 padrón of free blacks and mulattoes in

Santiago and its jurisdiction (presumably the Valley of Guatemala) lists 148 individuals: 130 mulattoes, 18 blacks. Slightly over half (68) of the mulattoes were either married (61) or widowed (7), while only a third of the blacks (6) were either married (5) or widowed (1). "Blas Hidalgo y Francisco de Morales escribanos que fueron de probincia de la ciudad de Santiago de Guatemala con el señor fiscal y con los escribanos de número," AGI, Guatemala 57, fols. 27–29. Thanks to Wendy Kramer for pointing out this useful document.

16. The persistence of lower than expected free black–Indian naboría marriage after 1625–48, when data are missing from the Sagrario, may suggest that marriage bonds between the two never exceeded expected levels. Though quantitative data about free black marriage in the mid-sixteenth century are lacking, the audiencia complained to the Crown in 1571 that some blacks, free or slave, had fathered children by Indian women and claimed they were exempt from personal tribute because they were not Indians. Audiencia a la Corona (Santiago: 6 September 1571), AGI, Guatemala 9. In apparent response, the Crown issued a royal cédula on 18 May 1572, ordering that children of blacks and Indian women be "counted so that they paid tribute." Pardo, *Prontuario*, 146.

17. Free black–mestizo marital ties in the Sagrario might have been stronger still were Chipilapa, a barrio located in the parish's eastern section and known in the eighteenth century for its heavy concentration of free blacks and mulattoes, not included in Sagrario marriage registers. While it is likely that a higher percentage of free blacks took marriage vows in Chipilapa than in the rest of the Sagrario, their relative independence, like that of free black parishioners in San Sebastián and Los Remedios, probably worked to discourage free black–mestizo contacts. While this argument might seem to contradict the broad theme of upward mobility and wider intermarriage possibilities, it must be remembered that anyone identified as a free black in parish registers was subject to racial discrimination by most sectors of Spanish colonial society.

18. In the sixteenth century, before miscegenation became widespread, black slaves filled niches (as cowboys, mayordomos, and domestic servants) later taken by mulatto slaves. Various AGCA documents suggest the shift would have occurred whether or not slave imports into Guatemala had declined in the seventeenth century, since the Hispanicized mulatto held a number of distinct advantages over the bozal.

19. For the dramatic post-1680 rise in legitimacy among the city's gente ordinaria, especially outside the central Sagrario, see appendix 3.

20. Marriage totals (see table 6) suggest the city's free mulatto population constituted a plurality of all gente ordinaria in every decade from 1650 to 1770.

21. A pardo infantry (militia) captain, Juan de Dios Aristondo, was named maestro mayor de arquitectura and *fontanero* (chief water official) on 27 October 1741. LC 31, AGCA, A1 1793 11.787, fols. 365v and 366v. See also Markman, *Colonial Architecture of Antigua Guatemala*, 57; and Ernesto Chinchilla Aguilar, *Historia del arte en Guatemala*, for mention of numerous prominent casta and Indian designer-builders. The shoemaker was among fifty infantrymen sent to man the Castillo del Río de San Juan de Granada in 1724. AGCA, A2 109 2102.

22. AGCA, A1 1577 10.221, fols. 5-8.

23. "Señor. El Sargento mayor Felipe de Fuentes vecino de la ciudad de Santiago de Guatemala refiere es hijo natural del Capitán Don Francisco de Fuentes y Guzmán y de María de Alvarado parda libre," AGI, Guatemala 74. The words "Consejo en 27 mayo 1680" appear on the document's cover.

24. Baptismal tables in appendix 3 demonstrate that free castas, at least those in Santiago de Guatemala, were not bastards as often as one is led to believe. For a discussion of the problem and data from late eighteenth-century Oaxaca, see Woodrow Borah and Sherburne F. Cook, "Marriage and Legitimacy in Mexican Culture." See also Bowser, "Colonial Spanish America," 38–39 and n. 83. As for illegitimacy, Mörner concludes: "More research is needed on the frequency of illegitimacy in colonial Latin America. It is particularly interesting because of the sad conditions in this respect in Latin America today." *Race Mixture*, 67, n. 57.

25. Precisely when free mulatto–Indian marriage weakened is impossible to pinpoint without Sagrario records for the 1620s, 1630s, and 1640s.

26. Indian women who married non-Indians in León married mulattoes "almost exclusively." Brading and Wu, "Population Growth and Crisis," 7.

27. It is often difficult to determine if Indians cited in gente ordinaria parish registers are tributaries or naborías. While marriages between Indian tributaries of the city appear to have been recorded in barrio or monastery chapels, tributaries who married blacks, castas, or naborías were apparently included in either tributary or gente ordinaria registers. A majority of Indians who worked and resided in the Spanish households of the Sagrario were probably naborías.

28. Free mulatto–mestizo marriage indices may in fact understate marital ties between the two, given the impact of widespread miscegenation on parish record keeping.

29. Mörner, *Race Mixture*, 58. Castizo–free mulatto unions are recorded in the "Others and Unidentified" column of the free mulatto marriage tables in appendix 1. Early seventeenth-century Castilians used "castizo" to describe those of good lineage. Américo Castro, *The Spaniards*, 51. Adapted to Spanish America's multiracial society and socioracial terminology, "castizo" was nonetheless reserved for those who fell short of the elite Spanish phenotype. It was thus both compliment and insult.

30. Free mulatto–castizo marriages numbered two in the 1720s, nine in the 1730s, fourteen in the 1740s, fourteen in the 1750s, and twenty-five in the 1760s. While such totals are too small to apply the Tilly formula, their distribution—twice as many in the peripheral San Sebastián as in the central Sagrario—confirms patterns of casta miscegenation and upward mobility, especially outside Santiago de Guatemala's core. John Chance found a small number of male and female castizos listed in the marriage registers of Oaxaca's Sagrario Parish for 1693–1700, three decades before castizos first appear in Santiago de Guatemala's marriage registers. *Race and Class*, 122, 136–37.

31. Important evidence the Sagrario's Spanish were of purer descent than San Sebastián's comes in the form of figures showing the Sagrario suffered Spanish population declines while San Sebastián registered increases simultaneous with the growth of the free mulatto, mestizo, and castizo populations there. But evidence that Spanish population declines in Los Remedios

were coupled with a rise in that parish's free mulatto-Spanish intermarriage index seems to be at odds with this interpretation. Perhaps the Spanish of Los Remedios moved elsewhere in the city to escape the frequent flooding of the Pensativo. LC 28, AGCA, A1 1790 11.784, fols. 219v, 221–22. A minor 1732 earthquake may also have prompted their departure. AGCA, A1 4000 30.314 (originally undated document dated 1732 by J. Joaquín Pardo).

32. One focus of contact may have been the weaving trade, which appears to have been centered in small *talleres* (workshops) in San Sebastián. Because free mulattoes and Spaniards alike became apprentice and master weavers, working hand in hand and living near their shops, the two may have intermarried more than they would have otherwise. San Sebastián's marriage registers (APSS) include numerous entries in which weavers are named as grooms, *padrinos* (godparents), or witnesses.

33. See table 8. See also AGCA, A1 210 5002, fols. 5–5v.

34. "New Spaniards" is used here to describe individuals who passed from the ladino, mestizo, and castizo segments into the Spanish segment in much the same way as the "new Christians" passed, through conversion, from the Jewish caste into that of the Christians in fourteenth- and fifteenth-century Iberia. See Castro, *Spaniards*, 53, 68, 72, passim, for a discussion of the Spanish *converso* (convert). Also see Stanley Payne, *A History of Spain and Portugal*, 1:208–12, for a discussion of conversos throughout the peninsula. The European Spanish of late seventeenth- and eighteenth-century Guatemala did not despise those new to their ranks to the same degree as their predecessors did. Nor were they jealous of the upstarts' wealth and influence, because the new Spanish of the later colonial period had so little. The new Spanish of the sixteenth century, however—mestizo sons of conquistadores, for example, who were granted their fathers' encomiendas—*were* resented by the established Spanish vecinos for contesting their social and economic standing. On increased marriage of Spanish men and women to castas in Mexico City's Sagrario Parish (and elsewhere in New Spain), see Seed, *To Love, Honor, and Obey*, 146ff.

35. Despite population decline due to intermarriage and a number of other factors, it would appear that the intramarriage index for barrio tributary Indians would have been comparable to that for nontributary Indians.

36. While indices for marriages between Indians and free mixed groups failed to continue their rise after 1669 (the Indian–free mulatto index actually fell during this period), they remained at higher than expected or near expected levels through the 1760s. Nevertheless, growing numbers of Indians married free mulattoes and mestizos beginning in the final decades of the seventeenth century. These increases are not reflected in Indian marriage indices with these groups since the number of free mulatto and mestizo marriages increased dramatically after about 1670. Total Indian marriages also grew in number, but not as fast.

37. The precipitous decline of Indian–black slave marriage indices after 1720 is probably associated with the decline of the city's black slave population during that period, itself linked with a sharp drop in the African slave trade a decade or so before. Mulatto slave totals began to decline around the same time, but the fall was more gradual, which may explain why Indian–mulatto slave ties were stronger than Indian–black slave ties.

38. The low number of free blacks who married in any one decade helps explain the erratic course of this index.

39. This is only an assumption, given the lack of data about the gender of Indians who married. However, since so many Indian naborías were servants, and since nearly every account of household makeup in Spanish colonial America suggests servants were mostly women, it is reasonable to assume that a high percentage of Santiago's naborías were women. The predominance of Indian women in Spanish-headed households can at least be seen in the series of Sagrario censuses, ca. 1680, in the APS. For a comparison of male and female intermarriage rates in late eighteenth-century New Spain, see Brading and Wu, "Population Growth and Crisis," 7–9. More recent studies on Spanish, especially Spanish creole, marriage to upwardly mobile castas include Chance, *Race and Class*; and Seed, *To Love, Honor, and Obey*. Precious little is known about the selection of marriage partners in Spanish American multiracial societies. Were the patterns found in Spanish peninsular culture predominant among the Indians and castas or did Amerindian and African patterns come to play an important part in the selection process? What impact did soci<
racial differences have on this process? For a classic discussion of courtship and marriage in Spain and Spanish America, see George M. Foster, *Culture and Conquest*, 125–42. This study would have been enriched by greater consideration of the gender of marriage partners, especially in cases of intermarriage. But this added variable might have unduly complicated the collection and analysis of such a large quantity of data.

40. The American-born slave of mixed descent, by contrast, had a better chance of passing out of the mulatto group. This was especially true in the late seventeenth and eighteenth centuries, when the line that separated mulatto from mestizo became blurred and ladinos began to make their presence felt.

41. Only in the 1630s and from the 1710s onward did Tilly measures of free mulatto endogamy exceed those for mestizo endogamy.

42. Weakening this hypothesis somewhat is evidence that increases in mestizo-Spanish marriage indices in the Sagrario and San Sebastián were less dramatic than declines in mestizo intramarriage indices there. But in Los Remedios, as in the city at large, the decline in mestizo intramarriage was of the same magnitude as the climb in mestizo-Spanish marriage, giving the hypothesis greater validity.

43. The only decennial exception, the 1720s, saw the mestizo–free mulatto index exceed the mestizo-Indian index by a single point.

44. Entry, of course, was contingent on Indians' escaping tributary status.

45. Ladino growth was hardly restricted to the capital. The region's trade centers and areas of commercial crop production also witnessed such growth. Free mulatto–Indian relations there may have been an even bigger factor in ladino creation than free mulatto–mestizo unions.

46. AGCA, A3 1749 28.130, fol. 229 (30 October 1778). The absorption of the free mulatto by the mestizo, or rather the amalgamation of the two groups, has since erased distinctions that were once obvious. Today anyone seen in Guatemala City who fits a black or mulatto phenotype is most likely

a relatively recent immigrant from the Atlantic coast, Belize, or the West Indies.

47. Only in the 1740s and 1750s did the composite mestizo–mulatto slave marriage index fall significantly below the expected level. The slight drop below the expected level in the first decade of the eighteenth century was followed by a three-decade recovery to previous levels.

48. If it were true that most American Spaniards (often of mixed ancestry) lived in the peripheral parishes and most European Spaniards lived in the central Sagrario, it would follow that the former had a greater tendency to marry free castas than did the latter. The highest decennial total of composite Spanish marriages occurred in the 1680s, decades after the number of Spanish unions peaked in the Sagrario. In San Sebastián, by contrast, total Spanish marriages peaked in the 1750s (see appendix 1 and table 6). Perhaps the city's European Spanish declined in number after 1670, while the American Spanish population continued to expand.

49. Evidence of this eighteenth-century phenomenon may be found in all parishes of the city, but it was most obvious in San Sebastián (app. 1). Also see table 18, in chapter seven, below.

50. Peter Smith coined the term "marital proximity." Personal communication (June 1974).

CHAPTER SIX **Supplying the City: The Casta Economic Revolution**

1. In the case of towns held in encomienda by the Crown, deliveries of tribute items were made to Spanish Royal Treasury officials in the plaza mayor; in the case of those held by individuals, tribute was brought to the encomenderos' houses.

2. Certain tribute items—eggs and chickens, for example—were usually sold or proffered without regard to habitat.

3. See Cortés y Larraz, *Descripción geográfico-moral,* for a discussion of the various crops grown in the towns (parishes) of the region. For a systematic summary of Cortés y Larraz's data, see Francisco de Solano, "La economía agraria de Guatemala." On Indian agricultural production and specialized trades by towns in the late seventeenth century, see Fuentes y Guzmán, *Obras históricas,* 1:218–342. For a less systematic discussion of the above, see Gage, *Travels.* For an innovative study on the sixteenth-century importance of various ecological zones in the alcaldía mayor of Zapotitlán and Suchitepéquez, see Elías Zamora Acosta, "El control vertical de diferentes pisos ecológicos."

4. Blacks, presumably slaves, were considered to be a principal cause of disorder in the market as early as 1537. In November of that year the cabildo tried but failed to prevent them from entering the market. Remesal, *Historia general,* 1:57.

5. See n. 1 above; and "Las tasaciones . . . [1549]," AGI, Guatemala 128.

6. A typical decree, like that issued by the cabildo on 6 May 1590, ordered that all persons bringing foodstuffs to the city be allowed to bring them freely to sell in the public market. AGCA, A1 1751 11.737, fol. 10. Other examples include LC 22, AGCA, A1 1784 11.778, fols. 131–32v (Cabildo: 23 January 1693); and AGCA, A1 1508, fol. 69 (1743). For similar cabildo

concerns in late colonial Guadalajara, see Eric Van Young, *Hacienda and Market*, 93-94.

7. AGCA, A1 2364 17.878 (1715); and AGCA, A3 888 16.364 (1771).

8. MacLeod, *Spanish Central America*, 311.

9. Towns held by the Crown in encomienda were rarely required to plant a specified amount of wheat since Indians lacked the necessities for plowing (oxen and plows) and threshing (horses or mules). Petapa was one exception. See "Las tasaciones . . . [1549]," AGI, Guatemala 128, fol. 247. For examples of encomienda towns that raised wheat as part of their tribute obligations, see "Las tasaciones . . . [1549]," AGI, Guatemala 128, fols. 91-92, 102, 105-6, 119, 124, 127, 133-34, 146, 167, 181, 192, 194-95, 200, 218, and 246-47. No encomienda towns came into Crown hands until after Pedro de Alvarado's death in 1541. Kramer, "Politics of Encomienda Distribution," 215-16.

10. MacLeod, *Spanish Central America*, 119-42.

11. Between 1560 and 1568 records (though incomplete) show that as many as forty-four land titles were granted specifically for wheat cultivation in the Valley of Guatemala. The heaviest concentrations were in the valleys of San Martín Jilotepeque (eighteen), La Hermita (thirteen), and Petapa (four). AGCA, A3 2863 41.694, 41.695, and 41.698. A good agricultural history of Santiago and its comarca is lacking, despite documentary evidence sufficient to produce a study of the scope and scale of Van Young, *Hacienda and Market*. For useful beginnings toward such a history, see Julio César Pinto Soria, "El valle central de Guatemala"; and Jorge Luján Muñoz, *Agricultura, mercado y sociedad*.

12. Audiencia a su Majestad (Santiago: 26 November 1603), AGI, Guatemala 11. Some Indians, of course, continued to grow wheat in the Valley of Guatemala. For details on Indian wheat growing in San Juan Comalapa during the late seventeenth century, see AGCA, A1 5762 48.242. Fuentes y Guzmán, writing in the late seventeenth century, actually complained of Indian use of communal labor to harvest their wheat, while he and his fellow creoles had to hire repartimiento labor to harvest theirs. That the repartimiento labor was subsidized did not enter his mind. *Obras históricas*, 1:356. Wheat growing among the Indians of the Quezaltenango and Totonicapán regions appears to have been more common than in Santiago's comarca, perhaps because there was less competition from Spanish labradores. For mention of Indian wheat farmers in Quezaltenango, see AGCA, A1 195 3947 (1705).

13. Repartimiento in both Guatemala and New Spain appears to have been instituted just as the Crown prohibited encomenderos from exacting servicio ordinario from the Indians they held in encomienda. For examples of such prohibitions in Guatemala, see "Las tasaciones . . . [1549]," AGI, Guatemala 128; for examples in Mexico, see Gibson, *Aztecs under Spanish Rule*, 226. For details of agricultural repartimiento in both, see Lesley Byrd Simpson, *The Repartimiento System of Native Labor*, 93ff.; MacLeod, *Spanish Central America*, 206; Gibson, *Aztecs under Spanish Rule*, 231-35; and Van Young, *Hacienda and Market*, 240-45. For details on the distribution of Indian labor for wheat production in the late seventeenth century, see Pilar Hernández Aparicio, "Problemas socioeconómicos en el valle de Guatemala"; and Luján Muñoz, *Agricultura, mercado y sociedad*.

14. AGCA, A1 4077 32.355 (1578), A1 5762 48.242 (1606), A1 5762 48.243 (involving the hiding of wheat by Indian *trigueros* [small-scale wheat growers] of San Juan Comalapa in 1695), A1 39 959 (1753), and A1 39 961 (1753). While wheat prices of three and three-fourths to five pesos, or thirty to forty reales, per fanega were considered excessive in 1556 (Audiencia a la Corona [Santiago: 31 April 1556], AGI, Guatemala 9), a fanega of wheat cost five to six pesos during a period of scarcity more than two centuries later. A3 33 663 (1770). Wheat shortages were particularly acute in 1696, when wheat cost thirty to thirty-six pesos per fanega, due in part to hoarding by regatones. Don Antonio Varona y Villanueva, Síndico y Procurador General de la ciudad, a su Majestad (Santiago: 24 January 1697), AGI, Guatemala 215, fol. 1v.

15. Gage, *Travels*, 206–7. Cabildo and church alike also used the wheat storage facilities in San Lucas. See, respectively, LC 10, AGCA, A1 1772 11.766 (1614), fols. 194 and 198; and AGCA, A3 2121 32.051 (1556–57). On grain speculation in eighteenth-century Guadalajara, see Van Young, *Hacienda and Market*, 92.

16. One cannot easily divide Santiago's elite into (rural) labradores and (urban) mercantilists, as has been done for other parts of Spanish America: many prominent individuals were both, as well as cabildo members. Audiencia al Rey (Santiago: 30 April 1601), AGI, Guatemala 11. For another viewpoint, see Frederick B. Pike, "Aspects of Cabildo Economic Regulation." Webre's fine research suggests that in the seventeenth century many cabildo seats were held by recently arrived Spanish peninsular merchants who focused more on commerce and moneylending than landholding. "Cabildo Membership."

17. See, for example, Relación de Matías Tejero, Escribano Público y del Valle de Guatemala (December 1622), AGI, Guatemala 66, fols. 1–3v.

18. One notable exception occurred in mid-1746, when the combination of drought, grain shortages, and a typhus epidemic dealt Santiago a serious blow. LC 32, AGCA, A1 1794 11.788, fols. 138–41.

19. For a description of where wheat and other crops were cultivated in Guatemala and El Salvador, see "Testimonio de las cartas respuestas . . . [ca. 1770]," AGI, Guatemala 948. See also Cortés y Larraz, *Descripción geográfico-moral*, vols. 1–2; and Francisco de Solano, "Economía agraria de Guatemala," 298–300.

20. LC 10, AGCA, A1 1772 11.766, fols. 47v and 51 (Cabildo: 30 April and 6 June 1610, respectively). In late 1694 the cabildo asked the president of the audiencia to suspend auctions of grain, collected as tribute in the corregimientos of Atitlán, Tecpanatitlán, Quezaltenango, and Huehuetenango, until officials could establish how much Santiago and the surrounding Valley of Guatemala would require. LC 22, AGCA, A1 1784 11.778, fols. 319v–20v (Cabildo: 14 December 1694).

In January 1771 Santiago's alguacil mayor charged that Quezaltenango's alcalde mayor and a number of its prominent vecinos (including one Don Ignacio de Urbina) were not only buying up large supplies of wheat and holding it for future resale, but blocking Indians from buying wheat to carry to the capital. LC 47, AGCA, A1 1800 11.803 (Cabildo: 16 January 1771). Similar practices had apparently been tolerated for years. Some thirty years before, for example, Urbina was reported to have bought 4,000 fanegas of wheat with plans to hold it until prices rose in Chiapas, Soconusco, or Santiago. AGCA, A3 2360 34.775 (1740).

21. Among the smugglers was a presumed Spaniard ("por el traje parecía español") believed to have smuggled fourteen mule loads of wheat out of Santiago in February 1705. AGCA, A1 4014 30.762. Ten years later the cabildo expressed concern at reports that two Peruvians were in the Quezaltenango region buying up large quantities of wheat. LC 26, AGCA, A1 1788 11.782, fol. 147 (Cabildo: 22 January 1715).

22. In December 1699, to cite one exception, Indian traders (from Patzún and Tecpán Guatemala) and their cargo were seized on the suspicion they had plied Indian growers with alcohol before buying their wheat. No proof of the charge was presented, but the Indian muleteers lost their wheat and were remanded to Santiago for punishment. "Causa de oficio contra los yndios de los Pueblos de Pasón [Patzún] y Tecpán Guatemala sobre regatones de trigo," AGI, Escribanía de Cámara 377A, pieza 26. On *regatonería* (reselling) in wheat and flour in eighteenth-century Guadalajara, see Van Young, *Hacienda and Market*, 70–71.

23. AGCA, A1 2198 15.753, fols. 22–23. A transcription of these ordinances, passed by the cabildo on 9 October 1551, was kindly made available by Don Manuel Rubio Sánchez, former director of the AGCA.

24. Bakers are listed in a *diezmo* (tithe) account book for the years 1656–57, AGCA, A3 2121 32.051. They include Spanish and free mulatto women, one free black woman, one free mulatto man, and one Indian woman (who lived in the house of a Spanish bread-baking family). Most such records remain uncatalogued in the AHA.

25. Despite higher wheat prices, the panaderos were expected to sell a pound and a half of bread for one real. Spanish authorities, in effect, required the panaderos to maintain prices even when their costs skyrocketed. On the abuses of bakers in Guadalajara, see Van Young, *Hacienda and Market*, 68. Adulteration of highly priced foodstuffs (coffee, beef) when prices rise is commonplace in modern-day Guatemala City.

26. Also, the Spanish feared that direct buying from Indian wheat growers might deplete seed supplies needed for the next planting. LC 24, AGCA, A1 1784 11.778, fols. 142–43 (Cabildo: 7 April 1693).

27. LC 24, AGCA, A1 1784 11.778, fols. 147v–48 (Cabildo: 21 April 1693).

28. For examples of these two supply methods, see "Las tasaciones . . . [1549]," AGI, Guatemala 128, fols. 151, 193, and 256.

29. For mention of the auctioning of foodstuffs paid in tribute to Santiago's Spanish vecinos, see Cuentas de 1566, AGI, Contaduría 967; and Cuentas de 1576, AGI, Contaduría 968. From the 1540s onward, Spanish encomenderos used auctions to convert tribute items into cash. MacLeod, *Spanish Central America*, 131.

30. Maize was distributed among *tortilleras* (tortilla makers, mostly Indian women) in such a way that the nonelites were almost always assured a steady, cheap food supply. In the mid-1690s, however, after highland Guatemala suffered poor grain harvests for three or more successive years, maize became so scarce that tortilla prices, at their worst levels, quadrupled. Auto del Presidente de la Audiencia, Don Gabriel Sánchez de Berrospe (Santiago: 27 June 1696), AGI, Escribanía de Cámara 373A, cuad. 8. The poor, as a

result, were priced out of the market for a time, and the number of Indian tortilleras plummeted. Of the remaining tortilleras, most regularly found themselves surrounded by hoards of people eager to buy despite the cost. Wheat and bread prices during the mid-1690s, by contrast, climbed twentyfold at their worst point. These shortages coincide with shortages, drought, and serious frosts in central Mexico, indicating that broad weather patterns may have been to blame. The agricultural crisis was made more serious by epidemics in both Mexico and Guatemala during this same period. See appendix 5 and Gibson, *Aztecs under Spanish Rule*, appendixes 4 and 5.

31. Santiago was spared food riots altogether, apparently because maize prices only rarely caused great hardship (see n. 30 above). For food riots in Mexico, see Gibson, *Aztecs under Spanish Rule*, appendix 5. On the relationship between maize prices and urban riots, see Chester L. Guthrie, "Colonial Economy, Trade, Industry, and Labor," 113–15, and "Riots in Seventeenth-Century Mexico City." For the impact of maize price fluctuations on a Spanish American colonial society, see Enrique Florescano, *Precios del maíz*. A valuable source on the maize supply in late seventeenth-century Guatemala is Luján Muñoz, *Agricultura, mercado y sociedad*, 67–74.

32. The eastern valleys around Lake Amatitlán were also maize-growing areas. To offset shortages and high prices, the cabildo agreed in September 1736 to order the Indian tributaries of the towns there to plant maize. LC 31, AGCA, A1 1793 11.787, fols. 53v–54 (Cabildo: 4 September 1736). Five years later efforts were again made to supplement the city's supply by commissioning large plantings of maize on the Pacific coast, in Escuintla. This effort ended in disaster when the crop was badly damaged in a six-day rain storm. LC 31, AGCA, A1 1793 11.787, fols. 278v–79 (Cabildo: 6 May 1740) and 336–36v (Cabildo: 27 October 1741).

33. See, for example, AGCA, A3 2536 37.193 (1693); and Pardo, *Efemérides*, 68 (4 March 1659).

34. AGCA, A3 2530 36.962 (1721).

35. Regarding enforcement of prohibitions against the regatones, see, for example, AGCA, A3 2357 34.706 (1692); and AGCA, A3 2360 34.790 (1756). The latter notes that the regatones brought their wares not to the public plaza but to their houses or to *mesones* (taverns), where they would be resold once again, at still higher prices.

36. AGCA, A1 2211 15.793.

37. AGCA, A3 888 16.364 (1771).

38. See, for example, AGCA, A3 2386 35.238, concerning porquero activities from 1 August 1734 to 31 July 1735. The assignment of particular Indian communities to supply pork and lard to the vecinos of Santiago appears to have originated with mid-sixteenth century servicio ordinario obligations. See Sherman, *Forced Native Labor*, 92, 197–98, 201; and Lutz, "Introducción histórica."

39. Regarding shakedowns, especially by servants of Spanish vecinos, see AGCA, A3 2536 37.089 (1634). For one official response to this kind of harassment, see Auto del Presidente, Sr. D. Joseph Vázquez Prego Monteros y Sotomayor (Santiago: 1 February 1753), AGCA, A1 1509 (Providencias del Gobierno, 1752–1821), fols. 23ff.

40. One rare mention appears in the minutes of a 13 October 1772 ca-

bildo meeting, where it was charged that *vendedores aventureros* (illicit mutton vendors, in this case) often gave more ounces of mutton for a real than the city's butcher shops, because they dealt in stolen meat. LC 48, AGCA, A1 1801 11.804, fol. 126.

41. Although the Spanish initially raised sheep in the valleys east of Santiago, these lands may have been given over to wheat and sugar by 1650, forcing obligados to buy flocks as far afield as Oaxaca, in New Spain, and the western corregimientos of Huehuetenango and Quezaltenango. The libros de cabildo contain numerous references to auctioning off the obligation to supply mutton to Santiago. For the announcement of the auction of the city's mutton supply in the western highlands during the 1650s and 1660s, see LC 16, AGCA, A1 1778 11.772, fol. 319v (Cabildo: 4 September 1654); LC 18, AGCA, A1 1780 11.774, fols. 86–86v (Cabildo: 6 October 1665), 168v–69 (Cabildo: 2 September 1667), and 234v–35 (Cabildo: 14 June 1669). For similar announcements in the valleys of Oaxaca and Tehuantepec in New Spain during the early 1660s, see LC 17, AGCA, A1 1779 11.773, fols. 260v (Cabildo: 6 March 1660) and 412–12v (Cabildo: 31 October 1662). For a brief description of sheep raising in the Valley of Mixco and elsewhere around Lake Amatitlán, ca. 1630, see Gage, *Travels*, 185. See also Lovell, *Conquest and Survival*, 121–26.

42. The establishment of additional butcher shops in San Sebastián and Santo Domingo was suggested in 1652. LC 16, AGCA, A1 1778 11.772, fol. 191 (Cabildo: 13 September 1652). And by the early 1680s another butcher shop was proposed, for San Francisco. LC 20, AGCA, A1 1782 11.776, fols. 97v–98 (Cabildo: 28 January 1681). Each appears to have opened soon after the proposal was put forth.

43. See, for example, LC 21, AGCA, A1 1783 11.777, fols. 196v–97 (Cabildo: 4 March 1687). The cabildo tried at times to determine the number and ownership of all cattle entering and leaving the city. LC 24, AGCA, A1 1786 11.780, fols. 51–51v (Cabildo: 29 November 1701); LC 30, AGCA, A1 1792 11.786, fols. 128v–29 (Cabildo: 5 May 1733); and AGCA, A3 2357 34.714 (1699). Using this information in combination with matadero records would have made it possible to discover who was illegally slaughtering cattle (and thus depriving Crown and city of revenues), but no such systematic survey was ever conducted.

44. The alcabala was instituted in the late 1570s. Pardo, *Efemérides*, 22.

45. Regarding meat supplied through the matadero's back door, see LC 20, AGCA, A1 1782 11.776, fols. 97v–98 (Cabildo: 28 January 1681); and LC 30, AGCA, A1 1792 11.786, fols. 59v–60 (Cabildo: 16 August 1732). On the slaughter of more cattle than called for under contract, see LC 20, AGCA, A1 1782 11.776, fol. 59 (Cabildo: 26 March 1680); AGCA, A3 2536 37.095 (1698); and AGCA, A1 2212 15.806 (1723).

46. For rustling and clandestine slaughter by castas, see LC 31, AGCA, A1 1793 11.787, fols. 59v–60 (1731); AGCA, A1 2456 19.068 (1738); AGCA, A1 1981 13.529 (1749); AGCA, A1 411 8.665 (1761); and AGCA, A1 6072 59.720 (1758).

47. These outposts, poorly constructed and often unattended, were virtually an invitation to steal meat. AGCA, A3 2536 37.124 (1756).

48. AGCA, A3 2536 37.122 (1755).

49. AGCA, A3 2362 34.831 (1764).

50. At 1697 prices, the revendedoras were required to give buyers three and a half pounds of beef for one-half real and double that amount for one real. AGCA, A1 2211 15.793 (1697).

51. AGCA, A1 6072 54.714 (1700).

52. For a transcript of the petition, see AGCA, A3 2357 34.714.

53. This suggests that the mulatas revendedoras began peddling beef in the mid-seventeenth century or even earlier. Confirming their contention is LC 16, AGCA, A1 1778 11.772, fol. 191 (Cabildo: 13 September 1652). Presumably non-Spanish women (with appealing nicknames) participated in the beef trade in late eighteenth-century Guadalajara. Van Young, *Hacienda and Market*, 55.

54. AGCA, A3 2357 34.714 (1715).

55. The cabildo charged in response that the revendedoras' beef came from sources other than the matadero (and, presumably, the carnicerías).

56. The decision coincided with the seizure of a mestiza widow with seven children for selling carne adobada in the plaza. Later released, the woman was stripped of her huipil (usually only worn by Indian women), given ten lashes in the central plaza, and jailed. AGCA, A3 2357 34.714.

57. Given that the revendedoras continued to work in the central plaza, right under the noses of cabildo and audiencia officials, they must have had little difficulty selling beef in Spanish and casta residential areas of the city.

58. Spanish officials did not fail to stop the black market for lack of trying. Witness the number of edicts banning regatonería: AGCA, A3 2357 34.714 (1699–1747); LC 23, AGCA, A1 1785 11.779, fol. 215 (Cabildo: 4 September 1699); Pardo, *Efemérides*, 103 (Cabildo: 4 September 1703); LC 24, AGCA, A1 1786 11.780, fols. 225v (Cabildo: 15 April 1704) and 259v–61 (Cabildo: 20 January 1705); LC 26, AGCA, A1 1788 11.782, fols. 143 (Cabildo: 8 January 1715) and 164–64v (Cabildo: 9 April 1715); LC 27, AGCA, A1 1789 11.783, fols. 171 (Cabildo: 11 August 1719) and 212–12v (Cabildo: 17 January 1721); LC 30, AGCA, A1 1792 11.786, fols. 59v–60 (Cabildo: 16 August 1732); LC 31, AGCA, A1 1793 11.787, fols. 99v–100v (Cabildo: 28 February 1737); LC 32, AGCA, A1 1794 11.788, fol. 124 (Cabildo: 27 May 1746); AGCA, A3 2360 34.791 (1748); AGCA, A1 6072 54.719 (1755); AGCA, A3 2536 37.136 (1761); AGCA, A3 2536 37.137 (1761); and AGCA, A1 263 5784, fol. 103 (1764). One document indicates a degree of official flexibility with regard to the regatones. A top city official suggested on 18 April 1760 that peddlers be allowed to sell meat when supplies were plentiful. LC 37, AGCA, A1 1797 11.793, fol. 38v. For the socioracial background of matadero and carnicería officials, see AGCA, A3 2357 34.714 (1700); and LC 20, AGCA, A1 1782 11.776, fols. 97v–98 (Cabildo: 28 January 1681).

59. A real in 1686 bought eight pounds of beef from the carniceras regatonas of the plaza, but fourteen pounds (probably somewhat less) in the city's official carnicerías. Fuentes y Guzmán, *Obras históricas*, 1:203. Revendedoras reportedly gave seven pounds per real in 1697 (when peddling was legal if meat was purchased from the obligado), six to seven pounds per real in 1699 (the year peddling was prohibited), and just fourteen ounces per real in 1780 (by which time the earthquake-shattered city was called Antigua Guatemala). By comparison, official weights per real were eight to ten pounds in 1695–96, thirteen pounds around 1710, and five to six pounds in 1780.

Francisco de Paula García Peláez, *Memorias para la historia,* 2:188; and Lutz, *Historia sociodemográfica,* appendix 9.

60. LC 20, AGCA, A1 1782 11.776, fols. 97v–98 (Cabildo: 28 January 1681); LC 21, AGCA, A1 1783 11.777, fols. 153–54 (Cabildo: 8 April 1686); AGCA, A1 2211 15.793 (1697); AGCA, A1 6072 54.714 (1700); AGCA, A3 2360 34.789 (1748); and AGCA, A3 2362 34.831. The cabildo in addition heard complaints that the carnicerías often closed early, leaving many families no recourse but to buy their beef from peddlers. AGCA, A3 2357 34.714 (1715).

61. Sevillan merchants managed to win a prohibition on wine imports from Peru between 1615 and 1685, so many of the Peruvian supplies during that period were smuggled into Santiago. See MacLeod, *Spanish Central America,* 265ff., for an excellent discussion of the importation and smuggling of wine.

62. See Cuentas de 1565, 1566, and 1567, AGI, Contaduría 967; Oficiales reales Don Juan de Castellanos Horozco and Don García de Castellanos a su Majestad (Santiago: 28 March 1585), AGI, Guatemala 45; Oidor Bartolomé de Cañas Villafane a su Majestad (Santiago: 12 October 1616), AGI, Guatemala 12; AGCA, A1 4084 32.407 (1590); and AGCA, A1 4093 32.469 (1608). See also Pardo, *Efemérides,* 22, on the need to ban taverns from Indian barrios (1575).

63. For examples of free castas' holding wine and tavern licenses, see LC 21, AGCA, A1 1783 11.777, fols. 172 (Cabildo: 3 September 1686) and 213v (Cabildo: 8 July 1687); Cuentas de 1690, AGCA, A1 2219 15.916; and LC 24, AGCA, A1 1786 11.780, fol. 155 (8 June 1703). In 1689–90 a total of twenty-one tavern licenses were issued, three of which were held by mulatas (one Peruvian), one by a Spanish woman, and seventeen by Spanish men. Cuentas de 1690, AGCA, A1 2219 15.916. See also Luján Muñoz, *Agricultura, mercado y sociedad,* 39–43.

64. LC 22, AGCA, A1 1784 11.778, fol. 256v (Cabildo: 7 July 1693); LC 31, AGCA, A1 1793 11.787, fol. 200v (Cabildo: 27 February 1739); LC 32, AGCA, A1 1794 11.788, fol. 1v (Cabildo: 14 January 1744); and AGCA, A1 2250 16.335, fol. 116v. As early as 1658 cabildo members tried to exclude blacks, mulattoes, and mestizos from owning taverns or pulperías. LC 17, AGCA, A1 1779 11.773, fol. 154 (Cabildo: 19 February 1658). It appears that free casta women were suspected of combining liquor sales with prostitution, though no evidence exists to support this conclusion. Thus one mestiza, Catalina de Aldana, was considered a good candidate for a liquor license in 1686 because she was an "elderly woman." LC 21, AGCA, A1 1783 11.777, fol. 172 (Cabildo: 3 September 1686).

65. Alcoholic drinks besides wine and chicha included *caldos* (winelike spirits brought from Spain or Peru); *guarapo* (fermented sugarcane juice); *aguardiente* (brandy or other strong spirits); *aguardiente de caña* (sugarcane brandy, a stronger version of guarapo); and *mistela* (a drink made with wine or aguardiente, water, sugar, and aromatic spices such as cinnamon). For brief descriptions, see *Diccionario de la lengua española,* 40, 228, 409, 882; *Velázquez Spanish and English Dictionary,* 37, 129, 460; and Ruth Bunzel, "The Role of Alcoholism in Two Central American Cultures," 366. For a discussion of chicha consumption in 1820s Guatemala, see Dunn, *Guatimala,* 102.

66. In 1753 one asentista was awarded sole rights to produce aguardiente

de caña, dispensable only in the city's four official taverns, beginning in 1755. LC 38, AGCA, A1 1798 11.794, fols. 35ff. (Cabildo: 28 May 1762). For related cabildo discussions, see LC 36, AGCA, A1 1797 11.792, fols. 183ff. (Cabildo: 13 July 1759); and LC 37, AGCA, A1 1797 11.793, fols. 52v (Cabildo: 11 June 1760) and 129 (Cabildo: 27 February 1761).

67. Criminal records show an increase in charges against *chicheros* (chicha bootleggers) at about the time the aguardiente de caña monopoly was established (see n. 66 above). See, for example, AGCA, A2 140 2576 (1741), detailing a prosecution for the illegal manufacture of chicha and aguardiente. While this may be due to increased Spanish vigilance, it may also be attributable to the loss of criminal (and other) records from earlier periods. Official searches for hidden stills probably resulted in the destruction of only a fraction of their total, especially when illicit production outside the city proper is taken into account. For an early case of chicha manufacture on the outskirts of the city, see LC 18, AGCA, A1 1780 11.774, fols. 96v–100 (Cabildo: 11 February 1666). Spanish officials often inspected licensed taverns to determine whether they were selling bootleg liquor. Tavern owners claimed the searches were unjustified. See AGCA, A1 4007 30.519 (1745), and AGCA, A1 2285 16.627 (1751). For a more detailed discussion of clandestine liquor production in the eighteenth-century city, see Lutz, "Santiago de Guatemala."

68. Cortés y Larraz, *Descripción geográfico-moral*, 1:24–34; AGCA, A2 141 2577 (1747); AGCA, A2 146 2679 (1760); and AGCA, A2 146 2686 (1761). For a study on the relationship between drinking and crime in New Spain, see Taylor, *Drinking, Homicide, and Rebellion*.

69. Crime, in effect, provided a degree of social mobility for those who found legitimate routes blocked by established elite groups. For an exploration of this concept in the modern U.S. context, see Daniel Bell, "Crime as an American Way of Life."

CHAPTER SEVEN **Conclusion**

1. See Hoetink, *Caribbean Race Relations*; and Palmer, "Negro Slavery in Mexico." Other exponents of the plural society model who stress the coercion used to hold together heterogeneous societies include M. G. Smith, *Corporations and Society*, 152 and passim; and Pierre L. Van den Berghe, "Racialism and Assimilation in Africa and the Americas," 424–32.

2. Hoetink, *Caribbean Race Relations*, 97 (italics Hoetink's). Subsequent research on plural or segmented societies, with the exception of Palmer's, has not improved on Hoetink's.

3. See Palmer, "Negro Slavery in Mexico," 29–30. Palmer states that prior to the mid-seventeenth century New Spain could be defined as a plural or segmented society that later evolved into a multiracial society. Palmer says of a multiracial society: "The cleavages that exist between the races are not as great as those that obtain in a plural society. Differences there are, but some common institutions play integrative roles in the society. As in the case of colonial Mexico, a common religion could play this role. Miscegenation could also be a characteristic of such a society. In a multiracial society, phenotypical criteria are most important factors determining one's place in that society."

4. Hoetink, *Caribbean Race Relations*, 106.

5. On the ranking of Indians and black slaves in Spanish America, as well as differences between "legal condition" and "social status," see Mörner, *Race Mixture*, 60. Chance refines Mörner's system, noting "that the relative positions of Negroes and Indians in the hierarchy varied from place to place in colonial Latin America, according to different population proportions. Blacks were more likely to occupy the bottom rung of the prestige ladder in areas where they substantially outnumbered the Indians." *Race and Class*, 128-29, n.

6. I am using homogeneity here not in the sense used by Robert Redfield in his folk-urban continuum but, rather, to describe the results of biological and cultural blending that occurred in Santiago's more popular (or nonelite) barrios. On Redfield see Richard G. Fox, *Urban Anthropology*, 10-11. For additional discussion of homogenization see Anthony D. Smith, *State and Nation in the Third World*.

7. For a fuller discussion of this process, see Lutz and Lovell, "Core and Periphery."

8. See Pinto Soria, *Valle central*; and Luján Muñoz, *Agricultura, mercado y sociedad*.

9. Hoetink, *Caribbean Race Relations*, 106.

10. Hoetink, *Caribbean Race Relations*, 102.

11. See Webre, "Cabildo Membership"; Joba, "Santiago"; and Gustavo Palma Murga, "Núcleos de poder local," for discussion of ongoing Spanish immigration. After independence European (including Spanish), followed later by North American, immigrants continued to fill niches in the elite. Unlike the colonial elite, which was overwhelmingly Spanish, the postindependence elite was dominated by Germans, Britons, a new wave of Spaniards, and citizens of the United States. See suggestive research on this subject by Marta Elena Casaús Arzú, "La metamorfosis de las oligarquías centroamericanas," and *Guatemala: Linaje y racismo*.

It would appear that these later immigrants maintained closer ties with their mother countries and other foreigners than with the local elite, because of cultural and religious differences, greater ease of travel (with the advent of the steamship) and communication, and in-country diplomatic representation by their home countries. This broke, to some extent, the earlier pattern of peninsular-creole intermarriage described by Webre for the seventeenth century. This subject awaits future research.

12. By the 1770s Santiago had nine convents and beaterios for women. Markman, *Colonial Architecture of Antigua Guatemala*.

13. Chance and Taylor find that in late eighteenth-century Antequera, two-thirds (twenty-one) of twenty-nine master craftsmen in some twelve gremios were either creoles or mestizos. Chance and Taylor, "Late Colonial Period," in Chance, *Race and Class*, 167.

14. This claim is based on a reading of diverse AGCA documents. See also Stephen Webre, "Water and Society in a Spanish American City."

15. Jeffrey Kaplow, "The Culture of Poverty in Paris," uses "laboring poor" to describe the urban nonelite in late eighteenth-century Paris.

16. MacLeod, "Indian Riots and Rebellions." On Spanish fear of uprisings by Indians in the vicinity of Santiago or by the urban castas, see Mar-

tínez Peláez, *La patria del criollo*, 286–92. Spanish fear seems unjustified, with hindsight.

17. For a convincing analysis of the importance of these factors in a seventeenth-century Spanish American urban setting, see Stephanie Bower Blank, "Social Integration and Social Stability in a Colonial Spanish American City." Blank, 56, suggests that ties of compadrazgo were much closer between independent nonelites (castas, blacks, and Indians) and the dominant Spanish than they were between dependent nonelites and the ruling elite. For a brief but broader discussion of compadrazgo and extended family networks in the context of Latin American urban history, see Richard M. Morse, "Some Characteristics of Latin American Urban History," 333–34.

18. The bibliography and newspaper clippings on this bleak subject grow by the day. One invaluable source is Robert M. Carmack, ed., *Harvest of Violence*. The term *selective genocide* is used by John Western in his preface to *Outcast Cape Town* (quoting but not citing the work of René Lemarchand), xiii, to describe the horrific experience of the Hutu people of Burundi, "an African Holocaust that weeded out *all* the formally educated and even minimally literate people among the Hutu."

19. On MacLeod's dichotomy, see *Spanish Central America*, 228–31, 308; Adriaan C. van Oss, *Catholic Colonialism*, 48; and Lutz and Lovell, "Core and Periphery." For analysis of recent events in Indian areas, see Carmack, ed., *Harvest of Violence*.

20. Lutz and Lovell, "Core and Periphery."

21. See, for example, Demetrio Cojtí Cuxil, "Lingüística e idiomas mayas en Guatemala"; and Irma Otzoy and Enrique Sam Colop, "Identidad étnica y modernización."

22. On the Guatemalan Maya's centuries-long struggle for survival, see W. George Lovell, "Surviving Conquest." Also see W. George Lovell and Christopher H. Lutz, "Conquest and Population."

23. Europeans and North Americans now function in the niche formerly occupied by Spaniards.

24. Chance, *Race and Class*, 175.

25. Chance, *Race and Class*, 176.

26. Seed, *To Love, Honor, and Obey*, 17, 24.

27. Seed, *To Love, Honor, and Obey*, 25.

28. Lowell Gudmundson Kristjanson, "Mecanismos de movilidad social," and "'Black' into 'White' in Nineteenth Century Spanish America."

29. Claudia Quirós Vargas, *La era de la encomienda*.

30. Quezaltenango, situated in the western highlands, was more Mesoamerican with its large Indian population but, at the same time, similar to the three Salvadoran cities listed in table 19 in terms of the size of its Spanish population. The significant ladino population of Quezaltenango (50.3 percent), however, placed it between the two Mesoamerican cities and Santiago—larger than the former two but smaller than the latter one.

31. Late nineteenth- and early twentieth-century national censuses, though not known for their accuracy, suggest Indians by then represented less than 10 percent of Guatemala City's total population. See Julio César Pinto Soria, "Guatemala de la Asunción."

32. The standard works on the relocation of the city are Cristina Zilbermann de Luján, *Aspectos socio-económicos del traslado*, and Inge Langenberg, *Urbanisation und Bevölkerungsstruktur*.

APPENDIX 7

1. The Crown saw free blacks and free mulattoes as an additional source of revenue. Since they were viewed as more prosperous than Indians, they were charged a higher per capita tribute. (Royal Cédula: Madrid, 27 April 1574), AGCA, A1 1512, fol. 447.
2. Contaduría records in the AGI for the Audiencia of Guatemala have suffered fire damage and are often incomplete, the exception being the latter third of the sixteenth century. Similar records have yet to be located in the AGCA.
3. Cuentas de 1577, AGI, Contaduría 968. In 1577 Juan Fernández Nájara el mozo (the younger), who served as the official Nahuatl interpreter of the audiencia, was appointed to collect the naboría tax since he "knew better than anyone else the debtors who are blacks, mulattoes and Indians." Some time after his appointment Juan Fernández died without leaving any possessions. Apparently he had been unsuccessful in collecting the tribute. Shortly afterward an investigation of the problems involved in collecting the naboría tribute was ordered. See Cuentas de 1580 regarding the failure to collect tribute in 1579.
4. Cuentas de 1579 and 1582, AGI, Contaduría 968.
5. Cuentas de 1592, AGI, Contaduría 966.
6. AGCA, A1 4588, fols. 99ff.
7. El Presidente Don Juan Miguel Agurto a la Corona (Santiago: 3 July 1683), AGI, Guatemala 28.

GLOSSARY

Adobado. Pickled, especially meat
Aguardiente. Brandy
Aguardiente de caña. Sugar cane brandy
Aguas calientes. Hot springs
Alcabala. Sales tax
Alcalde, alcalde ordinario. Mayor
Alcalde mayor. District officer; senior official or head of a cabildo in a town
Alcaldía mayor. District
Alférez. Commandant of the militia
Alguacil. Constable
Alguacil mayor. Chief constable
Almud. ¹⁄₂₄ fanega, especially maize
Alternativa. An ancient custom by which two competing groups annually rotate leadership posts
Amparo. Official decree of support
Arriero. Muleteer
Asentista. Slave contractor
Aserradero. Saw pit
Asiento. Contract, monopoly on African slave imports
Audiencia. Royal court
Ausente. Absent tributary
Barrio. Residential district
Bozal. Newly arrived African slave
Caballería. Land area 600 × 1000 paces, approximately 104 acres
Cabildo. City council, council building
Caldos. Winelike spirits

Calidad. Quality; used to describe persons of "pure" Spanish descent
Camino de Petapa. Petapa road
Camino real. Main road
Camisa. Shirt
Capellanía. Chaplaincy
Capote. Man's short cloak
Carga. Load, roughly 230 pounds
Cargador. Bearer
Carne salada. Salted beef
Carnicería. Butcher shop
Carretero. Cartwright
Casa de recogidas. House of detention for women
Casado tributario entero. Married entire tributary; that is, a husband and wife from the same parcialidad, barrio, or other tribute-collecting jurisdiction
Castizo. Spanish-mestizo offspring
Cédula. Directive, order, decree
Censo enfiteusis. Contract by which a house or land is subject to the payment of an annual pension of 5 percent as interest on a principal based on all or part of a property's cash value; censos held by religious institutions, cabildos, and cofradías
Cerro. Hill
Chicha. Alcoholic drink made from maize fermented in either sugar water or fruit juice and brown sugar
Chichero. Chicha bootlegger
Chino. Male of probable Filipino-Chinese descent; also a Spanish-American of mixed blood, especially one quarter Indian and three quarters black
Cocoliztli. *See* **Gucumatz**
Cofradía. Lay religious brotherhood, sodality
Colegio. Boarding school
Comarca. District or region
Compadrazgo. Relationship between godparents and parents of a child
Converso. Jewish convert to Christianity; Christian of Jewish ancestry; new Christian
Copista. Copier or paleographer of archival manuscripts
Corregidor. Magistrate of a corregimiento
Corregimiento. Jurisdiction
Creole. American-born Spaniard or slave of African descent; *see* **Negro criollo**

Criado. Servant
Criatura. Infant
Cronista. Chronicler
Cuadrilla. Gang, especially of slaves
Cura doctrinero. Priest in an Indian parish
Deán. Ecclesiastical dean
Demora. Miner's eight-month work period; coincided with dry season in Guatemala, 1 October–1 June
Derechos de esclavos, derechos de negros, derechos reales. Taxes on African slave imports; per capita slave tax paid by supplier or holder of asiento
Despacho. Order
Diezmo. Tithe
Doctrina. Indian parochial jurisdiction
Doncella. Maiden
Dueña. Female owner
Encomendero. Grantee of an encomienda
Encomienda. Grant or use of Indians for tribute and labor
Escribano. Notary
Escribano público. Public notary
Escribano real. Royal notary
Estancia. Small cattle ranch
Expediente. Document
Expuesto en la puerta. Left in the doorway; orphan child
Extramuros. Outside the walls
Fanega. 1.60 bushels, or 116 pounds
Fardo. Bundle
Fiel. Overseer, especially of butcher shops
Fiscal. Local Indian official charged with enforcing Indian religious obligations; also audiencia official
Fontanero. Chief water official
Frijoles. Beans
Gallina de castilla. Castilian or European chicken
Garita. Customs station
Gente ladina. Ladinos; persons of mixed descent
Gente ordinaria. Ecclesiastical term used in parish registers for common people; everyone except Spaniards and Indian tributaries, i.e., castas, slave and free, as well as naborías, black slaves, and free blacks
Gente parda. Mulattoes, especially militiamen
Gobernador. Governor

Gremio. Guild
Guarapo. Fermented sugarcane juice
Gucumatz. Pestilence, possibly pulmonary or bubonic plague
Habitante. Spaniard without vecino status
Hacendado. Rancher
Hermita. Hermitage
Hijo de la iglesia. Child of the church; church orphan
Hijo natural. Natural offspring
Hombre noble. Nobleman
Hortelano. Gardener
Huérfano. Orphan
Huipil. Blouse; usually worn by Indian women
Indio ladino. Hispanicized Indian; bilingual Indian; naboría
Informe. Report
Invierno. Rainy season, May to October in highland Guatemala
Labor. Farm, wheat farm
Labor de panllevar. Wheat farm
Laborío, laboría. Independent Indian; also a free black or free mulatto; tribute paid by laborío; called "naborío" in the late sixteenth century
Labrador. Farmer, especially Spanish wheat farmer
Ladino. Casta with some Spanish heritage, if only cultural
Libertado. Freedman of African descent
Libro de cabildo. Cabildo book
Licenciado. Person with a university degree
Lugar. Place
Macehual. Nahuatl for "peasant or commoner"
Maestro mayor de arquitectura. Chief architect
Mandamiento. Distribution of Indians for rural and urban labor
Mandato verbal. Spoken order
Mantelina. Woman's short cloak
Mantequero. Lard maker and dealer
Mantilla. Shawl
Matadero. Slaughterhouse
Mayordomo. Foreman
Medio solar. Small house lot, half lot
Mercader. Merchant
Mesón. Tavern
Mestizaje. Race mixture
Milpa. Rural agricultural settlement, especially near the city
Milpas altas. High milpas

Mistela. Spiced liquor
Monte. Woodland
Morisco. Quadroon
Mulata. Female mulatto
Mulata revendedora. Female mulatto peddler, especially of beef
Muleque. African slave under the age of five
Municipio. Municipality
Naboría, naborío. Hereditary Indian servant working for Spaniards; naboría used to describe general group or an individual woman; naborío also used for tribute paid by Indian naborías, free blacks, and free mulattoes in the sixteenth century
Natural. Native
Negrero. Slave trader
Negro criollo. American-born black; usually used in reference to slaves
Negro libre. Free black
Novenario. Public worship
Obispo. Bishop
Obligado. Contractual meat supplier
Obraje. Indigo plantation
Oficial. Artisan
Oficial real. Royal Treasury official
Oidor. Judge
Padre de menores. Father of minors
Padrino. Godparent
Padrón. Tributary census
Panadero, panadera. Bread baker
Paniaguado. Hanger-on
Parcialidad. Community of Indians; barrio; ethnolinguistic group
Pardo. *See* **Gente parda**
Partida. Entry in a parish register
Pastor. Shepherd
Peninsular(es). Spanish born, as compared with creole (criollo) or American born
Peonía. One-half caballería
Peso. Basic unit of money: eight reales or two tostones
Peste. Epidemic, pestilence
Pieza de India. Young adult male slave meeting certain size and weight criteria
Plebe común. Commoners
Porquero. Pork dealer and butcher

Principal. Member of the Indian hereditary nobility; elder
Procurador. Attorney or legal representative
Pueblo. Town
Pulpería. Small grocery store legally permitted to sell wine
Real. One-eighth peso or one-quarter tostón
Reducción de indios. Center of concentrated or "reduced" Indian population; term used in mid-sixteenth century
Regatón. Intermediary, middleman; often used disparagingly by city officials
Regatonería. Reselling by regatones
Regidor. Alderman
Regidor mayor. First regidor
Regidor segundo. Second regidor
Repartimiento de indios. *See* **Mandamiento**
República de los españoles. Spanish republic or community
República de los indios. Indian republic or community
Reservado(s). Reserved or exempted from tribute payment and related labor obligations
Revendedor. Peddler, often illicit
Rezago. Outstanding tribute obligation or debt
Rogativa. Supplication
Ronda. Patrol
Ropa de la tierra. Indian-made clothing
Sacate. Fodder, literally "grass"
Sambo. *See* **Zambo**
Sarampión. Measles
Sargento mayor. Sergeant major
Señor. Lord, especially Indian hereditary noble
Señor de las tierras. Lord or owner of the lands
Servicio. Contribution
Servicio del tostón. One-half silver peso or four reales; part of Indian tribute
Servicio ordinario. Ordinary service; Indian labor
Síndico general. City attorney
Solar. Building lot
Tabardillo. Typhus
Taller. Workshop
Tameme. Indian porter
Tasación. Tributary count or census
Terrazgo. Land rent
Tesorero. Treasurer

Teupanteca. Nahuatl for "servant of the house of God"
Tiangues, tianguis. Market
Tianguesillo. Little market; name of possible location of Santiago in 1541
Tienda. Store
Tierra caliente. Hot zone, literally "hot land"; between sea level and 800 meters
Tierra fría. Cold zone, literally "cold land"; between 1500 and 3000 meters
Tierra templada. Temperate zone; land between 800 and 1500 meters
Tortillera. Tortilla maker, woman vendor of tortillas
Tostón. Four reales
Traza. Urban plan with street layout
Traza nueva. New traza, urban plan
Tributario entero. Full tributary or family head
Triguero. Small-scale wheat grower; refers to Indian
Troje. Granary
Vecino. Citizen of a Spanish urban center; also used to refer to non-Spanish residents of barrios, towns, and cities
Vendedor aventurero. Illicit vendor
Verano. Dry season, November to April in highland Guatemala
Viruela. Smallpox
Visita. Subordinate church or parish jurisdiction; inspection tour
Yerbatero. Grass cutter
Zacate. *See* **Sacate**
Zambo. Person of mixed Afro-Indian descent; seldom used in Santiago and surrounding region

BIBLIOGRAPHY

LIKE most works on colonial Latin America, this study relies heavily on archival sources, in part because published primary sources contain questionable data so often repeated by chroniclers and historians that they now have an aura of truth.

Archival research for this study was concentrated in the Archivo General de Centroamérica (AGCA) and various ecclesiastical archives in Guatemala City, as well as in Seville's Archivo General de Indias (AGI). Don J. Joaquín Pardo's impressive AGCA card catalog documents sources of every type and classification, giving the historian a detailed picture of daily events. The AGI's holdings, by contrast, present more of an overview (see Dakin and Lutz, below, on the Nahuatl memorias dating from the 1570s, for the exception to the rule).

Access to the Archivo Eclesiástico de Guatemala (AEG)—now known as the Archivo Histórico Arquidiocesano "Francisco de Paula García Peláez" (AHA)—was severely restricted during the 1970s, a situation that no longer prevails under the enlightened direction of Lic. Ramiro Ordóñez Jonama. While the AEG was thus used on a very limited basis, no such restriction applied to the archive of the Order of La Merced (then officially called the Archivo Eclesiástico de Guatemala—Sección Mercedaria, or AEG-SM, and identified here as AHA-SM), which yielded useful details on Santiago's residential patterns. Crucial marriage and baptismal data came from the city's four parish archives (see "Introduction" to the appendixes for extant data).

The notes to each chapter reveal the depth of the archival research. Published sources appear below.

Aguirre Beltrán, Gonzalo. *La población negra de México, 1519–1810: Estudio etnohistórico.* Mexico: Ediciones Fuente Cultural, 1946.
Altman, Ida. *Emigrants and Society: Extremadura and America in the Six-*

teenth Century. Berkeley, Los Angeles, and London: University of California Press, 1989.
Annis, Verle L. *The Architecture of Antigua Guatemala, 1543–1773.* Bilingual ed. Guatemala: University of San Carlos of Guatemala, 1968.
———. "El plano de una ciudad colonial." *Revista de Antropología e Historia de Guatemala* 1, no. 1 (Jan. 1949): 48–57.
Arana, Tomás de. *Relación de los estragos y ruinas que ha padecido la ciudad de Santiago de Guatemala por los terremotos y fuego de sus volcanes en este año de 1717.* Repub. in *La Sociedad Económica* 26–33 (22 April–18 June 1876).
Archer, Christon I. "Military." In *Cities and Society in Colonial Latin America,* ed. Louisa Schell Hoberman and Susan Migden Socolow, 197–226. Albuquerque: University of New Mexico Press, 1986.
———. "Pardos, Indians and the Army of New Spain: Inter-relationships and Conflicts, 1780–1810." *Journal of Latin American Studies* 6, no. 2 (Nov. 1974): 231–55.
Asturias de Barrios, Linda. *Comalapa: Native Dress and Its Significance.* Ixchel Museum, no. 3. Guatemala: Ediciones del Museo Ixchel, 1985.
Bancroft, Hubert Howe. *History of Central America.* 3 vols. San Francisco: History Company, 1886–87.
Batres Jáuregui, Antonio. *La América Central ante la historia.* 3 vols. Guatemala: Tipografía Sánchez y de Guise, 1920.
Bell, Daniel. "Crime as an American Way of Life: A Queer Ladder of Social Mobility." In Daniel Bell, *The End of Ideology,* 115–36. Glencoe: Free Press, 1960.
Blank, Stephanie Bower. "Social Integration and Social Stability in a Colonial Spanish American City, Caracas (1595–1627)." Ph.D. dissertation, University of Wisconsin–Madison, 1970.
Boletín Climatológico. Guatemala: Observatorio Nacional, 1971.
Borah, Woodrow. *New Spain's Century of Depression.* Ibero-Americana, no. 35. Berkeley and Los Angeles: University of California Press, 1950.
———. "Trends in Recent Studies of Colonial Latin American Cities." *Hispanic American Historical Review* 64, no. 3 (Aug. 1984): 535–54.
Borah, Woodrow, and Sherburne F. Cook. "Marriage and Legitimacy in Mexican Culture: Mexico and California." *California Law Review* 54 (1966): 946–1008.
Borg, Barbara E. Jones. "Ethnohistory of the Sacatepéquez Cakchiquel Maya, ca. 1450–1690 A.D." Ph.D. dissertation, University of Missouri–Columbia, 1986.
Borhegyi, Stephan F. de. "Archaeological Synthesis of the Guatemalan Highlands." In *Archaeology of Southern Mesoamerica,* ed. Gordon R. Willey, *Handbook of Middle American Indians,* vol. 2, pt. 1, 3–58. Austin: University of Texas Press, 1965.
———. "Estudio arqueológico en la falda norte del volcán de Agua." *Revista de Antropología e Historia* 2, no. 1 (Jan. 1950): 3–22.
———. "Settlement Patterns of the Guatemalan Highlands." In *Archaeology of Southern Mesoamerica,* ed. Gordon R. Willey, *Handbook of Middle American Indians,* vol. 2, pt. 1, 59–75. Austin: University of Texas Press, 1965.

Boswell, John. *The Kindness of Strangers: The Abandonment of Children in Western Europe from Late Antiquity to the Renaissance.* New York: Vintage Books, 1990.
Bowser, Frederick P. *The African Slave in Colonial Peru, 1524–1650.* Stanford: Stanford University Press, 1974.
———. "Colonial Spanish America." In *Neither Slave nor Free: The Freedman of African Descent in the Slave Societies of the New World,* ed. David W. Cohen and Jack P. Greene, 19–58. Baltimore and London: Johns Hopkins University Press, 1972.
———. "The Free Person of Color in Mexico City and Lima: Manumission and Opportunity, 1580–1650." In *Race and Slavery in the Western Hemisphere: Quantitative Studies,* ed. Stanley L. Engerman and Eugene D. Genovese, 331–68. Princeton: Princeton University Press, 1975.
Brading, David, and Cynthia Wu. "Population Growth and Crisis: León, 1720–1860." *Journal of Latin American Studies* 5, no. 1 (May 1973): 1–36.
Browning, David. *El Salvador: Landscape and Society.* Oxford: Clarendon Press, 1971.
Bunzel, Ruth. "The Role of Alcoholism in Two Central American Cultures." *Psychiatry* 3, no. 3 (Aug. 1940): 361–87.
Carmack, Robert M. "La estratificación quicheana prehispánica." In *Estratificación social en la Mesoamérica prehispánica,* ed. Pedro Carrasco et al., 245–77. Centro de Investigaciones Superiores, Instituto Nacional de Antropología e Historia. Tlalpán, D.F.: SEP/INAH, 1976.
———. *Quichean Civilization: The Ethnohistoric, Ethnographic, and Archaeological Sources.* Berkeley, Los Angeles, and London: University of California Press, 1973.
———. *The Quiché Mayas of Utatlán: The Evolution of a Highland Guatemalan Kingdom.* Norman: University of Oklahoma Press, 1981.
———. *Toltec Influence on the Postclassic Culture History of Highland Guatemala.* Middle American Research Institute, pub. no. 26. New Orleans: Tulane University Press, 1968.
———, ed. *Harvest of Violence: The Maya Indians and the Guatemalan Crisis.* Norman and London: University of Oklahoma Press, 1988.
Carmack, Robert M., John Early, and Christopher H. Lutz, eds. *The Historical Demography of Highland Guatemala.* Pub. no. 6. Albany: Institute for Mesoamerican Studies/State University of New York, 1982.
Carmagnani, Marcello. "Demografia e società: La struttura sociale di due centri minerari del Messico settentrionale (1600–1720)." *Rivista Storica Italiana* 82, no. 3 (Sept. 1970): 560–91.
Carroll, Patrick. "Estudio sociodemográfico de personas de sangre negra en Jalapa, 1791." *Historia Mexicana* 89 (July–Sept. 1973): 560–91.
Casaús Arzú, Marta Elena. *Guatemala: Linaje y racismo.* San José, Costa Rica: Facultad Latinoamericana de Ciencias Sociales, 1992.
———. "La metamorfosis de las oligarquías centroamericanas." Paper presented at Latin American Studies Association meetings, Crystal City, Virginia, 3–6 April 1991.
Castro, Américo. *The Spaniards: An Introduction to Their History.* Trans. Willard F. King and Selma Margaretten. Berkeley: University of California Press, 1971.

Chance, John B. *Race and Class in Colonial Oaxaca.* Stanford: Stanford University Press, 1978.
Chance, John B., and William B. Taylor. "Estate and Class in a Colonial City: Oaxaca in 1792." *Comparative Studies in Society and History* 19, no. 4 (October 1977): 457–84.
———. "Estate and Class: A Reply." *Comparative Studies in Society and History* 21, no. 3 (July 1979): 434–42.
———. "The Late Colonial Period, 1750–1812. In John B. Chance, *Race and Class in Colonial Oaxaca,* 144–85. Stanford: Stanford University Press, 1978.
Chevalier, François. *Land and Society in Colonial Mexico: The Great Hacienda.* Ed. Lesley Byrd Simpson. Trans. Alvin Eustis. Berkeley and Los Angeles: University of California Press, 1966.
Chinchilla Aguilar, Ernesto. *El ayuntamiento colonial de la ciudad de Guatemala.* Pub. no. 37. Guatemala: Editorial Universitaria, Universidad de San Carlos de Guatemala, 1961.
———. *El primer reparto de tierras para labranza: Guatemala, 1528–1538.* Guatemala: Unión Tipográfica, 1984.
———. *Historia del arte en Guatemala.* 2d ed. Guatemala: Ministerio de Educación, 1965.
———. *Historia y tradiciones de la ciudad de Amatitlán.* Guatemala: Ministerio de Educación Pública, 1961.
Cojtí Cuxil, Demetrio. "Lingüística e idiomas mayas en Guatemala." In *Lecturas sobre la lingüística maya,* ed. Nora C. England and Stephen R. Elliott, 1–25. Antigua Guatemala: Centro de Investigaciones Regionales de Mesoamérica, 1990.
Cook, Sherburne F., and Woodrow Borah. *Essays in Population History,* vol. 1, *Mexico and the Caribbean.* Berkeley and Los Angeles: University of California Press, 1971.
Cortés y Larraz, Pedro de. *Descripción geográfico-moral de la diócesis de Goathemala.* 2 books. Biblioteca "Goathemala," vol. 20. Guatemala: Sociedad de Geografía e Historia de Guatemala, 1958.
Curtin, Philip D. *The Atlantic Slave Trade, A Census.* Madison: University of Wisconsin Press, 1969.
———. *Economic Change in Precolonial Africa: Senegambia in the Era of the Slave Trade.* Madison: University of Wisconsin Press, 1975.
Dakin, Karen, and Christopher H. Lutz, eds. *Nuestro pesar, nuestra aflicción: Memorias en lengua náhuatl enviadas a Felipe II por indígenas del Valle de Guatemala hacia 1572.* Mexico: UNAM and CIRMA, 1996.
De la Peña, José F., and María Teresa López Díaz. "Comercio y poder: Los mercaderes y el cabildo de Guatemala, 1592–1623." *Historia Mexicana* 120 (April–June 1981): 469–505.
Delgado Pang, Hilda. "Guatemalan Ethnographic Textiles: Background Data and State of the Art." In *Ethnographic Textiles of the Western Hemisphere,* ed. Irene Emery and Patricia Fiske, 89–105. Washington, D.C.: Textile Museum, 1976.
Diccionario de la lengua española. 19th ed. Madrid: Real Academia Española, 1970.

Dorta, Enrique Marco. "Ganadería y abastecimiento en Cartagena de Indias (1766)." *Revista de Indias* 30, nos. 119–22 (Jan.–Dec. 1970): 473–502.
Dunn, Henry. *Guatimala, or, the United Provinces of Central America, in 1827–1828.* New York: G. and C. Carvill, 1828.
Dusenberry, William H. "The Regulation of Meat Supply in Sixteenth-Century Mexico City." *Hispanic American Historical Review* 28, no. 1 (Feb. 1948): 38–52.
Estrada Monroy, Agustín. *Datos para la historia de la iglesia en Guatemala.* 3 vols. Biblioteca "Goathemala," vols. 26–28. Guatemala: Sociedad de Geografía e Historia de Guatemala, 1972–79.
Eversley, D. E. C. "A Survey of Population in an Area of Worcestershire from 1660 to 1850 on the Basis of Parish Registers." In *Population in History: Essays in Historical Demography*, ed. D. V. Glass and D. E. C. Eversley, 394–419. Chicago: Aldine Publishing Co., 1965.
Farriss, Nancy M. *Maya Society under Colonial Rule: The Collective Enterprise of Survival.* Princeton: Princeton University Press, 1984.
———. "Nucleation versus Dispersal: The Dynamics of Population Movement in Colonial Yucatan." *Hispanic American Historical Review* 58, no. 2 (1978): 187–216.
Feldman, Lawrence Herbert. "A Tumpline Economy: Production and Distribution Systems of Early Central-East Guatemala." Ph.D. dissertation, Pennsylvania State University, 1971.
Feldman, Lawrence H., Robert E. Brown, and Susan Garzon. "Alien Spouses in Eighteenth Century Guatemala: Implications for Language Change and Distribution." *Anthropological Linguistics* 29, no. 4 (Winter 1987): 409–24.
Florescano, Enrique. *Precios del maíz y crisis agrícolas en México (1708–1810).* Mexico: El Colegio de México, 1969.
Foster, George M. *Culture and Conquest: America's Spanish Heritage.* Viking Fund Publications in Anthropology, no. 27. Chicago: Quadrangle Books, 1960.
Fowler, Jr., William R. *The Evolution of the Ancient Nahua Civilizations: The Pipil-Nicarao of Central America.* Norman: University of Oklahoma Press, 1989.
Fox, Richard G. *Urban Anthropology: Cities in Their Cultural Settings.* Englewood Cliffs: Prentice-Hall, Inc., 1974.
Fuentes y Guzmán, Francisco Antonio de. *Obras históricas de D. Francisco Antonio de Fuentes y Guzmán.* Ed. Carmelo Sáenz de Santa María. 3 vols. Biblioteca de Autores Españoles, vols. 230, 251, and 259. Madrid: Ediciones Atlas, 1969–72. (All references to *Obras* are from the *Recordación florida*, with the exception of those to Sáenz, "Estudio preliminar.")
———. *Recordación florida: Discurso historial y demonstración natural, material, militar y política del reyno de Guatemala.* 3 vols. Biblioteca "Goathemala," vols. 6–8. Guatemala: Sociedad de Geografía e Historia de Guatemala, 1932–33.
Gage, Friar Thomas. *Thomas Gage's Travels in the New World.* 2d ed. Ed. J. Eric S. Thompson. Norman: University of Oklahoma Press, 1969.
Gall, Francis, comp. *Diccionario geográfico de Guatemala.* 4 vols. Guatemala: Instituto Geográfico Nacional, 1976–83.

García Peláez, Francisco de Paula. *Memorias para la historia del antiguo reino de Guatemala*. 3 vols. Biblioteca "Goathemala," vols. 21–23. Guatemala: Sociedad de Geografía e Historia de Guatemala, 1968–73.

Gerhard, Peter. *The Southeast Frontier of New Spain*. Princeton: Princeton University Press, 1979.

Gibson, Charles. *The Aztecs under Spanish Rule: A History of the Indians of the Valley of Mexico, 1519–1810*. Stanford: Stanford University Press, 1964.

———. "Rotation of Alcaldes in the Indian Cabildo of Mexico City." *Hispanic American Historical Review* 33, no. 2 (May 1953): 212–23.

———. *Tlaxcala in the Sixteenth Century*. Reissued ed. Stanford: Stanford University Press, 1967.

Gudmundson Kristjanson, Lowell. "'Black' into 'White' in Nineteenth Century Spanish America: Afro-American Assimilation in Argentina and Costa Rica." *Slavery and Abolition* 5, no. 1 (1984): 35–49. (Also published in translation as "De 'negro' a 'blanco' en la Hispanoamérica del siglo XIX: La asimilación afroamericana en Argentina y Costa Rica," *Mesoamérica* 12 [Dec. 1986]: 309–29.)

———. "Mecanismos de movilidad social para la población de procedencia africana en Costa Rica colonial: Manumisión y mestizaje." In Gudmundson Kristjanson, *Estratificación socio-racial y económica de Costa Rica: 1700–1850*, 17–78. San José: Editorial Universidad Estatal a Distancia, 1978.

Guillemín, Jorge F. *Iximché: Capital del antiguo reino cakchiquel*. Guatemala: Instituto de Antropología e Historia, 1965.

Guthrie, Chester L. "Colonial Economy, Trade, Industry, and Labor in Seventeenth-Century Mexico City." *Revista de Historia de América* 7 (1939): 103–34.

———. "Riots in Seventeenth-Century Mexico City: A Study of Social and Economic Conditions." In *Greater America: Essays in Honor of Herbert Eugene Bolton*, ed. Adele Ogden and Engel Sluiter, 243–58. Berkeley and Los Angeles: University of California Press, 1945.

Haslip-Viera, Gabriel. "The Underclass." In *Cities and Society in Colonial Latin America*, ed. Louisa Schell Hoberman and Susan Migden Socolow, 285–312. Albuquerque: University of New Mexico Press, 1986.

Hernández Aparicio, Pilar. "Problemas socioeconómicos en el valle de Guatemala (1670–1680)." *Revista de Indias* 37, nos. 149–50 (1977): 585–637.

Historia Belemítica. Introduction by Carmelo Sáenz de Santa María. Biblioteca "Goathemala," vol. 19. Guatemala: Sociedad de Geografía e Historia de Guatemala, 1956.

Hoberman, Louisa Schell, and Susan Migden Socolow, eds. *Cities and Society in Colonial Latin America*. Albuquerque: University of New Mexico Press, 1986.

Hoetink, Harry. *The Two Variants in Caribbean Race Relations*. Trans. Eva M. Hooykas. London and New York: Oxford University Press, 1967.

Hollingsworth, T. H. *Historical Demography*. Ithaca: Cornell University Press, 1969.

Indice de los documentos existentes en el Archivo General del Gobierno. Guatemala: Archivo General del Gobierno, 1936.

Isagoge histórica apologética de las Indias Occidentales y especial de la provincia de San Vicente de Chiapa y Guatemala de la orden de predicadores. Biblioteca "Goathemala," vol. 13. Guatemala: Sociedad de Geografía e Historia de Guatemala, 1935.
Jickling, David. "Los vecinos de Santiago de Guatemala en 1604." *Mesoamérica* 3 (June 1982): 145–231.
Joba, Dorothy Jane. "Santiago de los Caballeros, 1604–1626: Society and Economy in Colonial Guatemala." Ph.D. dissertation, University of Connecticut, 1984.
Jones, Grant D. "The Last Maya Frontiers of Colonial Yucatan." In *Spaniards and Indians, in Southeastern Mesoamerica: Essays on the History of Ethnic Relations,* ed. Murdo J. MacLeod and Robert Wasserstrom, 64–91. Lincoln: University of Nebraska Press, 1983.

———. *Maya Resistance to Spanish Rule: Time and History on a Colonial Frontier.* Albuquerque: University of New Mexico Press, 1989.
Juárez y Aragón, J. Fernando. "En el homenaje de la municipalidad de Antigua al Obispo Marroquín." *Anales de la Sociedad de Geografía e Historia de Guatemala* 36, nos. 1–4 (Jan.–Dec. 1963): 52–56.
Juarros, Domingo. *Compendio de la historia de la ciudad de Guatemala.* 3d ed. 2 vols. Guatemala: Tipografía Nacional, 1936.
Kaplow, Jeffrey. "The Culture of Poverty in Paris on the Eve of the Revolution." *International Review of Social History* 12 (1967): 277–91.
Konetzke, Richard. "Documentos para la historia y crítica de los registros parroquiales de las Indias." *Revista de Indias* 7, no. 25 (1946): 581–86.
Kramer, Wendy J. "The Politics of Encomienda Distribution in Early Spanish Guatemala, 1524–1544." Ph.D. dissertation, University of Warwick, Great Britain, 1990.

———. *Encomienda Politics in Early Spanish Guatemala, 1524–1544: Dividing the Spoils.* Dellplain Latin American Studies, no. 31. Boulder, San Francisco, and Oxford: Westview Press, 1994.
Kramer, Wendy J., W. George Lovell, and Christopher H. Lutz. "Fire in the Mountains: Juan de Espinar and the Indians of Huehuetenango, 1525–1560." In *Columbian Consequences: The Spanish Borderlands in Pan-American Perspective,* ed. David Hurst Thomas, vol. 3, 263–82. Washington, D.C., and London: Smithsonian Institution Press, 1991.

———. "Las tasaciónes de tributos de Francisco Marroquín y Alonso Maldonado, 1536–1541." *Mesoamérica* 12 (Dec. 1986): 357–94.
Langenberg, Inge. *Urbanisation und Bevölkerungsstruktur der Stadt Guatemala in der ausgehenden Kolonialzeit: Eine sozialhistorische Analyse der Stadtverlegung und ihrer Auswirkungen auf die demographische, berufliche und soziale Gliederung der Bevölkerung (1773–1824).* Cologne and Vienna: Böhlau Verlag, 1981.
Laslett, Peter, and Karla Oosterveen. "Long-term Trends in Bastardy in England: A Study of the Illegitimacy Figures in the Parish Registers and in the Reports of the Registrar General, 1561–1960." *Population Studies* 27, no. 2 (1973): 255–86.
León-Portilla, Miguel, ed. *The Broken Spears: The Aztec Account of the Conquest of Mexico.* Trans. from Nahuatl into Spanish by Angel María Garibay K., Eng. trans. Lysander Kemp. Boston: Beacon Press, 1962.

Libro viejo de la fundación de Guatemala y papeles relativos a D. Pedro de Alvarado. Prologue by Licenciado Jorge García Granados. Biblioteca "Goathemala," vol. 12. Guatemala: Sociedad de Geografía e Historia de Guatemala, 1934.

Lockhart, James. *Spanish Peru, 1532–1560: A Colonial Society.* Madison: University of Wisconsin Press, 1968.

López de Velasco, Juan. *Geografía y descripción universal de las Indias.* Biblioteca de Autores Españoles, vol. 248. Madrid: Ediciones Atlas, 1971.

López de Zorita, Alonso. *Breve y sumaria relación de los señores de la Nueva España.* In *Nueva colección de documentos para la historia de México,* ed. Joaquín García Icazbalceta, vol. 3. Reprod. of 1891 edition. Mexico: Editorial Salvador Chávez Hayhoe, 1941.

Love, Edgar F. "Marriage Patterns of Persons of African Descent in a Colonial Mexico City Parish." *Hispanic American Historical Review* 51, no. 1 (Feb. 1971): 79–91.

Lovell, W. George. *Conquest and Survival in Colonial Guatemala: A Historical Geography of the Cuchumatán Highlands, 1500–1821.* Kingston and Montreal: McGill-Queen's University Press, 1985.

———. *Conquista y cambio cultural: La sierra de los Cuchumatanes de Guatemala, 1500–1821.* Serie Monográfica, no. 6. Antigua and South Woodstock, Vt.: Centro de Investigaciones Regionales de Mesoamérica, 1990.

———. "Disease and Depopulation in Early Colonial Guatemala." In *"Secret Judgments of God": Native Americans and Old World Disease in Colonial Spanish America,* ed. Noble David Cook and W. George Lovell, 49–83. Norman and London: University of Oklahoma Press, 1992.

———. "Surviving Conquest: The Maya of Guatemala in Historical Perspective." *Latin American Research Review* 23, no. 2 (1988): 25–57.

Lovell, W. George, and Christopher H. Lutz. "Conquest and Population: Maya Demography in Historical Perspective." *Latin American Research Review* 29, no. 2 (1994): 133–40.

Lovell, W. George, Christopher H. Lutz, and William R. Swezey. "The Indian Population of Southern Guatemala, 1549–51: An Analysis of López de Cerrato's *Tasaciones de Tributos.*" *The Americas* 40, no. 4 (April 1984): 459–77.

Lovell, W. George, and William R. Swezey. "Indian Migration and Community Formation: An Analysis of *Congregación* in Colonial Guatemala." In *Migration in Colonial Spanish America,* ed. David J. Robinson, 18–40. Cambridge: Cambridge University Press, 1990.

Luján Muñoz, Jorge. *Agricultura, mercado y sociedad en el corregimiento del valle de Guatemala, 1670–80.* Cuadernos de Investigación, no. 2–88. Guatemala: Dirección General de Investigación, Universidad de San Carlos de Guatemala, 1988.

———. "El desarrollo demográfico de la ciudad de Santiago de Guatemala, 1543–1773." *Universidad de San Carlos* (Publicación anual) 1 (1970): 239–51.

———, gen. ed. *Historia general de Guatemala.* 5 vols. Guatemala: Fundación para la Cultura y el Desarrollo (in press).

Lutz, Christopher H. "Evolución demográfica de la población no indígena, 1524–1700." In *Historia general de Guatemala*, ed. Jorge Luján Muñoz, vol. 2, 249–58. 5 vols. Guatemala: Fundación para la Cultura y el Desarrollo, 1993.

———. *Historia sociodemográfica de Santiago de Guatemala, 1541–1773*. Guatemala: Centro de Investigaciones Regionales de Mesoamérica, 1982.

———. "Introducción histórica." In *Nuestro pesar, nuestra aflicción*, ed. Dakin and Lutz, xi–1.

———. "Evolución demográfica de la población ladina [1700–1821]." In *Historia general de Guatemala*, ed. Jorge Luján Muñoz, vol. 3, 119–34. 5 vols. Guatemala: Fundación para la Cultura y el Desarrollo, 1994.

———. "Population History of the Parish of San Miguel Dueñas, Guatemala, 1530–1770." In *The Historical Demography of Highland Guatemala*, ed. Robert M. Carmack, John Early, and Christopher H. Lutz, 21–35. Publication no. 6. Albany: Institute for Mesoamerican Studies/State University of New York, 1982.

———. "Santiago de Guatemala (1700–1773)." In *Historia general de Guatemala*, ed. Luján Muñoz, vol. 3, 185–98.

Lutz, Christopher H., and W. George Lovell. "Core and Periphery in Colonial Guatemala." In *Guatemalan Indians and the State, 1540–1988*, ed. Carol A. Smith, 35–51. Austin: University of Texas Press, 1990.

McCaa, Robert. "*Calidad, Clase*, and Marriage in Colonial Mexico: The Case of Parral, 1788–90." *Hispanic American Historical Review* 64, no. 3 (Aug. 1984): 477–501.

———. "Modeling Social Interaction: Marital Miscegenation in Colonial Spanish America." *Historical Methods* 15 (Spring 1982): 45–66.

McCaa, Robert, and Stuart B. Schwartz. "Measuring Marriage Patterns: Percentages, Cohen's Kappa, and Log-Linear Models." *Comparative Studies in Society and History* 25, no. 4 (Oct. 1983): 711–20.

McCaa, Robert, Stuart B. Schwartz, and Arturo Grubessich. "Race and Class in Colonial Latin America: A Critique." *Comparative Studies in Society and History* 21, no. 3 (July 1979): 421–33.

McFarlane, Anthony, "Riot and Rebellion in Colonial Spanish America." *Latin American Research Review* 17, no. 2 (1982): 212–21.

MacLeod, Murdo J. "Ethnic Relations and Indian Society in the Province of Guatemala, ca. 1620–ca. 1800." In *Spaniards and Indians in Southeastern Mesoamerica: Essays on the History of Ethnic Relations*, ed. Murdo J. MacLeod and Robert Wasserstrom, 189–214. Lincoln: University of Nebraska Press, 1983.

———. "Indian Riots and Rebellions, 1530–1720: Causes and Categories." In *Columbian Consequences: The Spanish Borderlands in Pan-American Perspective*, ed. David Hurst Thomas, vol. 3, 375–87. Washington, D.C., and London: Smithsonian Institution Press, 1991.

———. *Spanish Central America: A Socioeconomic History, 1520–1720*. Berkeley, Los Angeles, and London: University of California Press, 1973.

MacLeod, Murdo J., Robert Wasserstrom, eds. *Spaniards and Indians in Southeastern Mesoamerica: Essays on the History of Ethnic Relations*. Lincoln: University of Nebraska Press, 1983.

Marín-Tamayo, Fausto. *La división racial en Puebla de los Angeles bajo el régimen colonial*. Puebla: Centro de Estudios Históricos de Puebla, 1960.

Markman, Sidney David. *Colonial Architecture of Antigua Guatemala*. Philadelphia: American Philosophical Society, 1966.

———. "The Non-Spanish Labor Force in the Development of the Colonial Architecture of Guatemala." In *Actas y memorias*, 36º Congreso Internacional de Americanistas, vol. 4, 189–94. 4 vols. Seville: 1966.

Martínez de Pereda, Guillermo. "Relación geográfica del valle de Goathemala, 1740." *Boletín del Archivo General del Gobierno* (Guatemala) 1, no. 1 (Oct. 1935): 7–8.

Martínez Peláez, Severo. *La patria del criollo: Ensayo de interpretación de la realidad colonial guatemalteca*. Guatemala: Editorial Universitaria, 1970.

———. *Motines de indios (la violencia colonial en Centroamérica)*. Cuadernos de la Casa Presno, no. 3. Puebla: Centro de Investigaciones Históricas y Sociales, Universidad Autónoma de Puebla, 1985.

Miles, Sarah W. "The Sixteenth Century Pokom-Maya: A Documentary Analysis of Social Structure and Archaeological Setting." *Transactions of the American Philosophical Society* n.s. 47, pt. 4 (1957): 735–81.

———. "Summary of the Preconquest Ethnology of the Guatemala-Chiapas Highlands and Pacific Slopes." In *Archaeology of Southern Mesoamerica*, ed. Gordon R. Willey. *Handbook of Middle American Indians*, vol. 2, pt. 1, 276–87. Austin: University of Texas Press, 1965.

Molina, Antonio de. *Antigua Guatemala: Memorias de Fray Antonio de Molina*. Guatemala: Unión Tipográfica, 1943.

Mörner, Magnus. "El mestizaje en la historia de Ibero-América: Informe sobre el estado actual de la investigación." *Revista de Historia de América* 53–54 (June–Dec. 1962): 127–69.

———. *La corona española y los foráneos en los pueblos de indios de América*. Instituto de Estudios Ibero-Americanos, pub. series A, no. 1. Stockholm: Almqvist and Wiksell, 1970.

———. "La política de segregación y el mestizaje en la Audiencia de Guatemala." *Revista de Indias* 24, nos. 95–96 (1964): 137–51.

———. *Race Mixture in the History of Latin America*. Boston: Little, Brown and Company, 1967.

Morse, Richard M. "Latin American Cities: Aspects of Function and Structure." *Comparative Studies in Society and History* 4, no. 4 (July 1962): 473–93.

———. "Recent Research on Latin American Urbanization: A Selective Survey With Commentary." *Latin American Research Review* 1, no. 1 (Fall 1965): 35–74.

———. "Some Characteristics of Latin American Urban History." *American Historical Review* 67, no. 2 (Jan. 1962): 317–38.

Nadal, J., and E. Giralt. *La population catalane de 1553 à 1717: L'immigration française et les autres facteurs de son développement*. Paris: Ecole Pratique des Hautes Etudes. VIᵉ Section Centre de Recherches Historiques, 1960.

Newson, Linda A. *The Cost of Conquest: Indian Decline in Honduras under Spanish Rule*. Dellplain Latin American Studies, no. 20. Boulder and London: Westview Press, 1986.

———. *Indian Survival in Colonial Nicaragua*. Norman and London: University of Oklahoma Press, 1987.

Nueva recopilación de leyes de los reynos de las Indias. Facsimile of 1791 ed. 3 vols. Madrid: Consejo de la Hispanidad, 1943.
Orellana, Sandra. *The Tzutuhil Mayas: Continuity and Change, 1250–1630.* Norman: University of Oklahoma Press, 1984.
Osborne, Lilly de Jongh. *Guatemala Textiles.* Middle America Research Institute, no. 6. Department of Middle American Research. New Orleans: Tulane University, 1935.
———. *Indian Crafts of Guatemala and El Salvador.* Norman: University of Oklahoma Press, 1965.
Oss, Adriaan C. van. *Catholic Colonialism: A Parish History of Guatemala, 1524–1821.* Cambridge, London, and New York: Cambridge University Press, 1986.
———. "Central America's Autarkic Colonial Cities (1600–1800)." In *Colonial Cities,* ed. Robert J. Ross and Gerard J. Telkamp, 33–49. Dordrecht, Boston, and Lancaster: Martinus Nijhoff Publishers for the Leiden University Press, 1985.
Otzoy, Irma, and Enrique Sam Colop. "Identidad étnica y modernización entre los mayas de Guatemala." *Mesoamérica* 19 (June 1990): 97–100.
Palma Murga, Gustavo. "Núcleos de poder local y relaciones familiares en la ciudad de Guatemala a finales del siglo XVIII." *Mesoamérica* 12 (Dec. 1986): 241–308.
Palmer, Colin A. "Negro Slavery in Mexico, 1570–1650." Ph.D. dissertation, University of Wisconsin–Madison, 1970.
Pardo, J. Joaquín. *Efemérides para escribir la historia de la muy noble y muy leal ciudad de Santiago de los Caballeros del Reino de Guatemala.* Sociedad de Geografía e Historia. Guatemala: Tipografía Nacional, 1944.
———. *Miscelánea histórica: Guatemala, siglos 16 a 19; vida, costumbres, sociedad.* Colección "Realidad Nuestra," no. 6. Guatemala: Editorial Universitaria, 1978.
———. *Prontuario de reales cédulas, 1529–1599.* Guatemala: Unión Tipográfica, 1941.
Pardo, J. Joaquin, Pedro Zamora Castellanos, and Luis Luján Muñoz. *Guía de la Antigua Guatemala.* Publicación especial, no. 15. Guatemala: Sociedad de Geografía e Historia, 1968.
Payne, Stanley. *A History of Spain and Portugal.* 2 vols. Madison: University of Wisconsin Press, 1973.
Phelan, John L. *The Hispanization of the Philippines: Spanish Aims and Filipino Responses, 1565–1700.* Madison: University of Wisconsin Press, 1967.
———. *The Kingdom of Quito in the Seventeenth Century: Bureaucratic Politics in the Spanish Empire.* Madison: University of Wisconsin Press, 1967.
Pike, Frederick B. "Aspects of Cabildo Economic Regulation in Spanish America under the Hapsburgs." *Journal of Inter-American Economic Affairs* 13 (1959–60): 67–83.
Pinto Soria, Julio César. *El valle central de Guatemala (1524–1821): Un análisis acerca del origen histórico-económico del regionalismo en Centroamérica.* Cuadernos de Investigación, no. 7. Guatemala: Dirección General de Investigación, Universidad de San Carlos de Guatemala, 1987.

———. "Guatemala de la Asunción: Una semblanza histórica." In Gisela Gellert and Julio César Pinto Soria, *Ciudad de Guatemala: Dos estudios sobre evolución urbana (1525–1950)*, 49–80. Guatemala: Centro de Estudios Urbanos y Regionales, Universidad de San Carlos de Guatemala, 1990.

Putte, Jan Van de. "Phénomènes séismiques et volcaniques au Guatemala." *Ciel et Terre* (Bulletin of the Société Belge d'Astronomie) 39–40 (1923–24).

Quirós Vargas, Claudia. *La era de la encomienda*. Historia de Costa Rica. San José: Editorial de la Universidad de Costa Rica, 1990.

Recinos, Adrián, Delia Goetz, and Dionisio José Chonay, eds. *The Annals of the Cakchiquels: Title of the Lords of Totonicapán*. Norman: University of Oklahoma Press, 1953.

Relaciones históricas y geográficas de América Central. Introduction by Manuel Serrano y Sanz. Colección de Libros y Documentos Referentes a la Historia de América, vol. 8. Madrid: Librería General de Victoriano Suárez, 1908.

Remesal, Fr. Antonio de. *Historia general de las Indias Occidentales, y particular de la gobernación de Chiapa y Guatemala*. 2d ed. 2 vols. Biblioteca "Goathemala," vols. 4 and 5. Guatemala: Sociedad de Geografía e Historia de Guatemala, 1932.

Sáenz de Santa María, Carmelo. *El licenciado don Francisco Marroquín: Primer obispo de Guatemala (1499–1563)*. Madrid: Ediciones Cultura Hispánica, 1964.

———. "Estudio preliminar." In *Obras históricas de D. Francisco Antonio de Fuentes y Guzmán*, ed. Carmelo Sáenz de Santa María, v–lxxxii. 3 vols. Biblioteca de Autores Españoles, vol. 230. Madrid: Ediciones Atlas, 1969.

Saint-Lu, André. "Movimientos sísmicos, perturbaciones psíquicas y alborotos socio-políticos en Santiago de Guatemala." *Revista de Indias* 42, nos. 169–70 (July–Dec. 1982): 545–58.

Samaha, Joel. *Law and Order in Historical Perspective: The Case of Elizabethan Essex*. New York: Academic Press, 1974.

Samayoa Guevara, Héctor Humberto. "Historia del establecimiento de la orden mercedaria en el reino de Guatemala, desde el año de 1537 hasta 1632." *Revista de Antropología e Historia de Guatemala* 9, no. 2 (June 1957): 30–42.

Sanchiz Ochoa, Pilar. *Los hidalgos de Guatemala: Realidad y apariencia en un sistema de valores*. Publicaciones del Seminario de Antropología Americana, vol. 13. Seville: Universidad de Sevilla, 1976.

Schwartz, Stuart B. "The Manumission of Slaves in Colonial Brazil: Bahia, 1684–1745." *Hispanic American Historical Review* 54, no. 4 (Nov. 1974): 603–35.

Seed, Patricia. "The Social Dimensions of Race: Mexico City, 1753." *Hispanic American Historical Review* 62, no. 4 (Nov. 1982): 569–606.

———. *To Love, Honor, and Obey in Colonial Mexico: Conflicts over Marriage Choice, 1574–1821*. Stanford: Stanford University Press, 1988.

Seed, Patricia, and Philip F. Rust. "Across the Pages with Estate and Class" and "Estate and Class in Colonial Oaxaca Revisited." *Comparative Studies in Society and History* 25, no. 4 (Oct. 1983): 721–24 and 703–10.

Sherman, William L. "A Conqueror's Wealth: Notes on the Estate of Don Pedro de Alvarado." *The Americas* 26, no. 2 (Oct. 1969): 199–213.

———. "Dissent among the Bishops of Central America over Indian Policy." Paper delivered at the American Historical Association meetings, San Francisco, 29 December 1973.

———. *Forced Native Labor in Sixteenth-Century Central America.* Lincoln: University of Nebraska Press, 1979.

———. "Indian Slavery and the Cerrato Reforms." *Hispanic American Historical Review* 51, no. 1 (Feb. 1971): 25–50.

———. "Indian Slavery in Spanish Guatemala, 1524–1550." Ph.D. dissertation, University of New Mexico, 1967.

———. "Some Aspects of Change in Guatemalan Society, 1470–1620." In *Spaniards and Indians in Southeastern Mesoamerica: Essays on the History of Ethnic Relations*, ed. Murdo J. MacLeod and Robert Wasserstrom, 169–88. Lincoln: University of Nebraska Press, 1983.

———. "Tlaxcalans in Post-Conquest Guatemala." *Tlalocan* 6, no. 2 (1970): 124–39.

Shorter, Edward. "Illegitimacy, Sexual Revolution, and Social Change in Modern Europe." *Journal of Interdisciplinary History* 2, no. 2 (Autumn 1971): 237–72.

Simpson, Lesley Byrd. *The Emancipation of the Indian Slaves and the Resettlement of the Freedmen, 1548–1553.* Studies in the Administration of the Indians in New Spain, pt. 4. Ibero-Americana, no. 16. Berkeley and Los Angeles: University of California Press, 1940.

———. *The Repartimiento System of Native Labor in New Spain and Guatemala.* Studies in the Administration of the Indians in New Spain, pt. 3. Ibero-Americana, no. 13. Berkeley: University of California Press, 1938.

Smith, Anthony D. *State and Nation in the Third World: The Western State and African Nationalism.* Brighton, England: Wheatsheaf Books, Ltd., 1983.

Smith, M. G. *Corporations and Society.* London: Gerald Duckworth and Co., 1974.

Solano, Francisco de. "La economía agraria de Guatemala, 1768–1772." *Revista de Indias* 31, nos. 123–24 (Jan.–June 1971): 285–327.

Stanislawski, Dan. "Early Spanish Town Planning in the New World." *Geographical Review* 37, no. 1 (Jan. 1947): 94–105.

———. "The Origin and Spread of the Grid-Pattern Town." *Geographical Review* 36, no. 1 (Jan. 1946): 105–20.

Strauss, David J. "Measuring Endogamy." *Social Science Research* 6 (1977): 225–45.

Szecsy, Janos de. *Santiago de los Caballeros de Guatemala en Almolonga: Investigaciones del año 1950.* Guatemala: Instituto de Antropología e Historia de Guatemala, 1953.

Taracena Arriola, Arturo. "Contribución al estudio del vocablo 'ladino' en Guatemala (S. XVI–XIX)." In *Historia e antropología de Guatemala: Ensayos en honor de J. Daniel Contreras R.*, ed. Jorge Luján Muñoz, 89–104. Guatemala: Facultad de Humanidades, Universidad de San Carlos de Guatemala, 1982.

Taylor, William B. *Drinking, Homicide, and Rebellion in Colonial Mexican Villages.* Stanford: Stanford University Press, 1979.

———. *Riot, Rebellion, and Revolution: Rural Social Conflict in Mexico.* Princeton: Princeton University Press, 1988.
Thomas, David Hurst, ed. *Columbian Consequences: The Spanish Borderlands in Pan-American Perspective.* 3 vols. Washington, D.C., and London: Smithsonian Institution Press, 1989–1991.
Thompson, J. Eric S., ed. See Gage, Friar Thomas
Thomson, Guy P. C. *Puebla de los Angeles: Industry and Society in a Mexican City, 1700–1850.* Dellplain Latin American Studies, no. 25. Boulder, San Francisco, and London: Westview Press, 1989.
Tilly, Charles. *The Vendée: A Sociological Analysis of the Counterrevolution of 1793.* 2d ed. New York: John Wiley and Sons, 1967.
Tobar Cruz, Pedro. "La esclavitud del negro en Guatemala." *Revista de Antropología e Historia de Guatemala* 17, no. 1 (Jan. 1965): 3–14.
Valdés Oliva, Arturo. *Lenguas indígenas de Guatemala.* Cuadernos del Seminario de Integración Social Guatemalteca, no. 8. Guatemala: Ministerio de Educación, 1965.
Van den Berghe, Pierre L. "Racialism and Assimilation in Africa and the Americas," *Southwestern Journal of Anthropology* 19, no. 4 (Winter 1963): 424–32.
Van Oss, Adriaan C. See Oss, Adriaan C. van
Van Young, Eric. *Hacienda and Market in Eighteenth-Century Mexico: The Rural Economy of the Guadalajara Region, 1675–1820.* Berkeley and Los Angeles: University of California Press, 1981.
Vázquez, Francisco. *Crónica de la provincia del Santísimo Nombre de Jesús de Guatemala.* 4 vols. Biblioteca "Goathemala," vols. 14–17. Guatemala: Sociedad de Geografía e Historia de Guatemala, 1937–44.
Vázquez de Espinosa, Antonio. *Compendium and description of the West Indies.* Trans. Charles Upson Clark. Miscellaneous Collections, vol. 102. Washington, D.C.: Smithsonian Institution, 1942.
Velázquez Spanish and English Dictionary. Chicago and New York: Follet and Co., 1962.
Villacorta C., J. Antonio, and Carlos A. Villacorta. *Arqueología guatemalteca.* Guatemala: Tipografía Nacional, 1930.
Webre, Stephen. "Las compañías de milicia y la defensa del istmo centroamericano en el siglo XVII: El alistamiento general de 1673." *Mesoamérica* 14 (Dec. 1987): 511–29.
———. "The Social and Economic Bases of Cabildo Membership in Seventeenth-Century Santiago de Guatemala." Ph.D. dissertation, Tulane University, 1980.
———. "Water and Society in a Spanish American City: Santiago de Guatemala, 1555–1773." *Hispanic American Historical Review* 57, no. 1 (Feb. 1990): 57–84.
Western, John. *Outcast Cape Town.* Minneapolis: University of Minnesota Press, 1981.
Wolf, Eric. *Sons of the Shaking Earth.* Chicago: University of Chicago Press, 1962.
Wortman, Miles L. *Government and Society in Central America, 1680–1840.* New York: Columbia University Press, 1982.

Wrigley, E. A. *Population and History.* New York: McGraw-Hill Book Company, 1969.

Zamora Acosta, Elías. "El control vertical de diferentes pisos ecológicos: Aplicación del modelo al Occidente de Guatemala." *Revista de la Universidad Complutense* 38, no. 117 (1979): 245–72.

Zilbermann de Luján, Cristina. *Aspectos socio-económicos del traslado de la ciudad de Guatemala (1773–1783).* Serie Publicaciones Especiales, 31. Guatemala: Academia de Geografía e Historia de Guatemala, 1987.

Zorita, Alonso de. See López de Zorita, Alonso

INDEX

Abarca, Nicholás de, 50
Acatenango (volcano), 9, 259n.34
Agua (volcano), 7, 9, 258n.24, 259n.37; Indian settlement on (*see* Santa María de Jesús Aserradero)
Aguardiente de caña, 153, 306n.65, 306–307n.66, 307n.67
Alcabala, 150, 304n.44
Alcaldes, 43, 44; Indian, 35, 36, 38–41, 52, 53, 57, 62, 97, 98, 265nn.58,60
Alcaldes mayores, 43
Alcaldes ordinarios, 16, 49, 51, 101, 146, 260–61n.57
Alcohol, 152, 160. *See also* Aguardiente de caña; Alcoholism; Bootlegging; Chicha; Drunkenness; Liquor; Taverns; Wine
Alcoholism, 42, 153
Aldana, Manuel de, 56
Alguaciles, 43; Indian, 35, 37, 41, 43, 266n.63
Almolonga (barrio; pueblo), 6, 7, 65, 258nn.17,23; Indians of, 274n.67; Mexicanos of, 7, 24, 28, 73, 261n.1. *See also* San Miguel Escobar (milpa; barrio); Santiago in Almolonga
Almolonga, Valley of, 259n.36
Alms, cattle sale–related, 150
Alonso, Joan, 26
Alotenango, Valley of, 10
Alternativa, Guatimalteca campaign for, 36–41
Alvarado, María de, 125
Alvarado, Pedro de, 3–8, 13–14, 17, 24, 29, 37, 40; death of, 8, 13–15, 300n.9; emancipation of slaves, 19; Indian allies of, 7, 65, 258n.21, 274n.67; Mexican auxiliaries of, 28, 65, 72, 261n.1; mines of, 19, 20; in Santiago in Almolonga, 258n.19; slaves of, 19, 83, 84

Alvarez, Alonso, 260n.44
Alvarez, Juan, 13, 260n.47
Alvarez, María de, 13, 260n.47
Amatitlán, Lake, 303n.32
Angola, 86, 281n.29
Annis, Verle L., 11
Antequera (Oaxaca, Mex.), 163, 165, 166, 168, 308n.13
Antigua [Guatemala], Guat., 162, 292n.120, 305n.59. *See also* Santiago de Guatemala; Santiago in Panchoy
Antonelli, Juan Bautista, 8, 11, 259nn.29,41
Apprentices, castas as craft, 160
Aqueducts, Indian laborers on, 23
Argueta Santizo, Hernando de, 270n.24
Arias Dávila, Gaspar, 28
Arrieros. *See* Muleteers
Artisans: casta, 142, 160; free mulattoes as, 125, 128; Indian, 4, 5, 15, 24, 25, 66 (*see also* Artisans, naboría); mestizo, 136; naboría, 96, 98; slaves as, 21; Spanish, 136
Asentistas, 84. *See also* Gómes, Juan
Aserradero, the. *See* Santa María de Jesús Aserradero
Assault (crime), 42, 153
Atitlán (corregimiento), 301n.20
Atlantic Ocean, Panchoy access to, 9
Auctions, commodity, 147, 301n.20, 302n.29, 304n.41
Audiencia: vs. barrio desegregation, 50; and beef trade, 150–51; and Cárdenas case, 59–60; dissolution of, 261n.58; free Indian labor for, 23; and Mendoza case, 60, 272n.52; and migrant Maxeños, 287n.76; and Monzón case, 56–60, 271nn.38,40; power transferred to, 16; royal direction ignored by, 49;

and San Francisco cabildo and church repairs, 73, 276n.91; Santiago as seat of, 103–106; tributary counts by, 64; and wheat trade, 147
Ausentes, 49, 53–62, 75, 271n.38. *See also* Tribute, evasion of
Aztecs, 4, 273n.63

Bakers, 142, 143, 146–47, 302nn.24,25; house servants as, 146; tricks of, 147. *See also* Bread; Panaderas; Wheat
Baptism, 82, 86, 124, 282n.35, 284n.56
Barahona, Sancho de, 27
Barrio(s): K'iche'-established (*see* Santa Cruz, Barrio de); population trends in, 63–70, 274n.69, 275nn.73,75 (*see also* San Francisco, Barrio de, population decline in); of república de los indios, 24–26; taverns in, 152, 153. *See also* La Merced, Barrio de; San Antonio, Barrio de; San Francisco, Barrio de; San Gerónimo, Barrio de; Santa Cruz, Barrio de; Santa Lucía del Espíritu Santo, Barrio de; Santiago, Barrio de; Santo Domingo, Barrio de
Bastards, free castas as, 296n.24
Beans. *See* Frijoles
Beasts of burden, 53. *See also* Horses; Mules; Oxen
Beaterios, 308n.12
Becerra, Bartolomé de, 27
Becerra, Pedro de, 31
Beef, 149–52, 302n.25, 304nn.42,43,47, 305nn.50,53, 55–59, 306n.60. *See also* Carne salada; Cattle
Belize, 299n.46
Belly, law of, 56, 74, 88, 95, 97, 272n.48, 277n.100, 282–83n.41, 286n.69
Berkeley School, 64, 273n.63
Blackmail, tribute-related, 71
Black market, 141–43, 147, 149–53, 305n.58. *See also* Bootlegging
Blacks, 109, 267n.84; of Antequera, 165; of Costa Rica, 166; free (*see* Free blacks); as ladinos, 269n.20; of Latin America, 308n.5; marriage patterns of, 295n.15, 296n.27 (*see also* Black slaves, marriage patterns of; Free blacks, marriage patterns of); Indian women and, 289n.94; in parish records, 82; of república de los indios, 42; in Santiago militia, 43; as slaves (*see* Black slaves); as tavernkeepers, 306n.64; and tribute, 79. *See also* Black slaves; Free blacks; Mulattoes; Prejudice, racial
Black slaves, 7, 43, 45, 87–91, 142, 159, 162, 268nn.3,4; with Alvarado, 83; American-born (*see* Negros criollos); of Costa Rica, 166; decline in numbers of, 112; freed (*see* Free blacks); importation of, 83–88, 90, 91, 132, 156, 162, 280n.21, 280–81n.26, 281nn.27,29, 281–82n.30, 295n.18, 297n.37; and Indians contrasted, 91, 283n.49; as labor mayordomos, 290n.106; maize as staple of, 147; market disruptions by, 299n.4; marriage patterns of, 86–89, 91–94, 115–17, 120, 124, 131, 136, 138, 140, 282nn.37,39,40, 282–83n.41, 283n.49, 284nn.56,59,60, 294nn.6,7,12–14, 297n.37; and mulattoes compared, 86–91; postings of, 295n.18; as status symbol, 46; as sugar workers, 270n.27; violence toward, 88. *See also* Bozales; Muleques; Piezas de Indias
Blacksmiths, Indian, 15
Bobadilla, Ignacio de, 27
Bootlegging, 49, 63, 153–54, 307n.67
Bozales, 85, 86, 88, 160, 282n.35, 295n.18
Branding, of Indian slaves, 20
Brandy, 306n.65
Brazil, 157, 285n.63
Bread, 146, 147, 303n.30. *See also* Bakers; Wheat
British, as Guatemala immigrants, 308n.11
Brokers, mulattoes as, 46
Buildings, Indian upkeep of public, 23
Building trades, free mulattoes in, 125, 128
Burning alive, as Spanish technique, 5
Burundi, 309n.18
Bustamante, Francisco, 262n.12
Butchers, Indians as, 142. *See also* Carnicerías; Matadero
Butter, 142

Caballería, 259n.28
Cabildos, 16, 49, 107–108, 260–61n.57, 261n.58; vs. casta crime, 143, 299n.6; disintegration of, 156; Indian, 34–36, 265nn.55,58; makeup of, 301n.16
Cabrera, Gabriel de, 29, 30
Cacao, 4, 142, 290nn.100,103. *See also* Chocolate
Caldos, 306n.65
Camino de Petapa, 9
Camisas, 270n.28
Campeche, New Spain, 84
Canales, Valley of, 10
Canary Islands, emigrants to Santiago from, 108
Candelaria (parish), 80, 269n.21; creation of, 94; free blacks of, 92; growth of, 279n.13; ladinos of, 63; marriage patterns in, 89, 127–28, 138, 140, 283n.42; mestizos of, 63; mulattoes of, 63, 284n.60
Candelaria, Barrio de la. *See* Santo Domingo, Barrio de
Capotes, 54
Cárdenas case, 58–61, 272n.50, 286n.69
Cargadores, 146, 148
Caribbean Sea, social mobility in islands of, 157
Carmona, Juan de, 27
Carne salada, 150
Carnicerías, 149–52, 304nn.42,47, 305nn.55,59, 306n.60
Carpenters, Indian, 15

INDEX 337

Cartagena, Colombia, 86
Cartago, Costa Rica, 168
Cartwrights, Indian, 15, 20, 142
Casa de Recogidas, 100
Castas, 46, 48, 79–112, 156, 159, 160, 162, 165, 168, 268n.4, 309n.17; of Antequera, 163, 165; barrios invaded by, 51, 52, 63, 68, 69, 71, 276n.82; in beef trade (*see also* Revendedoras); as bootleggers, 153–54; and bread, 146–47; of Costa Rica, 166; and crime, 141, 143–44, 148–50, 153, 303n.35 (*see also* Black market; Castas, as bootleggers); derogation of, 285n.68; drinking habits of, 152; free, 287n.78, 296n.24; Indians displaced by, 45 (*see also* Mestizaje); of Jocotenango, 63; of Latin America, 166–68; and liquor trade, 306n.64 (*see also* Castas, as bootleggers); maize as staple of, 147; in maize trade, 148; marriage patterns of, 140, 294n.10, 296nn.27, 30, 298n.39, 299n.48; Mexican, 165; mortality patterns of, 284n.55; naborías and, 97; naborías of, 96; in parish records, 82; rise of, 52, 112, 141; in Santiago commerce, 142–44, 148; in Santiago infantry, 43, 267n.83. *See also* Castizos; Laboríos; Ladinos; Mestizos; Mulattoes
Castellanos, Francisco de, 31, 264n.48
Castilian. *See* Spanish (lang.)
Castillo del Río de San Juan de Granada, 295n.21
Castizos, 127, 129, 160, 165, 296nn.29-31; of Antequera, 163, 165; ascendence of, 135; marriage patterns of, 140; mestizos into, 133; as "new Spaniards," 297n.34; "passing" of, 137
Catalonia, French emigrants to, 285n.67
Cathedrals. *See* Churches
Catherine, Saint ("La Bienaventurada"), 27
Catholicism. *See* Roman Catholic Church
Cattle, 21, 85, 107, 108, 143, 290n.100; to black market, 150, 304n.43; rustling of, 150, 152; scarcity of, 289–90n.99. *See also* Beef; Cowboys; Estancias; Haciendas
Cavalry, Santiago municipal, 43
Ceballos, Pedro de, 26
Censo enfiteusis, 13
Censuses, 79–80, 278n.4; tribute-related (*see* Padrones). *See also* Tasaciones
Cerrato, Alonso López de, 16–19, 22, 39; antislavery efforts of, 17, 21, 261n.60, 262n.12; as Indian advocate, 18, 263n.28, 273n.65; vs. Juan Rojas, 263n.28
Chance, John B., 293n.2
Chapels, 6, 29, 35, 156, 279n.13
Charcoal, 142, 143
Cháves, Bernardino de, 40–41
Cháves, Diego de, 62
Cháves, Juan de, 27, 264n.31
Chiapa de los Indios, 271n.32
Chiapas, Mex., 145–46, 267n.87, 290n.102
Chicha, 153, 306n.65, 307n.67

Chicheros, 307n.67
Chickens, 148; payment of terrazgos and/or tribute, 22, 26–28, 30, 31, 141, 148, 263n.17. *See also* Eggs
Children: abandoned, 97, 287n.78; casta, 95, 285n.66; contracted as servants, 60–61, 272n.51; death of, 82; indenture of wayward, 288n.90; Indian, 285n.66; as slaves, 90, 94, 283nn.46,47, 285n.61; tribute and San Francisco, 74–76, 277nn.100,101. *See also* Expuestos en la puerta; Hijos de la iglesia; Hijos naturales; Muleques
Chimaltenango (dist.), 260n.57
Chimaltenango, Valley of, 10
Chinese, Spanish vs., 47, 268n.7
Chipilapa (barrio), 62, 92, 295n.17
Chocolate, 286n.74
Cholutecan Indians, 258n.21
Churches, 62, 80, 160, 269n.12, 279n.6; barrio, 35; earthquake-ravaged, 82; exactions of, 55, 97, 268n.8; Indian slave-built, 261n.5; of San Francisco barrio, 73, 276n.91; vecino bequests to, 22. *See also* Chapels
Cinnamon, 306n.65
Ciudad Vieja. *See* Almolonga (barrio; later pueblo, after 1541)
Cloth, Indian-provided, 22
Clothing, 143; of rural Indians, 53, 270n.28. *See also* Dress; Ropa de la tierra
Cobos, Francisco de los, 84
Coffee, 302n.25
Cofradía, 38; of church of San Gerónimo, 59; document of, 40; dress of, 270n.28. *See also* Cofradía del Nombre de Jesús
Cofradía del Nombre de Jesús, 38
Colegio de Doncellas, 100
Colegio de San Juan de Letrán, 288n.87
Colegios, 100, 288nn.85,86
College(s): as terrazgo recipients, 22, 28, 262nn.5,10
Commerce, of Santiago, 141–54
Communion, Holy, 287n.78
Compadrazgo, 161, 309n.17
Concubines, 94, 131, 289n.94. *See also* Prostitution
Conquistadores: Indian, 39–40; passing of, 17; progeny of, 99, 287n.81, 297n.34. *See also* Alvarado, Pedro de
Convents, 48, 62, 159, 268–69n.12, 279n.6, 308n.12; records of, 279n.13; as terrazgo beneficiaries, 28, 29; vecino bequests to, 22
Cooks, naborías as, 286n.74, 289n.94. *See also* Bakers
Corregidores, 16, 97
Corsicans, of Santiago, 108
Costa Rica, 166
Cowboys, black/mulatto slaves as, 295n.18
Creoles, 17, 102, 141, 159, 160, 163, 266n.71, 287n.83; of Antequera, 163, 308n.13; decline of, 108; exodus from Santiago of, 107; marriage patterns of, 136, 308n.11; peninsulares

and, 36, 108, 291n.113; "pure," 109, 292n.121; wheat of, 300n.12
Criados, 92, 159, 280n.18
Crime: among Indians (see Law and order, in república de los indios); as way up, 307n.69. See also Castas, and crime
Cruz, Bartolomé de la, 75, 265n.60
Cueva, Francisco de la, 8, 16, 19
Curas doctrineros, 41

Death, registration of, 280n.14
Díaz del Castillo, Francisco, son of Bernal Díaz del Castillo, 290n.105
Disease, 68, 71, 78, 106, 160, 162, 275nn.73,77,80, 284n.56, 288n.89, 303n.30; as barrio spectre, 52; and death, 82; Indians ravaged by, 14, 15, 17, 64, 66. See also Measles; Pandemic, great; Smallpox; Thyroid condition; Typhus
Dominica, María, 58
Dominicans, 11, 21, 62, 65; freed slaves recruited by, 263n.23; terrazgos exacted by, 262nn.5,10. See also Remesal, Antonio de; Santa Catalina Bobadilla; Santa Cruz, Barrio de; Santa María de Jesús Aserradero; Santo Domingo, Barrio de; Santo Domingo de los Hortelanos
Dress, status and, 98. See also Clothing
Drought, 82, 149, 301n.18, 303n.30; in Mexico, 148, 303n.30
Drunkenness, 42, 153, 285n.68. See also Alcoholism
Dueñas, Miguel de, 30–31
Dunn, Henry, 281n.30
Dyestuffs, 143

Earthquakes, 73, 82, 278n.6, 280n.15, 291n.115, 292n.120, 297n.31, 305n.59; fatalities due to, 82; Santiago destroyed by, 63, 169
Economy, of Santiago, 141–54
Eggs, 30, 143, 148, 299n.2
El Salvador, 85, 86, 166, 309n.30
Encomenderos, 106–107, 290nn.103,104; auctions used by, 302n.29; Cerrato vs., 273n.65; dominance of, 17; and Indian slaves, 15–17; royal, 299n.1, 300n.9; and servicio ordinario, 300n.13; and tribute, 141, 299n.1
Encomiendas, 5, 103, 289n.99, 297n.34
Endogamy. See Marriage, endogamous
England: criminal patterns in sixteenth-century, 267n.81; parish records in, 279n.12. See also British
Epidemics. See Disease; Pandemic, great
Escobar, Juan de, 31
Escobedo, D. Fernando de, 291n.116
Escribanos, 50
Escuintla, Guat., 291n.116, 303n.32
Espinosa, Tomasa de, 55
Espíritu Santo (barrio). See Santa Lucía del Espíritu Santo, Barrio de
Estancias, 8, 90, 108

Europeans: in Guatemala, 309n.23; as Santiago immigrants, 308n.11
Exogamy. See Marriage, exogamous
Expuestos en la puerta, 280n.18

Fieles, carnicería, 150
Filipinos, as Spanish allies, 268n.7
Firewood, 21, 23, 28, 30, 142
Fish, 142
Floods, 82, 297n.31
Flowers, trade in, 143
Food riots, 148, 303n.31
France, parish records of, 279n.12. See also Paris; Vendée
Franciscans, 11, 21, 25, 263n.23, 276n.83. See also San Francisco, Barrio de; Santa María de Jesús Aserradero
Free blacks, 46, 47, 90–92, 160, 268n.4, 284n.52; as bakers, 302n.24; barrios invaded by, 51, 52; of Chipilapa, 62; diminishing numbers of, 119–20; earnings of, 96; and laborío tribute, 54, 270n.31, 286n.73; marriage patterns of, 115, 119–22, 124, 125, 131–33, 135, 136, 138, 140, 294n.6, 294–95n.15, 295n.16,17, 298n.38; in Santiago commerce, 142–43. See also Free mulattoes; Libertados
Free mulattoes, 91–95, 98, 129, 284nn.59,60, 285nn.63,64,66–68, 286n.70; as bakers, 146, 302n.24; in beef trade, 152; Indians replaced by, 154; of León, 126; marriage patterns of, 101–103, 115, 117, 119, 120, 122–29, 131–35, 137, 138, 140, 294n.9, 294–95n.15, 295n.20, 296nn.25,28–30, 297nn.31,32,36, 298nn.41,43, 45; mestizo absorption of, 298–99n.46; opportunities for, 128; population gains of, 112, 117; privileged, 124, 295n.21 (see also Fuentes y Alvarado, Felipe de); stigmatized, 125; as tavernkeepers, 153, 306n.63; upwardly mobile, 125, 128; in wheat trade, 146
Friars, 18, 262n.12, 279n.13. See also Dominicans; Franciscans; Mercedarians; Monasteries
Frijoles, 143
Fruit, 141, 153
Fuego (volcano), 9, 259n.34
Fuentes y Alvarado, Felipe de, 125
Fuentes y Guzmán, Francisco, 125
Fuentes y Guzmán, Francisco Antonio, 125

Gage, Thomas, 259n.31
Gallinas de castilla. See Chickens
Gascón, Juan, 29
Genocide, selective, 161, 309n.18
Genoese, of Santiago, 48, 108
Gente ordinaria. See Blacks; Castas; Castizos; Laboríos; Mestizos; Mulattoes; Naboríos; Slaves
Gente parda. See Mulattoes
Germans, as Guatemala immigrants, 308n.11
Gobernadores, Indian, 36, 53, 265n.57
Godínez, Juan, 26, 28
Gods, Mayan, 4

INDEX   339

Gold, 5, 7, 15, 20, 257n.13; Peruvian, 14
Gómes, Juan, 281n.29, 282n.33
Gracias a Dios, Hond., 16
Grain, 141, 142, 145, 301nn.18,20, 302n.30. See also Wheat
Granada, Nic., 274n.67
Grass, Indian-harvested, 23. See also Yerbateros
Gremios, 149
Grillos (Genoese banking and slave-trading family), 281n.27
Grubessich, Arturo, 293n.2
GSK method, 293n.2
Guacalate River, 9, 10, 259n.28
Guadalajara, Mex., 305n.53
Guarapo, 306n.65
Guatemala, 169; Mexico and, 279n.11; mines of, 15; natives of (see Guatemala Indians); population patterns in, 106–108, 291n.116 (see also Santiago in Panchoy, population patterns in); Spanish conquest of, 3–17, 24, 31, 40–41, 65 83 (see also Alvarado, Pedro de; Marroquín, Francisco); today, 161–63, 309n.18; university of, 125 (see also "Indian West"; "Ladino East"). See also Guatemala Indians; Santiago de Guatemala
Guatemala, Valley of, 10, 145, 157, 291n.116, 295n.15, 300nn.11,12
Guatemala City, Guat., 169, 287n.79, 298–99n.46, 302n.25, 309n.31
Guatemala Indians, 4, 166, 168–69; contemporary persecution of, 161–62, 309n.18; "independent," 54, 268n.8; isolation of rural, 53; nobility of (see Principales); of Quezaltenango, 309n.30; of Santiago de Guatemala (see Santiago Indians); Santiago supplied by, 141–42; as slaves, 19–21, 261n.60, 261–62n.5, 282n.38 (see also Santiago Indians, as slaves); Spanish surnames of, 264–65n.54; and wheat trade, 144–47, 300n.12, 302nn.22,26. See also Maya Indians; Santiago Indians; Servicio ordinario; Tamemes
Guatimalteca Indians, 19, 21, 261n.1, 262nn.8,10; of La Merced barrio, 25; of San Francisco barrio, 24, 36, 63, 71–76, 276n.85, 277n.97; of Santo Domingo barrio, 24, 36–41, 266n.63; of Santa María Concepción Almolonga, 30; tribute exemptions for, 274n.67. See also Parcialidad de los Guatimaltecas de Jocotenango
Guzmán, Gascón de, 29, 264n.39

Habitantes, 289n.97
Hacendados, 149, 150, 152
Haciendas, 53, 85, 88–90, 97, 290–91n.106
Hanging, as Spanish punishment, 5
Havana, Cuba, 84
Hidalgo, Alonso, 31
Hijos de la iglesia, 280n.18
Hijos naturales, 99, 280n.18, 287n.81. See also Bastards
Hoarding, 143, 145

Hoetink, Harry, 155–59, 161, 307n.2
Homogeneity, socior180cial and cultural, 157, 165, 308n.6
Honduras, 9, 14, 15, 84–86, 290n.102
Horses, Spanish, 3
Hortelanos, Indians as, 28
Hospitals, 6, 22, 30, 31, 261n.5
Huehuetenango (corregimiento), 301n.20, 304n.41
Huérfanas, 261n.5
Huipil[es], 270n.28; punitive loss of, 305n.56
Hutu, 309n.18

Ibarra, Lucía de, 124–25
Ice, imported, 142
Illegitimacy, 82–83, 90, 99–102, 280nn.16–18, 287n.83, 288–89n.91; advantage of, 286n.70; among black slaves, 88; conquistador contributions to, 99, 287n.81; curse of, 125; in Mexico, 165; in modern Latin America, 296n.24; naborías and, 96. See also Hijos naturales
Indians: of Antequera, 165; and black slaves contrasted, 91; Colonial Latin American, 166, 168, 308n.5; of Costa Rica, 166; of Guatemala (see Guatemala Indians); hispanicized (see Ladinos); ladinos and, 278n.4; of León, 126, 296n.26; Mesoamerican, 165–66; Mexican, 258n.21 (see also Aztecs; Mexicanos); of Santiago de Guatemala (see Santiago Indians). See also Guatemala Indians; Maya Indians; Mexicanos; Santiago Indians; Slaves, Indian
"Indian West," 162, 166, 169
Indigo, 53, 85, 89, 290n.100
Indios ladinos. See Ladinos; Naborías
Infantry, Santiago municipal, 43
Intermarriage Index (Tilly), 113–14
Itzá Indians, 93, 284n.57
Iximché, Guat., 4–6, 258n.14. See also Santiago in Iximché
Izalcos (prov.; part of modern El Salvador), 290n.103

Jails, 6, 23, 35, 43; for women (see Colegio de Doncellas)
Jalapa, Guat., 145
Jews, Christianized, 297n.34
Jilotepeque, Valley of, 10
Jocotenango (pueblo), 21, 148; casta pressure on, 269n.13; growth of, 110; as maize market, 148; population trends in, 69; Spaniards of, 63; tributaries of, 69, 273n.61; Utatleca sector of, 21, 286–87n.76. See also Parcialidad de los Guatimaltecas de Jocotenango; Parcialidad de los Sacatecas de Jocotenango
Jocotenango, Valley of, 9, 19–21, 259n.36, 262n.6
Judges, 43; Indian, 51

Kaqchikel (lang.), 142
Kaqchikel Indians, 3–6, 30, 31. See also Guatimalteca Indians
K'iche' (lang.), 142, 286–87n.76
K'iche' Indians, 3–4, 6. See also Utatleca Indians

Labores, 8, 90, 97, 108, 290n.106
Labores de panllevar, 107
Laborío (tribute), 54–57, 61, 74, 95, 277n.96, 286nn.69,73
Laboríos (independent Indian, free black, or free mulatto), 54–58, 61, 74, 79, 270n.31. See also Naborías
Labradores, 144, 300n.12, 301n.16
Lacandón, Chiapas, Mex., 284n.57
Ladino (term), 103, 135, 269n.20; as label, 162–63
"Ladino East," 162, 166, 169
Ladinos, 54, 95, 160, 161, 163, 169, 268n.11; barrios invaded by, 50, 273n.62; castas and, 59; of Central America, 166, 168; of Chipilapa, 62; dress of, 97; emergence of, 101–102, 135, 298nn.40,45; Indians and, 278n.4; marriage patterns of, 140; mestizos as, 103; mulattoes as, 103, 124, 294n.9; as "new Spaniards," 297n.34; population gains of, 108, 124; of present-day Guatemala, 161–63; of Quezaltenango, 309n.30; "passing" of, 137; in wheat trade, 146, 147. See also Blacks; Mestizos; Mulattoes
La Ermita (also La Hermita), Valley of, 169, 300n.11
La Merced, Barrio de, 25, 35; ausentes of, 58; desegregation of, 63; padrón-juggling in, 55–58, 271n.37; residential patterns in, 268n.8; Spanish intrusion into, 270n.24; tributary losses in, 66, 68, 69, 275n.74
Languages, of rural Indians, 53. See also Nahuatl
Larceny, servants and, 43
Lard, 22, 142, 149, 303n.38
Larios, Alfonso, 26
Las Animas (solar), 276n.82
Las Casas, Bartolomé de, 39
Las Mesas, Valley of, 10
Las Vacas, Valley of, 10
Latrines, forced labor in, 22, 23
Laundresses, naborías as, 286n.74
Law and order, in república de los indios, 41–44
Laws of the Indies, 49, 57. See also New Laws
León, Juan de, 29, 31, 32
León, Mex., 126, 296n.26
Libertados, 45, 92
Libros de cabildo, 11, 259n.40
Lima, Peru, 282n.37
Liquor, 49, 63, 144. See also Brandy; Chicha
Lopes Corso, Jacome, 86, 282n.32
López, Sebastián, 271n.35
Los Remedios (parish), 80, 269n.21, 279n.7; creation of, 284n.59; free blacks of, 91–92, 295n.17; free mulattoes of, 94, 284n.59;
growth of, 279n.13; illegitimacy in, 83, 101, 102, 288n.91; marriage patterns in, 89, 102, 122, 127, 128, 131–33, 135–38, 140, 289n.92, 298n.42; mortality in, 284n.55; Spaniards of, 296–97n.31
Lumber, 22. See also Firewood; Santa María de Jesús Aserradero

McCaa, Robert, 293n.2
Macehuales, 4, 5, 66
MacLeod, Murdo, 64
Magdalena River. See Guacalate River
Magistrates, 43
Maize, 4, 141, 143, 147–48, 302–303n.30, 303n.31; on black market, 144; liquor from, 152 (see also Chicha); terrazgo/tribute paid in, 21–22, 26–32, 147, 148, 263n.17, 274n.67, 303n.32. See also Milpas; Tortillas
Málaga. See Santo Domingo, Barrio de
Mandamientos de indios, 22–23
Manila, Philippines, 47, 268n.7
Mantelinas, 54
Mantequeros, 149
Manumission, mechanics of, 285n.64. See also Free blacks; Free mulattoes
Market, of Santiago, 142–43, 299n.4. See also Black market
Marriage, 83, 113–40, 280n.19; catastrophe-inspired, 82, 280n.15; endogamous, 113, 122, 129, 132–33, 136, 138, 140, 293n.2, 298nn.41,42; exogamous, 68, 113–40, 275n.78, 292n.2, 294n.5 (see also Miscegenation); records of, 280n.15; and tributary status, 74–76, 276–77n.94, 277nn.97,98,100–103,105; unrecorded, 82
Marroquín, Francisco, 7, 8, 19, 29, 258n.23; as Alvarado executor, 19–21; as Mercedarian champion, 260n.44; as mestizo advocate, 100, 288n.85; power of, 16
Martín, Isabel, 50
Masons (artisans), Indian, 15
Massacres, of Guatemalan Indians, 162
Matadero, 143, 149, 150, 152, 305n.55
Maxeños (vecinos de Santo Tomás Chichicastenango), 286–87n.76
Maya (lang.), 4
Maya Indians: government of, 4; Mixtecs absorbed by, 274n.67; mulattoes vs., 93, 284n.57; response to invasion by, 258n.14; as Spanish slaves, 7, 8, 14–16 (see also Naborías); in twentieth century, 161–63, 258n.14. See also Itzá Indians; Kaqchikel Indians; K'iche' Indians; Tz'utujil Indians
Mayordomos, 107, 290n.106, 295n.18
Measles, 93, 280n.14
Meat, 143; on black market, 144. See also Beef; Carnicerías; Matadero; Mutton; Pork
Mendoza case, 60–61, 272nn.50–53
Mercedarians, 11, 21, 260n.44; exactions of, 25, 55, 268n.8, 271n.36; freed Indian slaves recruited by, 263n.23; records of, 289n.96;

INDEX   341

in Santiago in Almolonga, 11. *See also* La Merced, Barrio de; San Gerónimo, Barrio de; Santa Lucía del Espíritu Santo, Barrio de
Merchants: creole, 141; Utatlecas as, 25–26. *See also* Traders
Mesones. *See* Taverns
Mestizaje, 45–78, 91, 95, 101, 113, 166, 281n.30; in Costa Rica, 166; cultural vs. biological, 61–62. *See also* Castas; Indians, marriage patterns of; Mestizos; Miscegenation; Spaniards, marriage patterns of Santiago
Mestizos, 43, 45, 46, 89–103, 129, 156, 158–60, 286n.70, 287n.83, 287–88n.84, 288nn.85–88, 288–89n.91, 289nn.94–95; of Antequera, 163, 308n.13; in beef trade, 152; and endogamy, 293n.2; free mulattoes absorbed by, 298–99n.46; of Guatemala, 291n.116; Indians into, 98, 132; Indians replaced by, 154; as labores mayordomos, 290n.106; as ladinos, 269n.20; of León, 126; marriage patterns of, 93, 101–103, 117, 119, 120, 122, 127, 129, 132–40, 287n.83, 289n.92, 295n.17, 296n.28, 297n.36, 298nn.41,42,43,45, 299n.47; as militia volunteers, 291n.116; mulattoes and, 298n.40; mulattoes "passing" as, 95, 98; as "new Spaniards," 297n.34; "passing" of, 99, 137; population gains of, 112; as regatones, 142; in Santiago infantry, 43; as tavernkeepers, 153, 306n.64; and tribute, 59, 99; upward mobility of, 129. *See also* Castizos; Mestizaje
Mestizos (term), 102, 287n.83
Mexía, Antonio, 13, 260n.46
Mexicano (lang.). *See* Nahuatl
Mexicanos: of Almolonga, 7, 24, 28, 73, 261n.1; as Alvarado allies, 28, 65, 72, 261n.1; as conquistadores, 39–40; intercommunity marriage among Guatemala, 73; tribute exemptions for, 274n.67. *See also* Mixtec Indians; Tlaxcalteca Indians
Mexico: climatic variations in, 303n.30; disease in, 275n.73, 303n.30; food riots in, 148; Guatemala and, 279n.11; Indians of (*see* Aztecs; Indians, Mexican; Mexicanos; Mixtecs); marriage patterns in, 165, 279n.12; as "multiracial society," 307n.3; sixteenth-century, 64, 273n.63; Spaniards in, 4, 6, 168, 257n.5; university of, 125. *See also* New Spain
Mexico City, Mex., 86, 288nn.86,87
Migration, centrifugal/centripetal, 291n.114
Militia(s), 43, 125, 128, 270n.31; Guatemalan civil, 291n.116
Milpa de Juan de León, 15
Milpas, 8, 15, 259n.31
Mines, 261n.5, 262nn.11,13; Honduran, 85; of New Spain, 14, 15
Miscegenation, 45–47, 63, 90, 95, 109, 155, 156, 162, 163, 165, 168, 285n.62, 295n.18, 296n.30, 307n.3; in Antequera, 165; legacy of, 73; Marroquín for, 288n.85. *See also* Castas; Marriage, exogamous; Mestizaje

Mistela, 306n.65
Mixco, Guat., 53, 277n.95
Mixco, Valley of, 10
Mixtecas, Barrio de los, 28. *See also* San Gaspar Vivar
Mixtec Indians, 28, 65, 258n.21, 274n.67, 275n.79
Mixtón Indians, 8
Moctezuma, 4, 257n.5
Monasteries, 150
Moneylending, 301n.16
Monroy, Diego de, 29
Monroy, María de, 29
Monterroso, Francisco de, 29
Monterroso, Luis de, 29
Monzón case, 55–60, 271n.37, 272n.52
Morales, Sebastián de, 260n.47
Moriscos, 165
Mortgages, 160
Mulattoes, 267n.84, 281n.30; of Antequera, 163, 165; barrios invaded by, 269n.16, 273n.62; as beef peddlers, 150–51; and black slaves compared, 86–91; categorization of, 46, 95, 286n.70; of Chipilapa, 62, 295n.17; derogation of, 285n.68; earnings of, 96; and endogamy, 293n.2; free (*see* Free mulattoes); of Guatemala, 291n.116; vs. Indians, 93, 284n.57; and laborío tribute, 54, 270n.31, 286n.73; as ladinos, 269; of León, 126, 296n.26; marriage patterns of, 295n.15 (*see also* Free mulattoes, marriage patterns of; Mulatto slaves, marriage patterns of); mestizos and, 298n.40; in militia, 43, 44, 291n.116; role in New Spain of, 46 (*see also* Free mulattoes); as slaves (*see* Mulatto slaves); Spanish preference for, 94, 285n.65; as tavernkeepers, 306n.64; and tribute, 56, 79 (*see also* Monzón case; Mulattoes, laborío tribute of). *See also* Free mulattoes; Mulatto slaves
Mulatto slaves, 43, 142, 268n.3, 283nn.41,49; American-born, 132; decline in numbers of, 112; freed (*see* Free mulattoes); marriage patterns of, 86–89, 91–94, 115, 117–20, 122, 124, 131, 133, 135, 136, 282nn.37,39,40, 282–83n.41, 283n.49, 284n.56,59,60, 294nn.6, 12–14, 297n.37, 299n.47; niches filled by, 295n.18
Muleques, 281n.29
Mules, 300n.9
Muleteers, 53, 146, 302n.22
Murder, 42, 153, 273n.62
Mutton, 149, 304nn.40,41

Naborías, 7, 21, 46, 54, 96–99, 142, 156, 270n.31, 298n.39; census omission of, 65; contract, 97, 286nn.74,75, 289n.94; Dominicans and, 65; hereditary, 96–97; and laborío, 286n.73; marriage patterns of, 96, 98, 99, 115–17, 119, 120, 126–27, 129–32, 138, 140, 294n.8, 295n.16, 296n.27, 298n.39; in parish

records, 82; population gains of, 112; and tribute, 79. *See also* Mendoza case
Nahuatl (lang.), 24–25, 38, 39, 142
Native Americans. *See* Indians
Negros criollos, 45. *See also* Criollos
New Laws (1542), 16, 17
New Spain, 273n.63; disease throughout, 71; migrants to Santiago from, 98; parish records of, 279n.12 (*see also* Registrations, parish); repartimiento in, 300n.12; sheep of, 304n.41; slavery in, 88, 282n.39; societal nature of, 307n.3. *See also* Mexico
"New Spaniards," 129, 136, 158, 297n.34
Nicaragua, 9, 14, 166
Nobility, Indian, 283n.49
North Americans: in Guatemala, 309n.23; as Guatemala immigrants, 308n.11. *See also* United States
Nuestra Señora de la Piedad, Chapel of, 26
Nuestra Señora de los Remedios, Parish of. *See also* Los Remedios

Oaxaca, Mex., 166; castizos of, 296n.30; creole/peninsular relationship in, 291n.113; marriage patterns in, 293n.2; mestizo woman passing into upper-class, 289n.95; migrants to, 287n.77; migrants to Santiago from, 98; sheep of, 304n.41. *See also* Antequera
Obligados, 149
Obrajes, 53, 85, 89
Officials, castas as minor, 142
Oidores, 17. *See also* Audiencia
Orphans, 287n.78; disease-created, 288n.89; mestizo, 100–101, 287–88n.84, 288nn.86,88, 288–89n.91, 289n.94; as naborías, 97
Oxen, 300n.9
Ozaeta y Oro, Pedro de, 49, 269n.16

Pacific Ocean, Panchoy access to, 9
Padrones, 52, 55
Palmer, Colin, 155, 307nn.2,3
Panaderas, 146
Panaderos. *See* Bakers
Panama, 86
Panchoy, Valley of, 258n.23; access to, 9–10, 259n.37; climate of, 9; nature of, 8–10, 259nn.33,36; Spanish colonization of, 8, 258–59n.28 (*see also* Santiago in Panchoy, founding of). *See also* Guacalate River; Pensativo River; Santiago in Panchoy
Pandemic, great, 66, 275n.74
Paniaguados, 46, 90
Parcialidad (term), 261n.1
Parcialidad de los Sacatecas de Jocotenango, 19, 20, 35
Parcialidad de los Utatlecas de Jocotenango (settlement), 19, 20, 35, 54
Parcialidad de los Guatimaltecas de Jocotenango (settlement), 19–21, 35, 36, 265n.58.

See also Parcialidad de los Sacatecas de Jocotenango
Pardos, of Antequera, 165. *See also* Mulattoes
Paris, Fr., 308n.15
Parishes. *See* Candelaria; Los Remedios; Sagrario; San Sebastián
Pasture, lands of non-Spanish poor converted to Spanish vecino, 48
Peninsulares, 107, 108, 156–57, 159, 160, 292n.121, 308n.11; of Costa Rica, 166; creoles and, 36
Pensativo River, 9, 22, 62, 297n.31
Peonías, 259n.28
Peraza de Ayala, Antonio (Conde de la Gomera), 50
Pérez Dardón, Juan, 27–28
Peru, 7, 14, 88, 152, 282n.39, 285n.61, 306n.61
Peruvians: as barrio tavernkeeper, 306n.63; in Guatemala wheat trade, 302n.21
Petapa (parish; town; valley), 108, 277n.95, 291n.116, 300n.11
Petén, Lake, 93
Philip II, king of Spain, 40
Philip III, king of Spain, 35
Philippines, 47, 268n.7
Piezas de Indias, 83–85, 281nn.26,29, 282n.30
Pigs, 149. *See also* Lard; Pork
Pipil (lang.), 38, 266n.66
Pipil Indians, 5
Plaza mayor, 6, 10
Plebe común, 284n.54
Plows, 300n.9
Police, 43, 267n.85. *See also* Rondas
Poor, Spanish attentions to, 261n.5
Poqomam (lang.), 142
Pork, 22, 149, 303n.38
Porqueros, 149
Porres, Diego de, 267n.83
Portugal, 84, 281n.29
Portuguese, of Santiago, 48, 108
Poultry, 143, 144. *See also* Chickens
Poverty, crime and, 42
Prejudice, racial, 46, 47, 162, 295n.17
Principales, 32–35, 264n.53
Prisons. *See* Jails
Prostitution, drinking and, 306n.64
Proximity, marital, 140, 299n.50
Puebla, Mex., 166, 168
Pulperías, 152, 153, 306n.64

Quadroons, of Antequera, 165
Quezaltenango (corregimiento; alcaldía mayor; city), 145, 146, 300n.12, 301n.20, 302n.21, 304n.41, 309n.30
Quinizilapa, Lake, 31, 66
Quiñónez Osorio, Alvaro, 266n.72

Racism, Spaniards and, 47. *See also* Prejudice, racial
Rain, maize lost to, 303n.32
Ramírez, Matheo, 37, 265–66n.62

INDEX 343

Records, parish, 283n.50, 289n.96
Regatonería, 148
Regatones, 142, 148, 149
Regidores, 35, 43, 266n.63
Regidor mayor, 37
Registers, parish. *See* Records, parish; Registrations, parish
Registrations, parish, 80–82, 279nn.12,13, 280n.15
Religion: Catholic (*see* Roman Catholic Church); Mayan, 4
Remesal, Antonio de, 11
Repartimiento de indios, 22, 52, 54, 55, 95, 96; as labor system, 145; used to harvest wheat, 300nn.12,13
República de los españoles, 45, 47–51
República de los indios: administration of, 32–41, 52 (*see also* Law and order, in república de los indios); barrios of, 24–26; decay of, 45–78, 156; and mestizaje, 45–78 (*see also* Castas); residential patterns of, 46–53; as slum, 268n.10. *See also* Barrios
Revendedoras, 150–52, 305nn.50,53,55,57,59
Reyes, Domingo de los, 36–37, 265–66n.62, 266n.63
Rezagos, 55
Roads, Indian labor on, 23
Robbery, of Indian traders, 143, 148. *See also* Larceny; Regatonería; Theft
Rodríguez, Blas, 75, 278nn.107,108
Rojas, Juan, 26, 263n.28
Roman Catholic Church. *See* Chapels; Churches; Convents; Friars; Monasteries; Sacraments
Rondas, 43–44, 56
Roofs, fire-resistant, 268n.10
Ropa de la tierra, 286n.76
Rust, Philip F., 293n.2

Sacate, 22, 143
Sacateca Indians, 20, 262n.8, 265n.58. *See also* Parcialidad de los Sacatecas de Jocotenango
Sacatepéquez, Valley of, 10
Sacatepéquez-Amatitanes (dist.), 260–61n.57
Sacraments, Catholic, 271n.36. *See also* Baptism; Communion; Marriage
Sáenz de Mañozca y Murillo, Juan de Santo Mathías, 37–38
Sagrario (parish), 80, 279n.13; black slaves of, 86, 282n.35, 283n.43, 284n.51; disease in, 93; free blacks of, 91; illegitimacy in, 83, 88, 101, 280n.18, 284n.56, 288n.91; marriage patterns in, 89, 101, 102, 122, 126–29, 131–33, 135–38, 140, 295n.17, 296n.30, 298n.42, 299n.48; mortality in, 284n.55; mulattoes of, 93–94, 117, 284n.59, 294n.12; naborías of, 96, 287n.78; population makeup of, 83; Spaniards of, 128, 140, 280n.18, 296n.31, 299n.48; wealth of, 280n.18. *See also* Chipilapa (barrio)
Salas, Tomás de, 38

Salt, 5, 142
Sambo (term), 267n.1
San Alejo, Hospital of, 28
San Andrés Ceballos (milpa; pueblo), 26
San Andrés Deán (milpa; pueblo), 26, 69
San Antonio, Barrio de, 25, 35, 49, 69, 263n.26
San Antonio Aguas Calientes (milpa; pueblo), 27
San Bartolomé Becerra (milpa; pueblo), 27, 69
San Bartolomé Carmona (milpa; pueblo), 27, 29
San Carlos, Royal University of, 51, 125; as terrazgo recipient, 51
San Cristóbal (milpas; pueblos), el Alto and el Bajo, 27–28, 110, 263n.18; ronda, officials of el Bajo, 43–44
San Dionisio de los Pastores (milpa; pueblo), 19, 20, 262n.6
San Felipe de Jesús (milpa; pueblo), 28, 35, 54–55, 69, 99, 110, 271n.34
San Francisco (parcialidad), 30. *See also* Santa María de Jesús Aserradero
San Francisco, Barrio de, 24–25, 36, 62; alcaldes of, 265n.60; butcher shop of, 304n.42; castas of, 74, 277n.97; desegregation resisted by, 49–50, 52, 269n.18; free blacks of, 277n.100; mestizos of, 36, 63, 71, 265n.60, 274n.67; monastery of, 13; mulattoes of, 74, 75, 277n.100; naborías of, 74, 75, 277n.100; population decline in, 275n.80; tributary trends in, 66, 68–78, 275n.74, 276n.82, 277nn.97,98. *See also* Chipilapa
San Gaspar Vivar (milpa; pueblo), 28, 274n.67, 275n.79. *See also* Barrio de los Mixtecas
San Gerónimo, Barrio de, 25, 35, 58–60, 63, 69, 263n.25, 272n.50
San José, Costa Rica, 168
San Juan Amatitlán, Guat., 53, 99, 108, 270n.27, 291n.116
San Juan Comalapa, Guat., 300n.12
San Juan del Obispo (milpa; pueblo), 27, 29, 76, 278n.13
San Juan Gascón (milpa; pueblo), 29
San Juan Sacatepéquez, Guat., 108
San León, Marcos de, 58
San Lorenzo Monroy (milpa; pueblo), 29
San Lucas Cabrera (milpa; pueblo), 29, 35, 69
San Lucas Sacatepéquez, Guat., 145
San Luis de los Carreteros (milpa; pueblo), 19, 20
San Luis Jilotepeque, Guat., 145
San Martín Jilotepeque, Guat., 108, 300n.11
San Mateo Cabrera (milpa; pueblo), 30
San Miguel Dueñas (milpa; pueblo), 30–31
San Miguel Escobar (milpa; barrio), 31
San Miguel Milpas Altas (milpa; pueblo), 29, 31. *See also* Milpa de Juan de León
San Miguel Totonicapán, Guat., 146
San Pedro del Tesorero (milpa; pueblo), 31, 264n.49
San Salvador (prov.), 9, 168, 291n.115

San Sebastián (parish), 80; free blacks of, 91, 284n.52, 295n.17; free mulattoes of, 93–94, 284n.59, 285nn.66,67, 296n.31; growth of, 279n.13; as hermita, 278–79n.6; illegitimacy in, 83, 101, 102, 280n.18, 288n.91; marriage patterns in, 89, 101, 102, 126–33, 135–38, 140, 294n.12, 296n.30, 298n.42, 299nn.48,49; measles in, 280n.14; mestizos of, 296n.31; mortality in, 284n.55; mulattoes of, 284n.59 (see also San Sebastián [parish], free mulattoes of); naborías of, 96; population trends in, 93; Spaniards of, 296n.31; weavers of, 297n.32

San Sebastián, Barrio de, 269n.21, 279n.6; butcher shop of, 304n.42

Santa Ana (milpa; pueblo), 26

Santa Catalina (milpa), subordinate to Barrio del Espíritu Santo, 263n.27

Santa Catalina Bobadilla (milpa; pueblo), 27

Santa Catarina Barahona (milpa; pueblo), 27, 260n.54

Santa Cruz, Barrio de, 25–26, 35, 62, 263n.28, 272n.55

Santa Cruz Chinautla, Guat., 277n.95

Santa Cruz del Quiché, Guat., 25

Santa Cruz Utatlán. See Santa Cruz del Quiché

Santa Isabel Godínez (milpa; pueblo), 28, 35, 110

Santa Lucía (hermitage), 260n.43

Santa Lucía del Espíritu Santo, Barrio de, 25, 35, 48, 66, 68, 69, 263n.27

Santa Lucía Monterroso (milpa; pueblo), 29, 263n.18

Santa María Concepción Almolonga (barrio; pueblo), 29–30, 40

Santa María de Jesús Aserradero (milpa; pueblo), 30

Santa María Magdalena (milpa; pueblo), 30

Santa María Magdalena Analco (milpa; pueblo), subordinate to Barrio del Espíritu Santo, 263n.27

Santiago (Saint James), 6

Santiago, Barrio de, 25, 35, 63

Santiago de Guatemala. See Antigua [Guatemala], Guat.; Santiago in Almolonga; Santiago in Iximché; Santiago in Panchoy

Santiago in Almolonga: destruction of, 7, 258nn.23,24, 278n.6; founding of, 80; layout of, 6–7, 258nn.19,20, 259n.39; location of, 6, 258nn.17,24; Spanish population of, 258n.20. See also San Miguel Escobar (milpa; barrio)

Santiago Indians, 48, 49, 109, 155–60, 162, 168; ascendency of, 112; as bootleggers, 153, 154; and crime, 153; decline in numbers of, 103, 110; displaced by castas, 45, 141 (see also Mestizaje); drinking habits of, 152; free mulatto/mestizo replacement of, 154; and maize, 147; marriage patterns of, 117, 125–27, 131–35, 294nn.7,8, 296n.25,27, 297nn.35–37, 298nn.39,43,45 (see also Naborías, marriage patterns of); migrant, 156–57; omitted from census, 79; in Santiago commerce, 143, 144; as slaves, 19–21, 46, 65, 261–62n.5 (see also Tcupantecas); Spanish-created settlements of, 19–32 (see also República de los Indios); Spanish fear of, 161, 309n.16; wine denied to, 152. See also Guatimaltec Indians; Mexicanos; Sacateca Indians; Tlaxcalteca Indians; Utatleca Indians

Santiago in Iximché, 5–6

Santiago in Panchoy: abandoned, 169; administration of (see Alcaldes ordinarios; Corregidores); audiencia in, 16, 260–61n.57; destruction of, 63, 70; founding of, 10–13, 80, 259n.38; importance of, 106; layout of, 10–13, 259nn.38,41, 260nn.42–44; migrants to, 97–99, 107, 286–87n.76; non-Spanish Europeans of, 108, 291n.111; population patterns in, 86, 103–12, 292nn.119, 120. See also Alvarado, Pedro de; Cerrato, Alonso López de

Santiago Spaniards, 79, 93, 103–109, 155–60, 162, 278n.1, 284n.54, 291n.116, 291–92n.118, 292n.119, 296–97n.31; as bakers, 146; barrios invaded by poor, 50, 51, 63, 69, 71; and black market, 144; black slaves impregnated by, 90, 283n.46; as bootleggers, 153, 154; crime and poor, 153; drinking patterns of, 152; European-born, 109 (see also Peninsulares); illegal activities of, 144, 153, 154; immigrant, 158–60, 308n.11 (see also Peninsulares); marriage patterns of, 117, 119, 120, 127–29, 131–33, 135–40, 292nn.118,119, 294nn.10,14, 297nn.31,32, 298n.42, 299n.48; as militia volunteers, 291n.116; naborías of poor, 96; as república de los indios lawbreakers, 42–43, 266–67n.78; and Santiago commerce, 143; as slave owners, 89; as tavernkeepers, 306n.63. See also Alvarado, Pedro de; Creoles; Habitantes; Ladinos; "New Spaniards"; Peninsulares; Vecinos

Santiago Utatleca. See Parcialidad de los Utatlecas

Santiago Zamora (milpa; pueblo), 31–32

Santo Domingo (island), 17, 83

Santo Domingo (parcialidad), 30. See also Santa María de Jesús Aserradero

Santo Domingo, Barrio de, 24, 36, 63, 149, 269n.12, 274n.67; butcher shop of, 304n.42; cabildo of, 35; children of, 278n.114; "gentrification" of, 48; hermitage of, 80; infantry of, 57; Mexicano/Guatimalteca conflict in, 36–41; Mexicanos of, 24, 36–41, 266n.63; monastery of, 13; naborías of, 65; Spaniards of, 63; tributary trends in, 70, 276n.82. See also Candelaria, Barrio de la

Santo Domingo de los Hortelanos (milpa; pueblo), 28, 35, 70, 276n.82

Santo Tomás, College of, 22, 28, 262nn.5,10

Santo Tomás Chichicastenango, 286–87n.76. See also Maxeños

Saraza y Arce, Francisco de, 50–51
Sawyers, Indian, 15
Schools, 160. *See also* Colegios
Schwartz, Stuart B., 293n.2
Seed, Patricia, 293n.2
Servants: in barrios, 159; black slaves as, 85–86, 90, 282n.38, 295n.18; casta, 43, 159; free blacks as, 92, 122; Indians as, 23, 32, 43, 46, 66, 142, 159 (*see also* Naborías; Teupantecas); mestizos as, 122; of modern Antigua, 292n.120; mulattoes as, 128, 295n.18; Spanish, 142
Servicio ordinario, 22, 23, 300n.13
Sheep, 143, 149, 262n.6, 304n.41. *See also* Mutton
Shepherds, Indians as, 20
Shops, free blacks employed in, 92
Shrines, temporary (aftermath of 1717 earthquake), 82
Sicilians, of Santiago, 108
Silks, Mexican silver for Chinese, 268n.7
Silver: Guatemalan, 15, 19; Mexican, 268n.7; Peruvian, 14
Silvestre, Pascual, 37
Slavery: abolition of Indian, 19–21, 83, 261–62n.5, 280n.21; early African, 83–84; patterns of black, 89–90, 282n.38, 283nn.43,49 (*see also* Black slaves); Spanish sentiment against, 17–18. *See also* Asentistas; Slaves
Slaves: African (*see* Black slaves); as artisans (*see* Artisans, slaves as); children of, 90, 94, 283nn.46,47, 285n.61; expeditions seeking Indian, 284n.57; export from Guatemala of black, 282n.38; freeing of (*see* Free blacks; Free mulattoes; Slavery, abolition of Indian); household, 21, 262n.11 (*see also* Servants); Indian, 4–6 (*see also* Guatemala Indians, as slaves; Tamemes); mulatto (*see* Mulatto slaves); omitted from census, 79; and tribute, 79. *See also* Black slaves; Mulatto slaves; Slavery
Smallpox, 93, 275n.73
Smuggling: of black slaves, 85; of wheat, 145, 302n.21; of wine, 306n.61
Social mobility, 157–59
Societies: homogeneous, 155, 156, 161 (*see also* Homogeneity, biocultural); multiracial, 155, 156, 307n.3; segmented, 155, 157–58, 307nn.2,3
Solares, 6; of Santiago in Panchoy, 12–13, 260nn.44,45,47,48
Solís, Manuel de, 86, 282n.33
Somatic norm image, 285n.65
Sonsonate, El S., 85
Spain: and African slave trade, 84, 280–81n.26, 281nn.28,29; vs. barrio mestizaje, 49, 269n.15; Bourbon influence on, 279n.13; and "mestizo problem," 100, 288nn.85,86; migrants to New Spain from, 47 (*see also* Peninsulares); and New World Indians, 23, 24, 32, 46, 265n.58 (*see also* Laws of the Indies); vs. terrazgos, 262n.14; tribute-related rulings of, 295n.16; wine from, 152, 306n.61
Spaniards, New World: American-born (*see* Creoles); of Antequera, 163, 165; of Central America, 166, 168; cruelty of, 4, 5; of Guatemala, 163, 291n.116 (*see also* Santiago Spaniards); of León, 126; of Santiago de Guatemala (*see* Santiago Spaniards). *See also* Alvarado, Pedro de; Creoles; Habitantes; Ladinos; "New Spaniards"; Peninsulares; Spain
Spanish (lang.), 54, 97
Spanish conquest. *See* Guatemala, Spanish conquest of; Mexico, Spanish in
Spice Islands, as Alvarado goal, 14
Starvation, 66, 145
Strauss, David J., 293n.2
Street sweepers, Indians as, 22
Sugar, 53, 85, 88, 142, 143, 157, 162, 270n.27, 290n.100; as liquor ingredient, 152 (*see also* Aguardiente de caña; Chicha; Guarapo; Mistela); pasture converted to, 304n.41
Súñiga, Juana de, 60, 272n.51

Talleres, 297n.32
Tamemes, 16, 17, 141
Tasación(es), 66; of 1549, 64–65; 273n.65; of 1581, 66; of 1638, 72; of 1735, 278n.108; of 1754, 70
Taverns, 152, 153, 303n.35, 306n.63, 307nn.66,67
Taxes, 23, 85, 97, 281nn.28,29. *See also* Alcabala
Taylor, William B., 293n.2
Tecpanatitlán (corregimiento), 301n.20
Tenochtitlán, Mex., 6
Terrazgos, 21–32, 51, 262–63n.17; church renovations via, 276n.91; exemption from, 24–27; ladinos and, 273n.62
Teupantecas, 28
Theft, in república de los indios, 42. *See also* Robbery
Thompson, J. Eric S., 259n.31
Thread, 143
Thyroid condition (goiter), 277n.102
Tiendas, 261n.5
Tilly, Charles, 113–15, 293n.4
Timber, 8, 142. *See also* Firewood; Lumber
Tlaxcalteca Indians, 24, 30, 65, 71–76, 258n.21, 274n.67, 276n.85; as conquistadores, 39, 40
Tobacco, 143
Toluca, Mex., 265n.58
Tortillas, 147, 286n.74, 302n.30
Tortilleras, 302–303n.30
Tortuguero (barrio), 268n.11
Totonicapán (region), 145, 146, 300n.12
Town hall, 6
Towns: ladino, 53; Maya, 5
Traders: Indian, 141, 143, 302n.22; mestizo, 136; mulattoes as, 46
Traza, 6

346 INDEX

Tribute, 55, 79, 141, 147, 148, 273n.65, 274n.67, 299nn.1,2, 302n.29; absentee payment of, 97, 271n.35, 287n.76; age and, 56, 60–62, 74, 272n.53, 274n.69; declines in, 65–78, 275n.74; for encomenderos, 5, 15–17; evasion of, 49, 52–62, 66, 97 (see also Ausentes; Cárdenas case; Mendoza case; Monzón case); exemption from, 40, 55, 59, 62, 65, 74–75, 99, 266nn.72,73, 272n.55, 274n.67, 276n.91, 277n.100, 278nn.107,113 (see also Tribute, age and); from Indian communities, 23–32, 35, 265n.60, 298n.44; imposition of tribute, 262–63n.17; Indian slaves as, 20; Juan Rojas pursuit of, 263n.28; labor as (see Laboríos); mechanics of, 24, 263n.19, 277n.97; mestizaje effect on, 49–50; race and, 279n.10; used as proof of ancestors' slave status, 40, 266n.73; vecinos and, 106. See also Laborío; Naborías; Padrones; Rezagos; Tasaciónes; Taxes; Terrazgos
Trojes, 145
Trujillo, Hond., 281n.29
Typhus, 301n.18
Tzeltal Revolt, 267n.87
Tz'utujil Indians, 3, 5, 6

United States: immigrants to Guatemala from, 308n.11; social mobility in southern, 157
Universities: free mulatto offspring seek entry in, 125
Urbina, Ignacio de, 301n.20
Utatlán, Guat., 3–4
Utatleca Indians, 20, 21, 25–26, 62, 261n.1, 262nn.5,8, 263n.28. See also K'iche' Indians; Parcialidad de los Utatlecas de Jocotenango

Vecinos: bastards raised by, 280n.18; and black market, 144; Dominicans as rivals of, 24, 263n.23; "free" Indians abused by, 23; households of, 46; inequities among, 258–59n.28; military obligations of, 43; of Mixco, 277n.95; naborías of, 97; and "new Spaniards," 297n.34; orphans indentured to, 100–101, 288n.90; pious generosity of, 22; population of, 103, 287n.82, 289n.97; pork for, 303n.38; of Quezaltenango, 301n.20; of Santiago in Almolonga, 7, 8, 103, 258n.20, 259n.39; of Santiago in Panchoy, 10, 13–16, 39, 48, 106–107, 109, 117, 262n.11; and slaves, 21, 46, 86. See also Conquistadores; Encomenderos
Vegetables, 22, 141, 143
Velázquez, Juan, 50, 51
Vendée (dept.), Fr., 113, 114
Veracruz, New Spain, 84
Villalobos (Guat. audiencia president), 290n.104
Viruelas. See Smallpox
Visitas, 82
Vivar, Diego de, 28
Volcanoes. See Acatenango; Agua; Fuego

Water: as barrio concern, 160; disease due to impure, 66; Indians as suppliers of household, 23. See also Ice; Rain
Weavers, 297n.32
West Indies, 299n.46
Wheat, 21, 107, 108, 141–48, 157, 290n.105, 300nn.9,11, 301n.14, 301–302n.20, 302nn.21,22,25,26; on black market, 144; hoarding of, 145, 301nn.14,15, 301–302n.20; Indian-harvested, 22; market for, 146, 301n.14; pasture converted to, 304n.41; raised by Alvarado's former slaves, 261n.5; shortages of, 146, 303n.30; as tribute, 144, 145. See also Bread; Labores; Labores de panllevar
Whipping, women punished by, 151, 305n.56
Wine, 152, 266–67n.78, 306n.61
Women: in beef trade, 150–51, 305nn.53,55, 56; as convicts, 100; creole, 102; exempted from tribute, 272n.55; hispanicization of Indian, 289n.94; manumission patterns among slave, 94, 284–85n.61, 285nn.63,64; "passing" of mestizo, 102, 289n.95; shortage of Spanish, 102; and tribute, 272n.55
Wood, 143. See also Charcoal; Firewood; Lumber; Timber

Xiquilite, 290n.100. See also Indigo

Yerbateros, 23

Zambo (term), 267n.1
Zamora, Alonso de, 31
Zapoteca Indians, 40, 65, 258n.21

www.ingramcontent.com/pod-product-compliance
Lightning Source LLC
Chambersburg PA
CBHW022059150426
43195CB00008B/200